EX LIBRIS

CRUICKSHANK'S
LONDON

A Portrait of a City in 13 Walks

DAN CRUICKSHANK

HUTCHINSON
LONDON

1 3 5 7 9 10 8 6 4 2

Hutchinson
20 Vauxhall Bridge Road
London SW1V 2SA

Hutchinson is part of the Penguin Random House group of companies
whose addresses can be found at global.penguinrandomhouse.com.

Penguin
Random House
UK

Photographs and illustrations are from the author's or the publisher's
collections, apart from those on the following pages: vi (© Alamy); 523, 526
(© Getty); 335 (© iStock); 362, 429 (LSE Charles Booth's London Project),
365 (Pexels); 296 (Pixabay); 261, 273 (Wellcome Collection); 5, 30, 33, 40,
67, 93, 98, 114, 127, 134, 155, 213, 219, 242, 248, 261, 299, 338, 368,
488 (Wikimedia Commons); 11, 181 (Yale Center for British Art).

First published in the United Kingdom by Hutchinson in 2019

www.penguin.co.uk

A CIP catalogue record for this book is available from the British Library.

ISBN 9781847948229

Design and typesetting Roger Walker

Maps by Darren Bennett

Printed and bound by Firmengruppe APPL

Contents

Introduction   vii

The Temple of Mithras   1

1   Hampstead Heath: London's ancient birthright   9

The Tower of London   29

2   Norton Folgate to Bank: Medieval memories in the modern city   33

St Mary Magdalene, East Ham   71

3   Greenwich: The architecture of absolutism   77

Eastbury Manor House   117

4   Bank to St Paul's: Wren's London   124

Royal Hospital, Chelsea   169

5   Blackheath: Domestic architecture of the Stuarts and Georgians   176

Kew Gardens   211

6   The Regent's Canal: The rise of the waterways   218

The British Museum   243

7   King's Cross to Barnsbury: The late-Georgian estates   250

The Palace of Westminster   297

8   Notting Hill: The Victorian middle class goes west   304

Embankment   335

9   Kensal Green and Kensal Rise: Life and death in the Victorian city   341

St Pancras Station and the Midland Grand Hotel   365

10   Bermondsey: The industrial heart of London   370

Hampstead Garden Suburb   409

11   North Spitalfields: The last cry of outcast London   417

Oxford Street   451

12   Fleet Street to Trafalgar Square: London in the machine age   458

Dagenham Civic Centre   513

13   Brixton: Market forces in post-war London   518

Glossary   538

Notes   540

Key locations and buildings   547

Introduction

That 'great and monstrous thing called London' was how Daniel Defoe in 1724 warily defined the city he was about to describe.[1] London's population at the time was around 680,000. Since then, the metropolis has increased in density and expanded into its rural hinterland, with its population currently standing at nearly 9 million. What was already a 'monstrous' thing to Defoe nearly 300 years ago, as he contemplated telling its story, is now an organism so large that accurate, enlightening and relatively concise description seems beyond reach.

But the temptation to risk all and take a shot is great. I'm a Londoner, and I have been writing about London – and campaigning to save its physical and social identity – for over forty-five years. On and off, I have been toiling on this volume for over five. My goal has been to paint a picture of London and its buildings through a series of illustrated walks. I have wandered hundreds of miles, often going over the same ground many times, and each time finding something new (that, of course, is part of London's magic). I have spent months in libraries doing research, spoken to countless Londoners, and taken thousands of photographs – through the seasons and in different qualities of light. And through all, I have attempted to gain an understanding not only of London's history but also of its life – in its streets, cafés, pubs and markets. These places speak not only of London's vivacious character, but also reveal much about its past. My hope is that the resulting book is – in a sense – a user's guide to the city.

And there is no better way to offer this than through walks. Walking does not only make London's history and architecture more accessible to the reader – it can also reveal the dramatic juxtapositions that are so characteristic of this city. Essentially, once a location and route has been decided, the buildings select themselves, whether that's a nineteenth-century warehouse, a medieval terrace, or a psychedelically painted T-34 tank (all in Walk 10). To my mind this gives a pleasing objectivity to the choice of buildings described.

The challenge of aptly describing London is worth it, because this is one of the world's few truly great cities: a place that is many layered, complex, and with a rich mix of people and stories. London can delight, surprise, appal, break your heart – but it is rarely bland and hardly ever dull. It has a rough and raw beauty: while London might lack the finesse of Paris, antique grandeur of Rome or imperial presence of Vienna, it does have a tremendous soul – created in part by the waves of migrants that London has always received, embraced and succoured, and who have gradually transformed into Londoners themselves, enriching the city.

The book's structure evolved over the years as it gradually became clear that, with all the practical constraints of publishing, it would be impossible to cover all of London with the level of focus that is essential if the text is to rise above the coldly factual. As a result, while the book covers most of London – from Dagenham in the east and Notting Hill in the west, and from Hampstead Garden Suburb in the north to Brixton in the south – some of the most obvious locations have been omitted. This is sometimes because the obvious is already exhaustively covered elsewhere. But it is also because each walk is emblematic of a broader theme in London's history.

Take, for example, the development of London's mosaic of private estates between the late-seventeenth and early-nineteenth centuries. This is the process by which the capital's internationally admired Georgian streets and squares were created – and one that took place in a number of locations, including Bloomsbury, Mayfair, Canonbury and Marylebone. Each district has its own fascinating permutation of the same essential story – more, alas, than could ever be covered in a single volume. Instead, I focus on one representative example: the story of the New River Company Estate around King's Cross, and the smaller estates to its north (Walk 7). Between each of the book's long walks are shorter 'vignettes', which focus on small areas or individual buildings that are essential to include in any fully rounded story of the city.

Before diving into the walks, it is worth noting – to avoid disappointment or confusion – the things that this book is not. Firstly, this is not an exhaustive history of London. My goal has been to tell the city's story through its existing buildings, and that means that some historical periods receive more attention than others. Much of the book is about the nineteenth century, and this is as it should be. Just as Florence is essentially a Renaissance City of the fifteenth and sixteenth centuries, and Bath is a child of the eighteenth century, it was during the nineteenth century that London, as it expanded into its hinterland, and as industrial and commercial architecture flourished, became a great world city. It is a legacy that is still dominant.

Second, this is not a book about 'secret' London, nor about buildings and places open only to the few and privileged. There are no descents into sewer systems nor into palatial private houses or St James's clubs. Instead it is about the London you can see from the streets, public parks and gardens of the city. There is much discussion of the outsides of buildings, and of the interiors that can seen by all – some most easily, like churches and museums, and others with a little more effort, like theatres, pubs and hotels. This is a book about public London; the London that belongs to all of us.

And third, this is not, primarily, a book aimed at specialists. Rather it is for anyone with an interest in architecture and the city around them. I have tried to avoid using excessive architectural terminology, in the hope that all can appreciate the buildings and features that I mention. However, it is not possible to fully describe architecture without at least some references to pilasters, entablatures, pediments and the like – and for this reason I have included a short (and non-exhaustive) glossary, which defines some of the more specialist language that I use.

Finally, on the tone of the text. This book offers not only a selective portrait of the capital but also one that is personal. The text aims to be informative, but also at times campaigning, opinionated and, I hope, possessed by a sense of exploration, discovery and wonder. London is so large – and so diverse – that it is still possible, even for a long-term and inveterate London wanderer like me, to go to familiar places and still to be taken by surprise. This is hardly a fresh approach. When the American adventurer and novelist Jack London set out in 1902 to live among the 'natives' of Whitechapel he explained that 'I went down into the under-world of London with an attitude of mind which I may best liken to that of the explorer'. He wanted to offer descriptions of what he discovered based on the evidence of his own eyes rather than on 'the words of those who had seen and gone before'.[2] It remains a useful reminder that it is true observation that is important – that all memorable guides are based on first-hand experience, and that only from this can come fresh thinking.

So I hope this text not only informs but also inflames and inspires, launches readers on flights of fancy, and helps them tiptoe the thrilling line between London's history and its myths. But more than anything else, I hope this book sends its readers out into the city around them. If, on your travels, you encounter any errors in the text, or anything that you think I've neglected to mention or that has changed beyond recognition then please send me an email at cruickshankslondon@gmail.com. And if this book does make you feel compelled to walk the streets of London then, no doubt, I'll see you around.

This book has been long in the making and my debt to fellow London enthusiasts is enormous – for information, for insights, for suggestions about buildings and places to include. I would in particular like to thank Gavin Stamp, who over the years shared his enthusiasm for London and his immense knowledge in a most generous manner. I'm now only sad that Gavin will not see the fruits of our walks and talks. London books have, of course, played a key role in this endeavour, none more so than the volumes of the *Survey of London* and the London volumes of *The Buildings of England*. Together these are works of urban and architectural scholarship that are – in their scope and reliability – second to none, and that must always form the foundation of any book about London. But most of all I would like to thank my publishers and editors – Rowan Borchers and Nigel Wilcockson – whose commitment to this project has been astonishing and who, in most erudite and thoughtful manner, have shaped my deluge of text (naturally there is much to say about London) into a book. Finally, I would like to thank my long-suffering family – Marenka, Bella, Alexander and Inigo – for their support and indulgence.

Dan Cruickshank, August 2019

The Temple of Mithras

A few metres west of Bank station in the City lies one of the most ancient and sacred sites in London. The junction of Threadneedle Street and Poultry marks the course of the Walbrook – a small river that flowed from the north-east into the Thames. In Roman times, this was regarded as a holy place, where sacrifices were made to the gods. In those days, it meandered about 7 metres below existing ground level; by the sixteenth century it ran in subterranean culverts, and by the mid nineteenth century its water was appropriated to help flush out London's new sewer system – and the Walbrook was all but lost.

But the traces of the Walbrook that remain tell us much about the ancient history of London. Its route marked a key division in the Roman City. The land to the west of the river was, in the early years, generally informally built upon, with large areas left open to serve as gardens and paddocks; to the east was a grid of streets, more densely built upon, and the location of major public or institutional buildings such as the forum and the governor's palace.

This was Londinium, founded in the late 40s AD. In 55 and 54 BC Julius Caesar had invaded Britain, the second time with five legions, and, marching north from Kent, crossed the Thames, subdued British tribes, established client kings subservient to Rome, established a system of tributes to be paid to Rome and then withdrew. But in AD 43 Rome mounted a full-scale invasion as a prelude to occupation, ostensibly to quell growing turmoil in Britain that threatened the payment of tribute, though also no doubt to secure undisturbed access to valuable resources such as tin.

Emperor Claudius sent four legions across the Channel, one of which – II Augusta – was commanded by the future emperor Vespasian. By the mid first century, much of what is now southern England had been conquered. And, over the course of the next century, Londinium was to become the largest city in the Roman colony of Britannia – becoming the capital of the province soon after AD 61, following the suppression of Boudicca's uprising.

In the years that followed, the Walbrook would become a river of great importance. The City of London's wall was completed between

AD 190 and 225, and, as the built area of London expanded within it during the second, third and fourth centuries, the marshy banks of the shallow and meandering Walbrook were reclaimed and wharves and manufactories built along its western side. This small river, then, came to serve as a key location on the sea and river trade route linking Britain with continental Europe.

Today, the clearest signs of the old course of the Walbrook are around a huge late-modern building which houses the financial services empire Bloomberg. It is memorialised in direct and conventional manner, in a piece of public art that embellishes the building's Queen Victoria Street frontage. As a work of public art it is better than most, being very site specific and extremely evocative. Entitled *Forgotten Streams* and created by the Spanish artist Cristina Iglesias, the work shows – in several sections – large and very lifelike portions of river bed and marshy bank, packed with entwined roots and through which tumble small courses of water, as in a cascade. Bank and bed are made of bronze with the roots and plant tendrils being most delicately wrought.

The most exciting legacy of the Walbrook, however, lies underground. For in Roman times the river banks hosted not only quays and factories, but also a temple to the god Mithras. Built on of the reclaimed east bank of the Walbrook in the mid third century AD, the site was probably chosen because this small river was marshy – and so was perceived as equivalent to the River Styx, the mythological river that marked the boundary between the Earth and the Underworld and joined other rivers, such as the

The Walbrook in bronze: Cristina Iglesias's *Forgotten Streams* marks the course of the lost river.

Acheron, at a great marsh at the centre of the Underworld. Extraordinarily, this temple can still be seen today, in a dedicated museum underneath the Bloomberg building. The Mithraeum has been reconstructed almost on the original site and – as far as possible – to its original orientation, having been disassembled and relocated after its discovery in the 1950s. It is a triumph, returning to London an incredibly important and thought-provoking building from the Roman world, with an appropriate sense of respect, scholarship, awe and healthy theatricality.

Any visit to the Mithraeum – by booking only, but free – offers a tantalising glimpse of the idiosyncrasies of the Roman faith. For Mithras is a Persian god, whose veneration became popular in the Roman empire during the AD first century and with a life history and attributes strikingly similar to Christ. Some of this history is speculative, due to lack of firm knowledge from the ancient world about Mithras – it was, after all, a secretive 'mystery' cult open only to initiates. But it seems that both Mithras and Christ were born on 25 December, both offered their followers salvation (paid for by a sacrifice of holy blood), and in both religions the cross was sacred. Mithras, too, appears to have undergone some form of epiphany or rebirth in a cave, comparable to Christ's resurrection in his tomb after crucifixion. Did early Christians borrow from the mystery cult of Mithras? Perhaps, but it's more likely that the initiates of Mithras borrowed from early Christian rituals.

Such a mingling of traditions was possible because Roman religion was generally tolerant and inclusive: foreign gods were easily accommodated and often renamed to make them more Roman. Baal, the great creator God of the Middle East, was simply adopted by the Romans and his images and temples renamed in honour of Jupiter. This tradition of relaxed inclusiveness meant that the Romans were initially baffled – and then infuriated – when confronted by the monotheistic Jews and Christians who would not tolerate the existence of any gods but their own. Naturally the tolerant pagans become increasingly put out by the stridently intolerant monotheists, and thus Christianity was criminalised and its followers came to be regarded as members of a riotous, antisocial and anarchic cult – and were punished in the manner of all such criminals. Christians called the punishment persecution; the Romans no doubt saw it merely as justice.

The modern-day atmosphere of the Mithraeum, now dark and deep underground, is an apt recreation of the original temple. Mithras was worshipped in dark and secure places – no doubt to commemorate his epiphany within a cave – and with much ritual. The initiates had to undergo various secret ceremonies, some more or less frightening. There

The relief of Mithras slaying the astral bull, now in the Museum of London.

were likely seven grades of initiates, who acknowledged one another by means of secret handshakes. This was probably a male-only affair – no evidence of female initiates has been found – and through its mystery and initiations, the cult must have forged bonds and a sense of brotherhood, especially between legionaries serving on the hostile edges of the known world, such as Roman Londinium.

What we know about the cult of Mithras has largely been gleaned from a few surviving artefacts and inscriptions found at different sites. At the heart of this Mithraeum – as was presumably typical – would once have been a relief, now preserved nearby in the Museum of London, but partially evoked on glass inside the current temple. It shows Mithras slaying the astral bull, an act of sacrifice that maintained the cosmic order and controlled the fates of man. On the relief Mithras – the central figure wearing a Phrygian bonnet – is surrounded by a ring emblazoned with the signs of the zodiac. So Mithras was perceived as being at the centre of the cosmic wheel of the zodiac, which turned remorselessly through the year. Devotees believed that it was through the power and influence of the stars and planets that the gods ordered the lives of man.

The basilica plan – of a central nave with two narrow flanking aisles – was a common one in Roman public buildings, but its precise orientation (nearly but not quite recreated in the current museum) is revealing. An inscription dateable to AD 307–10 describes Mithras as the 'invincible Sun from the east to the west' – suggesting that the east–west axis of the Mithraeum was crucial (as with Christian churches), honouring the cycle from sunrise (birth), to sunset (death) and then the following sunrise (rebirth). Even more interestingly, though, the main door to the east has been manipulated slightly to the north, presumably to face sunrise, so that the cavern-like interior of the temple would be illuminated at dawn on certain days – likely when Taurus was in ascendency, so from late April to late May by our modern calendar.

The Mithraeum's tale has, since the fourth century, been rather chequered. Soon after partial reconstruction of the building around the time of the 307–10 inscription, it seems to have been rededicated to Bacchus, god of wine, fertility and theatre. We have no idea why. At this point, though, the heads of Mithras and some other items were carefully preserved by being buried below the temple's floor. This suggests an orderly and respectful change. But the next change was not so respectful. In the late fourth or very early fifth century the Mithraeum appears to have been abandoned – probably due to Christian intolerance – and then to have fallen into ruin, with the rest of Londinium, after the Romans left Britain in around AD 410.

It was only in the late 1880s that the first signs of the temple were rediscovered. The buried relief of Mithras with the bull was stumbled upon during building works. The temple proper was found by chance in 1954 when the bomb-damaged site was being cleared for a new office block. At about 7 metres below ground, the level of Roman London was reached and the builders discovered the ground floor and first metre or so of an ancient structure – prompting much publicity and excitement. But this did not save the temple. It was documented, dismantled and eventually the majority (but not all) of the stones put back together on a desolate and litter-blown raised terrace in front of the newly completed office block, about 100 metres away from its original site.

The present exhibition, which opened in 2017, is thankfully a more faithful and atmospheric reconstruction of the Mithraeum. First you enter a vestibule where recently discovered artefacts are displayed and explained, and then you descend via a flight of stairs or lift to a subterranean room, which includes explanations of Mithraic religion and architecture. Then, when the time is right, the group descends a few more steps to enter the dark chamber – around 9 metres below ground level, where the carefully reconstructed ruin resides. It's a dramatic presentation, with the atmosphere of sacred and shadowy gloom manipulated by subtle variations of light and by the sound of initiates, just invisible to the eye, chatting and chanting in Latin. Towards the end the light brightens so that you can inspect the ruins in greater detail. The imagination can easily run riot in this splendid addition to the City of London.

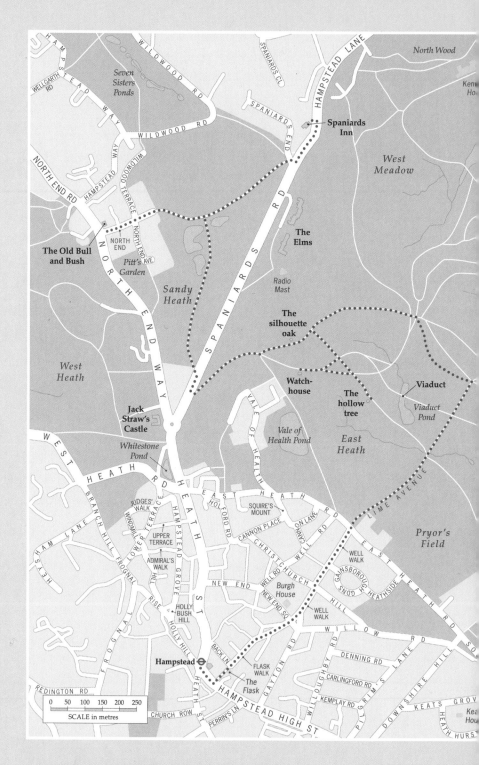

WALK 1

Hampstead Heath

London's ancient birthright

Hampstead Heath is a place that possesses a strange, at times almost unworldly, presence. At dusk or at dawn, it can feel like an ancient land, a wilderness remote from the vast city that bustles in the shadowy depths below. And sometimes, when walking through its groves and gullies, it is possible to experience a sense of isolation and calm that is amazing given the tens of thousands of people so close at hand.

At these romantic moments, it is easy to believe that this is where London started. This high land – standing well above the overgrown and boggy terrain nearer the Thames – was surely once sacred. Where else but in these ancient woods and mystic glades could the first Londoners have chosen to settle and build their temples? This is possible; there is much that is possible about Hampstead Heath. But, as with so many elemental and complex landscapes, nothing with the heath is quite what it seems.

There are indeed a few signs of ancient habitation. In 1976, an amateur archaeologist stumbled upon some worked flints on West Heath, sparking an excavation that found evidence of a Mesolithic settlement dating to around 7000 BC.[1] And the mythology of the heath often plays up its ancient heritage too: take the so-called 'tumulus', which some have claimed was the burial place of Queen Boudicca, who died around AD 61. (No hide nor hair of the unfortunate queen has ever been found here,

Looking out over the City from the heath.

and it now seems more likely that it was once the base of a seventeenth-century windmill.) For the most part, however, the heath has never been substantially built upon, and no evidence uncovered of any prehistoric works of any great significance. If Londoners did first settle here millennia ago, they did so in a most gentle manner.

The story of Hampstead Heath becomes more certain during the medieval period. A charter of around 974 records how King Edgar granted five hides of land around Hampstead to Mangoda, 'his faithful minister'.[2] The one unarguably ancient man-made feature of the land-scape was built by King Ethelred in 986: the 'Saxon Ditch', a boundary running from north-west to south-east. By the time of the Domesday Book of 1086, compiled after the Norman invasion, the land was held by Westminster Abbey as part of the manor of Hampstead. It was first identified as a 'certain heath' in 1312, and was known as Hampstead Heath by 1543.[3] The manor, meanwhile, passed into private hands in the twelfth century and it, and most of the constituent parts that now form the heath, remained in varied and changing ownerships into the twentieth century.

Throughout this period, much of the heath was already unfenced common land used for grazing, and so must have played a significant role in the lives of the more humble rural residents of the area. Such land was the birthright of the peasantry of England. In feudal times, most people worked on specific plots of land under the control of a lord, to whom they would pay dues. The common land, however, could be used by anyone in the manor – to pasture cattle, to fish, to search for firewood. Throughout the medieval period and beyond, conflicting interpretations of who owned the common land cropped up again and again. Often lords would spark riots by attempting to enclose the land and preventing peasants using it: in 1549, for example, one Lichfield man began a riot by ringing the village bell and proclaiming that 'every man that had any cattle within the town should bring them forth and claim their common'.[4] The great social historian E. P. Thompson once invoked an old Russian saying to summarise the relationship of the English peasantry to their landlords and the commons: 'We are yours, but the land is ours.'[5]

When walking upon the wildest and most natural parts of the heath, it is easy to conjure this past life as medieval common land. But this is only part of the story. For, like all of the great and ancient sections of London, the heath was born in the distant past, but remade and reformed much more recently. In fact, what we now know as Hampstead Heath

The heath was a constant source of inspiration for John Constable. This 1828 painting depicts the view north from the Branch Hill Pond, which once lay to the west of the Vale of Health.

has existed in its current form for less than a hundred years, and much of the original heathland no longer survives as open space. A cursory glance at a map of Hampstead reveals the different natures of the heath's component parts and suggests their origins.

As well as the heath proper, now rich in undergrowth, there are woods, rolling fields and pasture, cultivated parkland and picturesquely landscaped gardens. Broadly speaking, the western portion of modern Hampstead Heath is formed largely from old heathland with, from west to east, West Heath and Sandy Heath, both west of Spaniards Road and divided from each other by North End Way. To the east of Spaniards Road is East Heath, with the low-lying Vale of Health to its south. These heaths are now all quite densely covered with tall scrub and well-wooded, but to their east is the more open Pryor's Field, Hampstead Ponds and then the undulating Parliament Hill Fields. The northern portion of the heath is defined by the spectacular late-eighteenth-century Kenwood House and its art collection – long open to the public – together with its garden and grounds. Protuberant additions to the main body of the heath are Hampstead Heath Extension to the north-west and Golders Hill Park to the west, both respectively retaining their character of fields and parkland, with in Golders Hill Park the huge and spectacular Edwardian colonnaded pergola, complete with its temples and bridge.

Even the natural-seeming heathland has in fact been vastly manipulated by man, and in very modern times. The thick and romantically luxuriant undergrowth, which now gives character and a sense of mystery to much of West Heath and East Heath, is a relatively recent development. A glance at the 1894 Ordnance Survey map reveals that, a hundred or so years ago, the heath was generally open land, divided by rows of trees marking ancient field boundaries, with the only long-established woodland being to the north, at Kenwood. And perhaps even more surprising is the fact that much of the wild-seeming land on East Heath is the result of industrialisation, the gently undulating landscape a product of the time the heathland was levelled and turned into brick fields.

It was in this moment that a conflict began which has defined the heath ever since: between those who view it as an ancient inheritance to be preserved for all Londoners, and those who see it as a place ripe

Hampstead contains woodland and heathland, parkland and fields.

for commercial exploitation. The brickworks were the doing of the truly frightful Sir Thomas Maryon Wilson, who inherited 144 hectares in Hampstead – including much of the southern portion of the heath – in 1821, from his father. Sir Thomas senior had wanted the heathland preserved and in his will specified that it must not be built upon. His son, Sir Thomas junior, spent the next forty years or so trying, by any means possible, to get the terms of the will altered to allow building on the heath. When he repeatedly failed – thanks to much and mounting opposition – he undertook vindictive and arguably illegal actions to vent his spite and mortify his opponents.

The struggle for the heath came to its first head in the 1850s, when Maryon Wilson's lobbying for development reached a fever pitch. New opponents appeared, notably Gurney Hoare, an eminent banker, and the Vestry – the relevant local authority at the time – which argued that it was in the interests of the parish and the city that the government purchase and preserve the heath 'with such portions of the adjoining ground as are essential to its beauty'.[6] But they had little success until 1860, when Hampstead Heath station opened. The railway changed the fortunes of the preservationists: while it clearly made the land even riper for housing development, it also made the heath more attractive as a place of resort for Londoners – particularly for East Enders, who could reach Hampstead with ease after 1865, when stations opened at Broad Street and Dalston Junction. These people were very hard-pressed for fresh air in their narrow and crowded streets, so the availability and preservation of the heath for their recreation, health and tranquillity became a major issue, and one of political consequence and sensitivity. To entertain these visitors, a large fair near the Vale of Health became a regular feature – partly to compensate for the recent closure of those ancient and once vast gatherings held in Smithfield and Greenwich – which must have done much to remind Londoners of their ancient right to wander the heath. Maryon Wilson soon realised that his prospects for turning this new East Enders' playground into streets of smart and exclusive villas were dwindling. The forces of urban history were against him.

The struggle to save Hampstead's open spaces – its heathland, its woods and its fields – became one of the country's first great conservation battles. The leading campaigners – by now Gurney Hoare and the barrister and MP George Shaw-Lefevre – were able, articulate and well connected to centres of power and influence. Proposals to build no fewer than three railway routes across the heath were successfully opposed, but skirmishing continued until pressure from these campaigners led to the Metropolitan Commons Act of 1866 that gave the Metropolitan Board of Works – the pre-eminent institution for building public infrastructure – new powers to protect the heath. In 1869 Maryon Wilson died, and when it looked like his brother and heir, Sir John, might continue the battle, the MBW finally took definitive action. By means of the Hampstead Heath Act of 1871 the body bought nearly all that survived of the common land of the heath: East Heath, North-West or Sandy Heath, and West Heath – 90 hectares in all. The future of much of Hampstead Heath as an open public space was finally secured.

The full scale of this achievement is only visible when one looks to the land surrounding the heath today. The long, hard-fought and ultimately successful battle to save it set a precedent for the preservation of ancient landscapes across London. To the north of the heath are a remarkable collection of open spaces now hedged around by mostly late-nineteenth- and twentieth-century buildings. To the north-west there are two areas of ancient woodland that were spared during the construction of Hampstead Garden Suburb after 1906 (see p. 409) – the largest called Big Wood and the smaller called Little Wood, which together cover about 10 hectares.

More dramatic still is Highgate Wood, which consists of 28 hectares of ancient woodland that was once part of extensive hunting ground and park belonging to the Bishop of London. It contains superb hornbeams, some up to 500 years old, which are 'layered' – meaning their branches were once platted – suggesting they were used to reinforce a now lost system of hedges. Highgate Wood was saved from house builders during a tense battle, and has been owned since 1886 by the City of London, which now also manages and maintains Hampstead Heath. And that's not all – immediately to the east of Highgate Wood are the 21 hectares of Queen's Wood, a fragmentary surviving part of the great Forest of Middlesex, and further to the north are the ancient Coldfall Wood and Cherry Tree Wood.

The area's veteran trees live on not only in these public woodlands. The privately owned Turner's Wood, on the west side of Hampstead Heath Extension, is one of the most extraordinary pieces of old woodland to survive in London. It covers just 2.4 hectares and is a fragment of Bishop's Wood that was, like Highgate Wood, once part of the Bishop of London's hunting grounds. But it still contains beautiful oak, hornbeam and wild service trees and is divided by streams that are tributaries of the Decoy Brook, itself a tributary of the River Brent. The wood is now managed as a

Undisturbed woodland on the heath.

nature reserve and so is rich, in season, in wild flowers – with a beautiful carpet of bluebells in the spring – and in birdlife, including woodpeckers, tawny owls and kestrels. Traces of ancient forest also survive in the gardens of the palatial houses on each side of the long and winding Bishop's Avenue – also once part of the Bishop of London's hunting grounds. Since many of the adjoining gardens are nearly a hectare in size, they form a greatly disturbed but ancient woodland that is now in multiple private ownership and which the public has no hope of experiencing.[7]

Between them, these forests mean that north London contains, with Hampstead Heath included, around 400 hectares of ancient woodland, heathland, parkland and fields – much of it primary and virgin forest that has never been significantly altered by the hand of man. This is an astonishing treasure for a vast and old city like London to possess so close to its heart. And it is a heritage that most Londoners are keen to take advantage of: the 320 hectares of Hampstead Heath are now used by about 7 million people a year. This seemingly wild place has a remarkable openness and air of liberty that has created among the heath's regular users a bond of loyalty to the place, a proud sense of ownership, and a deep feeling of respect. For those who walk the heath, through the changing seasons, it's almost as if its glades and grottoes are one's own property to enjoy whenever the fancy strikes. In these moments, it is possible to imagine a line that connects the bustle of modern London with that of the medieval peasants who would once have claimed these slopes as their birthright.

THE WALK

The diversity of the walks offered by Hampstead Heath is as varied as its nature. They can be close and mysterious or open and bracing, offering spectacular views south and east to the city of towers. You can walk through sunlit glades, across meadows, through ordered plantations or plunge into the wildwood of the imagination, stumbling upon shattered and fallen trees and expecting any moment a fleeting glimpse of

Pan or his dryads. This walk offers one of the more introverted options, but to my mind one of the most characterful. It takes the rambler through the heart of the old heath and across the nineteenth-century battleground where Maryon Wilson arrayed his infamous brickworks.

Start by walking south along Hampstead High Street, before turning north on to Flask Walk. This soon becomes Well Walk, which takes us from the centre of Hampstead village towards the heath. As you come to East Heath Road, now fringed by late-nineteenth-century houses and mansion blocks, you pass in a sudden and most informal manner from town to country – from the streets of Hampstead on to heathland. You are now on land that has been part of the heath since time immemorial, although its current layout is rather more recent. In front of you is the Lime Avenue, a handsome if somewhat surprisingly formal ornament for this part of the Heath. The limes are tall, and the avenue – also known as the boundary path – curves slightly to make the vista more pleasingly picturesque. After around 250 metres, looking east, there is a fine prospect of Pryor's Field, delightful from spring to autumn when the views of this

A sudden and startling transition from town to country: entering the heath from Well Walk.

open glade are framed by lush foliage. But generally, the path is now bounded by tall scrub and other trees as well as by the limes. This is all relatively new. The 1894 Ordnance Survey map shows this area of East Heath as very open, with no hint of the avenue. The now-mature limes were not planted until 1905.

Continue north-east along the Lime Avenue for another few hundred metres (taking a compass on this walk would be a very good idea), until you reach the site of the 'Saxon Ditch', its location marked by an ancient, and seemingly now dead, beech tree of impressive appearance. The ditch could be part of an ancient drainage system or have marked the extent of King Ethelred's estate.

To your south-east lie the open fields of Parliament Hill, on most days bathed in light and offering spectacular views over the city. This is the site that modern Druids call Llandin, meaning a 'high-place of worship'. For them the visual line from here to the hill on which sits the Tower of London is the Midsummer's Day azimuth – the line on which the sun rises and reaches the pinnacle of its power, during the summer solstice. This has probably been the place from which Londoners have, for thousands of years, observed the cycle of the sun: its rise, decline and rebirth at the winter solstice. On this walk we don't go to this ancient, sacred ground but, instead, turn to the left – by a large fallen tree – roughly north-west along a well-beaten but 'unmade' footpath. There are two paths here, almost parallel but not quite. Take that to the left, the most westerly, past another fallen tree.

We now enter the enchanted heart of the old heath. This is a place that has for centuries enthralled foragers and nature lovers. The botanist John Gerard, who in the late-sixteenth century set out to record the plants of England, lamented in his magisterial *Herball* (1597) that the people of London no longer appreciated the goldenrod flower – which 'is extolled above all other herbes for the stopping of bloud in bleeding wounds' – since they had discovered it in Hampstead Wood. These days 'no man will give halfe a crowne for an hundred weight of it,' he wrote, 'which plainly setteth forth our inconstancie and sudden mutability, esteeming no longer of any thing, how pretious soever it be, than whilest it is strange and rare.'[8] An early introduction to the laws of supply and demand.

The 1894 Ordnance Survey shows that the tall, old trees around here

– mostly oaks but also beech, sweet chestnut, hornbeams and wild service trees that are from 150 to over 300 years in age – roughly follow ancient field boundaries. But now, with the thick shrub and saplings, these veteran trees appear to have arranged themselves into strange groups. Some seem to have gathered themselves to define sacred groves, others to mark Druidic circular enclosures that are veritable woodhenges. It's as if all is a mirage, with these venerable trees little more than figments of one's imagination, their appearance changing with the light – sometimes dappled in shade and dark, other times catching shafts of penetrating sun – so that on no two walks do they ever look quite the same.

Some trees, on the other hand, are so distinct that they form landmarks and become waysigns. I remember a large dead and fallen tree to the south of this path, marking the edge of a grove. Then, to the north-east, a beautiful oak, standing firm with spreading branches, and a fallen tree nearby. Turn east and you get to a broader path. After this the path divides, by an oak. Take the route to your left, which starts to curve gradually to the south-west, and then to the west. Walk slowly, enjoying the light, the shadows, the texture of the trees. Every season transforms the scene. In autumn, the ground is thickly carpeted with leaves in mottled tones of ochre; in winter, the trees are stark, skeletal and sculptural; in spring and summer, the leaf canopy is intense and the light enters through the shadow in dramatic shafts to create a chiaroscuro world.

To the north are the railings of Kenwood House park, then a grove in which pride of place is given to a vast and fallen oak tree, with its roots bent double and still partly bedded below the earth. Despite this tree's obvious predicament, it is yet alive, and each spring for as long as I can remember its old and stricken branches have given off young shoots.

———————◆———————

The path now divides again. The route to the right heads roughly north-west, near the course of the 'Saxon Ditch', passes through a pleasant glade, then crosses the drive to a villa called The Elms and joins Spaniards Road, with Sandy Heath beyond. But we take the left-hand path. Here one can imagine how the heath must have felt in the early nineteenth century, and begin to understand why Londoners were so desperate to save it from developers.

The silhouette oak.

As you walk south-west, the ground falls and then rises rapidly and a striking prospect appears. At the top of the path, set against the skyline, is a large oak with its spreading branches – seen to best effect in winter when denuded of leaves – forming a fantastic silhouette. It is quite a sight, viewed in the evening against the orange glow of a setting sun with walkers – black, stick-like figures against the illuminated sky – winding their way homeward over the rise and beneath the branches. It's like a suddenly animated image from a particularly fine piece of oriental porcelain.

Take a small detour, to the south-east of the silhouette oak, and you will soon arrive at a conical brick watch-house or ice-house built in the 1820s for Maryon Wilson. Beyond it is the Vale of Health and its pond, created in 1777 by a water company to drain the swampy terrain that was afterwards built upon to create a tiny hamlet secreted within the heath. Despite these works, this can still be something of a dank place on winter evenings. Take the path to the east, which leads to an 'unmade' path opposite a bench dedicated to the memory of Suzanne Sayer-Potts. This path, heading roughly south, comes to a splendid beech tree, one of my favourites on the heath. It is old, large and hollow – and still alive. And not just hollow. The tree's echoing and empty core – in which children have loved to hide for generations, to judge by its burnished surfaces – has two orifices. One of these is little more than a shapeless slash, but the other is roughly in the form of a slightly wobbly vesica piscis – that pointed oval shape beloved by the medieval Christian mind because its elemental fish-like outline seemed to echo one of the earliest images of Christ, who told his first disciples to be 'fishers of men'.

But the route of this walk is to the west of the silhouette oak. Here there is a fine wide field framed by clusters of tall trees, which possibly retain some of the pines or firs that John Constable (a Hampstead resident whose house survives at 40 Well Walk) drew in 1820. It would, too, have impressed William Blake, an obsessive wanderer over the heath, often on the way to visit his friend and patron John Linnell, whose weatherboarded cottage still stands to the north-west. The heath was for Blake a hallowed ground, where he could escape the noise and crowds of the city and dream his dreams. This is also the sort of glade, with its curtain of towering and beautiful trees murmuring in the summer evening breeze, that inspired John Keats: he lived nearby from 1817 until his fateful journey to Rome in 1820, writing of 'watching the sailing cloudlet's bright career', and mourning 'that day so soon has glided by,/E'en like the passage of an angel's tear.'[9]

Beyond this grove is Jack Straw's Castle, a former pub on the spot where Jack Straw, leader of the Peasants' Revolt of 1381, is said to have taken refuge after his uprising failed. The shift in atmosphere – albeit without the present roaring traffic – has likely existed for centuries. We have left the enchanted realm of the heath for the real world, in all its brutality. Next to the site of Jack Straw's Castle was set the gibbet, on the corner of North End Way, on which the rotting bodies of executed highway robbers were hung in chains as a warning to all tempted to chance their luck. At this frontier – Arcadian fields to the east, urban sprawl to the west – the Romantics' love for Hampstead Heath becomes all too understandable.

———————◆◆◆———————

But there is another side to this portion of the heath. For this was not only the ancient countryside that inspired Constable and Keats. It was this area that Thomas Maryon Wilson proposed to destroy when in the 1820s he launched a brutish and selfish campaign to build upon the Heath, and in the process destroy beauty and public amenity for private profit. The campaign was to be long, and close-run.

We have already caught a glimpse of Maryon Wilson's vision for the heath, in the form of the watch-house or ice-house, to the south-east of the silhouette oak. He also wanted to develop the area to the east of the lodge as a managed and exclusive estate, East Heath Park, comprising twenty-eight detached villas, each set in 2 acres of land and screened from its neighbours by clumps of trees. The proposal, much fought over, was on the cards for decades. And so this part of the heath is littered with Maryon Wilson's constructions: a road through his estate from the Vale of Health to Hampstead Pond, a wall near the Vale of Health to mark the park boundary, and – most surprising of all – a large, brick-built viaduct to carry the new road that, he hoped, would open the way to building and to great riches. The viaduct, a work of major and expensive civil engineering, was built between 1844 and 1847 and now carries no more than a path through the heath across the Viaduct Pond. The structure remains somewhat incongruous, but its harsh red brickwork has mellowed with age and it now appears a charming ornament, of almost Roman grandeur, in a picturesque parkland. It is extraordinary how time and changing circumstances can tame and transform the works of even the most ruthless of men.

At the time, however, all was most controversial. George Cruikshank's famous 1829 print, *London Going Out of Town or The March of Bricks and Mortar*, was in part a response to Maryon Wilson's greedy and selfish ambitions for the heath. It shows phalanxes of terraced houses, marching and animated chimney pots all going forth from the smoky city to attack the pristine high ground to the north of London. Farmland creatures and features – cattle, sheep and haystacks – are shown retreating in dismay and confusion. Meanwhile a group of trees on a distant skyline – just beyond a board marked 'Hampstead' and so presumably Parliament Hill – declare, 'Our fences, I fear, will be found to be no defence against these Barbarians, who threaten to enclose and destroy us in all "manor" of ways.'

Not all of Maryon Wilson's East Heath Park development was to take place on land that by tradition was part of the heath. It was also to include part of the already developed Vale of Health. But opposition focused

George Cruikshank's *London Going Out of Town* or *The March of Bricks and Mortar*.

on the loss of the ancient heathland. It was an effective tactic: despite lobbying and debate in the House of Commons and the House of Lords, where cronies offered support, Maryon Wilson repeatedly failed to get his father's will changed to allow him to develop the area. One consequence of Maryon Wilson's constant pressure was an ambitious but slightly cock-eyed government plan of 1853 to acquire part of the heath and the adjoining lands. This would have had the advantage of terminating Maryon Wilson's constant agitation and proposed bills to overturn his father's will, but could only be justified financially if the government itself turned developer. To explore possibilities a plan was drawn up by the eminent architect C. R. Cockerell. The resultant piece of city, called Hampstead New Park, was conceived in the spirit of John Nash's Regent's Park plan of forty years earlier and envisaged surrounding the heathland with new development rather than building through or over it.

All, however, came to nothing until the creation in 1855 of the Metropolitan Board of Works. It was urged to take on responsibility for the preservation of the heath and, over the course of the next fifteen years, the MBW would become the key body in its oversight. It was a long process. In 1857, a bill to bring the heath under MBW control was promoted but had no more luck than Maryon Wilson's efforts. The Metropolitan Commons Act of 1866, though, gave the MBW powers to

protect the heath and three years later, in 1869, Maryon Wilson died. The growing public acknowledgement of the importance of the heath prompted the government in 1871 to pass control of what is now the core of Hampstead Heath to the MBW.

Although the south-east portion of the heath did not become a housing estate or a long-term industrial site as Maryon Wilson would have liked, there are hints of the horrors that might have been – the brick viaduct, of course, and also the undulations in the land where brick earth was dug. But, miraculously, these now soft undulations only add to the impression that this is an undisturbed and ancient patch of countryside.

———————•:◆:•———————

By the beginning of the twentieth century, Hampstead Heath had come full circle: from its medieval origins as common land to commercial development opportunity, and back again. It's a story neatly encapsulated by the final portion of the walk, which takes us north to Spaniards Inn.

In the late nineteenth century East Heath became the site of a great annual Whitsun fair, which could stretch as far as Spaniards Road, to which we now walk. The crowd problem was exacerbated by the Bank Holidays Act of 1871, which created four bank holidays in England, Wales and Ireland: during the 1870s there were often as many as 50,000 people rollicking over the heath during their new spring and summer days off. In 1872, the year after this portion of the heath had finally been secured for public use, the fair was of particularly vast proportion. At many of these events, fires in the furze were a problem, as were noise, drunkenness and occasional violence. By the 1880s crowds could reach 100,000, when they spilled on to Parliament Hill Fields, and such numbers made accidents inevitable: in 1892, nine people died in a stampede to escape a sudden outburst of rain.

By this time, however, the government had realised quite how popular the heath was – and was going to even greater lengths to secure its future. Over the next few years, the heath would be expanded again and again, usually in response to threats from developers. Parliament Hill was acquired in 1888, Golders Hill Park in 1898 and Kenwood House and

---

Profiteering on the heath: Maryon Wilson's viaduct of 1844–7.

A postcard from the late-nineteenth century shows the view across the Vale of Health, complete with fairground.

its grounds in 1928. In this period 'Appy Ampstead' became a familiar slogan in the East End, and by 1900 the heath was the most popular open space in London.[10]

The effects of this expansion become clear when you continue west. The path across the grove from the silhouette oak comes out on Spaniards Road; cross over and walk a little to the north, and on your west is Sandy Heath, one of the most popular of Hampstead's leisure grounds until the early twentieth century. Take the path north-west on to Sandy Heath and then the one to the north-west, and soon you will come to the proof: the Old Bull and Bush, at the end of North End Way, became the subject of a popular music-hall song, 'Down at the Old Bull and Bush':

> *There's a little nook down near old Hampstead town:*
> *You know the place, it has won great renown.*
> *Often with my sweetheart on a bright summer's day*
> *To the little pub there my footsteps will stray . . .*
> *Come, come, come and make eyes at me*
> *Down at the Old Bull and Bush.*
> *Come, come, have some port wine with me*
> *Down at the Old Bull and Bush.*

The Old Bull and Bush is still open. The great joy of the heath, though, is that such modern reinvention has done little to harm the deeply historic atmosphere of its woods and fields. To give one example: just to the south of the Old Bull and Bush stands Pitt's Garden – so called because William Pitt the Younger retreated to a nearby house in the midst of one of his periodic bouts of debilitating anxiety. Architecturally it is now most memorable for its late-eighteenth-century arched gate, designed by James Paine; but even this charming structure is now dwarfed by a vast and ancient beech tree.

Down at the Old Bull and Bush.

The peculiar mixing of old and new is even better encapsulated a few hundred metres to the north. Walk north-east to the east end of Sandy Road, the main thoroughfare through Sandy Heath, and then for a hundred metres north along Spaniards Road. Here stands the Spaniards Inn, housed in a fine late-seventeenth- and early-eighteenth-century building. The pub is even older. It was first built in 1585, and in its garden sits a boundary stone marking the edge of the Bishop of London's estate – property of the Bishop of London since the Middle Ages.

The Spaniards Inn is as good a spot as any to finish this walk. As you sip your drink, reflect on the thread linking Mesolithic hunter-gatherers, medieval serfs and the revellers in the pub today. This alone, surely, makes Hampstead Heath not only one of the most remarkable terrains in London but one of the most remarkable stretches of open ground within the immediate environs of any great city in Europe.

The Tower of London

The Tower of London is one of the greatest medieval fortresses in the world. At times this can be hard to realise, as traffic thunders past and encircling office skyscrapers do their best to dwarf the fortress's ancient towers. But the reward, if you are in a receptive mood, is massive.

At the most obvious level the tower is the epitome of the evolving medieval and Tudor science of military design, reflecting theories about the use of redoubts and keeps, about defence through concentric systems of walls, and about how best to respond to the growing role of gunpowder and artillery from the sixteenth century onwards. But the tower is also so much more than a defensive outpost: it tells the story of England's princes and their palaces, and of the ways in which they have sought to legitimise their rule.

The multifaceted history of the tower is best told through the story of its central keep, the White Tower: the oldest and most recognisable feature of the complex. Started in about 1075, it was built to impress and intimidate the population of London. William of Normandy had gambled much on his military invasion of 1066, and his victory at the Battle of Hastings gained the English crown but in a most precarious manner. To hold the kingdom, William turned to architecture. Almost certainly designed by a Norman Benedictine monk named Gundulf, who William soon established as Bishop of Rochester, the White Tower reflected the Normans' desire to retain their new possession, England.

The location is, by its nature, of great strategic importance. Tower Hill plays a key role in commanding navigation along the Thames to the City – and the power that commands this trade route is the power that commands London. As such, the White Tower was designed to be as strong as possible, and is the definitive example of late-eleventh-century military architecture. But from the outset, the tower was more than just a place of military dominance. It was also a palace. As early as the twelfth century it was described as *Arx Palatina*[1] – fortified palace – and various details inside the tower proclaim that it was designed to be inhabited: notably the fireplaces in upper rooms that, with hearths and flues located within the thickness of the walls, allowed private chambers to be heated and as comfortable and convenient as possible.

The tower viewed from the Thames in 1647.

This opulence was all a way for William to hammer home the God-given nature of his power. The new king wanted to suggest that his military triumph was an expression of divine will – and his mighty new palace was a representation of his temporal and spiritual authority. Central to this project was the chapel of St John, one of the earliest and least-altered ecclesiastical interiors in England. The dedication of the chapel to St John the Evangelist is highly significant because in William's day it was believed that St John, one of the twelve Apostles, was the saint who had written the apocalyptic Book of Revelation. And this visionary biblical text – proclaiming the return of Christ and the descent from heaven of the New Jerusalem in the form of a mighty cube – seems to have been taken as a design guide for the chapel. Its sacred geometry is a permutation of *Ad Quadratum* – a geometrical system based on interlocking squares, seemingly related to the cubic imagery described in Revelation. And within this geometry, the royal dais, on which the king and queen would have sat, lies exactly opposite the altar. So the chapel is organised like a finely balanced set of scales. On one side sat the monarch, representing worldly power; on the other the altar, representing spiritual power.

Sacred geometry: inside the chapel in the White Tower.

William's White Tower established the future role of the Tower of London as a fortress of cutting-edge military design and opulent royal palace, in its organisation representing notions about kingship but also pioneering ideas of comfort and convenience. For example, Wakefield Tower, which stands at the middle of the south inner wall and was built from 1220 for Henry III, both enhanced the defences and served as part of a grand new palace, representing the magnificence of the Crown. And the massive Beauchamp Tower – which bulges out of the west part of the inner defensive wall – was added in the late 1270s as part of Edward I's strengthening of the tower, but was also a place of tremendous splendour and at times served as a high-class jail for eminent prisoners. Such enhancements, which continued until the nineteenth century, mean the tower incorporates eight centuries of regal pomp and ceremony.

The Tower of London, then, should not just be read as a means of defending and controlling the city. It is also architectural propaganda: a means of emphasising the spiritual legitimacy and splendour of the monarchy.

WALK 2

Norton Folgate to Bank

Medieval memories in the modern city

On one of the two surviving portions of the Copperplate map of the mid 1550s – the earliest surviving map of London – a large standing cross is shown looming over the main road running from north to south. This is 'Busshoppes gate Strete'.

The map ends abruptly north of the cross, but to the west is semi-developed countryside. A country lane winds tranquilly out to a windmill in the west on 'Fynnesbvrie Field', with pigs trotting along the track and some men practising archery in a field. To the south, however, all is different. After the cross, the main road and its hinterland almost immediately becomes more built-up. A few hundred

The Moorfields plate of the Copperplate map, with the 'Busshoppes Gate' to the south.

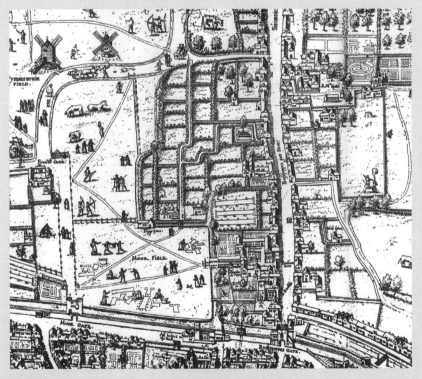

The ancient world collides with the modern: the view towards the site of the Bishop's Gate today.

metres later, the 'Busshoppes Gate' marks a route through the ancient city wall of London.

This standing cross, placed at the intersection of Bishopsgate and a road then known as Hog Lane, held enormous temporal and spiritual significance. It marked the north edge of the ward of Bishopsgate-without-the-Wall, delineating the point at which the City of London's authority ended. More importantly, the choice of a cross – rather than a simple boundary stone – proclaimed to all that the 'square mile' of the City was regarded as a sacred city: a place before the Reformation renowned for its encircling crown of monasteries and religious houses and its loyalty to the Virgin, and one that had been formed in semblance of the 'New Jerusalem' described in the biblical Book of Revelation. It was a view hinted at by John Stow, the antiquary and historian, who in the 1598 edition of his *Survey of London* stated that 'this famous Citie of London' was 'divided from East to West, and from North to South' like the sacred city of Jerusalem.

Clearly the City of London – with its Roman wall, seven gates and 109 churches – was already by the sixteenth century an ancient and holy place. Indeed, by the time of the Copperplate map and John Stow's *Survey*, London had been England's commercial centre for hundreds of years. Nearly five centuries after being abandoned by the Romans around AD 410, the City had been reoccupied by Alfred the Great in 886, its wall repaired and London – now Lundenburg – once more became a place of great importance. And after the Norman invasion of 1066, the City was granted its own charter that allowed Londoners to retain a level of autonomy over their affairs.

It was in this period that the City began to develop its idiosyncratic religious, commercial and political institutions, many of which are still in place to this day. Take, for example, the ward system. Stow tells us that there were originally, during Henry III's reign (1216–1272), '24 in all', each represented by an Elder man, or Alderman. This arrangement seems to have been inspired by the visionary Book of Revelation, which states that around Christ's throne – as he sat in judgement – were 'four and twenty elders'.[1] The connection is clear. The Aldermen of the City saw themselves as operating in a divine universe, as advisers to the Mayor, who sat in judgement but who owed 'fealty' to the divinely-appointed monarch, the representative of Christ on earth. The ward system still survives. So too does the Court of Aldermen.

What is even more remarkable, though, is how much the City's medieval past still lingers within the area once defined by its wall. There is the street plan, in places with a system of medieval alleys still intact, but also a significant amount of ancient fabric surviving – including long stretches of the wall itself, near the Tower of London and the junction of London Wall and Noble Street, with a fragmentary section still visible on London Wall near Bishopsgate. This is remarkable given the fires, twentieth-century bombing campaigns and ferocious waves of rebuilding that have beset the City. And ancient fabric can still be found in a number of churches – including those that dominate the Bishopsgate section of this walk, which is an area that largely escaped the Great Fire of 1666. Even some of the monasteries, although suppressed over 480 years ago, continue to have an influence on the way we experience the City today.

One example makes the point well. Whitefriars Street – a few hundred metres west of City Thameslink station on Ludgate Hill – marks the eastern edge of the Carmelite monastery that, until the Reformation of the 1530s, stretched west to Temple, and between Fleet Street and the Thames. Founded in 1150, the Carmelites' first home was in Palestine, near Mount Carmel, where Elijah was said to have occupied a crypt-like hermitage within the mountain. Known as the White Friars, they were located in London from 1253 after being forced to flee the Holy Land as the Crusader adventure finally collapsed. The monastery has long gone, but one can still find traces: a late-fourteenth-century vaulted crypt survives under 65 Fleet Street, now partly relocated and partly visible behind glass. The Carmelites perhaps intended this crypt to be an evocation of Elijah's distant, and no doubt fondly remembered, Mount Carmel grotto.

This monastic past had great influence on the function of the surrounding district until relatively recently. After the Reformation the Whitefriars area was, like much former monastic land, declared a Liberty – meaning it was to a limited degree self-governing and outside the jurisdiction of parish government. The result was that the Liberty of Whitefriars was recognised by parish and City authorities as a sanctuary, a reflection of its former monastic right to take in and protect a wide spectrum of offenders. All who entered the Liberty of Whitefriars fell outside the legal power of everyone but the Lord Chief Justice and the Privy Council. Inevitably, the area became a refuge for all manner of petty criminals, particularly those working in London's vast sex industry. The Liberty soon became known as 'Alsatia', because to the authorities it seemed to echo the lawless nature of Alsace, caught between Protestant Germany and Catholic France during the Thirty Years War (1618–48). Although a 1697 law abolished the Liberty's rights of sanctuary, the Liberty retained its status as a refuge for the poor and lawless into the eighteenth century and beyond, with Fleet Street remaining a hub of London's sex trade well into the nineteenth century.

This is just one example of the long legacy of the City's monastic past. Other buildings and place names, meanwhile, offer glimpses of its idiosyncratic commercial history. The Guildhall, which we encounter briefly on Walk 4, has for centuries been the beating heart of the City's official life. It is, in its way, the most remarkable building in the City.

Sacred and profane, side by side: Great St Helen's church is dwarfed by 30 St Mary Axe ('The Gherkin').

Constructed in 1411–30, it was likely inspired by biblical descriptions of the Holy of Holies in Solomon's Temple in Jerusalem (see p. 81). It has had many close encounters with radical change and even oblivion, damaged during the Great Fire of 1666 and gutted by fire bombs in 1940. But it endures, repaired and restored, the only one of the City's stone-built secular medieval buildings that survives to this day.

Today, of course, such treasures are not what catch one's eye when walking through the City. Looking out from the site of the standing cross of the Copperplate map – now the point where Worship Street meets Bishopsgate – no city walls, ancient gates or rolling fields are visible. Instead one sees the high-rise commercial district of the largest financial centre in Europe. The composition is visually cacophonous; indeed it's impossible to argue convincingly that it's a composition at all. The towers are crowded together in an almost absurd manner and each seems to strive for the maximum height possible within various planning and structural constraints. And yet, in its way, a walk through these buildings offers a most powerful perspective on the relationship between the City's medieval past and its present. It reveals London to be a place of extraordinary contrasts, where ancient and modern, large and small, homes and offices, the sacred and the profane stand side by side, and in their contrast unite to form the distinct character of the City.

THE WALK

This walk begins at Shoreditch High Street, meaning it can be joined up with a number of others in this book – at the beginning with Walk 11, or at the end with Walk 4. For now, though, our route is south along Wheler Street (recently renamed Braithwaite Street), and over to the junction of Commercial Street and Fleur-de-Lis Street.

When walking along Fleur-de-Lis Street you are walking over an ancient and important site. From 1197 to 1539 this land formed the northern edge of the Augustine Priory of the Blessed Virgin Mary, with its great church and main buildings lying just to the south, around what is now Spital Square. Hospital – abbreviated as 'spital – was the generic name for all institutional buildings that offered forms of hospitality to

Visual cacophony: the view west from Wheler Street.

the sick, injured, infirm and aged or those in need of medical aid such as women in labour. And so the fields just north of London's wall and the Bishop's Gate, in which the 'spital stood, became known as Spitalfields.

The Augustinians, who ran the priory, were one of the most prominent orders in medieval London. They were also fabulously rich. The ambition of the priory grew throughout the Middle Ages, with a new charter of 1235 indicating the acquisition of even more land, bringing the estate to about 13 acres. By 1453, when Anton van den Wyngaerde drew a panorama of London, an enormous squat tower had been built over the priory church which dominated the skyline to the north-east. Where Fleur-de-Lis Street now runs, with Elder Street joining it from the south, were the priory's orchard and garden, with the main water supply running in a conduit along what is now Blossom Street.[2]

All this would change with the Reformation. One of the most dramatic effects of Henry VIII's dispute with the Pope was the king's greedy obsession to acquire the wealth – in particular the buildings and land – of the monasteries. The interior and tower of St Mary's – one of the largest churches in London – were dismantled. This happened despite the pleas of the Lord Mayor of London, Sir Richard Gresham, to keep

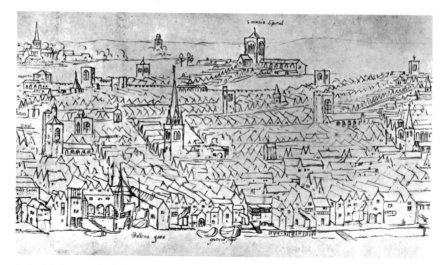

Part of Anton van den Wyngaerde's 1543 panorama of London. The Bishop's Gate is on the wall towards the left of the image; the church behind it is St Mary's Priory.

the capital's biggest hospital open. The only concession the king made was that the poor and infirm already lodged in priory buildings would be suffered to stay but no new inmates were to be admitted. Today, the only significant priory structure that survives in Spitalfields is the early-fourteenth-century charnel house, the remains of which can now be found just south of Spital Square.

The effects of the monastery on the layout of Spitalfields, however, would be long-lasting. While most of former monastic Spitalfields had, by the late seventeenth century, been covered with buildings, much of the old priory orchard and garden remained open land and was known as 'Porter's Close'. In 1716 the small estate of which the close formed a part was acquired by Isaac Tillard, a grandee among the French Protestant Huguenots who had settled in the area since the late seventeenth century. He and his family evidently had ambitions for this open space. The construction of speculatively-built terrace houses had been the main object of the Spitalfields estate owners during the second half of the seventeenth century and Tillard, seeing there was money to be made, joined in. But there was to be a difference. Tillard wanted the houses on his estate to be slightly larger and more architecturally impressive than most of the neighbouring seventeenth-century houses. He presumably believed there was a market for this more expensive product because in the early decades of the eighteenth century the silk industry in Spitalfields, dominated by Huguenot refugees, was doing very well indeed.

Tillard's speculation was shrewd. It has been estimated that by 1710 up to 80,000 Huguenots had fled Roman Catholic persecution in their French homeland. More than half of that number came to England, with most settling in London. So by the first decade of the eighteenth century Huguenots perhaps formed 5 per cent of the city's total population of around 575,000.[3] And this new community of wealth-generating merchants – working profitably in precious metals as well as silk – was welcomed by British authorities, even if regarded with some suspicion by tradesmen who feared their wages and profits would be undercut by these industrious Calvinists. The London historian John Strype probably expressed the majority view in 1720 when he wrote that, in Spitalfields, migrants have 'found quiet and security, and settled themselves in their several Trades and Occupations; Weavers especially' bringing 'a great Advantage . . . to the whole Nation, by the rich Manufactures of weaving Silks and Stuffs and Camlets' while also being 'Patterns of Thrift, Honesty, Industry, and Sobriety'.[4]

By May 1724 plans were in place to build Elder Street,[5] which is on your left as you walk west along Fleur-de-Lis Street. By 1725 it formed the main and central street in a small orthogonal grid of streets that the estate had laid out on Porter's Close. And, while the houses to the south around Spital Square were grand and formed the architectural and social jewel of the Tillard estate, those on Elder Street are also admirably well detailed, of good size and were originally inhabited by some of the area's leading merchants.

The south half of Elder Street remains largely intact, and it is the pair of facing terraces that you see as you walk west along Fleur-de-Lis Street. With their warm-coloured brickwork, well-wrought window arches, and diverse but erudite timber doorcases, they are a splendid example of London's domestic architecture of the 1720s (the houses in the street were built between 1725 and 1728). All were the result of speculations by different tradesmen, working on relatively short leases from the Tillard estate. The speculators tended to limit their expenditure and exposure to fluctuating markets, by constructing pairs of houses rather than larger groups. Much of the character of these buildings is due to the fact that

The east side of Elder Street, built 1725–8.

certain key details – such as doorcases and internal timber panelling and staircases – were left to the discretion of the first occupiers, and created to suit their tastes and pockets. This was typical of the manner in which Georgian London was built.[6]

And yet even in this exciting new world of migration and commerce, the effects of the monastery and the medieval world continued to be felt. Most of Elder Street lies in the Liberty of Norton Folgate – a self-governing urban entity, a little like that at White Friars, which was formed just after the Reformation from former monastic land that lay outside the ancient boundaries of the surrounding parishes. The northern tip of Elder Street is in the parish of St Leonard Shoreditch, which had been there since at least the twelfth century. And, to the south, the surviving fragment of the long, tall and uniform terrace of 1724, at 18, 16 and 10 Folgate Street, suggests in its scale and grandeur that this row was conceived as the formal entry from Bishopsgate into the Tillard estate – echoing one of the medieval routes of entry, via a gatehouse, from Bishopsgate into the St Mary's monastic precinct.

More recent architectural additions have been rather less respectful to Spitalfields' monastic past. Move west along the west portion of Fleur-de-Lis Street, which joins Blossom Street, now with a mix of mid- to late-nineteenth-century warehouses along its west side. At the time of writing this Blossom Street complex is being rebuilt, with some structures retained, as offices and retail buildings rising as high as fourteen storeys. Due to such schemes – in this case approved in autocratic manner by Boris Johnson, who, when Mayor of London, overturned a planning refusal from the democratically elected Tower Hamlets politicians – the historic character of Spitalfields is being fatally diluted.

⸻ ⋆◆⋆ ⸻

The next portion of the walk takes us along Norton Folgate, the name given to this portion of Bishopsgate. A narrow alley continues west from the end of Fleur-de-Lis Street through to Norton Folgate before it joins Shoreditch High Street to the north. This road, with its different names, follows the route of Ermine Street, the great Roman road running north to Lincoln and York that remained in use through the Middle Ages.

Today, the view south is extraordinary. As you emerge from the alley you will, almost immediately in front of you, see the tower – fifty storeys high and completed in 2018 – that loomed over you as you walked along Fleur-de-Lis Street. The tower contains private apartments, with the penthouses at the top on offer for £8 million. Like much of London's commercial architecture, the tower was designed by Foster + Partners (of London City Hall, the Gherkin, the Berlin Reichstag redevelopment and so on) and was conceived before the Brexit-related economic, political and social chaos of the last few years. It will be interesting, then, to see how quickly these apartments now sell – and at what prices. Immediately to the south of the tower is another new building, fifteen storeys high, very different in appearance but also designed by Foster + Partners. This is the London HQ for Amazon, in front of which is a minuscule square, or rather a plaza in the New York tradition. This apparent attempt to make the setting of these two buildings even faintly agreeable is little more than a gesture: the plaza is effectively the entrance forecourt for the Amazon office. Opposite these two new structures, on the other hand, stands – in the summer of 2019 – a mixed array of derelict buildings (two of which are early eighteenth century in origin and many destined to be destroyed as part of the Blossom Street scheme) and a row of low late-nineteenth-century structures that house shops and a pub. Modest in their scale and function, they are in striking contrast to the towers, spectres from the area's fast-disappearing past.

Even here, though, the ancient past of Norton Folgate rears its head. At the corner of Worship Street and Bishopsgate – the site of the boundary cross we encountered in London's earliest map – there stands a cast-iron heraldic dragon. For medieval Christians the dragon, like the griffin it resembles, was seen as a guardian or guide, and symbol of power and endurance – as made clear by the City's coat of arms, which includes dragons and a motto that reads *Domine dirige nos*, meaning 'Lord guide us'. More evidence that the City has for centuries seen itself as a sacred place, under divine guidance and protection. This creature has long been the City's emblem, and statues like this mark various of its boundaries.

Worship Street was once the Hog Lane that we encountered earlier. It is probable that William Shakespeare lodged here in the 1580s when involved, with Richard Burbage, in The Theatre, London's first purpose-built theatre since Roman times, founded in 1572 and based nearby. He may also have lodged on Norton Folgate itself. More certain is playwright Christopher Marlowe's association with the area. According to a 1581 warrant for his arrest, Marlowe lodged in Norton Folgate when a fatal brawl took place in Hog Lane, during which a local innkeeper's son named William Bradley was killed by Marlowe's friend Thomas Watson. Today the whole street is something of an architectural wasteland, the one exception being the remarkable terrace at numbers 91 to 101 that was designed in 1862 by Phillip Webb – William Morris's friend, architect and artistic collaborator – and is a rare example of Arts and Crafts architecture coming into the inner city: offering not wistful or fantastical homes, but practical nitty-gritty accommodation for a far-from-affluent neighbourhood.

Our route, though, is south along Bishopsgate. We soon come to Brushfield Street to the east, carved through the neighbourhood in the 1780s to improve links with the fruit and vegetable market that had existed in Spitalfields since the 1680s. From our location, you can just see Christ Church Spitalfields, constructed between 1714 and 1729 to the designs of Nicholas Hawksmoor. This is one of the 'Fifty New Churches' that a 1711 Act of Parliament ordered to be built in expanding parts of London (see p. 111), to proclaim the power of the church and state in places largely Victorian Revival building that is a loose imitation of the Victorian Gothic Revival structure that stood on the site. So a revival of a revival. But even

Nicholas Hawksmoor's
Christ Church, Spitalfields,
built 1714–29.

populated by Dissenters – or, as in Spitalfields, Protestants but not Anglicans, as was the case with the Calvinist Huguenots. The 1711 churches tended to be large and expensive to construct, which is why only a dozen or so were built before the project spluttered out in the late 1730s. But what churches they were. Even from a distance the powerful character of Hawksmoor's architecture is apparent. It is sculptural, bold – almost abstract in feel – with the emotional clout coming from the dramatic juxtaposition of pure, elemental forms. Even from Bishopsgate you can see that the west front of the church takes the form of a horizontal rectangle topped by a vertical rectangle, then by a cube supporting an obelisk-like spire. Both of the rectangles, each with an arch forming the centre of a tripartite composition, appear to be essays upon a Roman triumphal arch. The message seems clear: the church is a prayer in stone, representing the Christian belief that the soul can rise in triumph over death.

Such additions are, in City terms, relatively recent. But even such modern buildings are steeped in an older history. Continue south along Bishopsgate and to your left is New Street, which roughly marks the location of Hand Alley – in 1665, according to Daniel Defoe's *Journal of the Plague Year* (1722), the site of a pit for the disposal of the bodies of plague victims. Now it is dominated by the towering Bengal Warehouse, built for the East India Company in 1769–70, with its wide entrance gates and narrow forecourts. Here carts loaded with the wonders of the East would once have made their way into what was a walled and very secure mercantile enclosure.

Nearly opposite New Street sits Liverpool Street station, which arrived on this site in 1874. It stands largely on ground that from 1247 has been occupied by the Priory of Our New Lady of Bethlehem – better known as Bedlam. The priory specialised in the care of the mentally ill and survived the Reformation of the 1530s. This is one of the religious houses that the Lord Mayor of the time, Sir Richard Gresham, did manage to save so that – although no longer a Roman Catholic priory – it could continue to do its vital, worldly job, but now under City of London ownership and protection.

Bedlam continued on this site until the 1670s when it moved to nearby Moorfields, where it rebuilt itself in high style. Of course, the station holds no hint of this past – the Bishopsgate entrance is now marked by a 1980s

The pleasing bulk of the Barry brothers' Great Eastern Hotel.

Victorian revival building. But even revivals can be authentic in their way, and this 1980s building does the job.

Immediately to the south stands the more pleasing bulk of the Great Eastern Hotel, designed by Charles Barry Junior and E. M. Barry, the sons of the architect of the Palace of Westminster as rebuilt after the catastrophic fire of 1834 (see pp. 302–3). Clearly, rebuilding on top of lost medieval monuments ran in the family.

————◆◆◆————

You now start to enter a very different terrain, the crucible of the new high-rise City of London. Towers sprout all around. They dominate the next portion of the walk, and start at the south edge of Devonshire Row, which faces the Great Eastern Hotel and runs east from Bishopsgate.

The name Devonshire Row commemorates the fact that in the sixteenth century a magnificent mansion named 'Fisher's Folly' stood on the site. Jasper Fisher was a City merchant and goldsmith with great aspirations. After his death his mansion was occupied by various grand families including the Manners family, who were Earls of Rutland, and the Cavendish family, who were Earls of Devonshire. The Cavendish family came to prominence in the fourteenth century – Sir John Cavendish, while attending upon Richard II at Smithfield, probably dealt the death blow to Wat Tyler, the leader of the Peasants' Revolt of 1318. The dynasty became massively influential in the sixteenth century, when Sir William Cavendish – a close ally of Henry VIII's chief minister Thomas Cromwell – was able to enrich himself from the Dissolution of the Monasteries. By that time Bishopsgate, within and without the City wall, was a popular location for the mansions of aristocrats as well as prosperous merchants.

South of this site is Houndsditch, which appears on the 1550s Copperplate map as a narrow curving lane, lined with houses on its north side and the ditch or moat of the City's walled defences on its south. This part of Houndsditch now offers a very different experience, with the hotel and apartment tower rising to the north and immediately to the south the soaring, 230-metre-tall Heron Tower (or Salesforce Tower, as it has recently been renamed in less than elegiac manner). The Heron Tower was completed in 2011 and has a brash, no-nonsense appearance, with the zigzag bracing of its structural frame exposed and clad with dull silver metal. The architects were the American commercial practice Kohn Pedersen Fox. This office tower has a few public benefits. There is a bar on part of the ground floor that shares – with the reception – a vast fish tank full of strange creatures and on the upper floors are restaurants and bars (one open twenty-four hours a day) and a roof terrace, all of which offer good views over the City and East London.

Opposite, on Bishopsgate, is the church of St Botolph-without-Bishopsgate. There has been a church here since at least the thirteenth century. It then backed directly on to the City ditch, the defensive moat that surrounded the City's wall. The existing building is later, roughly the same date as Christ Church – it was started in 1724 and completed in 1729. Although St Botolph's is a far more economic exercise than Christ Church, both materially and intellectually, it is not without its charm. The architects were James Gould and George Dance the Elder, two surveyors and architects who drew on their extensive City connections to win a number of crucial commissions: Dance went on to design the Mansion House (see pp. 142–4). The main frontage to the church is to Bishopsgate, but this is also its east end and the location of the main altar. This presented the pair with a potential problem. By convention Christian churches offer a processional route from entry to altar so that, ideally, the main entrance and show front

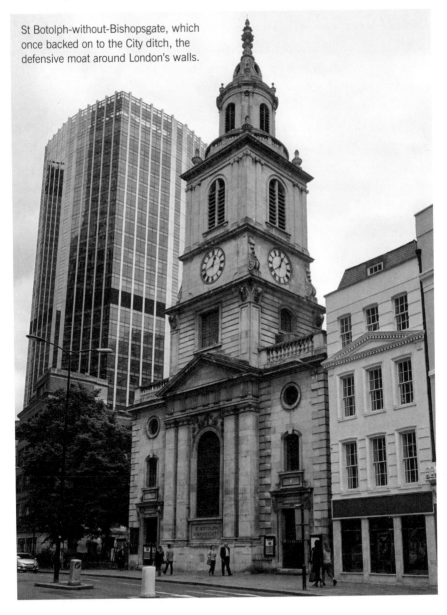

St Botolph-without-Bishopsgate, which once backed on to the City ditch, the defensive moat around London's walls.

should be at the west end. Here this could not be the case but, undaunted, the pair treated the east end as the main entry, with doors and entrance vestibules designed so that one sidles into the church and then turns to face the altar. Above the altar rises a square-plan tower, much in the manner of several of Christopher Wren's City churches.

Before continuing south along Bishopsgate it's worth walking a few metres east along Houndsditch to get a better view of one of the oddest high-rise buildings erected in recent years in the small patch of city. The building bellies out towards Houndsditch and towards parallel Camomile Street, and both curves meet at the top as an arch. When viewed from the east or the west, the structure, now called 70 St Mary Axe, takes the profile of a massive parabolic arch. Crude perhaps – but visually striking and the very personification of structural strength. Also crude but effective is the glazing. The curving north and south elevations are clad with slender ribs and are fully glazed with curtain walls. Look and wonder. It's one of those ideas for a building that pops up on an envelope but usually the next morning gets dismissed as being a bit too simplistic. But not here. The bold doodle has been built.

———————◆•◆•◆———————

As you continue south, you come to the location of the Roman and medieval wall around the City. At the junction of Bishopsgate and Wormwood Street stood one of the major gates in the wall – the long-lost Bishop's Gate. There is nothing of the gate to be seen, but standing nearby, on London Wall (as Wormwood Street becomes), there is a fragment of the City wall, thought to date from the Roman fortification of the City that took place around AD 190–225. Most of the wall visible here is wrought of seventeenth- and eighteenth-century brick but a small portion and lower levels are made of ragstone and there is even evidence of brick and tile that were laid in horizontal courses within the stone courses by Roman engineers to give improved stability.

It is haunting how the presence of the wall, although itself now virtually invisible, still makes itself felt. There is the street London Wall, of course, which follows the inner circuit of the wall, and which almost makes the ancient fortification tangible. And the names of the once all-important gates echo in street names – Aldgate, Bishopsgate, Moorgate,

A fragment of the Roman wall around the City.

Aldersgate. Perhaps more moving are the ancient buildings that nestle up to the wall, built when it was still a defining presence, cradling a world within its protective embrace and keeping the world outside at arm's length.

Take the church that stands immediately to the west, appropriately named All Hallows-on-the-Wall. This is the site of a thirteenth-century church that was rebuilt in 1765 to 1767 in a pioneering and solemn neoclassical manner inspired by antique precedent. It was designed by James Gould's grandson and George Dance's son, George Dance junior. He was an architect and planner of genius who went on to become the City's Architect and Surveyor. When he won the competition to design All Hallows he was twenty-four, and had just returned from a Grand Tour in Italy – and the building he produced is very much in the Roman manner. The most visible elevation, wrought of brick, is embellished with tall piers each topped by arches. Three of these arches contain semicircular openings, called lunettes, inspired by the design of Roman baths. The effect is severe: utilitarian yet in its way sublime. Inside the narrow church – really no more than a sliver of a building – the light from the lunettes plays upon the curved surface of the vault and its moulded

Delicate plasterwork adorns the roof inside All Hallows-on-the-Wall.

plaster decorations. The geometry and decoration of the vault are Roman in form, probably derived from the Temple of Venus near the Forum in Rome. But the complex lozenge-shaped decoration of the apse could also have been inspired by plates depicting Palmyra – particularly the Temple of Bel – that had been published in 1753 by Robert Wood in *The Ruins of Palmyra*. Islamic State has recently destroyed the prototype so this evocation is particularly precious. This is a most wonderful little church, often overlooked but inspiring.

As you return to Bishopsgate, take a moment to consider the names of these roads – Wormwood Street, on which you walk, and Camomile Street, a little to the east. The road names seem of ancient origin: both appear, as Wormwood and 'Camamile' Streets, on Ogilby and Morgan's City map of 1676, which also shows the Bishop's Gate and large runs of adjoining City wall still in existence. Wormwood and Camomile are herbs, both traditionally used as medicines. Camomile was brewed to make a bracing infusion that was (and is) an antidote to anxiety; its name, from the Greek via Latin, means 'Earth Apple'. Wormwood is more curious. Its leaves and flowers, and the oil made from them, have been used since ancient times to treat digestive disorders, depression and fever and have even been regarded as an aphrodisiac. The family name of the plant is *Artemisia* and one branch of the family is *absinthium*, a key ingredient in the production of the powerful psychoactive, hallucinogenic spirit absinthe.

Presumably these street names commemorate the fact that, in the distant past, they were the location of the City's herb market, with precious commodities brought from all over the known world. But there is another possibility, one that connects with ancient City lore. In keeping with the medieval perception of London as a sacred city there seems to have been – enshrined in its architecture, its customs and its legends – much reference to biblical texts. The fifteenth-century Guildhall – built, arguably, in the model of the Holy of Holies – contains images of the legendary giants Gog and Magog, who make an appearance in the Book of Revelation. So too does wormwood. The reference is most strange: 'a great star, blazing like a torch, fell from the sky' and 'the name of the star is Wormwood . . . waters turned bitter, and many people died from the waters'.[7] So perhaps Wormwood Street was once part of the biblical landscape of the 'Square Mile', which sought to suggest that the City was the New Jerusalem.

If Wormwood Street was part of a continuous 'miracle play' then presumably it was intended to conjure up the evil to come when – as the Book of Revelation warns – Satan was to be 'released for a little while' as a prelude to the apocalyptic End of Days that Christian doctrine claims will usher in the second coming of Christ. Wormwood Street today, with its roaring traffic, scuttling pedestrians and looming glass towers of Mammon does, it must be admitted, possess alarming qualities that mark it as a not unlikely location for the end of the world.

One of the most unsettling aspects of this piece of City is, as already observed, the visual cacophony and sense of profound chaos as towers rise seemingly without regard to one another. On the south-east corner of Bishopsgate and Camomile Street a new tower – glass-clad and of simplistic design (although no doubt of complex construction) – rises up to the sky, to join this community of commercial behemoths. As if to emphasise the inhumanity of such structures, the tower proclaims itself as merely 100 Bishopsgate. Essentially it is identified as just a number, and its creators think this is fitting. One looks, ponders the

Earlier worlds: the fourteenth-century St Ethelburga church sits nestled between much later buildings.

massive scale of the new tower – so much for the visionary New Jerusalem of medieval imagination – and scurries on.

Next to 100 Bishopsgate are reminders of earlier worlds. As if to emphasise the difference between the present and the past this survivor is diminutive – almost ridiculously so when seen in contrast with its towering neighbours. St Ethelburga-the-Virgin, facing on to Bishopsgate, is the third of the medieval churches to cluster around the Bishopsgate: St Botolph's just outside the wall, All Hallows adjoining the inner face of the wall and St Ethelburga's inside the wall. It is the only one to retain a significant amount of its medieval fabric and appearance, having escaped destruction in the Great Fire and in the eighteenth century, when most of its neighbours were rebuilt.

The dedications of these three churches are interesting. St Botolph was, until the rise of St Christopher in the late Middle Ages, the Christian church's dominant patron saint of travellers. St Botolph-without-Bishopsgate is one of several churches just outside City gates dedicated to that saint in medieval times. All Hallows – as its name reveals – was dedicated to all the saints and to those blessed with beatific vision and in direct communion with God. Ethelburga was a seventh-century abbess of Barking Abbey, way to the east of the City, and so is rather homely in its dedication. It is also homely in appearance. The existing building dates from the early fourteenth century and contains only a small nave and one aisle, and a west front built of rubble that features a door with a pointed arch and a modest but nicely detailed window.

The western half of the church was reassembled from its old stones after being blasted apart by the explosion in 1993 of a bomb planted nearby by the IRA. I was at home in Spitalfields when the bomb detonated, at about 10.30 a.m. and about half a kilometre away. The lights in my house all went out a split second before a massive and deep explosion. I raced to the window and saw, to the south, smoke in the sky and a hurricane of paper – I suppose the contents of the desks and filing cabinets of thousands of City workers who had just lost their offices. I went into the street and moved towards the pillar of acrid smoke, but with great caution. It occurred to me that there might be a second bomb. The sound of sirens filled the air and I could not venture far south along Bishopsgate before reaching a police cordon and being told to get back. All I could see was the eddying cloud of paper, rising high into the sky, and the desolate appearance of Liverpool Street station.

Subsequently I saw the strange things blast can do. It travels in straight lines, so fragile buildings near the explosion escaped damage because they were secreted around corners or in alleys or courts shielded from the direct blast. But I was amazed to see that some buildings as far away as Brick Lane had been damaged because they stood opposite wider, straighter streets, down which the energy of the blast had rushed – in zigzag fashion being bounced off stout structures – as it sought the course of least resistance. I found this interesting because it explained something that had long puzzled me. How had the fragile eighteenth-century glass in the windows of my Spitalfields home survived the bombing of the Blitz in late 1940? High-explosive bombs had been falling in large numbers half a kilometre away or less. Now I understood. Clearly, by a quirk of geography, my street was shielded from the blast that shattered more distant yet more exposed locations.

Immediately south of St Ethelburga's church is St Helen's Place. This is an oddity in the City: a broad and architecturally ambitious court, and an oasis of calm that is distinctly Parisian in feel, designed in the early 1920s by the Francophile London-based architects Mewes and Davis. Earlier in the century they had designed the Ritz Hotel in Piccadilly, inspired by the Rue de Rivoli in Paris. The grand and stone-faced buildings of St Helen's Place conjure up associations of a vast Parisian mansion, with pavilions and *cours d'honneur*.

The court stretches back from the sites of 60–64 Bishopsgate on which the London headquarters of the Hudson's Bay Company had stood. The buildings of the court were completed in 1926 to house the company – which has long since moved out – but its role in their creation explains the otherwise somewhat baffling ornament. For example, the court is entered by passing beneath a building and through a screen of Doric columns. Above these columns is a frieze embellished with stone-carved details of a most exotic kind: some feature wolves' heads, others snowshoes, feathered war bonnets, quivers of arrows, moose horns, axes and powder horns. These, of course, were the stock in trade of the Hudson's Bay Company. It was founded by Royal Charter in London in 1670 and soon controlled the fur and hunting trade in much of North America, making it not only the largest land-owner in the world but also – through its network of trading posts, trade routes and alliance with native peoples and settler communities – the de facto government in much of Canada.

More explicit reference to the connection of this building with the Hudson's Bay Company is the coat of arms moulded on the ceiling of the entrance block, with beavers, fox and elk (apparently no one in London in the 1670s knew what moose or caribou looked like so made do with elk), and a motto in Latin that reads 'skin for leather' (a reference to Job 2:4 – 'skin for skin'). This was to leave no one in doubt that honest trade was a holy business. To top it all off, and to leave no doubt either about the animal upon which much of the financial success of the company was based, there is a small turret above the entrance that holds up a weathervane topped by an image of a beaver – the hapless creatures whose skin was the company's crowning glory.

Again, though, even this most twentieth century of plazas has its links with the medieval past. For the south range of the court now houses the Leathersellers' livery company. The company's charter dates from 1444, although it was only recently moved here, and is now housed in contemporary splendour. It used to control the leather trade in London but it has long lost its regulatory role. Now it supports charitable activities and spends its time promoting leather goods. The interior has been designed by Eric Parry, one of Britain's more interesting architects and a champion of contemporary design spiced with a flavour of history. It is well worth seeing, but it must be said is a trifle too tasteful – especially if you like your livery halls to be brimming with opulent and charmingly over-the-top Baroque ornament, such as the Armourers' Company on London Wall, with its splendid displays of seventeenth-century breastplates, helmets and pikes.

Back on Bishopsgate, adjoining Mewes and Davis's imposing stone-clad frontage to the south, is a fascinating group of buildings. Numbers 50, 48 and 46 Bishopsgate are the only early domestic and commercial buildings to survive on this stretch of the street and give some idea of its appearance in the eighteenth and nineteenth centuries. The plots indicate that they too have a link with the ancient past – they are relatively narrow and deep, a typical medieval urban arrangement. The most remarkable is Number 46. In this busy City street, full of commercial architecture, much of it modern and high-rise, we have a modest eighteenth-century house – probably dating from around 1740 – and only a little later than those that survive a world away in the backwater streets of Spitalfields. The house's brick front has been rebuilt, probably in the late twentieth century and not particularly well (the bricks' colour and the detailing around the window jambs are wrong), but inside panelling survives on the first-floor landing and in the second-floor front room, once no doubt the main bedroom of the shopkeeper or merchant who would have lived here.

And to the south stands an even more remarkable building. Great St Helen's, now an amorphous open space flanked by high-rise commercial towers, marks the route to an almost miraculous

The west front of Great St Helen's, a church in two halves. The north door dates to the sixteenth century, the south to the fourteenth.

ancient structure. St Helen's church, like St Ethelburga, survived the Great Fire of 1666 and wartime bombing. Originating in the twelfth century and largely rebuilt in the early thirteenth century, the church is now one of the architectural glories of London. In 1210 it became the priory church for Benedictine nuns and from that time a favoured place for opulent burials – so that it is now second only to Westminster Abbey in the number of memorials within its walls.

The west front of the church, which dates from the early thirteenth century, tells its story. Rather strangely, there are two doors of almost equal size, each topped by a large fifteenth-century window and divided by a centrally placed buttress of the usual stepped profile. The arrangement was necessary because, until the priory was closed in 1538 during the Reformation, the building was in essence two churches. The nave entered by the door to the north was used by the nuns, and the nave to the south was used by the parishioners. The row of arches running through the church, once closed off with timber panelling, divided the two. The external buttress resists the thrust of the arcade.

The south side of the church is a marvellous thing. The rubble stonework is like a collage of history, patched and mended through the centuries. Particularly fine is the west elevation of the south transept, with its array of small thirteenth-century windows. The somewhat self-consciously odd stone-made door surround was added in the mid 1990s to the design of Quinlan Terry, who at that time reordered the interior after serious damage by IRA bombs in 1992 and 1993. But there is a second, even more glorious, stone door surround on the south side of the church. The door is dated 1633 and is a wonderful example of a classical style that flourished in London and its environs in the mid seventeenth century, favoured particularly by merchants and men of wealth. Such classical architecture is the child of the Italian Renaissance, which from the early fifteenth century, in increasingly coherent and erudite manner, sought to give rebirth to the culture of Rome. This meant a return to ancient Roman architecture, and by implication that of Greece. As we will see time and again in the chapters that follow, this classical architecture was – both in the ancient past and during the Renaissance – a living thing, evolving and adapting to different cultures and traditions.

The door surround on this church has much in common with the Baroque and Mannerist style that evolved in the sixteenth century in Italy and the Low Countries, distinguished by an inventive and often idiosyncratic use of the classical language of design. In the 1630s this would have been in striking contrast to the simpler and more orthodox

The Renaissance comes to London: the classical door surround on the south side of St Helen's.

style of classicism being promoted by the Stuart court and aristocracy, as seen in Inigo Jones's designs for the court in Whitehall, St James's and Greenwich (see pp. 80–81). This preference for Mannerist Baroque in the City can be seen as a statement of cultural independence by merchants whose tastes veered more to the exotic and ornamental – as witnessed here by the vigorous use of the classical language. The architrave and half-pilasters framing the door are particularly characterful, as is the delightful chubby-faced and winged cherub that adorns the pediment.

There's one other detail worth brooding on. Immediately to the south of the 1633 door is a cast-iron bollard, and this is a genuine cannon, up-ended so that it's not the muzzle that pops up above ground but the rounded 'knob' at its rear. Look hard and you can also see, just at ground level, the remains of the trunnions – the pivots on which the cannon was placed in its carriage. It's a splendid thing, and has probably stood on or near this location for a couple of centuries or more, guarding the church's congregation from wayward carts or carriages.

———◆•◆•◆———

Now back to Bishopsgate and, immediately to the left (south), is another of the City's new generation of ultra-sleek and ultra-tall commercial towers. Known as 22 Bishopsgate – another example of the sinister-feeling City fashion for giving overpowering buildings numbers not names – it rises 278 metres in sixty-two storeys and was designed by PLP Architecture. It's hard to comprehend the demand for yet another commercial tower in this small patch of the City. This building will add around 120,000 square metres of office and 4,000 square metres of retail space to the City's stockpile, although much of the space in this block is intended to be shared and form the base for a community of independent entrepreneurs. A relatively worthy intention, though from the artistic point of view it is hard to feel much affection for this tower. It lacks character, with its sheath of all-embracing glass merely breaking backwards and forwards in slight manner.

More interesting is the site on which the tower stands. Part of it is on the location of one of the City's most famous houses. Crosby Place was constructed in 1466 for a City merchant named Sir John Crosby on land that he had leased from the prioress of St Helen's. It was a palatial complex that fronted on to Bishopsgate, whose three gables concealed a large court behind, a mansion on the east side and a great hall on the south. The hall was an ostentatious piece of work, being stone-built, with a tall bay window lighting the high table at the east end and a fine, ornamental, timber roof structure. This urban palace survived the Great Fire of 1666, which spared the north-east corner of the City, and, in reduced form and in increasingly incongruous manner, lived on until 1910 when it finally succumbed to commercial pressure and the demolition squad. But even then the great hall was spared complete oblivion and was carefully dismantled and reconstructed on Chelsea Embankment. For a century it served as a public hall but in 1989 was sold by Kensington and Chelsea to a businessman who eventually made it the centrepiece of his vast neo-Tudor mansion that, in its broad composition, seems inspired by Crosby Place.

This is a strange fate for a hall that has played a prominent role in Britain's history. Crosby died in 1476 – his monument survives in St Helen's church – but before his death he leased his mansion to the Duke of Gloucester, a key member of the Yorkist faction in the dynastic Wars of the Roses, to serve as his London home. This was natural. During the wars Crosby was a prominent Yorkist, and had led the defence of the City in 1471 when attacked by Lancastrian forces, and so it was fitting that Gloucester – an ambitious pretender to the throne – should occupy the City's most notable Yorkist mansion. And it was in this mansion – indeed in its hall in the

An 1804 sketch of the decaying Crosby Hall.

early 1480s – that meetings took place and stratagems set in place that led to the duke seizing the throne as Richard III. When he set himself up as Lord Protector, having confined the young Edward V to the Tower, Crosby Place became the nation's centre of power. As the chronicler Raphael

Holinshed put it, 'Little by little all folke . . . drew unto Crosbies in Bishops gates Street, where the Protector kept his household.'[8]

Shakespeare, in his tragedy *Richard III*, gives the house an important role. When Richard starts his pursuit of Anne Neville, seeing marriage to her as a useful stepping stone to the throne, he invites her to 'repair to Crosby Place'. This is something of an anachronism because, historically, this courtship probably took place before Richard had moved into Crosby Place – but Shakespeare would not, of course, let mere factual accuracy stand in the way of a good scene. Shakespeare must have known the mansion well. New research shows that he lived near what is now 35 Great St Helen's in the 1590s, when the play was written – a significant move up in the world because St Helen's was a rich parish, occupied by eminent public figures and wealthy merchants, and so was a world away from the home around Norton Folgate that he lived in previously. Consequently Shakespeare not only knew Crosby Place but no doubt also recognised that its architectural grandeur – in a setting of wealth and power – expressed precisely Richard's unbridled ambitions.

The first hint of the house is near the beginning of the play. Richard accosts Anne – the wife of the slain Lancastrian Prince of Wales who, in Shakespeare's opinion at least, was killed by Richard – as she escorts the body of Henry VI, her dead husband's father, to burial. Richard succeeds in ensnaring Anne and the scene ends with his chillingly cynical observation, 'Was ever woman in this humour woo'd? Was ever woman in this humour won? I'll have her; but I will not keep her long.' The scene directions in the play merely state that the action takes place in a London street but I fancy that in Shakespeare's imagination it occurred near St Helen's church, adjoining Crosby Place. Shakespeare's second significant mention of the mansion comes when Richard has dealings with the men he hires to murder the princes in the tower. He tells them, 'when you have done repair to Crosby Place,' thus making it the epicentre of Yorkist evil, and a site calculated to curdle the blood of Lancastrian, or by Shakespeare's time Tudor, loyalists.

There is even a legend that it was at Crosby Place that Richard was offered the crown in 1483. While most contemporary historians think that this happened at Baynards Castle, which stood on the Thames near Blackfriars Bridge, John Strype in his 1720 edition of the *Survey of London*

Gibson Hall, embodiment of the spirit of the mid-nineteenth-century City.

states unequivocally that the 'citizens' – meaning the denizens of the City – went to Crosby Place to beg Richard to accept the crown. So, where towers now rear up and workers bustle in my mind's eye, I can't help but see Richard's spectral mansion and Anne's sad cortège making its way across the small churchyard in front of St Helen's, and fancy that I can taste the pungent atmosphere of deadly intrigue and sense the hunger for power. But perhaps that's just the City.

We now enter a part of the City with a different atmosphere. The skyscrapers dissipate and more staid nineteenth-century buildings become the norm. Threadneedle Street, to the west, is particularly remarkable in its architectural coherence – mercantile, classical in design and largely late nineteenth and early twentieth century.

At the junction is Gibson Hall – 15 Bishopsgate – one of the City's finest surviving mid-nineteenth-century commercial buildings. Designed by John Gibson, it was opened in 1865 as an extraordinarily opulent neo-Renaissance banking hall. Inside there are columned walls, glazed domes in the ceiling and a rich array of Italianate detail. Outside huge Corinthian engaged columns rise from a plinth, framing the single-storeyed building's wide arched windows. Above them are carved panels depicting the sort of industries, professions and crafts that the bank helped to finance – including mining, manufacturing, commerce and agriculture. Complementary stone-carved figures of large size stand on top. All is most impressive. That such a grand and erudite classical building should be constructed on a key site at the height of the Gothic Revival says much about the tastes of City men at the time. Not only were they traditional but also the classical language spoke of solidity, pedigree and reliability. The architectural product of the Gothic Revival – that got under way in earnest in the 1830s as designers sought to produce increasingly accurate interpretations of medieval buildings – could look too flimsy and ecclesiastical for the tastes of the City's commercial clients.

And it is also typical of the spirit of that curious age that the directors of the bank, an institution exercising the financial innovations of mid-nineteenth-century capitalism, chose to garb their building in carved panels depicting various money-making activities which avoid reference to modern technology. 'Navigation', for example, shows not an iron-hulled, steam-driven ship – the wonder of the 1860s – but a timber-made sailing ship. And naturally the panel depicting 'Arts and Architecture' shows not pioneering iron-framed buildings or Gothic forms, but bare-breasted muses venerating a Roman capital at the top of a column.

Opposite Gibson Hall is 39 Threadneedle Street, which turns the corner with Bishopsgate well through the simple device of treating the corner as a curved classical temple. This is achieved in minimal manner. Until 1874, when this building was constructed, the site was occupied by St Martin Outwich, originally a medieval church that survived the Great Fire but fell into ruin. It was rebuilt in powerful classical style between 1796 and 1798 by Samuel Pepys Cockerell, one of the most interesting architects of his generation. Cockerell's church had an oval nave, which presumably provided the new architect with the germ of the idea for his curved corner design.

G. H. Hunt, the designer of the existing building, was a provincial architect and, like many architects at the time, had a most eclectic bent. He designed Tudor-style timber-framed country houses, the stone-built, Baroque municipal buildings of 1890 in Gloucester and – as here – would on occasion indulge in a bit of neoclassicism. For a while he was in partnership with Thomas Verity, one of the most able theatre and restaurant designers in late Victorian London. The Bishopsgate building is a testimony to Hunt's talent. It is faced with mellow stone and the windows arched to suggest a Roman podium. The curved corner is further emphasised because it is ornamented by columns with capitals formed with carved acanthus leaves, in the manner of the Tower of the Winds in Athens. This building is always satisfying to contemplate and, for me, a source of quiet pleasure. It's so civilised, all is cleverly understated and so seemingly conventional and old-fashioned to the point of being dowdy, yet with a flash of ready wit that makes its familiar classical forms dance into life. It is at the centre of a group of several nineteenth-century commercial palazzi, all proclaiming that, in the Victorian City, Renaissance classicism was the style to instil financial confidence.

Now go west along Threadneedle Street and observe that, immediately to the north, is a small opening called Adam's Court. This is worth exploring. You pass the side elevations of two twentieth-century commercial buildings and arrive in a usually deserted and relatively recently created garden court, with a sunken lawn. On one side is a noble loggia, backing on to Threadneedle Street, and facing it is one of the architectural wonders of the City, the garden elevation of the City of London Club. Designed in 1832 by Philip Hardwick, who a few years later designed the arch at Euston station, it was conceived as a City-based gentleman's club to rival those being built in St James's. But this City permutation was not based around politics, intellectual pursuits or

G. H. Hunt's foray into neoclassicism at 39 Threadneedle Street.

travel but around trade and business. It's a solid and admirable building, a mix of Italian Renaissance and Greek Revival – predictable for the time and the type of building – but also with a nod to the English eighteenth-century Palladian tradition that recreated the classical forms of the sixteenth-century Venetian architect Andrea Palladio (see pp. 185–6). Take, for example, the garden front, which is dominated by three huge windows that are an inventive permutation of what was known as the 'Venetian window' – tripartite in design with its centre portion arch-topped – beloved by Renaissance architects such as Palladio.

As ever in the City, though, medieval fabric and imagery sneak their way into the apparently nineteenth-century architecture. On the south side of Threadneedle Street is a stone-made doorcase that frames an elaborate coat of arms. This – number 30 – leads to the hall of one of the prime City livery companies, the Merchant Taylors'. The door, and the commercial block on Threadneedle Street that screens the hall, dates from the 1840s. The hall itself, though, has ancient origins. The Merchant Taylors located themselves here in 1347, and their hall survived the Great Fire and was the City's only largely intact medieval hall until severely bomb-damaged during the Second World War. Parts survive, including portions of a late-fourteenth-century crypt, but most was reconstructed by Sir Albert Richardson, an admired conservation architect and classicist during the early post-war years. There are the remains of a medieval kitchen, as well as a 1920s cloister, and a simple range of late-seventeenth-century buildings.

———————◆•◆•◆———————

A little further west stands the final and, perhaps, most historically important building of the walk. This is the former Royal Exchange, in some senses the place where the modern City, as the nation's financial centre, has its origin. The construction of a merchants' exchange, to act as a centre of commerce in the City, was the idea of the merchants Richard Clough and Thomas Gresham. Inspired by continental examples, the pair determined to make the building large and grand to express the nobility of honest trade. When Queen Elizabeth opened the Exchange in 1571, she granted it a royal pedigree, and something even more valuable – permission to deal in alcohol. The exchange flourished and became the focus of the City's trade in goods, with merchants meeting and doing deals within the colonnades that flanked the building's large, central court.

The late-sixteenth-century building was destroyed in the Great Fire then rapidly rebuilt. But when the 1669 replacement in turn burned down, in 1838, it was decided that something new should be attempted. A competition was held for a new building, which was won by William Tite, the City-born son of a merchant. His design, organised as four ranges set around an open court – as with the previous exchanges – was conceived as a grand classical composition with a mighty columned portico on its west side. At the east end was a tall tower to assure the exchange made its mark on the City's skyline. This exchange was opened in 1844 by Queen Victoria as the financial heart of the City and, like its predecessors, was intended to make a bold architectural display.

Tite's basic idea was to design a classical building that greatly contributed to this hugely symbolic part of London. For Victorians the site represented *The Heart of the Empire*, as the artist Niels Møller Lund titled this bustling intersection in his atmospheric painting of 1904, which offers a view from the roof of the Royal Exchange looking west towards St

Niels Møller Lund's *The Heart of the Empire* (1904), from the Royal Exchange with the Mansion House in the foreground.

Paul's (now in the City's Guildhall Art Gallery). At that time the exchange remained the empire's financial heart because around this meeting of major City thoroughfares were also located the Bank of England, the headquarter buildings of major banking houses and the Mansion House, the official residence of the elected 'prince' of the Square Mile, the Lord Mayor of London.

And yet, for all its pomp, the exchange has had a chequered history. For much of the last 160 years or so it has been in search of a long-term identity and future, often being little more than a warren of City offices. By the early 1980s changing patterns of trade, and the uncertain fortunes of the City as a world marketplace, meant that the Royal Exchange – by then in poor repair – had most uncertain prospects. Business revived when its main tenant became the London International Financial Futures Exchange, with the courtyard becoming its primary trading floor. But things changed again in 2001 when the building was remodelled, with the courtyard given over to cafés, restaurants and shops that, until then, had been confined to small spaces created within the long north and south elevations.

The result made an already strange structure even more peculiar. The architecture of the building has always been somewhat unresolved – which is surprising, given Tite's seemingly safe strategy of bestowing upon his design a massive, conventional, classical presence. Somehow, it doesn't quite work. The reason, I think, relates to a profound architectural truth – so much is going on that the boldness of the essential idea is obscured and compromised. Despite the building's apparent gravitas, there is a certain lack of confidence, expressed by the fact that much of the overabundant ornament appears frivolous, irrational and illogical.

The architectural model Tite had in mind, of course, was the second-century AD Pantheon in Rome, or the eighteenth-century Panthéon in Paris. These buildings are characterised by a bold simplicity, in which the essential idea of triangular pediment, majestic colonnade and dome dominate. But Tite, who achieved a really fine eight-column-wide portico, just couldn't leave things alone. Succumbing to the over-ornamental spirit of the age, he felt compelled to trick-out his building with trivial, fiddly, irrelevant and ultimately annoying details. Take, for example, the sections of wall flanking the columns at the front. They are ornamented,

The view west along Threadneedle Street. On the left the Royal Exchange, on the right the Bank of England and in the distance the Mansion House.

from bottom to top, with banded rustication – the style in which stone channels break up the wall – with areas of plain stone walling and a carved ornamental panel, with a carved floral swag linking the capitals of the pilasters, and finally with a horizontal entablature topped by a balustrade. It is too much – distracting and too visually dominant – when all that is required is for the magnificent portico to stand in solitary and unchallenged splendour. As the modernist architect Mies van der Rohe is said to have observed in the mid twentieth century, 'Less is more.' The Royal Exchange – with its tremendous history, its dominant site and evident architectural and artistic aspirations – ought to be one of London's best-loved Victorian buildings. But it is not. This says it all.

In many ways, though, the overwrought Royal Exchange is a fitting end to this walk. After all, what could be a better embodiment of the City of London than this: a noble and ancient institution whose great historic importance and dignity is to a degree undermined by its currently dominant and somewhat ephemeral use as shops and restaurants? These, after all, are the streets in which medieval treasures like St Helen's and Guildhall are nestled within an ever-growing number of ever higher commercial tower blocks. It makes every walk through the City of London a fascinating, if disconcerting, experience.

St Mary Magdalene, East Ham

The Domesday Book of 1086 records a settlement called Hame to the east of London. The name denotes a hamlet on a dry area of land between marshland and rivers – in this case the Rivers Lea, Thames and Roding. And it is a name that lives on in West Ham and East Ham, the old and once marshy borderland between London and Essex. This is a land crossed by ancient roads, and littered with haunting fragments of the past.

It can be difficult, when walking through East Ham today, to remember that this is an ancient village. It is a diverse and vibrant suburb of London, but one which at first glance has little going for it in the way of architecture: as the great architectural historian Nikolaus Pevsner put it in his survey, *The Buildings of England,* 'Much of East Ham is dull.'[1] However, a few miles south of the Tube station, the high street offers up a man-made wonder. To the south-east a low and broad medieval church tower comes suddenly into view, across the variegated rooftops of modern buildings. The church is set some little way back from the droning traffic, with its stubby west tower set square on to the road.

The pair of tall, narrow and semicircular-topped arches on the west elevation of the tower instantly proclaim this church to be something very special. Pointed arches instead of semicircular arches started to come into general use during the second half of the twelfth century, and became standard from the early thirteenth century – so this church must be twelfth century. The arches are in the Romanesque style, so named because its forms and details retain a lingering memory of Roman classical architecture. (The style is also sometimes called 'Norman' because in the nineteenth century it was believed, generally erroneously, that it had been introduced into England by the Normans after 1066. Even more confusingly, in the eighteenth century the style was often called 'Saxon'.)

Remarkably, the church's original form remains intact, with only minimal alteration through nearly 900 years. Certain stone and timber details and building methods – such as the apse at the east end to the chancel and the wide, semicircular arch between chancel and apse – suggest that construction started at the east end somewhere between 1130 and 1150; a west tower was built perhaps in the early thirteenth century and altered in the fifteenth and sixteenth centuries; and a few windows were added in the seventeenth and mid nineteenth centuries. But all in all this is one of the oldest, least-altered and most fascinating medieval churches in London.

Even the church's doors reveal much about its history. That to the west, now concealed inside the thirteenth-century tower but still with its Romanesque semicircular arch, would have been used during special festivals – such as Palm Sunday and Easter – when the congregation would have processed around and through the church. The south door, which remains the more usual entrance, also retains its original semicircular arch. But even more intriguing is the door in the south wall of the apse in the east, which was perhaps inserted or enlarged in the thirteenth century. This is the 'priest's door', which allowed clergy to enter and leave the chancel and apse without having to leave the sacred space at the east end of the church, and without passing through the profane space of the nave occupied by the laity. In the twelfth and thirteenth centuries, the central nave was regarded as a secular space, rather like a village hall, separated from the altar by a partition called a rood screen. Clerics celebrated Mass almost for their own benefit, with the laity loitering beyond the screen, in the hope of receiving a little spiritual fallout or a few blessings from the priests.

The fourth door is in the east end of the north side of the church. It looks considerably later than the other three and its lower portion is now bricked up. This opening seems to be related to a peculiar feature of the church, a small hatch through the chancel's north wall. According to one reading of the surviving physical evidence,

The north side of the apse, perhaps once home to an anchorite.

near this door was located the cell (or 'anchorhold') of an anchorite – a person who out of religious conviction chose to withdraw from the world, immuring themselves in a room attached to the eastern portion of a church. Within this cell, which they seldom or ever left, the anchorite held solitary communion with God and, through prayer, hoped to atone for the sins of the world. They perhaps communicated with the world via a grille – through which they were given food and passed spiritual insights to all who would listen. And through a small window into the chancel they witnessed Mass being celebrated and partook of the Eucharist. All external trace of the anchorhold and its grille has gone, leaving just the enigmatic window or hatch to remind us what might have been, although there is a diminutive cell within the thickness of the wall – but surely not large enough for even the most self-mortifying of religious fanatics.

Also worth studying while outside are the windows. Original, small, semicircular-headed windows from the twelfth century survive in the north and south nave walls. With their narrow width these windows show how dark and mysterious the interior would have been in the twelfth century, with the church's walls embellished with boldly coloured wall paintings – fragments of which survive. The design of the windows also suggests that the church would have been a defensible space, their narrowness and height helping to protect villagers sheltering inside from attackers. East Ham's proximity to the Thames, and its remoteness from London, must have long made it vulnerable – or at least feel vulnerable – to seaborne raiders.

One early window, in the south wall of the chancel, is set low, below the cill level of the large seventeenth-century window. This window is a puzzle, as it compromises the defensive potential of the church. One possible explanation is that it acted as a squint to allow those excluded from the building, because of disease or some social evil, to catch a glimpse of Mass being celebrated. Changing ground levels means that this window is now set just above the level of the surrounding churchyard. Originally, though, all would have been considerably above ground and flood level: the ground has been raised over the centuries by the large number of bodies buried on the favoured south-east side of the church. The ground level to the north – by tradition the Devil's side – is lower, suggesting far fewer burials.

The south wall of the chancel. Note the squint on the left and the 'priest's door' on the right.

Once you have explored the outside, enter the church via the south door (it is wise to ring up in advance to ensure that it will be open). Medieval glories abound. Look first at the timber structure forming the roof – so often in medieval churches the roofs have been reconstructed or obscured, but here we have an intact example of carpentry from the first half of the twelfth century (the apse), and the thirteenth and fourteenth centuries, although alterations are said to have been made in the early seventeenth century and the timbers of the chancel roof were damaged during the war. But even more fascinating is the intersecting row of semicircular arches on the chancel's north wall. This type of design – in which a pointed arch emerges from the overlapping of semicircular arches – seems to have appeared first in Anglo-Norman Romanesque architecture around 1100, during the construction of the choir of Durham Cathedral. But the source is not Norman: the motif is found earlier, in Anglo-Saxon architecture in England and in Muslim architecture, especially in Spain.[2]

These forms and details, ancient and mysterious in their origin and meaning, are particularly inspiring when contemplated alongside a small, wooden figure set against the chancel arch. The figure is ancient, although only acquired in the 1930s, and shows St Mary Magdalene, to whom the church is dedicated. In the early twelfth century Mary had certain striking and idiosyncratic associations. She was regarded as the most ardent female disciple of Christ, was present at the Crucifixion and was the first person to see and speak to Christ after his Resurrection. But she was also thought by some to have been a 'fallen woman', and in the twelfth century she was often presented as a penitent temptress or prostitute saved by Christ. Christian scholars could not even agree which passages in the Bible referred to her or to other Marys – notably Mary of Bethany who anointed Christ's feet with oil. Were they one and the same person?

It was perhaps this ambiguous position in Christian lore that led Mary to crop up in some of the most esoteric myths of the Middle Ages. Some Christians – notably the Gnostic Christian sect of the Cathars – believed her to be the wife of the 'earthly' Christ, although this was considered a terrible heresy by the church. There was a legend that Mary Magdalene had gone to the south of France after Christ's ascent, carrying the Holy Grail and blessed with the gift of healing with balm and oils. And for reasons now lost in obscurity she seems to have become one of the patron saints of the mysterious military order, the Knights Templar. It seems that the cult of Mary symbolised – for some at least – arcane knowledge stretching back to the gods and goddesses of the pre-Christian era. And here is this exotic woman, represented by a little effigy set within an ancient building in a field not far from the roar of the A13.

Perhaps the masons who created the church would have thought it fitting that, centuries later, St Mary Magdalene East Ham would become the grave-site for one of the greatest mystic thinkers of the eighteenth century. For St Mary Magdalene contains the remains of William Stukeley, a pioneering antiquarian and archaeologist who did much good work of discovery, interpretation and preservation at Stonehenge and Avebury in Wiltshire. Stukeley was also a doctor of medicine, an ordained clergyman, a Freemason and a leading member of the neo-Druid movement – who argued that Druidic beliefs were an early expression of British culture. And this man, who died in 1765 and had a living in Bloomsbury, chose to be buried in the churchyard in East Ham. Why? No one knows for certain nor, sadly, does anyone now know where exactly his grave is. But we can guess his reasons. Stukeley is here, no doubt, because he felt there was something very special about this old church and its churchyard. Perhaps he believed it was an ancient British sacred site, or that in its unpretentious antiquity the church bestowed distinction on all buried here.

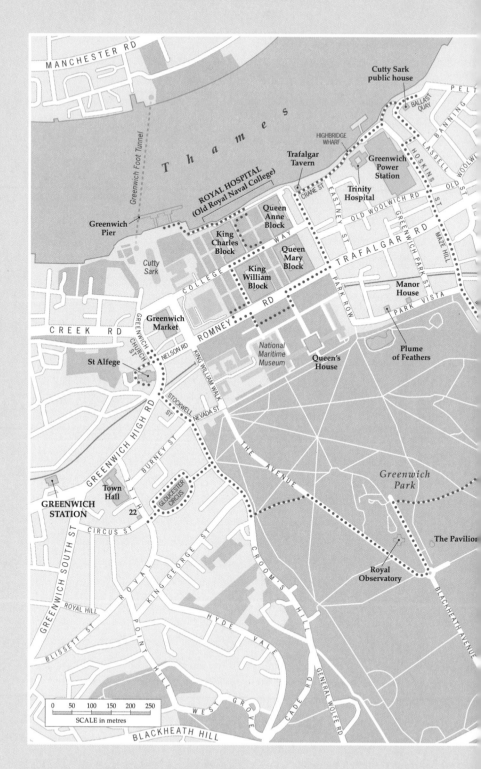

WALK 3

Greenwich

The architecture of absolutism

Greenwich is the great architectural jewel on the Thames. Although embedded within the vast fabric of London, the area retains the air of a self-contained maritime and royal town of ancient origin – buildings, river and landscape unite in a way that is strangely rare in the city, creating a place that is of huge artistic significance. Walking through these streets today, one can discern in the buildings the political history of England and of Britain from the sixteenth to the early eighteenth century, told through a number of architectural masterpieces.

The Thames at Greenwich has been, from time immemorial, a mighty ornament. Its dramatic curve – the steep plateau rising to Blackheath in the south, set in contrast with the flat and marshy land of the Isle of Dogs on the north bank – would have made the site of Greenwich emblematic: an ethereal Camelot set against the bustling and worldly City of London. But the area's emergence as a place of great political import came later. In the early fifteenth century the manor of Greenwich was given by Henry V to the Duke of Exeter. On the duke's death in 1426 it passed to the Duke of Gloucester – Henry VI's uncle – who in the early 1440s rebuilt the manor house on its riverside site, where the Old Royal Naval College (originally the Royal Hospital for Seamen) now stands. Only in 1447 did the manor pass back to the Crown, and then to Henry VI's powerful French wife, Margaret of Anjou. She is best remembered as one of the key champions of the Lancastrian cause during the Wars of the Roses. But she was also a lover of learning and the arts, founding Queen's College, Cambridge in 1448. She seems to have enlarged – certainly improved – the existing manor house and it was she who christened it La Plaisance – or, as the Tudors came to call it, Placentia.

An ethereal Camelot above the worldly city: the view north from Greenwich Park, looking over the Queen's House and the Royal Hospital.

The name Plaisance means pleasant or highly acceptable. This is just what the site is, perched on the hinge-point of the Thames, offering distant views towards the countryside of Essex, Surrey and Kent and towards London's riverside hamlets. And subsequent Tudor monarchs clearly agreed with Margaret's assessment. In around 1500, Henry VII enlarged the riverside complex, and it was here that the future Henry VIII was born in June 1491. As a youth, Henry loved to hunt in the park that sprawled to the south from the river, and which has now been incorporated into Greenwich Park. When king, from 1509, Henry VIII developed and beautified Placentia so that it started to be regarded as a royal palace of great state rather than merely as a royal retreat. It was here that Henry married Catherine of Aragon in 1509, and Anne of Cleves in 1540. It was here that the future Queen Mary was born in 1516, and Queen Elizabeth in 1533. And it was here that, in 1536, the death warrant was signed for the execution of Henry's second wife, Anne Boleyn.

What made Placentia so appealing to Henry? It certainly wasn't his only choice of home – all told, he had acquired or created around sixty palaces by his death. But Greenwich in particular seems to have chimed with his Arthurian fantasies. A number of medieval and Tudor monarchs wanted to present themselves as incarnations, in one way or another, of the legendary King Arthur. For Henry, a key aspect of this fantasy involved the rebirth of England as a mighty military power, and Greenwich was the best site from which to make the dream a reality. Henry set up a sprawling network of naval bases in what is now south-east London, with Greenwich at the centre. In 1513 he founded the great shipbuilding and naval victualling yard at Deptford to the west; to the east, at Woolwich, he founded a dockyard that by the 1540s had evolved into an armaments factory, specialising in ordnance. At Placentia itself Henry established an armoury, where hand-picked craftsmen from centres of excellence in Milan and Germany created state-of-the-art armour. And, to flatter his Arthurian dreams, Henry created a jousting ground, complete with medieval-style towers, so that jousts could take place as he fancied they did at Camelot. By the time of his death in 1547, Placentia was a large and rambling structure, still essentially Gothic in feel, with a long river frontage rising almost vertically from the water.

A romantic complex indeed. But such irregular and meandering structures did little to inflame the imaginations of later generations of observers. In 1613 James I – the first Stuart monarch, who united England and Scotland under a single king – gave Placentia and the manor of Greenwich to his wife, Anne of Denmark. Evidently she did not like what she saw. By then, tastes had changed dramatically. It was believed that palatial structures should be altogether more classical in their design, with greater symmetry and with features imbued with the character of Rome and the world of antiquity. As well as being old-fashioned in appearance, Placentia – no doubt rising from a jumble of vernacular buildings clustered outside its walls – was probably in serious disrepair.

Anne accepted the gift but chose not to occupy the giant and mouldering building. Instead in 1616 she commissioned a small and compact new home set south of Placentia, on higher ground. Somewhat oddly, the new building was designed to bridge a public road and thus – perhaps symbolically as well as practically – united separated parts of the royal park, which sprawled to the south. The architect James and Anne selected for the task was Inigo Jones, the king's court architect and designer of elaborate and festive theatrical performances called masques. At Greenwich he designed a villa – which is to say a modest house for occasional and pleasurable use – in the Italian Renaissance manner. The result was a jewel of a building that captured the architectural taste of the

A temple to the divine right of kings: the Queen's House.

time, and presented James and Anne as monarchs with a finger on the pulse of European fashion.

The choice of style, however, was not just an aesthetic one. What James and Anne had commissioned was political architecture; the Queen's House, as it became known, had a spiritual meaning with profound implications for the nature of James's rule. The new king was obsessed with the notion of rule by divine right, believing that kings had divine virtues, being nothing less than God's chosen emissaries on earth, and as such should have near unlimited power. And his buildings were part of a campaign to sustain his self-proclaimed semi-divine status. In royal houses in Europe during the sixteenth century, classical architecture of a harmonious and rational type came to be seen as God's gift to man. On closer inspection, then, it becomes apparent that the Queen's House is a powerful example of the architecture of rule by divine right.

The link between classical architecture and divine right seems opaque now, but it would have been clear to James's contemporaries. The Bible, it was thought, should be taken as a design guide, especially when it came to creating sacred buildings and royal palaces – and the most important biblical texts were those chronicling the creation of King Solomon's Temple in Jerusalem. This was a vast sacred building that was built by man but designed by God, intended to house the Arc of the Covenant: God's throne on Earth, and the receptacle of the Tablets of the Law – the stones on which Moses had inscribed God's Ten Commandments. Of course, the architectural implications of biblical texts are hard to fathom – through the centuries they have been emulated in buildings that range from synagogues, domed prayer halls and mosques to Romanesque and Gothic Christian cathedrals. But what is clear is that harmonically related proportions were important – usually in the form of simple permutations or extensions of the square or cube, such as the 2:3, 2:1 and 3:1 proportions – and that the temple was organised around a number of courts that used these shapes.

During the Renaissance the biblical texts relating to Solomon's Temple were radically reinterpreted. The holy proportions were now taken to refer to classical forms, as opposed to the Gothic ones of earlier generations. And a newly classical vision of Solomon's Temple became the key building for monarchs obsessed with legitimising their positions.

By housing themselves, their heirs and their courts within recreations of God's house on earth, they sought to both allude to and justify their divine status – often to the dismay of their more constitutionally-minded subjects.

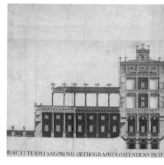

This new divinely ordained architecture reached its zenith in Spain in the late sixteenth century. In 1563, King Philip II began to build his own visionary evocation of Solomon's Temple with the vast El Escorial – the monastery and royal palace outside Madrid that was to serve as temporal and spiritual power base for his dynasty. The palace was designed by Juan Bautista de Toledo. By the early 1590s, King Philip was supporting the Jesuit scholar Juan Bautista Villalpando in his lavish visual 'reconstruction' of Solomon's Temple as a huge

classical palace, of geometric and proportional perfection, incorporating many square and rectangle courts and sumptuous classical elevations embellished with tiers of columns and pilasters. Part of Villalpando's argument was that classical architecture was not pagan in origin but emerged during the building of Solomon's Temple and thus was the direct gift of God. Published in 1598, the plans for Villalpando's buildings were to prove influential on a European scale – including in England.

Despite England's troubled relationship with Spain – the Armada of 1588 was within living memory – when James I became king of England in 1603 he displayed an admiration for Philip. James caused consternation among his puritan subjects when he launched lengthy (and ultimately futile) negotiations to marry his son, the future King Charles I, to Philip II's granddaughter. He was evidently also impressed by Philip's architectural ambitions and, it seems, by his vision of Solomon's Temple as remade for the modern age of divine kingship. James wanted his own Solomon's Temple-inspired version of the Escorial to serve, as it were, as a 'Holy Land' for the Stuarts. This palace was to be located in Whitehall, in London, replacing the existing Tudor Whitehall Palace that stood near the Palace of Westminster and St James's Palace. The proposed palace, again

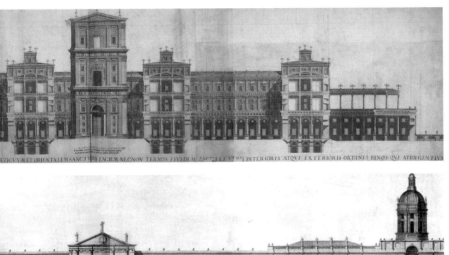

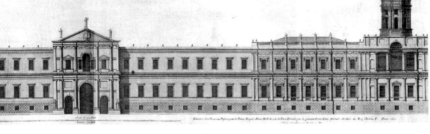

Top: Juan Batista Villalpando's classical reimagining of Solomon's Temple.
Above: Inigo Jones's second design for James I's Whitehall Palace.

masterminded by Inigo Jones with the assistance of John Webb, evoked in its plan, forms and details the Jesuit Villalpando's visionary recreation of the Temple of Solomon.

Between his palaces on Whitehall and in Greenwich, James made clear his aspirations for a distinctly absolutist aesthetic. And while both projects faltered during James's reign – the Queen's House was abandoned when Anne died in 1619, and only the Banqueting House of Whitehall Palace was ever completed – they would be reinvigorated after 1625 when James's son, Charles I, became king. In 1629, Charles resolved to complete the Queen's House, started for his mother, as a house for his wife, the French Roman Catholic princess Henrietta Maria: Jones came back on board, and completed the building in 1635. In Whitehall Charles brooded over the construction of the Stuarts' vast dynastic temple-like palace, with Jones's assistant John Webb producing an almost baffling array of subtly but significantly alternative designs. In the end, Charles only ever embellished the existing Banqueting House, with a series of specially commissioned ceiling paintings, completed in 1636 by Peter Paul

Rubens. Here, too, the aesthetic was distinctly absolutist: James I in one painting sits between spiralling Solomonic columns.

The end result of the Stuarts' vastly ambitious regime is well known. The conflict between the Crown and the people – personified by Parliament – came to a head in 1642, with the outbreak of the English Civil War. In Greenwich the Queen's House was soon abandoned and fell into disrepair, while in Whitehall the Banqueting House fulfilled a role that was beyond the imagination of those who had created it for festive and dynastic celebrations: in January 1649, Charles walked through the house's noble double-cube hall, beneath the Rubens ceiling, to the scaffold and his execution. But even as his death approached Charles had architecture on his mind. While imprisoned in Carisbrooke Castle during most of 1648 he requested, and was given, a set of the designs by Webb for the palace at Whitehall. Contemplating this project – once in his grasp – was evidently of some comfort.

The Restoration of the monarchy, when it came in 1660, soon proved to be the dawn of a Golden Age for Greenwich. Inigo Jones had died in 1652, but John Webb was very much alive. He renewed work on the long-dormant Whitehall Palace scheme but the financially embarrassed Charles II, no longer an absolute but a parliamentary and constitutional monarch, chose wisely not to pursue this provocative option; instead, in 1661, he pointed Webb towards Greenwich. The Tudor palace was by now a crumbling ruin and Charles – encouraged by his mother, the Dowager Queen Henrietta Maria – thought it a reasonable idea to replace this ancient and forlorn building with a new one that might measure up to the mighty royal works being created across the Channel by Louis XIV. In 1664 Webb was set to work and he produced the first part of the proposed royal palace, set slightly inland and to the east of Placentia. The structure survives and is now known as the King Charles Block. But it was not to be. Before construction of this block was completed Charles lost interest in Greenwich and it was not until the Glorious Revolution of 1688 – when the Protestant King William and Queen Mary secured the throne – that Greenwich became home to one of the most important and effective architectural creations in Britain.

The driving force seems to have been Queen Mary, one of the great but forgotten patrons of the arts in seventeenth-century Britain. She and

William did not want to live in Greenwich – they had already resolved to live in Kensington and Hampton Court and by 1689 building works were already under way. But what to do with Greenwich? The queen was a Stuart, Charles II was her uncle and Anne of Denmark her great-grandmother – she knew that Greenwich was dynastic land. However, instead of building a palace to rival Louis XIV's Versailles, she embraced the idea (already put forward by her father James II) of creating a charitable naval hospital for aged or injured sailors, in the manner of the French king's Hôtel des Invalides in Paris and of Charles II's Chelsea Hospital for soldiers (see pp. 169–75). This was not just to be a large almshouse – it was to be a building of palatial scale and high architectural ambition, worthy of its site and of its royal heritage and patronage. And thus in 1692 the idea of the Royal Hospital for Seamen, which now stands between the Queen's House and the Thames, was born.

The resulting vista, when one looks south through the Royal Hospital, offers a unique distillation of three centuries of cultural and political turmoil. First, in the distance, is the sprawling Greenwich Park, beloved hunting ground of Henry VIII; nearer sits the Queen's House, emblematic of the absolutist ambitions of the Stuarts; and in the foreground stands

Two centuries of English history: looking south through the Royal Hospital from the Thames.

the Royal Hospital, which reflects the more politically palatable designs of the monarchy after the Glorious Revolution. Together they form a landscape that tells the story of two centuries of English political history.

THE WALK

How best to arrive in Greenwich? The options are many. The Docklands Light Railway takes you into the very heart of the town, but you can also get off at the Isle of Dogs, contemplate the prospect of Greenwich from the north bank of the Thames, and then go beneath the Thames in a pedestrian tunnel that brings you on to the Greenwich riverside. It's best, though, to arrive by water. When approaching on one of the 'river taxis' – such as the *Monsoon Clipper* that sails from Westminster, London Bridge or Tower Hill – the majestic Royal Hospital gradually comes into view, offering a vision of the magisterial worldly power the kings and queens of England once held.

Before entering the hospital proper, walk along the Thames-side promenade to the east. At the centre of the Royal Hospital court, directly opposite the Queen's House, are some steps that, when the tide is low, lead down to the beach. This foreshore can offer some extraordinary insights into the long history of Greenwich and the Thames. The river here has been a highway for centuries, so many ancient artefacts that were jettisoned or lost by passing vessels continue to be washed up or uncovered. Most is trash – fragments of discarded clay pipes, or fragments of glass – but, of course, old trash can be most revealing. Yet even more exciting is the subtle evidence of the Tudor palace that once stood here. Look at the bricks and tiles closely, particularly

those you find at the western part of the foreshore. The bricks are thin and red in colour, and the tile fragments are thick and glazed a strong yellow with green or black flecks. These are demolition waste from the Tudor palace, and are part of floor surfaces upon which Henry VIII or Queen Elizabeth could have walked. Look and touch, but you must leave the bricks and tiles where you find them, for others to discover and enjoy. After all, such fragments have little meaning or significance when wrenched out of their historic setting.

From the top of the steps, look south to the Royal Hospital. The first building to visit, immediately to the west, includes the King Charles Block – the only part of Charles II's planned new palace that was built.

This structure tells us a great deal about shifting tastes in the middle of the seventeenth century. In some respects, the design echoes those Webb and Jones had produced for the unbuilt Whitehall Palace. But, in its boldly detailed and richly textured elevation, it had moved with the times and reflects the Baroque spirit sweeping Europe in the later

The west elevation of Queen Anne block, built in the early-eighteenth century in imitation of John Webb's King Charles Block opposite.

seventeenth century. Here this spirit is expressed by the rustication that covers the entire façade and by the huge triple keystones above the windows, symbolising strength. These ornamental and somewhat theatrical treatments are typically Baroque. Palatial quality is given to this monumental design by the central pediment and columns and the treatment of each end as a pilaster-clad pavilion, given extra height by the addition of an attic storey.

In Charles II's planned palace, the King Charles Block was to have been faced by a matching block to form a large court with its axis aligned with that of the Queen's House. But, of course, nothing else of Charles's palace was ever built. Instead, the development of the site stalled for twenty years, until the creation of the Royal Hospital.

The history is revealed by the courtyard of which the King Charles Block forms the west range. The range opposite it, of matching design and known as Queen Anne Block, was constructed between 1699 and 1730. Together they define a generous riverside court that plays a key role in the slowly evolving Royal Hospital. Here architectural uniformity and symmetry was all-important, which means that earlier styles were – when necessary – echoed in new work, as is the case with these two facing blocks, started thirty-five years apart. Viewed from the north this harmonious courtyard frames a vista through the palace that focuses on the Queen's House and the rising landscape to its south. The overall effect, in its scenic power, is stunning. Also note the way in which the narrow riverside elevation of Webb's King Charles Block has been extended to the west (in fact in 1712), and then the extended version duplicated in the river elevation of Queen Anne Block. The object, of course, was to give the hospital a strong and commanding elevation to the river, but one that takes its cue from Webb's existing building and that probably echoes his intentions. The story is complex, but the point is that what was eventually built works brilliantly. This is thoughtful and inventively pragmatic architecture at its best.

But this is no more than what one would expect from the architect in question. For the man responsible for realising the Royal Hospital was none other than Christopher Wren, who had honed his architectural genius by designing St Paul's Cathedral and the City churches – often in most difficult and demanding circumstances (see Walk 4). When Wren got to work in 1694, he and his team of designers – including his protégé Nicholas Hawksmoor – sought not just to realise Webb's idea for a mighty riverside court by duplicating the King Charles Block, but also to follow his plan for a linking range to the south. This southern range was to stand between the Queen's House and the Thames.

But all was not well. Mary seems to have intervened. Records are murky but it is likely that she did not want her grandmother's emblematic house – essentially the pioneering architectural monument to the Stuart dynasty – to be concealed from the view of those plying the great highway of the Thames, or the prospect of the Thames hidden by those using the house. So the south range – in Wren and Hawksmoor's version large in scale, domed and pedimented – was abandoned and the extraordinary idea was born that the palatial almshouse should be in two parts, each broadly a mirror image of the other, with the space between the parts forming a broad avenue or linear garden allowing views to and from the Queen's House. So involved was Mary in this design that Hawksmoor would later recollect that she was the 'real foundress' of the hospital, and that its architectural glory was the result of 'her Majesty's fix't intention for Magnificence'.

The resulting complex is remarkable, and often in the most peculiar ways. The grand open space in the middle works tremendously well. Indeed, it has often been noted that the spaces within the Royal Hospital – the courts, the avenue, the colonnades – are almost as spatially and architecturally rewarding as the buildings themselves. This is all very much in the spirit of Baroque architecture, where spaces are designed to have a dynamic, surprising and illusionary – often theatrical – character, when architectural 'scenes' are framed by columns or arches that play with perceptions of space. Take the narrowing of the central avenue as you pass south through the hospital. When the composition is viewed from the river, a somewhat false perspective suggests to the eye that the avenue is longer than it is and that the Queen's House is more distant.

———•◆•———

While Wren's approach to the Thames-side buildings was determined by the existing architectural style of the King Charles Block, elsewhere he was able to be more inventive. This becomes apparent in the domed and colonnaded buildings to the south. These two structures – King William Block to the west, and Queen Mary Block to the east – were under construction by 1698 and, of course, purpose-designed for hospital use. They display the hand of Wren most forcefully, with their long lines of columns and the pair of domes – placed with scenic brilliance – that mark the locations of the two main interiors. And what interiors they are. The chapel, within Queen Mary Block, and the great hall, within King William Block, are among the glories of the hospital. The interior of the chapel was created, following a fire, between 1779 and 1789 to the designs of James Stuart and is an exquisite, erudite and pioneering essay in neoclassical

Queen Mary Block, which houses the chapel of the Royal Hospital.

architecture. The hall has a stunning Baroque painted interior, packed with allegory, symbolism and historical references, created from 1708 to 1725 by the painter James Thornhill. And the way the two parts sit opposite one another can be seen as a division between the spiritual and temporal aspects of the hospital: between ministering to the old sailors' souls and keeping them in good spirits.

When standing between the domes, astride the Royal Hospital's main axis, all feels most uniform and harmonious. Just around the corner, however, everything changes. The west side of King William Block could be described either as deeply mannered or simply as wild. This elevation was likely the work of Hawksmoor: while there is no proof of his involvement, it is hard to imagine any other architect at the time being capable of such an odd and wilful design (John Vanbrugh, who we will meet in a moment, perhaps – but he only become involved with Greenwich after this structure was complete). The range, completed in 1702, is designed as a unified palace front, with the emphasis on its centre and the end pavilions. In striking contrast to the other buildings of the hospital, this elevation is made of brick, with stone used only for main architectural elements and as ornament. In the centre is a Doric portico, with closely spaced columns, rising four storeys from ground level, to support an entablature and an attic wall. The conceit might have been to evoke the feel of a Roman triumphal arch or, more probably, a Roman city gate.

In the very centre of this unusual elevation is a strange detail that has puzzled me for years. Above the main door are slabs of stone, plain-faced but with slightly recessed margins. It could be that these were intended to be carved, but the work was never completed. Yet I wonder if their meaning is rather more mystic. They look like the stones that face the retaining wall of the Temple Mount in Jerusalem, on which Solomon's Temple once rose. Hawksmoor was obsessed with history, especially 'primitive' Christianity and its sacred sites and buildings. Was Hawksmoor trying to link the hospital at Greenwich with the emblematic and inspirational Temple of Solomon? If so, this is a fascinating example of the myriad meanings read into Solomon's Temple during the seventeenth and eighteenth centuries. The Stuart monarchs saw it as a model for palaces for kings who claimed to rule by divine right, while others – like Hawksmoor –

The uncarved stone slabs on the west elevation of King William Block.

would have viewed it as a source of beauty that represented the origin of architecture. Designed by God, the temple, in its parts and proportions, offered inspirational clues to the manner in which the absolute beauty of God's creation could be echoed in the architecture of man.

Today, the hospital has a worldlier feel. You will notice that the grounds are no longer populated by old sailors. The Royal Hospital closed as a maritime almshouse in 1869, becoming in 1873 the core of the Royal Naval College, which itself closed in 1998. It is now overseen by a charitable foundation, with the buildings housing various academic institutions including the University of Greenwich and the Trinity Laban Conservatoire of Music and Dance. The result is that it is now generally accessible to the public – a fact that still remains faintly surprising to those of us who knew the buildings before 1998, when much of the hospital was guarded by Ministry of Defence security men and was out of bounds to casual explorers.

———————————◆———————————

Head south-west from Hawksmoor's Roman arch and exit the grounds of the hospital, crossing over the road and walking on to the lawns of the Queen's House. As you walk east, and pass in front of the house, take in its charmingly Renaissance character. It is hard, today, to imagine that this was the architecture of absolutism.

Inigo Jones had been to Italy, in around 1605 and again in 1613–14, and studied the works of leading architects including the great sixteenth-century Venetian architect Andrea Palladio (see pp. 185–6). Upon his return from Italy Jones was appointed Surveyor to the King's Works (probably due to the queen's influence because he had worked successfully for her brother, King Christian IV of Denmark), and in 1616 was commissioned to design the Queen's House.

Here the consequences of his Italian journeys are most clear. It is an incredibly competent evocation of northern Italy in central London. In many ways, the house is little more than an erudite copy of a foreign architecture – even its odd H-shaped plan, with a bridge-like central range straddling a road, is taken from Giuliano da Sangallo's Villa Medici at Poggio a Caiano which, dating from the 1480s, seems in many ways the model Jones took as his main inspiration. But imagine how alien it would have been to Londoners then, when the Queen's House would have been set amongst the still largely Gothic vernacular architecture – wrought of timber, brick and plaster – that would have dominated the city.

As with Palladio's villas, at the

The north side of the Queen's House of 1616–35. Its beauty lies in its harmonically related proportions.

Queen's House externally all is simplicity and symmetry. Beauty comes from the restrained use of classical detail and from harmonically related proportions that unite all parts – from window openings and the areas of wall between windows to floor plan. In his *I Quattro Libri del'Architettura* of 1570 Palladio offered seven ideal proportions, mostly generated from the square or cube, including the square and a half proportion (2:3) and the double square (2:1). Jones applied this theory with vigour. The overall proportion of the Queen's House is square – although in two parts each side of the road – and most of its rooms are square or double-square in plan, including the sublime double-height and galleried cubical hall, one of the finest and most influential Renaissance rooms created in Britain.

––––––––––––––◆•◆•◆––––––––––––––

From the Queen's House, walk east along the south edge of the Royal Hospital, and then north, along Park Row. We now encounter fewer grand royal buildings, and more modest architecture – structures that reveal a different side to the history of Greenwich. In the seventeenth and eighteenth centuries streets like this would have contained the homes of the residents of this tranquil Thames-side village.

If it's lunchtime or early evening when you leave the hospital, then the first stop must be the Trafalgar Tavern at the north end of Park Row, which marks the eastern edge of the complex. The Tavern rises directly from the Thames and is a splendid affair, faced with stucco and ornamented with a pair of large and very generously glazed bay windows and cast-iron balconies of elegant neoclassical design. It was built in 1837 and its architect was Joseph Kay, an important man in England's late-Georgian and early-Victorian building world. This pub is not without fame. It won renown for being one of the first places within easy reach of London to serve whitebait (the fry of fish such as sprat and herring) when the season started, and was evidently well known to Charles Dickens who used it as the location for a wedding breakfast described in *Our Mutual Friend*. But the Tavern closed in 1915, when it served as a refuge for aged sailors, and then became a working men's club, only reopening in 1965. The physical changes that occurred during this half-century of non-tavern use, combined with the standard taste of current pub companies – generally open-plan, with bland pastiche detailing – mean that, sadly, the interior of the Tavern does not quite live up to the promise of its very fine exterior. It does, however, still serve very good whitebait.

Head south along Park Row and turn east immediately behind the Trafalgar Tavern. This is Crane Street. It is narrow, paved, and takes you past another and far more discreet public house called the Yacht Tavern and a terrace of mid- to late-nineteenth-century cottages, until you get to High Bridge, which is the location of the Trinity Hospital. Like the Royal Hospital this was an almshouse – one of many such institutions built to accommodate aged, decayed or generally impoverished members of a guild, trade or profession or, as in this case, worthy but beset residents of a parish. According to an engraving above the door, the Trinity Hospital was for 'retired gentlemen of Greenwich' – those who had become poor by 'casual means', mind, and not through their own 'dissolute life'. The almshouse is a remarkable survival, and is significantly older than it looks. The face it presents to the world is a pleasing if somewhat meagre expression of the early-nineteenth-century Gothic Revival, with the stucco elevations probably dating from around 1812. But in fact it was founded in 1613 (not 1616, as proclaimed on its façade) by the Earl of Northampton, and was run by the Mercers' Company from 1621. A considerable amount of early fabric survives, although much is concealed from the casual observer. If the main door facing the river is open (which sadly is not often the case), take a look at the cloister-like central court around which the ranges of dwellings, hall and chapel are arranged. It is generously planted, and embellished with a fine ancient mulberry tree said to date to the seventeenth century. Central courts like this are typical of larger almshouses and reveal that the roots of this kind of building, with

Trinity Hospital, a refuge for the 'retired gentlemen of Greenwich' founded in 1613.

its charitable, communal and often religious function, lie in the monastic architectural tradition.

If you manage to find your way into the chapel make sure you see the very fine early-sixteenth-century Flemish-made stained glass – the acquisition of which shows admirable taste on the part of the Trinity – which depicts the 'Agony in the Garden', the Crucifixion and the Ascension. The window perhaps offers an alternative meaning to the name of the almshouse. The Trinity of the Father, the Son and the Holy Ghost is, of course, central to Christian theology; but the stained-glass's depiction of the three crucial scenes from the tale of Christ – betrayal, death, and resurrection – offer another take on the word Trinity.

Just east of Trinity Hospital is Ballast Quay. Its south side consists of small, mainly early-nineteenth-century terrace houses – two retaining delightful Regency balconies, complete with timber decorations. And to their west are a couple of intriguing late-seventeenth-century houses and the Cutty Sark public house (until 1951 the Union Tavern) which is the main architectural accent of the street. Formed by a pair of very modest houses, also early nineteenth century, the pub sports a truly splendid three-window-wide bay window of curved form that rises to the second storey. Even more so than the Trafalgar, the interior fails to live up to the promise of the exterior: between the exposed internal brickwork, the faux panelling on the walls, the crazy-paved floor and the vast and vulgar staircase, any sense of authenticity is destroyed. Nonetheless, if you sit outside on a fair day, with a pint of Young's bitter in your hand and with the exterior of the pub in your sights, you surely will be happy enough.

These days, the Cutty Sark pub cowers beneath the stunted towers of the gaunt early-twentieth-century Greenwich Power Station. From the riverfront look back at its pair of spectacular turbine halls, each gabled and lit by a huge, arched, Roman-style 'thermal' window. If this power station ever becomes redundant and these halls opened to the public, then they will become one of the most magnificent interiors on the Thames. For now, though, walk south along Hoskins Street, beside the eastern side of the building, before crossing Trafalgar Road and continuing along Maze Hill until you come to its corner with Park Vista.

Park Vista is, in many ways, one of the most charming and least known of Greenwich's many characterful historic roads. Much of the south side is formed by a wall, part of which screens a house called The Chantry that incorporates a brick-built Tudor outbuilding, once part of Placentia. Opposite is yet one more early public house – the Plume of Feathers – which claims a foundation date of 1691, making it the oldest still-functioning pub in Greenwich, with its origin as a tavern for those who made a living ushering livestock down the old drovers' road (now Romney Road) connecting Kent with south London and the City.

Even more striking are buildings constructed in the eighteenth century. East of the pub is a charming medley of Georgian houses, with a number of distinctive features. One short terrace has a plaque proclaiming it to be 'Park Place' and bearing the date 1791 – meaning that it makes remarkably early use of first-floor relieving arches, which take the weight off the windows below. A few houses to the east is the 'Manor House', also five windows wide but set back slightly from the street behind a small front garden. Its brickwork details, flat-headed windows, the overhanging cornice and the simple doorcase suggest a construction date no later than 1718. Particularly characterful is the gazebo on the roof, from which prospects of the river and the park could have been enjoyed.

Our route, however, is up the slope to the south. This is Maze Hill, which marks the east edge of Greenwich Park, with the west side of the road formed by park railings and wall. On the west side of the street is a terrace of 1807 that originally served as an infirmary, the Royal Naval Asylum School, which in the early nineteenth century occupied the Queen's House. This terrace was the work of Daniel Asher Alexander, an architect and engineer of remarkable ability and a pioneer of sparely detailed and utilitarian neoclassical design – every ornament with a practical function or distinct purpose – particularly known for his dockland architecture. This Maze Hill terrace is quintessential Alexander, representing his ability to reinvent what is essentially traditional street architecture. Take the severe-looking elevation that faces Maze Hill, beautifully wrought of pale brick, in which the space between ground- and first-floor windows bestows a strange nobility on the composition by hinting at unusually lofty ground-floor rooms.

The most remarkable building on this part of the street is still to come. Continue south a short distance and you arrive at the most interesting – if not most beautiful – piece of domestic street architecture in Greenwich. Vanbrugh Castle, on the corner of Westcombe Park Road, was designed in 1718 by the idiosyncratic – indeed in many ways maverick – architect Sir John Vanbrugh, now best known for his work on Blenheim Palace, Oxfordshire, and Castle Howard, Yorkshire. These are both designed in Vanbrugh's inventive, vigorous and sculptural English Baroque style: a style developed and refined by Nicholas Hawksmoor, who had worked for Vanbrugh. Vanbrugh acquired 12 acres of land in and around the park and designed and built a series of odd and characterful houses for members of his family. This house, which Vanbrugh built for himself, is the only one to survive.

Although famed for his Baroque classical country-house architecture, Vanbrugh preferred, when it came to creating a home for himself, something very different. The Maze Hill house possesses what Vanbrugh

A home with a 'Castle Air': John Vanbrugh's house on Maze Hill.

would have called the 'Castle Air', which is to say it attempts to evoke something of the romance of medieval castle architecture: there is a round central tower, and square-plan corner towers tipped with large-scale battlements. But the design was initially strictly symmetrical (apart from the off-centre main door), in conventional classical manner. These characteristics, combined with the almost utilitarian brick construction, mean the building looks more like an evocation of Rome than of the English Middle Ages. The east wing, however, was even more radical: designed by Vanbrugh only a few years or so after the castle was completed, it makes the building somewhat asymmetrical. In 1726 or so, this relaxed asymmetry and informality would have been highly novel in a building with any real architectural or social pretensions.

Now cut west into the park and head to the high land rising in the distance. This plateau offers a sensational prospect, looking north. In the foreground is the grassy remnant of a once formal garden created in 1662

for Charles II by André Le Nôtre, Louis XIV's favourite landscape architect, and the brains behind the garden at Versailles. This makes clear Charles's initial aspiration for Greenwich. Then there is the Queen's House, and its flanking colonnades and stucco-clad wings added in 1806–16, also to the designs of Daniel Asher Alexander; then the Royal Hospital and the Thames; then the Isle of Dogs on the north bank with a backdrop of the somewhat sinister array of commercial towers of Canary Wharf.

But nearer at hand is one of Greenwich's more remarkable public buildings, which you reach after about 500 metres: the Royal Observatory, now known as Flamsteed House, and named after the Astronomer Royal John

The view north from the Royal Observatory in 1842, with Flamsteed House on the left, and the Royal Hospital in the distance.

Flamsteed who was the first occupant of the observatory when it was completed in 1676. The building – again designed by Christopher Wren – is primarily a machine of science. Its main feature is a large double-height octagonal room, fitted with huge windows and the location of an array of powerful telescopes through which the heavens could be scrutinised. But it also has other functions. It marks the Prime Meridian – a line of longitude (essentially an arbitrary line, as opposed to the lines of latitude, determined by the Equator and the Earth's axis of rotation) that was accepted by most nations in 1884 as a key reference point defining the precise time of day, and time zones, as in Greenwich Mean Time.

The design of the observatory is striking because Wren utilised the 'vernacular' style he was to perfect for the rebuilding of a number of City churches (see Walk 4). Wren's 'vernacular' approach is characterised by the use of good-quality red brickwork, usually crafted with great skill, combined with a limited use of pale Portland stone for important features such as keystones, corner quoins and door surrounds. This largely brick construction was cheaper than facing a building entirely with finely cut and squared stone, and was used by Wren for structrues that were more humble in their purpose or for which a less formal or monumental look was appropriate. This meant that sometimes even the most ambitious buildings designed by Wren – such as Kensington Palace and his extensions to Hampton Court Palace – are in brick and stone, because for these projects a more domestic and less imperious architectural style was thought essential. The Observatory is one of Wren's earliest uses of this brick-and-stone approach, and can be seen as one of his exploratory works.

Flamsteed House, an early example of Christopher Wren's redbrick-and-stone vernacular style.

Of the various stone details in the Royal Observatory I find the blocks that make up the corners the most intriguing. They help reveal the origin of this style and suggest Wren's sources. For example, quoins in Italian Renaissance buildings like the sixteenth-century Palazzo Farnese, Rome, and stone quoins combined with red brick became a feature in northern French architecture in the very early seventeenth century, such as the Place des Vosges in Paris. Stone quoins and brick were a dominant element in English late-Elizabethan and Jacobean buildings, such as Hatfield House, Hertfordshire, and Charlton House, south London.

Indeed, Charlton House plays a peculiar role in the design of the observatory. The pair of square-plan turrets are strikingly like the turrets at Charlton House. Perhaps this was a conscious reference because the house was built from 1607 by the Crown to house the Dean of Durham and his royal charge, James I's eldest son Prince Henry, who died in 1612. Are these turrets, then, a reference to Charles II's long-dead infant uncle and to the Stuarts' all-embracing dynastic ambitions? One of the towers, though, fulfils a more functional role. On it stands a short mast and on this mast is a large red ball. Every day the ball rises up the mast and falls rapidly at 1 p.m. This was for ships moored on the Thames, and within visual contact, to set their timepieces. It was more than just a useful service but a vital necessity: accurate timekeeping was required to help determine longitude and thus the position of a craft on the ocean and the direction and location of its destination.

From the observatory take the central path through the park and head south. Soon you come to a café. Called the Pavilion and run by the Royal Parks, it is spacious, clean, neo-Georgian in manner with a charming wrap-around colonnade, but somewhat municipal – in the way most park cafés used to be. And really nothing wrong with that. If you are in need it's a most welcome oasis.

The next portion of the walk has a rather different flavour. In contrast to the powerful political architecture of the Royal Hospital and the observatory, we now enter a world of tranquil domesticity – albeit domesticity of the grandest kind. Walk west from the Pavilion café, around the south of the observatory complex, and cut down the wide avenue running from north-west to south-east, before turning west to leave the park via one of its west gates. You now stand on Croom's Hill, which contains some of the most impressive domestic architecture in Greenwich.

The southern portion of Croom's Hill is discussed in detail in Walk 5. For now, though, our route is to the north and towards the town centre. Immediately upon leaving the park, to the north-west, you come to 52 Croom's Hill – The Grange – which is a mid-seventeenth- and eighteenth-century house. While the main building is hidden from public gaze by high walls and a deep garden, its gazebo – perched above the road – is most visible. It's a charming thing, wrought of fine red brickwork with rubbed brick architrave and cornice to its main window, and with a pyramidal roof. Inside is a very good ornamental plaster ceiling, which looks splendid from the street when light floods into the building's single room through large windows to illuminate the pale interior. At dusk on summer evenings, as the sun sets, the gazebo can glow like a lantern. It is dated 1672 and was probably designed by Robert Hooke, a friend of Wren's with whom he worked on the design of the Monument in the City and several City churches. The owner of The Grange at the time was William Hooker – a City figure and later a Lord Mayor – which makes the Hooke connection plausible.

Almost all of the houses north of here warrant careful scrutiny, between them telling the story of two centuries of domestic architecture. Here, though, it will suffice to focus on just a couple. First, number 34, set back from the street and with a wing to its north that, with the projecting side of the late-eighteenth-century number 36, define a small front court. This is very much a Greenwich and Blackheath form, as exemplified by 25 Dartmouth Row (see p. 187). The doorcase has simple brackets supporting a cornice and a very fine and early fanlight, with its radiating bars made of wood treated as small, panelled and inverted obelisks. All must date from the 1720s or 1730s, although inside there is evidence of an even earlier house. Then comes number 32, which also dates from the early eighteenth century and also has a small front court defined by a wing. Most notable is the doorcase with its deeply carved brackets set on Doric pilasters, which *The Buildings of England* says has been reused from elsewhere. The carvings include a pair of scallop shells, which were popular decorative motifs in the late seventeenth and early eighteenth centuries.

Delicate details of Gloucester Circus, designed by Michael Searles.

But the most remarkable complex around Croom's Hill – which rather breaks with our Stuart and early-Georgian theme, but is too notable to be missed – is down a narrow street going off to the west from number 26. It is the work of Michael Searles, a prominent figure in the history of Blackheath and Greenwich who we will meet again in Walk 5. The north side of the alleyway includes a wall that is clad with what can only be described as a ghost elevation – pedimented, but with blank windows of rather grand design. Searles attached this elevation to the side of the existing Croom's Hill house to create a theatrical entry to a new residential development known as Gloucester Circus, built from 1791 to 1809.

It is one of Searles's most intriguing projects, not least because a set of early design drawings survive. These show various compositional permutations, with some incarnations of the circus formed by virtually free-standing houses and others by houses that are more fully linked to create a virtual terrace. The circus was only half built (the north portion is now of conventional mid-nineteenth-century construction) and Searles's houses have been much altered, but it would appear that originally he went for a compromise, giving the circus a most striking rhythm by alternating pairs of houses, designed as uniform blocks, some with arcaded ground-floor windows, linked by lower and recessed entrance blocks to single pedimented houses. These houses are also grouped as adjoining pairs, just to give added visual interest. The original arrangement is more obvious in the western portion of the circus.

A particular pleasure are the side elevations of the houses forming each end of the crescent. That to the east, near Croom's Hill, appears a little odd because it's truncated, with the upper portion built or rebuilt in plan manner leaving the lower portion of the elevation somewhat wrong-footed. The side elevation to the west was completed as intended. It is three windows wide (but all main windows are blank, as in the ghost elevation) with centre windows and door framed by piers that support an arch upon which reclines a pediment. Both of these end houses have bold and bulbous full-height bays, in typical Searles manner. These buildings are superb architecture – sculptural, minimal, visually powerful – and they represent Searles's determination to give speculative house building an added artistic element, which we will meet again on pp. 201–6.

A permutation of Michael Searles's Gloucester Circus.

While at the west end of the circus, take a brief look along the street it leads into: Royal Hill. This remains one of the most pleasing backwaters of Greenwich. Much of the town is now taken up by tourism, with the array of familiar shops and cafés that the tourist trade engenders around the world. But Royal Hill retains authenticity. It is like wandering into the Greenwich of the past: low-key, local in feel, and individual. Though that's not to say that it is entirely architecturally humble and anonymous – at its north end stands the tallest building in Greenwich, the Town Hall (or now former Town Hall, for it has long been abandoned by the municipality and is now in ever-changing mixed use), which is utterly and wonderfully alien to Greenwich, indeed alien to much of Britain. It was designed in

The view along Royal Hill to Greenwich Town Hall.

1939 in a most 'progressive' manner by a young architect called Clifford Culpin. He was evidently smitten by the Romantic brick-built modern architecture of the Netherlands and Scandinavia, particularly the works of the Dutch architect Willem Marinus Dudok, who had an obsession for odd, cubistic brickwork. The wonder is that Culpin persuaded the good burghers of Greenwich to go along with his dream. The old Town Hall has a tall, slim, square-plan tower – seemingly inspired by the tower of the town hall at Hilversum near Amsterdam, designed by Dudok and completed in 1931 – and bold, functional elevations. Sadly its interior was much altered in the 1970s by the council, before it moved out.

Of less idiosyncratic style is another building visible from the end of Gloucester Circus, number 22 Royal Hill. This very modest two-storey-high and one-window-wide stucco-fronted house of uncertain date contains a family butcher – a purveyor of 'traditional meat, poultry and game' (a rarity now in town centres increasingly dominated by look-alike chains of cafés and supermarkets). And beside it, at number 24, is a rare survivor of a now almost lost world of early-eighteenth-century vernacular building – so humble and slightly built that most were long ago swept away. The sash boxes in the windows, which are set on the same plane as the elevations, give a clue as to the building's age. This was a construction technique that fell from fashion in London during the early 1730s, with the late adoption of a provision of a Building Act of 1709 that boxes be set back four inches to prevent the spread of fire – a rule that was very slow to have effect outside the Cities of London and Westminster.

This marvellous little building, which is two rooms deep, has a centrally placed chimney stack serving back and front rooms, with a staircase beside it. Large and centrally placed brick-built chimney stacks are typical of late-seventeenth- and early-eighteenth-century London vernacular buildings, and contrived to serve two key functions. First, and obviously, they carried away smoke. But second, and almost as important, they acted as large and solid structural piers, in what were generally very slightly built houses. This small but very important house is currently derelict, and has been for many years. It is listed by the government as being of historic or architectural interest, but one can't help but feel that there is a tragedy here waiting to happen.

For somewhat more architectural fare, return to Croom's Hill – this time, for variety, walking along the other side of Gloucester Circus – and head north, taking note of number 24 on the north corner of the two streets: a very striking late-eighteenth-century design, with a full-height bay to its centre, flanked by second-floor lunettes. This structure is testament to the ability of anonymous eighteenth-century builder-architects to handle the classical language in a most deft, sophisticated and pleasing manner – these humble men were, as the poet Thomas Gray put it, 'village-Hampdens' and 'mute inglorious Miltons' who, if circumstances had been different, would no doubt have been famed and praised for their artistic skill and erudition. Also good is number 14, which is rather like a small country house and appears to date from the early eighteenth century. It possesses a distinct architectural presence, with its centrally placed pedimented doorcase and small paved court that helps create a sense of enclosure.

The builders of the houses on this stretch were clearly – and rightly – aware of the potential offered by the prospect. This is particularly clear to the north-east, along Nevada Street. To the east and south lies the beauty of Greenwich Park, so many of these houses sprout bays calculated to

Number 14 Croom's Hill, with its pedimented doorcase, seems to aspire to be a miniature country house.

provide occupants with splendid views. Rather shockingly, number 10 has fitted to its first-floor windows plastic sashes, which should be removed immediately. History and beauty demands it.

At the north end of Croom's Hill, on Stockwell Street, is an unsettling new arrival. It has been designed for the University of Greenwich, and, among other things, houses the Department of Architecture. The building is most alien in its aesthetic but this should not necessarily be a problem, given the generally mixed architectural character of this part of Greenwich; in many respects it is less alien than the 1930s former Town Hall. But with this Stockwell Street building it's not only the design that is startlingly different to any of its neighbours. Also discordant are the materials of construction. It is faced with glass and pale stone cladding, while its neighbours are brick and stucco (by tradition, in Greenwich stone is used for only the most important monumental buildings). Perhaps worse, the scale of this new arrival is far larger than any of the area's non-monumental and non-public buildings. The centre of Greenwich is special and rare, and its established character ought to be protected and enhanced, with new buildings subservient to old. But this building, rather than being self-effacing, seems determined to steal the show from its historic neighbours. This precious site in the centre of sensitive Greenwich has been treated as if it were in some more ordinary part of south London, where history is less evident. For me, this interloper does much to break the fragile spell that has been cast by the journey down Croom's Hill to the centre of the town.

———————◆•◆•◆———————

When this building is passed much happens. You walk over a deep railway cutting, running west–east from Greenwich station to Maze Hill, and then on the right, spread before you, is the town centre. In this final stretch of the walk, the nature of the architecture comes full circle: from the great political statements of the Queen's House and the Royal Hospital, past the charming mansions of Croom's Hill, and now back to political architecture of a very different kind – in the form of Nicholas Hawksmoor's St Alfege church, where this walk ends.

The town centre in its current form was recast in 1829–31 by Joseph Kay, the architect of the Trafalgar Tavern. This was a radical makeover because fifteenth-century monastic remains and, no doubt, an array of small-scale brick and timber buildings of vernacular design were replaced with large, stucco-clad houses and shops of very metropolitan neoclassical design. Perhaps the word for Kay's work is 'strident', and so arguably this Regency new town centre offers some comfort to the architects of the new building on Stockwell Street and some precedent for their assertive design. But, on the other hand, there remains – after nearly 200 years – something awkward and odd about Kay's architecture. It still seems too big, too orchestrated, as if it were envisaged and built for a larger, more urban canvas.

Things are not helped by the basic plan. Essentially Kay created no more than one hollow block of roughly square form, which loosely echoed the previous layout – so no crescents, circuses or urban flourishes. Within this hollow block he located an open market (now roofed over in a utilitarian and unbeautiful manner, but with a charming alley on its south side), with terraces added to the outer edges of the streets forming the

The west side of Greenwich Church Street. The building in the middle, number 17, likely dates to the late seventeenth century.

north (College Approach) and south (Nelson Road) edges of the box. The west side is formed by ancient Greenwich Church Street. Unfortunately traffic now hurtles in most noisy and visually disturbing manner around the edges of this box – with Nelson Road being the saddest because here Kay contrived to create his most urbane thoroughfare, with centre blocks dressed with Grecian Ionic columns.

Some idea of what was swept away for this ambitious 'improvement' scheme is suggested by what survives on the west side of Greenwich Church Street, north of the church. A sustained and irregular terrace contains a number of early buildings, of which number 17 is the most

remarkable. It is small – only two windows wide and the central pier between windows is only two and a half bricks wide (less than 2 feet), which is about as narrow as a brick pier can get if the nicety of brick bond and detailing are observed. Above the façade is a timber eaves cornice, and above both numbers 15 and 17 rises a steep, tile-clad roof. Inside there is a pair of central stacks – one serving the rear rooms of the pair of houses and the other serving the front rooms. Between the stacks is a pair of winding staircases. All is very typical of vernacular building of the late seventeenth century, from when this pair of houses must date.

But of course, the most eye-catching building on Church Street is St Alfege church itself. This is one of the great public buildings of Greenwich – built in 1711 to 1718 to the designs of Nicholas Hawksmoor, with significant contributions from John James, particularly the steeple that was not added to the top of the tower until 1730. There was a medieval church on this site but the decision was taken to rebuild using funds made available from the 1711 Act of Parliament to build 'Fifty New Churches' in London. Through a tax on coal, funds had been raised to help with the construction of St Paul's Cathedral and various City churches after the Great Fire (see Walk 4). But by 1711 this mighty project was virtually complete, so the tax revenue was diverted to the mission to build monumental churches in those parts of London that were expanding and that, more often than not, had populations dominated by various bodies of Dissenters or Nonconformists. These churches were political architecture. They were to make manifest the power of the established church that, united with the state, was determined to proclaim its presence and dominance in newly built or expanded quarters of the capital. And, as the Commissioners

The pilasters on St Alfege church were relatively conventional for Nicholas Hawksmoor, and by the second decade of the eighteenth century he had adopted a more abstract approach.

for the Act evidently believed, to be successful in their political aims, these new churches had to be big, architecturally impressive and – in consequence – expensive. As such, all are faced and detailed in beautiful Portland stone. These churches, like Egyptian mortuary temples, possess the sense that they were built for eternity.

St Alfege is visually striking, but not as idiosyncratic, abstract or strangely intoxicating as Hawksmoor's slightly later churches built under the 1711 Act – notably St Anne's Limehouse, St George-in-the-East and Christ Church Spitalfields (see p. 44), which commenced in 1714. You might think that the individualism of these later churches merely reflects the fact that Hawksmoor was hitting his stride. But there is a little more to it. St Alfege was Hawksmoor's first actual as opposed to theoretical design for the Commission, and there seem to have been certain controls exerted upon him. And these controls mean that the St Alfege's design

– as fanciful as it might seem – is more conventional than Hawksmoor's later designs.

The most obvious expression of this is the fact that the body of the church is dressed with a giant order of pilasters. Hawksmoor was not so conventional with his second-generation churches. He had used a giant order before – notably in 1702 at Easton Neston, a country house in Northamptonshire, where, as at St Alfege, the order rises majestically in a continuous fashion around the entire exterior of the building. But by the second decade of the eighteenth century Hawksmoor had moved on artistically – no doubt partly inspired by his former master Sir John Vanbrugh – to embrace a more elemental, abstract, sculptural and inventive interpretation of the classical language of architecture.

Despite the presence of the somewhat conventional giant order, St Alfege displays many of the more original ideas and obsessions that Hawksmoor was to develop in his slightly later churches. We have already encountered his obsession with early Christianity (see p. 91); in this church, he explored the notion of the 'primitive' basilicas of the Christians, by adding north and south transepts to the church to create a cross-shaped plan. The origin of Christian churches within the traditions of Roman basilicas also led Hawksmoor to ponder the manner of handling the tower and steeple – required by Christian convention and liturgy but, of course, unprecedented in the design of ancient basilicas. At St Alfege the solution was to place the west end of the body of the church against the tower (which in fact was inherited from the earlier church) so that the tower rises as a self-contained entity from ground level, and the temple-like body of the church appears visually (if not actually) detached from the tower. This avoids the oddity of the tower emerging in ungainly fashion from the top of the west end of the church, or being poised uncomfortably above a pediment.

The design of St Alfege also reveals how Hawksmoor worked as an architect, transferring ideas from one project to another, and in the process adapting, refining and enriching them. The portico giving the church the appearance of a mighty Roman temple when viewed from the town centre is based on a design that he had produced earlier for Wren for St Paul's Cathedral and that appears on the transept elevations of the early Great Model of the cathedral (see p. 159), but which ultimately did not appear on the cathedral itself. Likewise, early designs for the top stage of St Alfege's tower seem to have inspired his general approach to the later St George-in-the-East. No ideas, it seems, were ever wasted.

Time to enter the church. The portico of St Alfege is odd since it leads nowhere. It stands at the east end of the church so behind it is the altar

Hawksmoor grappled with how to reconcile the need for a steeple with his classical design for St Alfege.

and choir, making the location of a central main door here physically impossible, as well as liturgically undesirable. Instead, then, enter the church from the south. The interior of St Alfege was always something of a 'work in progress' in comparison with Hawksmoor's later London churches. It lacked power and the striking monumentality and sense of bold scale and geometry that distinguishes Christ Church in particular. And what you see now is mostly a generally faithful reconstruction after devastating damage during the Second World War. But some details survived, including the finely wrought ironwork.

Before leaving there is one external detail that must not be missed: a small but sublime example of Hawksmoor's love for the elemental. Outside each transept, the entrances to the burial vaults beneath the church are capped by triangular slabs of stone. They are primitive – almost brutal – in appearance, and reduce the elegance of the classical pediment to its bare essentials. These were the portals to Hawksmoor's underworld. Their raw and unadorned form says something about his attitude to the naked realities of death, the great equaliser. It is a fitting end to this walk, which, between the ruins of Placentia, the Queen's House and Charles II's doomed attempts at palace building, reveals much about the pride and arrogance of generations of monarchs. In these slabs of stone, Hawksmoor alludes to a truth that such buildings do not acknowledge: that in death, worldly power and wealth count for nothing, and ornament is just another form of vanity.

Eastbury Manor House

Eastbury Square is a leafy oasis that stands a few minutes' walk to the south of Upney station. Surrounded by dull interwar housing, mostly organised as semi-detached pairs set within front gardens, it is not at first apparent that this is an ancient park – and that secreted within it is an extraordinary Tudor mansion with a singular role in British history.

First walk around the house to sample its character. The north elevation is surrounded by large old trees which mean that, at most times of the year, it is almost lost in gloom. This is the main entrance front, which is flanked by two narrower wings, evidence that the house has an H-shaped plan, typical of the time. The wing to your left (the east) would once have contained the family's apartment; that to the west would have contained the three main service rooms – the kitchen, the buttery (for bottles), the pantry (for bread) – as well as low-status lodgings. In the middle, behind the entrance front, was the great hall, and, above it, the great chamber, which was the main room in which the family dined and entertained.

This north elevation has a Gothic flavour, with the door itself, set to one side, having a four-centred – or Tudor – arch: very traditional for the 1570s, when the house is said to have been completed, although in this instance topped in modish manner with a pediment. On the west side, however, all is much more classical. The elevation is flat-fronted, seven windows wide, and possesses harmonious repose and symmetry. But all changes again to the south: this elevation seems far more medieval, or at least early rather than mid or late Tudor. It has a slightly fortified appearance, not least because from within an inner court rises a five-storey, faceted tower (faced by the ruins of its pair), with the court itself screened by a formidable wall. The house, overall, has a rather antiquated appearance considering the period in which it was built – it opts for Gothic rather than stylish Renaissance details, which leads *The Buildings of England* to say that it 'must certainly be considered backward looking for the 1570s'.[1]

It's time to enter the manor. The best way in is via the court, now a small garden, in front of the west elevation. The ground level is fascinating.

Look first at the window openings, which contain fixed panels of small oblong panes of glass. This was the typical sixteenth-century way of doing things, when glass was expensive and large panes were almost impossible to make. But the most striking thing about this elevation is that there is no formally designed door, merely a small and very utilitarian opening inserted into the lower portion of one of the windows. This looks very much an afterthought or later addition. In fact a large number of the ground-floor windows of this elevation are blocked – probably to prevent servants in the kitchen wing looking at the family and its guests in the west garden.

There is access from the kitchen anteroom to the tower, which contains a staircase providing a direct connection between the kitchen and the first-floor great chamber where the family would have dined. The staircase is a wonderful thing, with hefty treads, each fashioned from a single baulk of oak, winding around a massive oak newel, almost an entire tree trunk, with limewashed brick walls. Its ultimate destination is a room perched above the house's roof ridge; its windows, set in each facet of the tower, must have offered a fine prospect, including distant views of the Thames and of the City of London, around 8 miles to the west.

When inside the house observe two particular details. First, look at the great chamber above the great hall. It appears originally to have been divided into two rooms. To the east is the painted chamber which retains impressive fragments of a *trompe l'oeil* scheme of 1600, while to

Entrance as afterthought: the peculiarly informal door to the house on the west front.

the west was an anteroom. A 1917 entry in the *Survey of London* records something intriguing about this western room. From it 'a door leads into a small room over the porch, where a trap door opens on a space some 3 ft 6 ins deep between the floor and the room and the ceiling of the porch below.' This small space was evidently intended to be habitable because it was lit 'by a loophole in the eastern wall', which suggests that it was a well-contrived hiding place. It could perhaps have been a 'priest's hole', as the occupants of the house in the late sixteenth and early seventeenth century were Roman Catholics and celebration of the Catholic Mass was illegal; these hiding places were where Catholic priests could flee in fear for their lives.[2]

And second, take note of the denuded interior of the manor. While there are some old decorative fragments – including of course the 'painted room' depicting an idyllic landscape with boating and fishing scenes, perhaps inspired by the marshy flatlands of Tudor Dagenham – in general little of the original interior survives. On the second floor are visible the bare bones of the timber partitions and roof structure – impressive, but nothing like how it would have appeared during the house's prime.

What accounts for these idiosyncratic features? Well, they are a reflection of the volatile history of Eastbury Manor, first as a possible Catholic safe house, and then as a neglected and nearly demolished country home. Its origins were regular enough. Until the Reformation, the land had belonged to an Augustinian abbey in nearby Barking; a man named Clement Sisley appears to have acquired the former monastic estate in 1556 from John Keele, and the house was built from the late 1560s into the early 1570s. By 1608 Sisley had sold the manor to Augustine Steward, but by this time Eastbury had entered the annals of British history by supposedly being involved in the scheme of November 1605 to assassinate King James I by detonating barrels of black powder underneath Parliament: the Gunpowder Plot.

Admittedly, the link between Eastbury and the plot is somewhat murky, marred by confusion and the absence of some crucial evidence. What we do know is this: in the early 1600s Steward had likely let the house to John Moore – an Alderman of the City of London and a committee member of the East India Company, who seems to have commissioned the murals in the 'painted room' (they incorporate his coat

The staircase, built around a newel that is almost an entire tree trunk.

of arms). Moore died in April 1603, but a number of members of his family probably continued to live in the house: namely his wife, a Spanish-born Roman Catholic called Maria and their daughter Maria Perez (or Margery Moore), who was married to a man called Lewis Tresham.

It is Lewis Tresham who forms the possible connection between Eastbury and the Gunpowder Plot. He hailed from a Catholic family: his father, Sir Thomas, had during the 1590s built the famed Triangular Lodge at Rushton, Northamptonshire – a peculiar building that has sometimes been interpreted as a shrine to the Holy Trinity and Catholicism. Lewis's older brother, Sir Francis Tresham, was among the key plotters; the leader of the conspiracy, Robert Catesby, was their cousin. But the possible links between Eastbury and the plot go even further. For Lewis Tresham was the brother-in-law of Lord Monteagle – and it was Monteagle who received the anonymous letter warning him to avoid the State Opening of Parliament if he valued his life. Puzzled more than alarmed, Monteagle alerted the authorities, and on 4 December the cellars at the Palace of Westminster were searched, Guy Fawkes found and the plot thwarted. Did Lewis write the letter? No one knows for certain, but it is possible – although it could also have come from the older brother Francis, or from a number of others who knew about the plot.

Nor can we be sure whether the plotters used Eastbury House to plan their attack on king and Parliament. But there is some intriguing evidence that places Barking – and by implication Eastbury – in the frame. On 9 November – just a few days after Fawkes's arrest and his brutal interrogation – a Barking fisherman asserted Fawkes had hired a boat (using the name of John Johnson) in which he and other plotters had travelled to and from the French port of Gravelines. Fawkes, it seems, planned to make Barking and the boat to Gravelines his escape route if the plot had succeeded. It seems likely that Eastbury was considered a safe house by the plotters, and a prime factor in persuading them to make Barking part of their perilous journey from Westminster to northern France. All that can be said with certainty is that, while Sir Francis Tresham was executed in December 1605, his head put on public display as a traitor, his younger brother survived and thrived. Lewis inherited his older brother's estates, was created a baronet in his own right in 1611, and lived into his sixties, dying in 1639.

In the early seventeenth century the house entered a period of steady, and then speedy, decline. In 1628, it was probably sold by Martin Steward to Jacob Price, the first of a series of owners throughout the century. By the late seventeenth century the house was old, unfashionable and no doubt relatively uncomfortable, and the country around it was becoming more heavily inhabited and less attractive for those with means and ambition. In 1714 it was acquired by a William Browne, presumably more for its land than as a home. Daniel Defoe, in his *Tour Thro' the Whole Island of Great Britain*, compiled in 1724–7, described it as 'a great house, antient, and now almost fallen down', and only worth a mention because it was 'where tradition says the gunpowder treason plot was at first contriv'd, and that all the first consultations about it were held there'.

By the later eighteenth century Eastbury Manor had ceased to be a much-loved family home but a piece of real estate, let, divided, mildly exploited and thoroughly neglected by its owners. As antiquarian Daniel Lysons observed of the manor in 1795, 'for almost a hundred years it hath been occupied by lessees and thereby degraded into a farmhouse' with its tenants presiding over such neglect that the house's 'ruin' was visibly 'hastening'.[3] The house had also been pillaged for timber and brick, which goes a long way to explain its currently greatly denuded interior. And although some works were undertaken in the early 1840s, and perhaps in the 1860s or early 1870s, to stabilise the crumbling ruin, it remained a multi-occupied farmhouse. During the First World War it was taken over by the government and used to manufacture observation balloons, and after the war – when Dagenham and Barking's farmland was fast being appropriated for the construction of housing estates and factories – it became marooned in an ever-dwindling patch of park, soon reduced to the mere garden you see today.

And so, by the early twentieth century, demolition seemed the inevitable fate of Eastbury Manor. But, after the destruction and suffering of the war, history and beauty seemed more precious and – luckily – many recognised that the gaunt wreck of the house was both beautiful and historic. The Society for the Protection of Ancient Buildings and the London Survey Committee (which had just published its monograph on the house) started to campaign for preservation, making the obvious point that its years of poverty had, ironically, made the manor more precious because it had been saved from fashion-driven alterations (if not from pillaging) – and so giving it a rare authenticity. Finally the National Trust stepped in, bought the house, and promptly leased it to Barking Council to run for the good of the local people. And broadly, a hundred years on, this is the position still. The Trust has done what it can to preserve what little of historic interest survives within the manor – notably the murals in the 'painted room' – while the London Borough of Barking and Dagenham runs it as a community venue, museum and café.

WALK 4

Bank to St Paul's

Wren's London

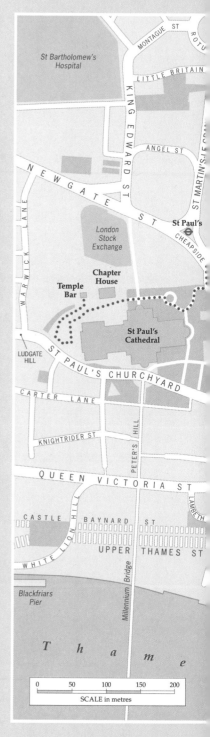

In late August 1666, Sir Christopher Wren submitted a plan for the elaborate repair and partial restyling of the ancient and battered St Paul's Cathedral. An astronomy professor at Oxford, Wren was a leading figure in a circle of prominent natural philosophers in London. In 1660, he had been involved in founding the Royal Society, and his early designs – notably for the Sheldonian Theatre in Oxford – had been well received. So when he submitted his new plans for the cathedral, they were accepted by King Charles II. Neither of the men could have known that, a week later, St Paul's would burn to the ground.

Starting in Pudding Lane on the night of Sunday 2 September, the Great Fire of London swept through the wooden buildings of the capital, reducing a huge swathe of the city to ruins – from the approximate location of Temple in the west to the Tower of London in the east, and to the north-east being halted along Bishopsgate within the wall. By Thursday, when the fire was extinguished, eighty-seven parish churches and around 13,000 houses had been destroyed, and thousands of Londoners had been forced into make-shift tents around the city.[1] It was the largest fire in the history of London.

London burning: an anonymous painting from *c.* 1675 depicts the Great Fire.

The diarist John Evelyn offers an account of the Great Fire that, even 350 years later, vividly recreates its horror. 'All the sky was of a fiery aspect, like the top of a burning oven, and the light seen above 40 miles round about for many nights,' he wrote.

> The noise and cracking and thunder of people, the fall of towers,
> houses, and churches, was like an hideous storm, and the air
> all about so hot and inflamed that at last one was not able to
> approach it, so that they were forced to stand still and let the
> flames burn on . . . The clouds also of smoke were dismal and
> reached upon computation near 50 miles in length. Thus I left it
> this afternoon burning, a resemblance of Sodom, or the last day
> . . . London was, but is no more![2]

While most Londoners mourned the loss of their city, however, a number of them were already planning its reconstruction. In the years after the Restoration of Charles II in 1660, London had become a vibrant centre of science and art – the haunt of scientists ranging from Robert Boyle to Robert Hooke to Isaac Newton. A number of these men saw the destruction of London as a chance to turn the capital into a rational and orderly city, which would embody the new age of science and optimism. Within a week of the fire being quenched, Charles II promised to rebuild 'a much more beautiful city than is at this time consumed' – and invited architects to offer new plans for the reconstruction of London.[3]

Five plans were rapidly submitted, all more or less rational expressions of a grid-city with squares of circular, polygonal or triangular piazza for public buildings, and all intended – with wide streets and masonry buildings – to be as hygienic and fireproof as possible. Hooke and Richard Newcourt proposed grid systems incorporating squares for churches and large marketplaces. One former army captain, Valentine Knight, proposed long streets running from east to west, divided by a canalised Fleet River and a reduced number. of north–south streets. And Christopher Wren, inspired by the sixteenth- and seventeenth-century Rome of the Popes, proposed a city composed of a right-angular grid of streets cut across diagonally by wide avenues emanating from a series of piazzas.[4]

In the end, the utopian schemes for a rebuilt London came to nothing. Property owners almost immediately asserted their right to rebuild on their old plots of land, and soon the City was being reconstructed

Christopher Wren's plan for rebuilding the City of London, inspired by Rome.

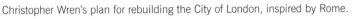

largely according to the existing street plan – albeit this time in brick and stone, not wood. Nonetheless, Wren remained at the forefront of the reconstruction of the city. In 1669, he was made Surveyor-General of the King's Works, the role chiefly responsible for overseeing the construction of government buildings. When, the following year, Charles passed a rebuilding Act that provided funding for the creation of new churches, Wren became the key figure in the reconstruction effort. In all, fifty-one new churches would be built.

This chapter takes us through a part of the City that contains a number of the most intriguing churches produced by Wren and his office, including his most famous work, the rebuilt St Paul's Cathedral. At the height of his productivity during the 1670s and 1680s, his office was large and efficient and it included many designers – among them, perhaps, his own daughter Jane. This team, together with the outstanding craftsmen Wren employed like Grinling Gibbons and Christopher Kempster, formed an inspiring college of building. Nicholas Hawksmoor trained with, and worked for, Wren (notably on St Paul's) while Robert Hooke – a member with Wren of the Royal Society – contributed to several Wren projects, almost as a means of pursuing experimental scientific enquiry. So Wren's City churches can be seen as a creative collaboration, but most share common and developing themes that make them into a powerful and coherent body of work revealing most clearly the guiding mind of a master: Wren.

Above all, Wren was striving for beauty in his architecture. And like many a Renaissance theorist and architect before him, Wren had pondered the nature of beauty at great length. In his *Tract 1 on Architecture*, written in the 1670s, he offered a definition: beauty in architecture is 'a Harmony of Objects, begetting Pleasure by the Eye'.[5] This reflected the quintessential Renaissance view. Beauty was not quite the subjective business it is today, but in fact existed in nature, and was the work of the Creator. All that was necessary in the bid to create beauty in the works of man was for the architect or artist to identify the origins and mechanisms of natural beauty and to emulate them. As Wren put it, 'geometry had an absolute value, given by nature and God'.[6]

No doubt Wren, like most Renaissance thinkers, believed that the Romans and the Greeks had, through observation, trial and error, and skilful imitation of nature, found the key to beauty, and recreated it in their buildings. In the late seventeenth century, it was thought that the best way to understand these classical principles was to study the sixteenth-century Venetian architect Andrea Palladio, who we met in the previous chapter: he had codified natural beauty and applied it in his buildings, which embodied the secrets of universal architectural beauty. The key was geometry, harmonically related proportions, and mathematics. As St Augustine observed as early as the fourth century AD, 'God is number', citing the account of God's creation of the world as explained in *The Wisdom of Solomon*, which states God 'ordered all things in measure and number and weight'.[7] For Wren – as with all Renaissance architects – classical architecture and the refined geometrical proportional systems that it embodied were the foundation of 'natural' beauty.

But Wren was also doing something new. He was primarily a man of science, and this somewhat mystic approach to beauty was not

Wren's masterpiece, the rebuilt St Paul's from the east.

enough. He wanted this essentially religious argument and theory to be underpinned by an element, at least, of empirical observation and by the 'geometrical Reasons of Optics'. He noticed that many things that were regarded as beautiful did not conform to the theory about the divine cause of beauty – which led him to argue that, as well as geometrical, rational, absolute and 'natural' beauty, there was also 'customary' beauty or beauty achieved through association.

In this argument, Wren was moving to the modern sense that, on occasion, beauty could be a subjective business, very much in the eye of the beholder. While 'natural' beauty relates to the physiology of the eye – which he thought recognises and responds to 'natural' beauty and to the forms generated by proportion and harmony – 'customary' beauty 'relates to the psychology of the mind'.[8] And so Wren developed a theory – that was not originally his own invention – to explain why things not naturally beautiful could be regarded as beautiful through custom, familiarity or associations.

Once you begin to appreciate the thinking underpinning Wren's architecture, his buildings become intriguing to consider at some length. Indeed, you can begin to understand them. Most agree – usually in a vague manner – that Wren's architecture possesses beauty, but now you can see different types of beauty. Some of his City churches are evidently pragmatic solutions to tricky problems, often to do with the difficult nature of the site or lack of money. Here the beauty might be more subjective, achieved through familiarity. Other churches are more perfect, and appear to connect more directly to profound objective ideas that are as old as architecture itself. Often these churches are distinguished by bold references to antique models or are permutations upon Wren's idea for 'centralised' churches of cubic volume with domes of various sorts set upon a cruciform arrangement of columns. You are about to see a couple of these. But which of these types of churches are more satisfying? Probably no consensus can be reached, and destruction and gruesome rebuilding, reordering and 'restoration' has irredeemably tainted his City work. But nothing is obvious, and it's hardly necessary to point out that the odd little compromised churches might be the more moving. See what you think – and feel – when we dip into Wren's churches during this walk.

THE WALK

At around a kilometre and a half, this is one of the shortest walks in the book. But it offers such a feast of architectural treats that it can nonetheless take some time to complete. It can easily be joined up with Walk 2, which finishes at the Royal Exchange, and can be expanded into Walk 12, which begins just west of where this route ends.

Our route starts opposite the Royal Exchange, with what would now be regarded as one of the greatest buildings in Britain – if it had been suffered to survive. This is the Bank of England, established in 1694. The story of the bank reveals much about the commercial changes sweeping the nation in the late seventeenth century. Founded six years after the Glorious Revolution – in which the Dutch Protestant King William of Orange deposed Britain's Catholic monarch, James II – it was created to fund the new king's ongoing war against his French rival, Louis XIV, specifically in response to the French naval victory in 1690 over an allied English and Dutch fleet in the Battle of Beachy Head. With triumphant French ships cruising in the Channel to the very mouth of the Thames estuary, and with a French-supported Jacobite invasion a real possibility, William had no choice but to rebuild and re-equip his fleet. And to do that money was needed – urgently. The plan was simple: the government was to raise loans of £1.2 million; in return, the lenders were incorporated into a bank that had the right to make loans and issue notes. Given the political aspect of the foundation of the bank, and its role in resisting a possible French invasion and the imposition of the ousted Catholic monarch James II, it comes as no surprise that the first governor of the bank was Sir John Houblon, a third-generation French Huguenot refugee. The Huguenots had suffered much at the hands of Louis XIV and the French Catholic authorities and were determined to oppose them in every way possible.

The first hundred years of the bank's architectural history is interesting but not exceptional. All would change, however, in 1788 when it appointed John Soane as its architect. During the following forty years or so Soane expanded and largely rebuilt the bank in sensational manner. His strategy was to create a number of single-storey, top-lit and often saucer-domed banking halls – interrelated but serving different

This 1810 watercolour reveals how John Soane's now-lost Bank of England once looked.

functions – within a lofty, solemn and secure stone-built perimeter wall, breached only by monumental doors. This formed part of Soane's broader project to reinvigorate the ancient language of classicism for the modern age. To do this, he sought to reduce the style to its bare essentials, relying on proportion, on a minimalist and a virtually abstract vocabulary of simple motifs – bold incised lines and right-angled fret patterns, for example – that imply the feel of (rather than literally recreate) antique classical architecture. The rationale was rooted in Soane's understanding of architectural history as a living thing, which should be used creatively rather than slavishly emulated. So, the atmosphere of his halls, vaulted and lit from above, was clearly informed by Roman bath architecture, yet they were not direct copies but inspired evocations.

Yet Soane's Bank of England can only now live in the imagination. In the 1920s the bank's directors took the decision to destroy the great work that their predecessors had commissioned. The architectural historian Sir Nikolaus Pevsner argued that the directors' decision resulted in 'the worst individual loss suffered by London architecture in the first half of the 20th century'.[9] Because Soane's buildings were generally single-storey, and top-lit so they could not be extended upwards, the directors chose gradually to destroy all within the perimeter wall and replace them with tall classical buildings with more office accommodation – an act of architectural vandalism undertaken between 1921 and 1937 by the essentially second-rate architect Sir Herbert Baker. As Pevsner pithily put it, to preserve only Soane's screen wall and 'scoop out all the rest strikes one as particularly distasteful'; to 'use Soane's masterwork as the footstool of a *Herbert Baker* seems unforgivable.'

What I find particularly irritating is the way in which Baker peddles the same favoured neo-Baroque details, seemingly without much thought or reference to site or function, in his various projects. Here he emphasises centre windows with feeble aedicules – the small shrines set into the wall, placed above the windows. Why? There seems no rhyme or reason and, as Pevsner notes, such whimsical and irrational motifs 'are entirely out of sympathy with Soane's forthright style'. Baker's interiors are, in part, an oddball homage to Soane that involves the recreation, in over-large scale and clumsy manner, of some of Soane's halls. This is probably the worst approach possible – not only did Baker connive at the destruction of Soane's masterpiece but also recreated some of its elements in a debased and clumsy manner, thus adding insult to injury. Some of Baker's interiors can be most disconcerting because on occasion he incorporated Soane details that had been salvaged from the ruins.

The closest one can now get to Soane's original vision comes by stepping into the Bank of England Museum, accessible from Bartholomew Street. In 1986 the bank – no doubt as an act of penance – recreated one of Soane's halls in a most exact and admirable manner. This is the Bank Stock Office of 1793, and is the central space of the museum. It's a beautiful thing – when not overwhelmed by interactive tat – that gives a very good idea of the architectural wonder that has been lost.

Here, though, we will suffice with a walk around the perimeter of the bank. What you can still see of Soane's exterior – the outer wall, built between 1795 and 1805 – remains most moving. Baker fiddled with it, and in so doing predictably diluted its power, but it is still a fascinating study in the expression of strength through architecture (it was essential that the bank not only be unassailable at times of riot but also look so, to deter the mob), and in the inspired use of antique precedent. The south stretch, facing Threadneedle Street, is the most architectural. Soane was

Soane was fond of imagining his buildings as ruins, as in this inventive 1830 painting of the Bank of England by Joseph Gandy.

wary of using columns – they were too obviously historic and evoked the sort of direct associations with the Greek and Roman past that he wished to avoid – but this section has a central colonnade set with the plane of the wall. The columns are of a Corinthian order as found on the early-first-century BC Temple of Vesta at Tivoli in Italy, an ancient building Soane much admired for its form, just proportion and fine detail. He seems to have particularly liked the unusually abrupt way in which the fluting was terminated at capital and base. Capping the bank's wall is an entablature topped by lion masks simulating the water spouts on the cornices on antique temples. It's all very erudite and incredibly beautiful, especially when sunlight plays upon the textures to create a dazzling array of abstract shadows. Soane, like most great architects, at one level conceived his buildings as freestanding sculptures, set in constantly changing light, with details burnished by the sun or emphasised by shadow, all calculated to move the senses in an almost visceral manner.

The windows within the central colonnade reveal that the wall is inhabited. This must have tickled Soane's fancy because he liked to imagine his buildings as ruins, in the manner of Pompeii. Indeed in 1830 he commissioned Joseph Gandy to paint a cut-away watercolour of the bank which takes the form of a vast bird's-eye view of the building in ruins. The romantic idea of the bank as an ancient classical ruin in the heart of the City – or perhaps an inhabited ruin like many of the Roman remnants in Rome or Diocletian's Palace at Split – seems to have beguiled Soane from the start of the project.

One of the most striking details of the Threadneedle Street wall are the false doors or windows of vast scale, defined by architraves that taper outward slightly from top to bottom in Egyptian and Grecian manner, indeed like the blank windows and doors found in the ruins of Egyptian mortuary temples and tombs. Their presence adds to Soane's ruin romance; it's almost as if the bank is an ancient city of the dead. Originally these windows were flanked by much smaller, square, blocked windows set above smaller blocked doors. For inexplicable reasons Baker removed all of these and replaced them with rustication. The presence of these blank, dead, unseeing eyes greatly enhanced the wall's ominous atmosphere.

———————————◆•◆•◆———————————

Walk now to the west wall facing Princes Street, which is the longest, simplest and most overwhelmingly sublime stretch. It is now almost ruthless, a cliff face of banded rustication, which was by tradition used to imply strength and permanence of construction. In the centre is a door, flanked by recessed columns, but originally here also were 'blind' windows and door – walled off and impassable – which were again expunged by Baker. What survives is a magnificent blocked door of monumental scale.

At the northern end of Princes Street, forming the corner with Lothbury, is Soane's recreation of part of the ruined round Temple of Vesta at Tivoli. This corner is the architectural jewel of the wall. As on the Temple of Vesta, it has a frieze with bucrania (ox skulls) and swags – symbolising sacrifice to the gods – and was originally topped by an intricately detailed and pedimented attic. This was created by Soane as an exquisite, archaeologically inspired, homage to history. But, naturally, Baker could not leave it alone. He cut arches through the wall next to Soane's temple and made it part of a pedestrian route. Now one walks through Soane's monument, below a shallow saucer dome with an opening at the top (an oculus) that was inserted by Baker, complete with a pompous inscription stating that in 1936 the bank made this route 'for the Citizens of London'.

Baker's intervention is not awful – in its way it's rather successful – but it is not Soane, and it contradicts Soane's intention. He created a sacrosanct shrine by embedding an evocation of an exemplary antique temple within the wall of the Bank of England. It was chaste, a work of lofty art to contemplate. Baker turned the shrine into a self-important thoroughfare for City workers.

We can take heart, though, from the magnificent building just to the south-west of the Princes Street wall – built at the same moment that Baker was brutalising the Bank of England. This is the former HQ of the Midland Bank, constructed in 1924 to 1929 to the design of Sir Edwin Lutyens, and it is one of the City's most rewarding pieces of early-

The sublime Princes Street wall of the Bank of England.

twentieth-century commercial architecture. It was, when completed, the City's great showpiece of high-class and contemporary commercial design, with an array of architect-designed furniture and fittings and a complex and masterful ground floor, in which Lutyens organised various halls and offices as if he were laying out a small ideal town. There are vistas, obelisks to frame views, variety and a pleasing sense of enclosure and even surprise – all possible because the building occupies a corner site and has doors on two of its sides, allowing 'avenues' to meet in the centre. This splendid ground floor now contains a series of restaurants and bars, with a hotel in the rooms above, and so is accessible to the public. The composition of the main wide elevation to Poultry consists of

a rusticated podium, with tall arched windows capped with a cornice and topped by a mezzanine storey that is fifteen windows wide.

In the Midland Bank, we see Lutyens attempting to design a tall, modern, commercial building, within the time-honoured constraints of classical composition. His solution was to construct a series of tiers, each itself a perfect classical composition. So, after the attic storey, Lutyens's composition restarts with a three-storey block containing tiers of windows united by being set within arched recesses. The piers dividing the recesses are rusticated and can be read as elemental pilaster, in the English Baroque tradition, and the arched top windows in this tier are the deepest and so suggest that the *piano nobile* – the principal floor – is at an usually high level. This composition is topped by a cornice, smaller than that below, and then the design starts for a third time. The upper two storeys are set back and treated as an almost independent pavilion, with a centre that is domed and breaks forward to Poultry where it displays a pediment and a deep arched window suggesting a room of noble proportion. Lutyens and Baker had once been colleagues, but had fallen out during the design and construction of New Delhi, for which Lutyens had been master-planner and lead architect since the city was got under way in 1911. Lutyens believed that Baker had, for selfish reasons, compromised the setting of the Viceroy's Palace – Lutyens's main project. Lutyens must have pulled out all stops to ensure his City bank HQ triumphed over Baker's, which of course it does.

The contrast between the two men's abilities becomes even more apparent with the north wall of the Bank of England, on Lothbury. This is the most altered part of the perimeter wall. Blank windows have again

Edwin Lutyens's design for the Midland Bank was the high point of early-twentieth-century commercial architecture in the City.

been removed and there are now three arched openings topped by pediments. Two are functioning doors and one contains a niche in which is mounted a statue of Soane. Walk to the end of Lothbury, and look along Bartholomew Lane to see the east wall. This is more ornate, much like the Threadneedle Street elevation – again the frieze is decorated with a fret or Greek key pattern, and there are huge blank windows framed by pilasters. But much has been lost. The stretches of wall on either side of the colonnade were previously fitted out with two tiers of blank openings, the upper being square windows: look hard and you can see newish rusticated stone marking the locations of these lost details. How did Baker dare destroy them? The Soane work he suffered to survive he mutilated, and for reasons that were entirely subjective. It really is an extraordinary – and depressing – business.

On Lothbury, we come to our first Christopher Wren church. St Margaret's Lothbury is one of his less-altered churches and, given the harrowing of his City that took place during the nineteenth century and the Second World War, its survival is something of a miracle. In the mid nineteenth century, as trains and improved transport made it possible for City families to move to the airy edges of London, all of Wren's churches came under threat. With greatly diminished parish populations what, many asked, was the point of these parish churches? Even Charles Dickens was defeatist. In *The Uncommercial Traveller* of c.1860 he suggested the inevitability of the passing of 'these deserted churches', which 'remain like the tombs of the old citizens who lie beneath them and around them, Monuments of another age'. But, despite everything, St Margaret's and thirteen of Wren's other fifty-one City churches survive – largely intact, internally as well as externally (although all altered to a lesser or greater degree). Of this precious band St Margaret's is one of the best and, somewhat awkward and irregular in its cramped plan, is an excellent example of Wren's pragmatic approach to design. In St Margaret's beauty is not absolute, as Wren explained it in his theory of aesthetics, for it is not a pure expression of rational geometry nor is it modelled on an exemplary ancient prototype. It is not an example of Wren's 'natural' beauty but of his more subjective 'customary' beauty.

St Margaret's Lothbury reveals Wren's impressive ability to adapt to the sites he was given.

St Margaret's was built from 1686 to 1690 and in plan takes the form of a squarish rectangle with a stubby nave and a single aisle to the south. This asymmetry was, of course, far removed from Wren's classical ideals for church design, but imposed by the awkward shape of the site he'd inherited, and the need – for practical reasons – to build on the entire plot so as to accommodate the parish congregation. On its south-west corner stands a tower topped by a pretty timber and lead spire that achieves the verticality and complex profile of Gothic towers and spires, but through a combination of the essentially classical motifs of an obelisk and a dome, the former sitting on the latter. It's a clever fusion of the two traditions and one that Wren and his 'college' of craftsmen mastered brilliantly when designing the City's post-fire silhouette.

The church's contribution to Lothbury is to offer its relatively plain south wall, pierced by a row of large semicircular topped windows, as a frontage aligned with neighbouring buildings. This is very literally street architecture, with the church being just part of a terrace and originally flanked by brick-built merchant houses and commercial buildings. Wren's grander churches tend to stand in space – at least partly so – and read as significant public buildings. The arrangement seen at St Margaret's was usual for Wren's more humble churches, where he often had to rebuild on the site of a medieval church (and often utilise the surviving structure) that had long been embedded deeply in the surrounding fabric of the City. Reusing existing fabric helped cut costs. A tax on coal imported into London was used to pay for the shells of the rebuilt City churches but money for interior fittings, and even for special exterior details, generally came from the parish. And if the parish and its parishioners were poor, or unwilling to subsidise the aggrandisement of their new church, then the building was generally finished in most modest manner.

Very broadly speaking, Wren and his assistants had two basic approaches when planning new churches, both of which could realise notions of 'natural' beauty. When circumstances were appropriate – relatively large and open, sites of roughly 2:1 or 3:1 proportion – churches were designed as permutations of the Roman and early Christian basilica form: typically with a nave flanked by lower aisles, separated from each other by a colonnade, with an apse at the east end, and timber galleries within the aisles and at the west end. When designing basilica churches Wren was consciously – and as we shall see – sometimes most literally emulating exemplary antique models.

And then there were the centralised churches. These were usually roughly square in plan, depending to a large degree on the proportion of the site, and were preferred when a significant amount of high-level daylight would be required to help illuminate the interior. In these cases the cubic volume of the church was furnished with columns that, by a system of entablatures and arches, were enabled to support a large, centrally placed, dome. The columns that supported the domes were not merely practical – they had a symbolic function, dividing the interior space to create an east–west main axis and a north–south cross axis that together defined a cruciform plan. Most satisfactory for a Christian place of worship, and a direct reflection of sixteenth- and seventeenth-century theories about the design of 'ideal' churches. Wren so liked square churches that his initial designs for rebuilding St Paul's Cathedral envisaged it as a mighty centralised church with a 'Greek cross' plan, with nave, chancel and transepts all of equal length.

The plan for St Margaret's is a common permutation of Wren's treatment for squarish sites that were too small for the creation of a centralised and domed church with cruciform main and cross axes.

Limited space only allowed for the construction of a single-aisled basilica, a most irregular solution but functional. It meant that the nave was of more traditional rectangular plan while the single aisle was adequate for the provision of a subsidiary altar or chapel if required.

On the inside, much of the church's Wren-period design remains intact. Box pews have long ago been replaced by ranks of soulless benches, as happened in virtually all Wren's churches. Box pews, rented by local families for their exclusive use, were frowned upon by nineteenth-century evangelical churchmen as a reflection of worldly hierarchies, with those with most worldly riches getting the best seats in God's house. This is an understandable reaction, but it has undermined the architecture of the church interior (the boxes' high partitions defined 'highways' through the nave, and drew attention to the main internal features). The joinery that survives, however, is particularly rich. Most of it is not quite what it seems: much comes from other City churches and was installed in St Margaret's in the late nineteenth century, such as the splendid screens, with open-work twisted columns and a central eagle, which were designed by Wren himself but for the now lost All-Hallows-the-Great. The communion rail, too, has been brought in, this time from St Olave Jewry, demolished in 1887 except for the tower.

***

Finish your loop of the Bank of England at the west end of Threadneedle Street at its junction with Cheapside. As we saw on p. 1, the junction of Threadneedle Street with Cheapside – the eastern portion of which is known as Poultry – and to their south Queen Victoria Street, is a very special place in the City, marking the course of the sacred River Walbrook. Here, from the mid third century AD, was located a temple to Mithras. In a no doubt unintended manner the rough location of the Roman governor's palace is today commemorated by the palace of the Lord Mayor of London – in a sense the City's governor – that lies just to the north.

The Mansion House, built between 1739 and 1742, not only stands near the site of its ancestor but also, with its mighty columned and pediment-topped portico, evokes it in a grand Roman manner. The commission was won by George Dance the Elder, who earlier had been involved in the design of St Botolph-without-Bishopsgate (see p. 48). It

Mansion House: George Dance the Elder's restless attempt at Palladianism.

was a victory against the odds. Dance was not only up against one of the great architects of the age, James Gibbs, who in the 1720s had designed the seminal St Martin-in-the-Fields (see p. 484) and was the author of the highly influential *Book of Architecture* published in 1728. He was also up against Giacomo Leoni, a Venetian country-house architect and the first English-language translator, between 1715 and 1720, of Palladio's *I Quattro Libri dell'Architettura*. But Dance's City connections – in 1735 he had been appointed the City's Clerk of Works and Surveyor for its Bridge House estate – as well as being City born and raised, steered him to triumph.

The building Dance created is an essay in the Palladian style of classicism, which came into fashion in the early years of the eighteenth century. In theory the style was more measured, more simple and more harmonically proportioned than the more inventive Baroque style that Dance had pursued at St Botolph's. Despite his best intentions it is evident that Dance could not quite pull off the transition. Though he used Palladian forms and details, Dance's Mansion House is showy, too compacted and burdened with ornament and ideas: the handsome portico seems almost to spill on to the street in front of it, and the side elevations, with their bizarre mix of details and windows of vastly differing scales and character, give this would-be Roman palace a very restless quality.

Immediately to its south is another Wren church – and in many ways his best. This is St Stephen's Walbrook. Upon its completion in 1679 the highly satisfied parishioners voted Wren a purse of gold as a gift for a job well done, and even James Ralph, generally a stern critic of English Baroque architects and architecture, conceded in his 1734 review of London's public buildings that St Stephen's 'is famous all over Europe . . . Italy itself can produce no modern building that can vie with this in taste or proportion.'[10] In 1758, John Wesley, a man better known for his interest in the world of the spirit than the world of architecture, observed in his diary that this 'little church' is 'neat and elegant beyond expression', and recalled a conversation the architectural pundit and Palladio fanatic Lord Burlington (see p. 212) had in Rome with an Italian architect who told him, 'My Lord, go back and see St Stephen's in London. We have not so fine a piece of architecture in Rome.' No doubt Burlington, who had routinely slighted Wren and his fellow English Baroque architects, was quite taken aback.

What is 'so fine' about St Stephen's? Well, just about everything – until we come to the late-twentieth-century contributions. But notably the joy of the church is all to do with what is inside. The exterior – almost windowless at lower level, and a montage of retained rough stonework from the medieval church on the site and utilitarian seventeenth-, eighteenth- and nineteenth-century brickwork – was originally shrouded by adjoining houses and shops. All that was visible externally was the main west porch and the tower and its crowning spire.

The church's focal point, then, has always been its interior. It is fascinating to contemplate, like being inside a large piece of sculpture or a finely tuned and precise piece of machinery, one in which strictly modulated light plays upon strictly modulated forms. This is one of Wren's centralised and domed churches – indeed the very best of the type – and here planes, implied cubes, cylinders and a semi-spherical dome relate to each other in most elegant and logical manner to create a sense of order and beauty in which all elements are in finely balanced visual harmony.

The view through the nave of St Stephen's Walbrook looking west, with Henry Moore's altar in the centre.

St Stephen's was built between 1672 and 1679, at the same time as Wren was working on St Paul's as well as numerous other City churches. Wren was at the peak of his powers, and St Stephen's is the ultimate expression of his notion of geometrically generated 'natural' or absolute beauty.

The experience of entering the church is most memorable. You leave the noisy world of man – rumbling traffic and bustling people – by entering a lofty lobby and ascending twelve steps to a sort of raised sacred acropolis, which is the floor level of the church. Suddenly all is serene, with pale-coloured architecture basking in the soft and gentle light, much falling from high-level arched windows and from handsome oval windows located at a lower level. The interior is dominated visually by an array of free-standing Corinthian columns set on pedestals. So at first impression this is a hall-church, offering a democratic space, without hierarchy of nave and lower aisles, popular at the time in the Calvinistic Low Countries. But all, in fact, is far more ambiguous.

Two groups of three columns – each group L-shaped in plan – stand at the east end of the church, and two groups of five columns stand at the west end of the church. These sixteen columns define the interior space with precision. The groups frame a main east–west axis and a north–south cross axis – so imply a cruciform plan – with a dome placed above the point where the axes cross. The additional columns at the west end of the church's oblong plan imply the presence of a nave, which gives this seemingly centralised church a stunted Latin-cross plan in the manner of more traditional churches.

The dome evidently gave Wren much to ponder. He likely viewed it as an opportunity to experiment with an approach that he intended to apply – at far larger and much more demanding scale – at St Paul's. At St Stephen's the columns support eight semicircular arches of matching size, which in turn support a circular Doric cornice, from which rises the dome.

St Stephen's gave Wren an opportunity to build a dome before starting work on St Paul's.

But this was not, by any means, the only choice of design Wren could have opted for. The design of a dome over a cubical base is a time-honoured form for tombs and sacred buildings in Islam as well as Christianity, with well-established symbolism: the cube or square represents the material world (the four seasons, the four elements), while the circle or dome, a geometrical form with no beginning and no end, represents the immaterial world to which the soul ascends. And as a result, over the years a number of different approaches to this type of dome had been attempted: in Byzantine buildings, for example, the dome is supported on pendentives and four wide arches, spanning between four piers (the approach adopted in the sixth-century AD Hagia Sophia in Istanbul).

But Wren wanted eight arches at St Stephen's and subsequently at St Paul's. Why? There are numerous possibilities. At a basic level a system of eight arches is easier to build and easier to stabilise: smaller arches exert a more modest horizontal thrust, and so reduce the need for thick outer walls or external buttresses. Such massive structures could have denied Wren the lightness of touch – almost weightless – that he evidently wanted to achieve to give this church an ethereal quality and spatial ambiguity.

So the decision could have been an aesthetic one. But in other ways, the eight-arch system is less visually and structurally logical than the four-arch system. Four arches reflect the four primary routes into the space beneath the dome – the main axis and the cross axis – but the eight-arch system means that four arches span nothing of significance (Wren tried to capitalise on these seeming non-essential arches by arranging high-level windows behind them so, during daylight, the arches appear to frame large lanterns). Perhaps, then, there was a more practical reason: Wren's aim was to see if the eight-arch system could be made to work visually before applying it to St Paul's.

What we do know is that Wren undertook a vast amount of research before and during the design of St Stephen's. The sources for this research were limited. Like most people of his generation Wren travelled little – it was too expensive, too time-consuming and too dangerous to travel just for leisure or pleasure. For most people of means one Grand Tour – usually to Italy – was generally the limit. But Wren did not even manage this. All he could organise was one brief journey to Paris in 1665, just after he had commenced his architectural career in earnest. He had to make do with reading: the Bible for Solomon's Temple, and architectural tomes to familiarise himself with the works of great Renaissance architects such as Alberti and Palladio, who presented not only their own or contemporary designs but also detailed information about seminal ancient buildings.

Wren also spoke to many travellers, with meetings often arranged through his Royal Society connections, and he would have seen many sketches of ancient sites and ancient structures. He was influenced by the Paris-born Huguenot jewel merchant, traveller, diplomat, artist and antiquarian Jean Chardin, who settled in London in 1681: Chardin had first gone to Istanbul and Persia in 1666 and from the 1680s started to publish the journals of his travels in the Middle East, which were to become a prime and authoritative source of information about life in the Ottoman and Persian empires. Wren knew Chardin and on several occasions met him with John Evelyn to discuss ancient architecture and ruins, including Persepolis.[11]

From the records of Wren's meetings with various travellers and architects, we know that he had a fascination with the architecture of the Ottoman empire, especially the Hagia Sophia. He would have become familiar with the great domed structures created in the mid sixteenth and early seventeenth centuries by Ottoman architects, such as Mimar Sinan. Of particular inspiration for Wren were surely Sinan's Süleymaniye Mosque complex in Istanbul, of 1550–57, with its prayer hall capped by a gigantic dome supported on four arches, and the Selimiye Mosque in Edirne of 1568–75, with its prayer hall roofed with a huge dome supported on eight arches rising from eight columns. Wren himself acknowledges this Ottoman influence in his writings. In his second *Tract on Architecture*, written in the 1680s, he said that for the vaulting of St Paul's he 'followed' techniques used at Hagia Sophia and which is 'yet found in the present Seraglio'[12] – a reference to the Topkapi Palace in Istanbul, built in the late fifteenth and late sixteenth centuries as a series of rooms – many vaulted – around courtyards. When wrestling with the problems of designing the domes of St Stephen's and of St Paul's, Wren would no doubt have been intrigued to draw on the solutions devised by Sinan and his peers.

Wren would also have taken inspiration from closer to home. The key comparison to the new St Paul's was the massive dome of St Peter's in

Rome, designed in the mid sixteenth century by Michelangelo, supported primarily on four large arches springing between four massive piers: Wren knew that at the very least his dome had to be as dominant and beautiful as that of the Vatican, so the Protestant faith would not appear eclipsed. And he would also no doubt have taken inspiration from the dome added from 1680 by Jules Hardouin-Mansart to Les Invalides in Paris. This consists of three shells, two of which are visible internally because the lower is furnished with a wide oculus through which part of the frescoed surface of the middle dome can be glimpsed. It was almost certainly the key influence for Wren's spectacular three-skinned dome at St Paul's, where the outer dome achieves an ideal hemispherical form by rising on a strong, but far from beautiful, cone-shaped middle dome made of brick and stone, laced with wrought iron. This in turn is masked from below by the third dome, designed to look beautiful from within the cathedrals.

In incorporating a dome as the central feature of his design, Wren was placing both St Stephen's and St Paul's within an ancient and holy architectural tradition. One can trace a direct link between the dome designs of the Renaissance and medieval round churches, which usually feature a central lantern, if not a dome, supported on rings of six or eight shafts or columns. These churches were inspired by the prototype of Christian round and domed churches with central circular arcades or colonnades – the Church of the Holy Sepulchre in Jerusalem, dating from the mid fourth century but repaired and extended into the mid twelfth century. By tradition this was the primary church in Christendom because it was believed to mark the sites of Christ's crucifixion and entombment. And this round form was in turn probably inspired by the 'Second' Temple in Jerusalem, rebuilt after the initial Solomon's Temple was destroyed by Nebuchadnezzar II in around 600 BC. According to Apocryphal biblical texts this 'Second' Temple – like the first supposedly divine in inspiration – was cubical or cylindrical in shape.[13] So, in simple terms, all round Christian churches – including Wren's St Stephen's – are in a sense evocations of the Second Temple in Jerusalem.

Before you leave St Stephen's, study the details. Most are not without a meaning related to the broad intentions of the building as a whole, although many might now be difficult to decode. Here, two examples will suffice. First, look for the cherubs with outstretched wings placed at

The sounding board above the pulpit in St Stephen's.

the top or bottom of a number of the capitals, as well as dancing around the domed sounding board above the pulpit. Cherubs were one of the most popular details in late-seventeenth-century British architecture and interior design. But to men of Wren's stamp, cherubs and the angelic choir were far more than just pleasing motifs. They had a very particular meaning. In Solomon's Temple, the Ark of the Covenant – which contained the Tablets of the Law given to Moses by God (see p. 81) – was, according to the Bible, guarded by six-winged seraphim, a higher order of angels than cherubs: Isaiah describes a vision of 'the Lord sitting upon a throne, high and lifted up . . . above it stood the seraphims: each one had six wings; with twain he covered his face, and with twain he covered his feet, and with twain he did fly. And one cried unto another, and said, "Holy, holy, holy, is the Lord of hosts: the whole earth is full of his glory."'[14]

Cherubs or seraphim being used to evoke associations with Solomon's Temple were common enough in late-seventeenth-century

British architecture (see Morden College on pp. 206–9 and the chapel in Chelsea Hospital on pp. 172–3). In St Stephen's the cherub keystones are probably meant to represent the angelic beings guarding the Ark in the temple's Holy of Holies, here represented by the area below St Stephen's heavenly dome. To Wren, this central space was of equal importance to the handsome – but relatively small – altar at the church's east end. Its openness suggests that it was the place of the immaterial, a place dominated by light and by the word of God. The New Testament makes much of the holiness of light, particularly in John's Gospel, where light and Christian virtue are synonymous: 'the light shineth in the darkness, and the darkness comprehended it not'[15] and 'while ye have the light, believe in the light, that ye may be the children of light.'[16] The importance of the word of God is made clear by Wren himself, not least by the fact that the pulpit here – large, well placed and, with its grand sounding board – is well designed to project the word. As Wren himself wrote, for the 'Romanists . . . it is enough if they hear the Murmur of the Mass, and see the Elevation of the Host, but [Protestant churches] are to be fitted for Auditories' in which congregations can 'both . . . hear distinctly and see the Preacher'.[17]

Much of the original atmosphere of St Stephen's has been lost in recent years. The centre of the open space now contains a large altar, which was added in 1978. To place an altar in this place of light and of the immaterial and invisible presence of God is a most strange thing to have done and suggests that the perpetrators of this act – no doubt well intentioned – had little idea about the probable meaning of Wren's design. It does not matter whether one likes or dislikes Henry Moore's large and amorphous altar-stone: the point is that no material object – beautiful, ugly, sacred or otherwise – should stand in this space.

The church's environs have also changed beyond recognition, thanks to the arrival of the new Bloomberg HQ (see pp. 2–3). One oddity of such grandiose late modernist architecture – where the only permissible ornaments come from the expression of the materials and means of construction – are the somewhat feeble attempts to relate it to the surrounding buildings. Here, a small roughly circular piazza has been created to the west of St Stephen's tower, which is a very good idea, but the new building possesses no power of rhetoric to relate the two

The view west along Cheapside, once an integral part of London's great sexual highway.

structures, and its somewhat pompous design does not have the ability to give this potentially charming City enclave a sense of place. The details and materials of the Foster + Partners' building are too large, and too alien to chime with Wren's complexity and subtlety.

———◆•◆•◆———

Walk from St Stephen's across the Bloomberg plaza and cut underneath the red-and-white-striped building, 1 Poultry, so you end up back on Cheapside/Poultry. This was once the greatest shopping street in the City, the preferred location for shops of silver and goldsmiths and purveyors of all manner of luxury goods. The street's name commemorates its origin because 'ceapan' in Old English means 'to buy'; Cheapside was thus a market street full of shops. But by the eighteenth century, it had taken on another purpose, as an integral part of London's sexual highway, running west from the Royal Exchange to St James's Park.

The sex industry in Georgian London was a trade of great value. It was regularly argued during the eighteenth and early nineteenth centuries that one London woman in five was, in one way or another, involved with the industry. More recent estimates have put the annual gross value of the sex industry in London at as much as £21,840,000[18] – making it one of the city's most important enterprises, which spurred urban growth and the expansion of many other London industries.

The prostitutes of Georgian London fell into a number of categories and they worked in different manners, ranging from impoverished and generally diseased streetwalkers to discreet high-class courtesans operating from their own establishments. The streetwalkers were the most numerous and visible aspect of the industry and their place of favoured patrol was Ludgate Hill and Fleet Street, west along the Strand and Charing Cross, to St James's Park. But the trade also expanded into the courts and streets off these thoroughfares, most notably the Piazza in Covent Garden and its purlieus that, in the eighteenth century, became known as the 'Square of Venus'.

In the 1720s Daniel Defoe left a startling account of a journey along this route, during which he was being constantly brought to a halt

> sometimes by the full Encounter of an audacious Harlot, whose impudent Leer shewd she only stopp'd my Passage in order to draw my Observations to her; at other times by Twitches on the Sleeve, Lewd and ogling Salutations; and not infrequently by the more profligate Impudence of some Jades, who boldly dare to seize a Man by the Elbow, and make insolent Demands of Wine and Treats before they let him go.[19]

It is no doubt significant that the first plate in William Hogarth's moralising series entitled *A Harlot's Progress*, dating from 1731, shows the Bell Inn on Wood Street, running north off Cheapside. Evidently, for Hogarth, Cheapside and its environs were part of London's sexual geography. The very name of the inn – a pun on *belle*, meaning beautiful young girl – is witty but also sinister. Hogarth appears to be presenting the inn as 'receiving house' for innocent country girls and the beginning of their brutal transformation into London harlots. Young Moll Hackabout standing alone before the inn, vulnerable in the great, bustling and heartless city, is easy prey for those with wicked intentions. In front of her there is a goose in a basket addressed to 'my lofing cosen in Tems stret in London' lying beside Moll's initialled trunk. Thames Street, in which Billingsgate Market stood, was a major thoroughfare of trade running parallel to the river. It contained the houses of honest and industrious merchants. It seems Moll has relations there and was planning to make her way to them with a goodly gift, perhaps to settle with them in safety.

But Hogarth shows her – trusting and defenceless – being hijacked by a smiling and patched aged bawd. This is the notorious Mother Needham, who is in the process of procuring Moll for a leering man standing outside the door to the inn. The man is thought to represent the ill-famed rake Colonel Charteris who, in 1730, had been tried and sentenced to death for raping a servant girl Needham had procured for him. While this tragic scene is being played out on Cheapside, and Moll is seduced into London's sex industry, a clergyman, distracted by some scribbles on a piece of paper, turns his back towards Moll while his horse nibbles hay. So much for the care of the church. The painting is full of strange and curious clues to its meaning. A pile of pots totters in the background – foretelling the fall of Moll – and at her breast she wears a rose, the ancient symbol of the Virgin Mary, the 'rose without thorns' and the epitome of purity.

Such an unremittingly extreme depiction of London's sexual highway was, of course, a caricature. Over the years, many writers would conjure up a more sympathetic portrait of London's prostitutes: in the 1780s, Francis Place, then an apprentice to a maker of leather breeches and later a social reformer, spent much time with 'the prostitutes who walked Fleet Street', and found them honest and even generous:

> on no occasion did I ever hear one of these women urge any one of these youths to bring her more money than he seemed willing to part from . . . the women were generally as willing as the lads to spend money when they were flush. With these youths and these women I sometimes spent the evening eating and drinking at a public house . . . and never had any serious quarrel with any one of my companions.[20]

Nor did Hogarth's portrait do justice to the full range of sexual encounters one could procure here. This was not just a place for hetero-

A plate from William Hogarth's *A Harlot's Progress* (1731): the innocent Moll Huckabout is ensnared by Mother Needham in the Bell Inn off Cheapside.

sexuals to buy sex. Around the Royal Exchange, which was rebuilt in 1669 after the Great Fire, well-muscled male riverside labourers offered themselves for hire. The London Spy described the scene in 1699: 'On the 'Change, [we] turn'd to the Right, and Jostled in amongst a parcel of Swarthy Buggerantoes, Preternatural Fornicators . . . who would Ogle a Handsome Young Man with as much Lust as a True-bred English Whoremaster would gaze upon a Beautiful Virgin.'[21]

Cheapside remains a wide and noble street but its architectural delights are now few and far between. The post-war rebuilding has been thorough and generally dull, and although still a shopping street its emporiums are humdrum. Be sure, though, to glance north along King Street to get a distant view of the entrance frontage of the Guildhall (see p. 37).

The ornate north door into St Mary-le-Bow.

Continue to the west and look left (south) into Bow Lane. Narrow, very slightly curving and lined with low-rise late-eighteenth- and nineteenth-century buildings, the lane is a rare survival from before late-nineteenth-century rebuilding, wartime bombing and crude post-war commercial redevelopment. Our route, though, is to the church a few metres to the west: the most monumental and archaeologically inspired of Wren's City parish churches, St Mary-le-Bow. This had long been a most important City church and Wren rebuilt it after the Great Fire in grand style. To the east the church is abutted by a secular building, but in Wren's initial plan this site was to be occupied by an annex of the church, in the form of an open structure formed of two arches, to match the arch framing the north door.

Both north and west doors of St Mary's are adorned in rich and almost uniform manner, and are most enjoyable to contemplate. Both include a Doric entablature, supported by columns that frame an arched opening, and in both cases this composition is set within an arched recess. These entrances really are most noble designs, but it's the slight difference of details between the two that appears significant. Notice the two pairs of cherubs that loll above each of the entablatures. All are different, or at least all have different attributes and activities: above the west door, one grasps a text and the other plays a lyre; above the north door both appear merely to slumber among the bountiful swags of flowers and fruits. These cherubs, acting as harbingers or guardians, suggest that once again Wren was evoking the imagery and associations of the Holy of Holies in Solomon's Temple.

Also consider the spire that Wren set upon his square-plan tower. It takes the form of a colonnaded rotunda, topped by brackets that support a smaller square-plan temple based on a Greek-cross, which in turn is topped by brackets that sustain an obelisk. This reflects a difficulty many seventeenth-century architects designing in the classical style had when it came to spires. There were few antique classical precedents to call upon when designing what was, essentially, a Gothic composition. So, like his fellows, Wren settled for the option of placing diminutive classical temples, combined with details such as urns and obelisks, upon his towers. By this method he attained spires that were Gothic in spirit but strictly classical in detail – as St Mary-le-Bow exemplifies.

The church itself was inspired by one of the classical masterpieces of the Roman world, the early-fourth-

Gothic in spirit but classical in detail: the tower of St Mary-le-Bow.

century AD Temple of Maxentius – in the seventeenth century a vast but partly obscured ruin on the Forum in Rome. The Renaissance had long regarded this mighty basilica as an exemplary building. It was illustrated in the Third Book of Sebastiano Serlio's influential *Five Books of Architecture*, published in parts from 1537 with Book Three appearing in 1540. It also appears, reconstructed and in scintillating manner, in Andrea Palladio's *Quattro Libri* of 1570. Serlio was a favoured crib sheet for Wren, especially at the start of his architectural career. St Mary-le-Bow was one of the first City churches rebuilt by Wren, starting in 1671, which perhaps explains why he used antique precedent so literally as a means of achieving absolute, 'natural' beauty.

Wren's decision to emulate the Temple of Maxentius might also have been down to one of the idiosyncrasies of its design. The Basilica of Maxentius is a most unusual basilica. Its nave, of rectangular plan, is defined on its two long sides not by colonnades but by walls that are each pierced by three large-scale arched recesses. These recesses – like chapels – take the place of conventional aisles. It was perhaps the presence of these six large arches within the Basilica that gave Wren the idea to use it as his model.

The pre-fire church on the site was known as Santa Maria de Arcubus, so called due to the noble arches inside – an attribute commemorated in the name of the church, with 'arcubus' rendered in the vernacular as 'bow'. It was within this church, below the arches, that the ecclesiastical court of the Church of England met, and from which it took the name the Court of Arches. The court moved on, becoming somewhat itinerant, but St Mary-le-Bow remains its formal and permanent home. Given the visual and symbolic power of these arches, what better way could Wren commemorate the old St Mary's, lost in the Great Fire, than by using an antique model, also notable for its arches, when designing the new church?

The church was badly bombed in the war and its interior is a generally faithful but somewhat reduced and amended recreation. Sadly it lacks character and its over-complex paint scheme does nothing to help, but it does, broadly, give a good idea of Wren's intentions. And the church possesses a secret that must be seen before you move on. Below the floor of Wren's church is a crypt that survives from a far earlier church on the site. Most dates from the late eleventh century, although post-war strengthening piers of brick and of concrete intrude to give parts of the crypt a rather oddly contemporary feel.

————◆•◆•◆————

Around 250 metres to the west of St Mary-le-Bow, we come to the north-east corner of St Paul's churchyard. It is a church with a long and gripping past. Historians speculate that, during the centuries that the City was largely uninhabited – between around AD 410 when the Roman legions left Britannia and AD 886 when King Alfred reoccupied the City ruins – Ludgate Hill, to the west of where we now stand, remained settled. It was here, according to legend, that St Paul's church was founded in 604. By the time of the Great Fire, then, St Paul's had stood nearby for over a millennium.

The story of the design and construction of the current cathedral is long, complex and told in many places. The original plan after the Great Fire was to retain and patch-up the ruins of the cathedral, and to keep the mighty and majestic colonnaded west porch that had been added to it in the 1630s to the design of Inigo Jones, and paid for by Charles I, and that was generally regarded as one of the architectural wonders of London. Wren, having drawn up proposals for the cathedral before the fire, was put in charge of its repair or rebuilding in 1668. By the early 1670s, however, it had been agreed that a new cathedral should be built and the remains of the old building cleared away.

But what form should the new cathedral take? Wren produced a series of proposals, including, in 1673–4, the superlative 'Great Model' design – so called after the 1:25 scale model that he produced, and which is preserved within the cathedral. This design was rejected by the clergy because its plan, with nave only slightly longer than chancel and transepts, did not reflect Anglican liturgical conventions and design traditions and perhaps, to some, its bold classicism made it look too disturbingly like contemporary Roman Catholic Counter-Reformation architecture of Italy. So Wren went back to the drawing board, coming up instead with the bizarre 'Warrant' design of 1675, with a traditional Latin-cross plan and long nave. The beloved west portico was retained, and a most ungainly diminutive dome crowned a tall spire almost Gothic in its eccentricity and unlike anything that would have been tolerated in Catholic, Renaissance Italy. This concoction seems to have subdued opposition from the clergy and duly received royal approval.

Construction started that year but the Warrant design was not built – thank goodness. In his contract Wren was granted the liberty to change details when necessary without seeking approval. This gave him the loophole lawfully to amend the design as construction proceeded. The result was a vast improvement over the Warrant design and is, despite its many idiosyncrasies, one of the greatest classical buildings erected in seventeenth-century Europe. The cathedral – a marvel of engineering and of Wren's wise pragmatism – was consecrated in 1697 and completed in 1711.

Wren's bizarre 'Warrant' design of 1675, which received royal approval but was abandoned soon afterwards.

Perhaps its greatest triumph is that, despite being conceived by committee and required to reconcile potentially conflicting requirements – and despite many dauntingly difficult structural challenges – the building manages to possess a noble, at times breathtaking, sense of architectural unity, purpose and power. The geometry of its form, its traditional Latin-cross plan dressed in splendid Renaissance garb, and its beautifully wrought details make the cathedral a thing to wonder at. And, of course, there is nothing more wonderful, nor more typical of Wren's invention and ambitions, than the dome. The aim was always to make it big, to outdo the dome on St Peter's in Rome. And big it certainly is, indeed so big that Wren had to add screen walls to raise the height of the aisles so that the cathedral would not look visually crushed by its soaring drum and dome. But more striking than its height is the dome's form and

Cherubs are a ubiquitous presence around the Cathedral, here nestling beneath the celestial dome.

the manner in which this was achieved. It is an ideal dome – perfectly semi-spherical and truly celestial – and the consequence of extraordinary and unsightly structural gymnastics that, in most satisfactory manner, are completely concealed from public gaze by the dome's immaculate outer skin. This is Wren at his most brilliant.

Many books have been written about the cathedral, so here we will just walk past and concentrate on some of the external features. On all four sides, the carved details can vary in workmanship. Yet they all tell parts of the same story. Like sacred buildings of different religions around the world, and through time, St Paul's is an attempt to create an image of paradise on earth – and in particular of the celestial New Jerusalem of the Book of Revelation, descended from heaven to earth, as a sign of Christ's sacrifice and power of redemption.

Look first at the east end, with its splendid bow marking the location of the internal high altar. In the centre is a vast, arched, east window, and this is topped by a keystone embellished with a beautifully carved cherub's head, framed by neatly folded wings. Similar heads, all slightly different, embellish flanking windows. So cherubs again.

When you turn to the detail, several themes become clear. First, notice that the cathedral's elevations are embellished by two tiers of

Top: cherubs hovering above the sacred heart, usually a Catholic image. *Above:* The enigmatic disc-and-snake symbolism could be an allusion to alchemy.

pilasters, the lower being in the ornate Corinthian order with the upper being in the slightly more simple Composite order. Wren, on his Great Model, envisaged the elevations of the cathedral dressed with a single giant order of pilasters rising from a deep pedestal to the height of the crowning cornice, with even taller giant columns forming the portico of the west front. What changed his mind? It could, of course, have been to do with cost: a series of single, giant columns would have required larger and more expensive stones. But there is another, more pleasing, explanation, hinted at by the brick-built structure to the north-west, the Chapter House, designed in 1712 by Wren or his office. The building's height relates exactly to that of the middle entablature on the cathedral. When taken alongside Wren's visionary 1666 plan for a rebuilt City of

London in the manner of Rome, we can guess that he envisaged the cathedral surrounded by smaller buildings designed to make it seem even more monumental. From a distance, St Paul's lower tier of pilasters would have been obscured – meaning the upper tier would rise, above the surrounding rooftops, looking like a great classical temple perched on its acropolis.

Now look at the details of the north elevation. You'll be struck, first, by the enormous number of cherubs. There is a pair seemingly in conversation, set above opulent swags of fruit and flowers; elsewhere cherubs' heads adorn each side of swords crossed over a book, the traditional emblems of St Paul; and across the building, the cherubs sit above the aisle windows looking serene, some almost ecstatic. And now look up, way above, to the colonnaded drum, and here you'll see yet more cherubs' heads – wings outstretched – nesting just below the celestial dome.

Often more interesting, thugh, are the images between the cherubs. You'll notice a pair towards the centre of the north elevation fly above a heart that seems to be spouting blood. This is the 'sacred heart', an image traditionally associated with Catholicism, and it hints at the fine line that Wren was walking when designing St Paul's: making the cathedral's fashionable Baroque architectural language – associated with the Catholic architecture of France and Italy – appropriate for Protestant worship.

For High Church Anglicans, who shared in much of the pomp and ceremony of Catholicism, it was uncontroversial to include imagery of this kind. But St Paul's was not a High Church cathedral. Henry Compton, who in 1675 was appointed Bishop of London, was staunchly anti-Catholic and wanted a church with a distinctly Protestant ethos and aesthetic: inside, as at St Stephen's Walbrook, the pulpit is more important than the altar (again suggesting that the word of God is more important than the Eucharist), and the large windows are filled with plain, rather than stained, glass – all designed to prevent the cathedral feeling like a Catholic world of mystic gloom and 'superstition'.

Because Wren was, as fashion demanded, working with the architectural language of the Baroque – which had been pioneered in the Roman Catholic countries of Europe – he could not altogether avoid an element of ambiguity, as suggested by the 'bleeding heart'. This, I suppose,

The black-and-white chequered floor within the north portico, likely a Masonic reference. The Chapter House is on the right.

confirmed the fears of the clerical critics of his pre-Warrant designs. With his white-painted interior and plain glass Wren did his utmost to give the Catholic rhetoric a Protestant tone. But sometimes the temptations were overwhelming. Take the curved porticoes of the north and south transepts. These are the cathedral's clearest reference to seventeenth-century Counter-Reformation Rome. The design appears to be derived from the main elevation of a Catholic church, Santa Maria della Pace, commissioned by Pope Alexander XII and designed in 1656 by Pietro da Cortona. Wren, it seems, simply couldn't help himself.

Continental and Catholic architectural references were not the only controversial or curious images that Wren was integrating into his designs. The spectacular interior of St Paul's has a decorative black-and-white chequered floor, as does the west portico and the transept porticoes. It is more than simply a charming design feature: black-and-white squares invariably adorn the floors of Masonic lodges. Symbolising the duality of Creation. That Wren was a Freemason is beyond doubt. John Aubrey wrote in his *Natural Historie of Wiltshire* (1691) of 'a great convention at St Paul's church of the Fraternity of the Adopted Masons, when Sir Christopher Wren is to be adopted a brother'. At the time many people involved with the building trades or the arts were Masons, most openly so. It was a society with its secrets, but it was Christian in its religion, and ethical in its intentions, with lodges modelled on the biblical description of Solomon's Temple that, naturally, Masons believed had a black-and-white chequered floor.

And there are other, more mystical allusions in Wren's design. Among the cherubs on the north side of the cathedral, you'll notice a pair supporting a fabric canopy, below which is an emblem composed of a single snake curling around a staff topped by a disc. This could represent Aesculapius, the Greco-Roman god of medicine. But the composition is peculiar, for the emblem of Aesculapius usually includes wings on the staff and two snakes. The circular disc and the single snake could, then, also be a veiled reference to the ouroboros – an image of ancient Egyptian and Greek magic – that shows a snake, circular in form, eating its own tail. In the seventeenth century this ancient image of repetition or perpetual change was a symbol of alchemy. Wren, like his friend and fellow scientist Isaac Newton, was fascinated by alchemy – Newton wrote more about alchemy than any other single subject. Our snake and coin image could, then, reveal much about the peculiar seventeenth-century intermingling of science, art and magic.

Moving further west there are more cherubs, whose heads, crowned with palm leaves, frame a book that is open, with its pages held in place by ribbons. The book is one of the emblems of St Paul, but this book probably has another meaning. It is perhaps the Book of the Law – the Ten Commandments – housed in the Ark of the Covenant, and the palm leaves could refer to the Christian festival of Palm Sunday, when Christ rode on a donkey into Jerusalem. But they could also symbolise the Holy of Holies in Solomon's Temple – where the Ark was lodged and guarded by seraphim and whose walls were embellished with columns with palm-tree capitals. So perhaps another piece of Masonic imagery.

Finally you come round to the west front. It must be said that, whatever the reason for Wren's two-tier system, it led to a profoundly odd arrangement here, with two separate colonnades, one above the other. The lower colonnade, with its twelve paired columns, is significantly broader than the upper colonnade, which incorporates eight paired columns that are of noticeably smaller scale than the one below. The lower portico, though, refers back to the original Inigo Jones design that Wren destroyed – except this time it has a dainty but completely inaccessible portico sitting on top of it. For rational classicists who believe that external ornaments should express internal arrangements or functions, it is all something of a disappointment.

Naturally, nothing else in the City can quite rival St Paul's. Before heading home (or on to Walk 12), though, be sure to see Temple Bar. It was designed by Wren in 1669 to act as a gate to the City – symbolic more than actual – and was located at the west end of Fleet Street, conceived as a Roman-style triumphal arch. But, as the traffic on Fleet Street increased, the arch started to get in the way. It was carefully dismantled in 1878, and in 1880 the stones were taken to Hertfordshire where they were reassembled on Theobalds Park – the estate of the brewer Henry Meux. There the bar stood, quietly decaying, until 2003, when it was purchased by

The peculiar west front to St Paul's.

a specially formed trust and with financial help from the City Corporation brought back to the City and painstakingly re-erected on this site as part of the ambitious Paternoster Square redevelopment. Here the bar now stands, a splendid testimony to the fact that great and lost architecture can, when there is a will, live again.

Royal Hospital, Chelsea

The story of the Royal Hospital begins in the 1670s, partly in response to the establishment by Charles II of a standing, regular, army – a predictable move on his part to increase his security and grip on the throne, considering what had happened to his father. It was clear that a significant aid to enlistment, and to solid loyal service, would be the founding of an establishment to care for aged, injured or infirm veterans. The immediate model for the hospital was the Hôtel des Invalides in Paris, construction of which started in 1670 on the orders of Louis XIV and which Charles II's eldest illegitimate son, the Duke of Monmouth, had visited in 1672. In late 1681, Charles instructed one of his administrators, Sir Stephen Fox, to get the project in motion, and very soon afterwards Sir Christopher Wren, Surveyor-General of the King's Works, was appointed as architect.

Wren worked fast. The chosen site was in semi-rural Chelsea, next to the Thames, within easy reach by river of the royal palaces at Whitehall and Hampton Court. It was also already in Crown ownership, and partly occupied by the largely redundant Chelsey College, commissioned by James I. By late January 1682 Wren had produced a draft plan that, after some amendments, gained final approval in May. By July, the college had been demolished, and in August the footings and foundations were under way for the construction of a hospital that, as Charles II declared, was 'for the relief of such Land soldiers as are, or shall be, old, lame, or infirme in ye Service of the Crowne'. The resulting structure stands just a few minutes' walk from Sloane Square station, and is best accessed from Royal Hospital Road to the north.

John Evelyn, who had been consulted by Fox and, like Wren, was a member of the Royal Society, described it in his diary on 25 May 1682: 'it was a Quadrangle of 200 foote square, after the dimensions of the larger Quadrangle at Christ Church, Oxford, for the accommodation of 440 persons with governor and officers.' The hospital was indeed, in some ways, like an Oxford or Cambridge college. But there is a significant difference. Unlike most colleges, the court at Chelsea is defined by only three ranges; the fourth, south side is left open. Wren had a particular reason for this arrangement: it allowed the centre block to be seen from the Thames to the south, and the open south side of the court provided a good view of the river from the hospital.

You will notice, though, that the hospital does not sit directly opposite the river – rather it sits at an angle. This is partly because Wren was wedded to particular axes, around which the hospital buildings and gardens are arranged in symmetrical manner; these axes were continued in the 1690s, to the north-west and outside hospital grounds, by the construction of Royal Avenue. It seems that, soon after William and Mary gained the throne in 1688, the idea emerged to run an avenue all the way from the Royal Hospital to the king and queen's newly acquired and reconstructed Kensington Palace, for which Wren was also the architect. The creation

A modest monumentality: the view south-east across the quadrangle, with the Thames on the right.

of a long, straight avenue between these two significant monumental buildings, offering sublime vistas of both, would have been a Baroque gesture worthy of Louis XIV. It would also have doubled as a most useful military road allowing loyal Chelsea veterans – who already had the job of guarding roads around the capital – to be rushed to Kensington Palace if necessary.

For reasons now unknown, works did not proceed beyond the construction of the Royal Avenue so that, over time, the heroic project disappeared into the realms of myth and misinformation. In 1805 Thomas Faulkner, in his *Historical and Descriptive Account of Royal Hospital and Royal Military Asylum in Chelsea*, wrote that 'there is a tradition . . . that it was the intention of Queen Anne to have extended [the] avenue through the fields to the gates of the palace at Kensington, but that this design was

prevented by her majesty's death. Had the plan been carried into execution it would certainly have formed a *coup d'oeil* not to be equaled in this kingdom.'[1] In fact, while in 1693 Wren did approve an estimate for the construction of a new road from Kensington Palace to the Royal Hospital at Chelsea, Queen Anne had nothing to do with the original idea. But she might have stopped its completion. The project, which was to be 8,059 feet long, 11 feet wide, did not proceed beyond King's Road.

Architecturally, one of the most intriguing aspects of the Royal Hospital is the way in which Wren achieved monumentality in a relatively modest manner. As we saw in the previous walk, during his rebuilding of the City churches he had refined an economic means of construction combining brick – which was relatively cheap to make and use – with the judicious use of a small amount of stone, usually for corners and architectural trim. The majority of the hospital's façades are made of handsome and well-laid grey/purple bricks, with the most striking decorative detail being the red-brick dressings and delicate arches that frame each window opening. It is particularly effective in the range containing the great hall and the chapel, which is in every way the centrepiece of the composition. It is essentially a single-storey building – as its massive semicircular arched windows reveal – and so there is no doubt that it contains the major, public rooms of the hospital. These huge, close-spaced windows give it a dramatic transparency and allow light to flood inside.

The porticoes in the centre of the main range form the principal architectural and symbolic feature of the hospital, and are in considerable contrast to the brick building they adorn. Built of stone, and timber painted to look like stone, these monumental portals are like a triumphal arch set astride the hospital's main axis, from the Thames and via Burton's Court and the Royal Avenue to King's Road. The visual importance of these porticoes is confirmed by the interior into which they lead. Here Wren seems to have anticipated architectural fashion by a hundred years, creating a stunning composition of a chaste clarity that would subsequently be associated with late-eighteenth-century neoclassicism. Octagonal in form and crowned by a faceted dome that is top-lit – like the Pantheon in Rome – by a central oculus, it is effectively a temple to the military virtues. Austere, simple, masculine.

The hall was organised in the manner of an Oxford or Cambridge college, with the pensioners dining at sixteen long tables and the governor, his staff and his guests seated at the raised high table. The chapel, meanwhile, has a barrel vault with plaster embellishments. These are discreet but of high quality – the oblong plaster panels, set along the wall below the springing of the vault, are especially good. Each panel is of broadly similar design but in its details individual and inventive, many with strange faces lurking in the foliage. The woodwork is fascinating, with oak panelling on which perch the heads of four-winged angelic beings. These heads, and the 3:1 proportion of the chapel's plan, indicate

Pensioners parade in the quadrangle.

that Wren had in mind the biblical description of the Holy of Holies in Solomon's Temple in Jerusalem, guarded by multi-winged seraphim. The Temple was the template for so many of Wren's sacred buildings (see pp. 81–2).

Even before the hospital was completed it was decided that more accommodation space was needed. Wren's solution was simple. He added four smaller-scale ranges to the main ones. All was to sit within a simple landscape that complemented the buildings, and reinforced the impression that the Royal Hospital was a key component in a great axial plan for west London. Not only was the main axis of the hospital continued north to King's Road, across what is now Burton's Court, it was also extended south and used to organise the gardens lying between the Royal Hospital and the Thames – which included a pair of right-angled canals that, in effect, brought the river right up to the southern terrace. The result was a simple and satisfying complex of buildings, which was immediately hailed as a great success. At the beginning of February 1685, just days before his death, Charles II visited the nearly complete Royal Hospital. He was pleased with what he saw, declaring, it was reported at the time, that'Fox and Hee [the king] had done that great worke.'[2]

All worked well at the Royal Hospital for over a hundred years. But by the first decade of the nineteenth century the nature of Britain had changed: its empire had expanded, as had its army, and it was locked in a prolonged war with Napoleonic France, which produced a steady flow of injured soldiers. So naturally the hospital also had to change, and the man who gave the change architectural expression was John Soane, who in 1807 was appointed Clerk of Works of the hospital. His first major commission came in 1809 when he was asked to design an infirmary. This was destroyed by bombing in 1941 but his stable block of 1814, which stood next to the infirmary, does survive, and reveals the extraordinary nature of Soane's early designs. As we saw earlier, he was determined to reinvigorate the traditions of classical design. To do this he stripped away much conventional ornament and relied on simple primary forms, proportion and almost abstract details to create structures that were novel and original, yet which still possessed a sense of classical nobility. The stables are spare, with the main elevation defined by a ripple of concentric arches set around openings in the wall. This building is now perceived to mark a key moment in the progression of Soane's architecture, combining elements of Roman gravity – rendered in Roman-style pale yellow brick – with his very personal reinvention of the classical tradition. Part of this exploration drew on the ancient language of death, inspired largely by the study of Roman sarcophagi. Consequently, and rather oddly, the stables look rather like an antique tomb.

Soane's idiosyncratic architecture is now much admired but at the time shocked and offended many – including his son, George, who in 1815 published a scathing article about his father's designs at Chelsea, dismissing one building as a 'monster in the art of building' and calling the collected work 'follies . . . too dull for madness [and] too mad for the soberness of reason'. Unsurprisingly this public rebuke from his own child caused a family rift that was never healed. It also seems to have been at least partly responsible for a significant shift in Soane's architectural direction in Chelsea. After 1815 the Royal Hospital Board instructed

Until the 1870s, the hospital fronted directly on to the Thames – as depicted in this evocative engraving from 1815.

Soane to design his Chelsea buildings to look 'similar' to Wren's work. The result of this more self-effacing approach is the long range of the 'Secretary's Office' on the eastern edge of the hospital, which adjoins the burial ground.

All changed again in the 1870s, when the construction of the Chelsea Embankment separated the hospital's garden from the river, transforming the overall effect of the grounds. Nonetheless, to walk around the Royal Hospital remains one of the great delights of London. This is architecture of great distinction, monumental but also humane. Your eye can linger on lovely details – the well-wrought brick, the plasterwork in the chapel. It is the epitome of understated erudition, of learning that does not need to assert itself. This is civilisation. As Thomas Carlyle, who lived near the hospital for many years, observed in the 1840s, 'it had always been a pleasure to me to see it' because 'it was quiet and dignified and the work of a gentleman'. Quite.

But perhaps most of all enjoy the fact that the Royal Hospital is not only a historic building but also a living building – for the life lived within it is still that for which it was designed and built over three centuries ago.

WALK 5

Blackheath

Domestic architecture of the Stuarts and Georgians

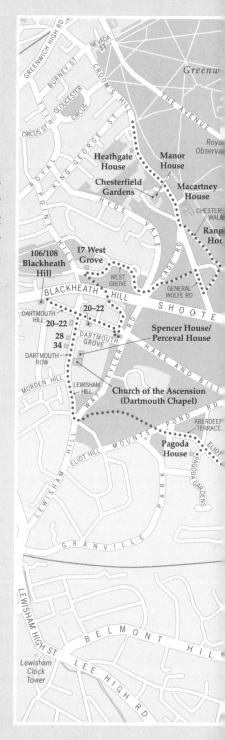

In 1683, the diarist John Evelyn attended a fair that had recently began to be held biannually on Blackheath. He wasn't impressed. While it was 'pretended for the sale of cattle', the real purpose of the new fair was more unscrupulous, Evelyn recorded.

> I think, in truth, [it is designed] to enrich the new tavern (the Green Man) at the bowling green, erected by [Andrew] Snape, his Majesty's farrier, a man full of projects. There appeared nothing but an innumerable assembly of drinking people from London, pedlars, etc.; and I suppose it is too neere London to be of any greate use to the country.[1]

It was an inauspicious start. Snape – a cleric, academic, and sometime head-master of Eton College who also held an honorific position in the royal household – was notorious for using his proximity to the king to get away with all sorts of nefarious schemes, including building

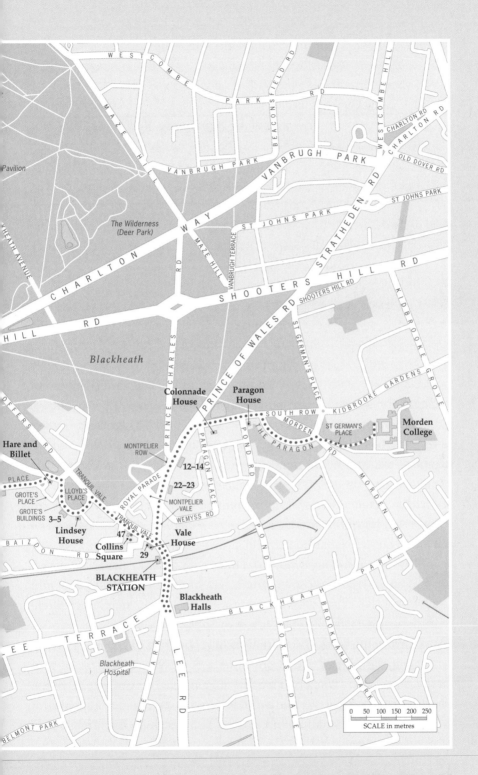

A medieval common with a Georgian aesthetic: the view across Blackheath today.

houses in Blackheath without permission. But the fair itself marked the beginning of a new chapter in the history of Blackheath – and of London. It had been authorised by Charles II himself, at the bequest of George Legge, the Baron of Dartmouth, who was one of the king's key military commanders. And it was the first step in an ambitious new commercial venture. Over the next few years, Dartmouth would undertake the speculative construction of a self-contained and high-class little town on the western edge of the heath, adjoining the existing and important east–west road known as Blackheath Hill.

Dartmouth himself was soon to fall from influence. After the Glorious Revolution of 1688–9, he was imprisoned in the Tower of London as a result of his close links with the deposed Catholic monarch James II. He died there in 1691. But his vision for a suburbanised Blackheath – an extra source of revenue for the Dartmouth family – outlived him, being pursued by his son William, made earl in 1711. Over the course of the next century, wave upon wave of speculative housing would be built around the heath, transforming it from a peripheral common outside London into an exemplary representation of Georgian taste, both on the Dartmouths' land and beyond.

The Dartmouths' scheme was, even in the late seventeenth century, hardly a new idea. Fifty years earlier, the Earl of Bedford with his architect Inigo Jones (see pp. 80–1) had, on the earl's estate in Covent Garden, created a self-contained miniature town organised around a forum-like square of grand houses, with smaller houses, shops and taverns on subsidiary streets and its own temple-like church and informal market. And although visionary in its design, this was all to be done for profit: most of the buildings would be paid for by speculating builders, working on leases granted by the estate that reverted to estate ownership after forty or so years. Little of the earl's Covent Garden still exists, but this pioneering scheme remained, in its essentials, the urban-development model throughout Britain and its colonies into the early nineteenth century (see pp. 493–5).

The Dartmouths' speculation at Blackheath, then, was very much in the adventurous and expansionist spirit of the age – comparable with the likes of Kensington Square, Soho Square and Hoxton Square, all of which were developed in the 1670s and 1680s as centrepieces of new quarters being built on the edges of London. And, while the Dartmouths were more modest than their fellow speculating landlords – they did not venture to build a land-consuming square, merely two streets joining at right angles – the houses they constructed were nonetheless large, fashionable and intensely urban. They must have formed a most sophisticated if unlikely West End-style outpost on what at the time was a rural road leading to a heath favoured by vagabonds, footpads and drovers.

All of this was catalysed by the extraordinary growth of London's population, which would go on throughout the eighteenth century. Between the 1670s and 1801 – when the first reliable census was taken – London went from being the home of about 527,000 to having a population of over a million. And schemes like the Dartmouths' were part of what made it all possible, reaching their zenith in the squares like those we see in Walk 7.

Most remarkably of all, however, this was not merely a revolution in property development. For the rise of the Georgian estates coincided with a transformation in domestic architecture. As the next few pages will reveal, this was the period in which classical domestic architecture became codified, regulated – almost mass-produced – to create harmonious and uniform streets, which often displayed an erudition previously found in civic and religious buildings (see Walk 3 and Walk 4).

This walk offers a tour through some of the best domestic architecture that the late seventeenth and eighteenth centuries have to offer. From the glorious 1690s manor on Croom's Hill – at first glance a simple structure, but in fact most subtle – to the early speculatively built houses of Dartmouth Hill, to the late-Georgian masterpiece the Paragon, it reveals how the combination of commercial shrewdness with architectural sophistication helped forge the London that we all recognise.

THE WALK

Our route is a detour from Walk 3, which takes us through Greenwich. It begins midway up Croom's Hill, at the west gate of Greenwich Park. Where the Greenwich walk heads north, culminating at St Alfege church, this route veers off to the south, to Blackheath. Unlike those in the Greenwich walk, its buildings are primarily domestic rather than grand political ones. When taken together, the two walks provide a most comprehensive tour through the architecture of the seventeenth and eighteenth century.

The first portion of this walk offers insights into the changing tastes of seventeenth- and eighteenth-century house builders, and of the clients

Francis Nicholson's *London from Blackheath* shows the view north-west from the top of Croom's Hill. In the distance, St Paul's Cathedral; in the foreground on the right, the south-west corner of Greenwich Park.

they were working for or whom they were trying to attract. Spanning well over a century of architectural change – from the 1630s to the 1790s – it reveals how the language of classical design became gradually more refined, almost more streamlined, as houses were produced in greater numbers and individual schemes got larger and more uniform. Mass production did play a role (this was, after all, the age of the Industrial Revolution), and components could be – and were – manufactured in bulk. Yet this mass production did not tend towards the cheap and nasty but towards the sophisticated and the erudite. This is one of the wonders of the Georgian age – as we will see. All the buildings stand on or near Croom's Hill, which is not only the most pleasing residential street in Greenwich but, given its location opposite the dramatic beauty of Greenwich Park, its sinuous form and the variety and quality of its earlier architecture, is one of the most visually satisfying streets in London.

Our first stop is one of the most curious structures in Greenwich. Heathgate House at number 66 is an extremely rare survival of early-seventeenth-century domestic architecture. It dates from 1635 and is designed in what has become known as the 'Artisan Mannerist' style. The term refers to buildings usually created for the merchant class and generally executed by artisan builders or masons, instead of by gentleman architects. Rather than having the studied simplicity of the brand of Renaissance classicism produced, for example, by Inigo Jones for the Stuart court (see pp. 80–1), such buildings display a more liberated approach to classical design, mixing sources and references but always tending to the ornamental, and usually most original. The sources tend to be Northern European, with a certain Baroque swagger, rather than coming directly from the Italian fountainhead – and often there is a lingering Gothic spirit, usually expressed by asymmetry and romantic profiles with abundant gables.

Heathgate House is a case in point: a free-standing mansion, it has a rather busy façade – full of surface decoration – in which the Gothic tradition fuses in curious but not unpleasing manner with then-novel classical features. There is a pair of crowning triangular gables, each topped with a neat little pediment, and look at the Doric pilasters on the first floor. By classical convention, pilasters should appear to have a supportive role, and rise from the ground, or at least from other pilasters. Here, however, they clearly have no such function – the ground floor is plain, and the pilasters thus declare themselves to be no more than mere decoration.

By the time our next house was built, however, the style of domestic architecture had changed. On the west side, and set back in a large front garden, overlooking a small green called Chesterfield Gardens and facing south towards Blackheath, is the Manor House – a splendid five-window-wide brick box of 1695, built for Sir Robert Robinson, Lieutenant Governor of Greenwich Hospital. It is simple in its details; most ornamental is the large-scale scallop-shell motif hovering above the door, a curious feature that delighted late-seventeenth-century designers – but, this time, has a more overtly classical inspiration.

The dominant concern of the designer here seems to have been the quest for absolute symmetry, and indeed the back elevation is as ordered as the front. There is an architectural perfection that makes this house harmonious, simple but sophisticated in form. Take, for example, the piers on each side of the first-floor centre window, which are ever so slightly wider than those between adjoining windows – designed to draw our attention to the centre of the façade – and slightly thinner than those at the ends – to make the edges of the building look reassuringly sturdy.

And the layout is equally rational. The house is more or less square in plan and of 'double-pile' arrangement, which means back rooms and front rooms on each floor separated by a central corridor or staircase lobby. The idea was to achieve greater privacy and convenience by avoiding the need to enter one room by passing through another. The concept was novel in England in the mid seventeenth century. The Manor House is all to do with subtlety, precision, proportion – indeed the scientific theory of optics is at work, related to Wren's notions about 'natural' and 'customary' beauty. It's a world away from the ornamental rough and tumble vigour of Heathgate House.

Further south, up the hill, lies Macartney House. It dates from the late seventeenth century, and has a walled garden court on its south side – overlooked by a pair of huge sashes. It is odd that there appears to be no main façade with considered architectural form or focus. In 1802, John Soane (see pp. 174–5) made additions and remodelled the interior, which is worth a look if you can – particularly the entrance lobby, with unfluted Doric columns – but it is difficult to do so since the house is now divided into flats. If you can't, head straight on south, and enter Chesterfield Walk, a path that curves to the south-east of Croom's Hill.

You soon come to the Ranger's House, standing on the edge of Greenwich Park with a large formal garden to its east. This reveals another shift in the style of domestic architecture. Dating from the 1720s, it is essentially a small and very dignified country mansion in the brick-built domestic idiom of the time but with a stone-faced centre, with single-storey Ionic columns. All most prim, proper and undemonstrative – until you notice the keystone above the front door. It's decorated with a rather wild-looking visage, probably a rendering of the Green Man, the pre-Christian personification of nature, the wildwood and fecundity. Generally speaking, there is much pleasing clarity about the design, making it read rather like an oversized doll's house. It was inherited in 1748 by Lord Chesterfield, and, although by the nineteenth century it had become home to the rangers of Greenwich Park – an honorary position appointed by the monarch – Chesterfield still gives his name to the path that leads to the house. It is open to the public.

Walk south-west from Ranger's House to get the first view of Blackheath itself. The common has a most evocative past, and a not

Ranger's House is prim, proper and undemonstrative – until you get to the details.

insignificant role in the history of the city. This great plain, south of London and on the road from Kent and the Channel, was an obvious rallying point for military forces. Most famously, it was here that Wat Tyler's supporters rallied in 1381 during the Peasants' Revolt, as did Jack Cade's men of Kent during their uprising in 1450. Each were, in their own ways, rebelling against the inequalities of the feudal system – in particular punitive and unfair taxation, and the abuses of inherited privilege and royal government based on the notion of rule by divine right. Both rebellions came to nothing but both were significant events in the evolution of a more equitable British society. So, for many, Blackheath remains holy ground.

Today, of course, the prospect is more Georgian than medieval – as suggested by the final two buildings in this portion of the walk. Cross Hyde Vale and in West Grove you will find one of the finest, and in some sense most melancholic, Georgian houses in Blackheath. Number 17 stands tall, proud and very much alone. It was built in 1788 by an architect and speculating builder named Michael Searles, who we met in Walk 3 and about whom you will hear a great deal more in a moment. All that needs to be said now is that this is a most gloriously built and ornamented terrace house – but clearly something went very wrong with the project.

Number 17 has a good front elevation but its side elevation, very visible from the heath, is merely rendered. This house was clearly the first move in the construction of a majestic terrace. But it was not to be. The 1780s was a difficult decade for speculation, with the war with the American colonies causing uncertainty.

What was built, however, is wonderful, the stuff of Georgian dreams. There are flat-arched first-floor windows set within a blank arcade suggesting an array of Roman-style relieving arches. This is a very early use of a motif that became tremendously popular – almost universal – after 1800. And the ground floor is also arcaded, a favourite Searles motif, with arched windows set within relieving arches. But the great glory is the beautiful and delicately detailed porch – wide, deep, almost free-standing – with an array of ironwork. Around the flat roof of the porch is a railing of most minimal and abstract form, with bars of serpentine pattern that are probably inspired by those found on Roman sarcophagi. This is an early example of the neoclassical language of death that became so popular in the early nineteenth century.

Walk back towards the heath, and cross the road on to Dartmouth Terrace. You'll soon see a fine and imposing pile of building placed between Dartmouth Grove and Dartmouth Hill: a pair of houses united into a single, monumental, stucco-faced composition. The pair has a five-window-wide, three-storey-high centre block topped by a pediment, and flanked by lower and narrower wings, each topped by half a pediment. So it looks like the taller, pedimented, central portion of the house has broken through, and divided the lower, also pedimented, portion.

Like many designs we have encountered in this book, the inspiration was Andrea Palladio, who used three permutations of this composition in sixteenth-century Venetian churches. Palladianism came back into fashion in the early eighteenth century, partly in response to the changing political climate (see pp. 212). In this house, that meant invoking elements of Palladio's Redentore, a church completed in 1592. It was a rational way of designing a façade that related the tall nave with the lower flanking aisles while keeping within the conventions of antique classical temple architecture, as Renaissance architects liked to do.

And yet, in other ways, the house is strikingly different to the earlier designs we have encountered on this walk. Note, for example, the stucco –

Andrea Palladio's Redentore reimagined for south-east London.

characteristic of later Georgian architecture, and distinct from the mellow but exposed brick that defines Macartney House and Ranger's House. This simulates the stone, or imitates the stucco cladding of Palladio's original design, and stops at the corners of the main front: the right-hand side and back are plain utilitarian brickwork. There are other most revealing details. The centre windows, which form the visual focus of the paired composition, are all blank, for the simple reason that behind the centre of the elevation is the party wall dividing the grand-looking building in two. The effect is charming. Clearly the architect's evident ambition was quietly undermined by the realities of the project.

Who was the designer? No one knows for certain but *The Buildings of England* argues that the houses can be 'plausibly attributed' to Thomas Gayfere Snr, who from 1766 was the master mason of Westminster Abbey. They were constructed in 1776, and are one of the earliest examples of the detached and architecturally united pair of houses that became such a popular building type in late-eighteenth- and early-nineteenth-century Blackheath and Greenwich.

———————

We now enter the heart of Dartmouth's estate, laid out in the late seventeenth century. The surviving buildings on Dartmouth Hill, however, are later. Numbers 20 and 22 are the grandest, and typical of late-eighteenth-century Blackheath houses – once again they are a detached pair of united design, each with a two-storey stucco-clad bay. They must date from around 1780. At the west end of the street, on the steep junction with Blackheath Hill, is a charmingly irregular group of eighteenth-century houses. Best are numbers 106 and 108, of matching design although not attempting to form a unified composition. Note the beautifully detailed doorcases, including elegant neoclassical medallions. Their vigorous sense of proportion and fine detailing give these small houses an almost monumental quality.

Our route, though, is on to the most important feature of Dartmouth's mini town. Dartmouth Row runs south off Dartmouth Hill and was originally formed by a terrace of very urban houses – complete with basement kitchens – on its west side. Set back in small front gardens, most of these would have enjoyed uninterrupted views of the heath to the east. And they are early. Most of the surviving examples here have their origins in the 1690s, although the majority have been more or less significantly altered, amended or rebuilt.

The most complete survival, suggesting clearly how most of the houses on the west side of the row would have appeared originally, is number 34. Five windows wide and three storeys high, its face is formed with bark-brown or purple bricks with red-brick dressings on the sides of the windows – very much the fashion for the time. Not so typical are the lintels that sit atop the windows. These are formed with well-cut red-brick segmental arches – that is, with a slight curve. If the house does indeed date from the early to mid 1690s, and there is every reason to believe that it does, then these segmental arches are unusual. Uncurved flat arches were generally preferred at the time by most speculating builders, with segmental arches only starting to appear in large number during the second decade of the eighteenth century. So apparently the houses of Dartmouth Row were on the cutting edge of fashion – even ahead of it – and most certainly not the dawdling country cousins of contemporary West End speculations.

More typical of the row – at least as far as their layers of alterations are concerned – are numbers 20 and 22, at its north end. Number 20 has a delicate Regency-era porch made of cast iron, but the size of the house's windows, their proportions and details suggest a 1690s origin; number 22 has a superb eight-panel front door and a doorcase that appears to date from the same decade. Number 28, meanwhile, offers an intriguing, if conjectural, explanation for the siting of the row, as well as insights about the fates that have befallen most of the surviving houses. Its most striking and unusual feature is the way the gable fronts on to the street, with the rest of the house at right angles to it. This sort of gable-fronted dwelling was common in London until the mid seventeenth century, at which point most house plans were turned 90 degrees – so that the gables were facing the party walls of neighbouring houses. Virtually no pre-1800 London houses survive with gables fronting the street.

The main door, on the other hand, seems later. It is ornamented by a doorcase with delicate and rather abstract neoclassical details that date it to around 1800. And the bricks also hint at a later date: the house seems to have been refronted in the late eighteenth century. So what is the construction date of this most unusual building? *The Buildings of England* merely suggests 1794, presumably the date of the brick refronting. But, when considered alongside the older details, one does wonder if this was an existing house around which the row was aligned when it was laid out in the 1690s. Certainly its L-shaped plan, with a small court, is a rural vernacular type familiar in the seventeenth century and survives in such ancient coastal towns as Cley next the Sea in Norfolk.

We now turn to the east side of Dartmouth Row, which was not entirely unbuilt upon in the early years of the development. Indeed the estate's most significant buildings stood on this side of the row. Strangely the domestic masterpiece of the street was placed on the east side, with its back towards the heath. When new – standing large and in near isolation – its presence must have been extraordinarily commanding.

One half of the domestic masterpiece of the Dartmouths' estate, Spencer House and Perceval House.

This is the building now known as Spencer House and Perceval House. It is said to date from 1689, so just before the houses on the west side of Dartmouth Row.

Now set back in a deep front garden, the building rewards careful study. Oddities abound, some no doubt a result of the house being divided into two dwellings in the nineteenth century – a fact revealed by the presence of two front doors, and a rooftop parapet marking a wall dividing the central block in two. After the division, one side was named Spencer House and the other Perceval House. The name harks back to the premiership of Spencer Perceval, prime minister from October 1809 until May 1812, when he was assassinated in the House of Commons lobby – making him the only British prime minister to have been murdered. Perceval was something of a local man, and was buried at St Luke's church in nearby Charlton. So it is tempting to think that his death dates the division of this house. But nothing here is quite as it seems: in fact it was not divided and renamed until the 1890s.

The detailing on the house is even more remarkable. The frieze above the larger, central door contains a somewhat frenzied scene, with a grimacing face sporting long and pointed ears, framed with swirling vegetation. This could be another representation of the Green Man, who we met at Ranger's House on Croom's Hill. But if so, this is a somewhat unusual rendering. More typical is the keystone on an adjoining first-floor window. This, in standard Green Man fashion, shows a head emerging from foliage. The Green Man has an enigmatic presence in many late-seventeenth-century London buildings – including Wren's St Paul's Cathedral – but quite why this ancient and apparently pagan image was popular is uncertain.

The Green Man is only one of a number of extraordinary keystones. Every window in the wide elevation of the house has one, and between them they offer a glimpse into the vivid imagination of London's late-seventeenth-century building world. The keystones are not peopled by celestial characters – like the seraphim or cherubs on the keystone at Morden College (see pp. 206–9) – nor do they appear to depict familiar and handsome gods and goddesses from the classical world. Rather they hint at an underworld, peopled by the inflicted and the grotesque, or – like the Green Man – evoke an ancient pre-Christian past.

Their meaning is now hard to fathom. Are they culled from obscure emblem books, the compilations of allegorical pictures that were popular in seventeenth-century England? Or do they relate to the theory of the humours and the temperaments, an ancient taxonomy of emotions that informed early modern medicine? Or are they in some secret manner connected to Freemasonry? It's hard to say.

While this bizarre imagery is not unique, it is rare, and most examples date from the very late seventeenth or very early eighteenth centuries. For example, 29 Queen Square in Bristol, dating from 1709 and built by a slave-trader named Nathaniel Day, sports similar keystones, with dolphins or smirking human heads formed by foliage. The keystones on the Dartmouth Row house generally lack this lightness of touch. Some are pretty neutral, but most are unsettling. One depicts a grim and frowning moustachioed face with unusually large ears, another a fawnlike or satyr face with alarmingly distorted features, while another simply shows a screaming man – mouth wide open.

Evocations of a pre-Christian past? The idiosyncratic keystones above the windows of Spencer House and Perceval House.

The success of the Dartmouths' estate was not, however, just about fine houses. Like all aspiring speculative developers, they wanted their miniature new town to have a sense of community – and, in particular, a church. And so, immediately to the south of Spencer and Perceval Houses, set forward on the pavement's edge, is a chapel. Founded in 1697 and originally named simply the Dartmouth Chapel, it seems to have been rebuilt in 1750 – from when the apse dates – with the nave and street frontage rebuilt yet again in 1834. It is now known as the Church of the Ascension, and reveals that, to the Dartmouths, their new estate was always intended to offer far more than just housing.

◆◆◆◆◆

The Dartmouth estate was the first major residential development on Blackheath. But it was far from the last. The next portions of the walk take us forward nearly eighty years, to a time when Blackheath had turned into one of the more desirable neighbourhoods of outer London, and was populated with a number of grand, classical houses. Walk south from Dartmouth Chapel and cut east across the south-western corner of the heath, between a copse of trees and a complex of buildings surrounded by greenery. As you come on to Aberdeen Terrace, the large three-storey houses begin almost immediately. Walk straight past, though, for we are holding out for an architectural treat that is altogether more peculiar.

After around 150 metres, you will come to a street on your right (south) called Pagoda Gardens. As the name hints, it contains one of the great curiosities of Blackheath, indeed of London. This is Pagoda House, which really is one of the most strange-looking Georgian houses to be seen anywhere in the country. It is not the presence of a pagoda that is unusual, however. The house was built in the 1760s, during a decades-long fashion for all things Chinese – in porcelain, silks and painted wallpapers – which had been a key part of the highly ornamental Rococo style since the 1740s. So there is nothing inherently odd about finding a pagoda lurking down a suburban side street in Blackheath. What's so unusual about this particular pagoda is its design. It is vastly squat, only one and a half times as high as it is broad. And this stubby base – rendered in rather common brickwork – is topped by a pyramidal roof that projects far over the walls, and is furnished with huge turned-up corners. The windows are also striking. On the more narrow façade facing the street there is a large round window at second-floor level; on the wide façade facing the garden the second-floor window is oval in shape. All most peculiar.

The design is uncomfortable rather than curious, and seems a somewhat amateur affair – which is surprising since the architect was almost certainly Sir William Chambers, famed for exquisitely detailed and academically correct neoclassical buildings such as Somerset House on the Strand. Chambers had developed a playful sideline in exotic and fashionably oriental architecture, notably the towering and many-tiered Great Pagoda in Kew Gardens, which was completed in 1762 for Princess Augusta, the wife of the dead Frederick, Prince of Wales, and the mother of George III (see pp. 213–6). The Blackheath Pagoda was probably designed in 1767, so is the somewhat stunted child of the more skilfully conceived Great Pagoda.

William Chambers' unusually amateurish stab at pagoda design.

But for all its clumsiness, the Blackheath Pagoda has had its share of excitement. It appears to have been designed as a garden building for Montagu House, which, until its demolition in 1815, stood on the southwest edge of Greenwich Park with grounds extending west across the heath. In the 1760s, when the house was likely built, the Earl of Cardigan was the occupant. There is even a legend that the pagoda was used as a summer house by Caroline, Princess of Wales, when her husband the Prince of Wales – later George IV – leased Montagu House around 1800. It was clear that the prince wanted a secluded, relatively distant residence for his wife: the two had hated one another from the moment they were married (George had been drunk at their wedding), and by the turn of the century were completely estranged. Rumours spread that Caroline was using Montagu House to entertain her lovers, and in 1806 the government launched a so-called 'delicate investigation' into allegations of her infidelity. By the 1810s the royal couple's relationship had got so bad that George effectively banned Caroline from seeing her daughter. It's an ironic history considering the iconography of the building: the curious Chinese symbol on the roof is said to mean 'House of Family Love'.

Caroline was not the only person to make use of the house. The historian Neil Rhind suggests that the pagoda was at one point used as a tea-house by the Society of Toxophilites, 'elegant and beauteous . . . Lady Archers' who referred to themselves as the 'British Amazons'. Interestingly, the Royal Toxophilite Society – which still exists – dates from 1781. One of its patrons was the very same Prince of Wales, the future Prince Regent whose wife would occupy the pagoda from 1800.

———◆•◆•◆———

Of course, such ostentatious and peculiar architecture is hardly representative of Georgian housing. To find more regular middle-class homes, we must leave Pagoda Gardens and walk east, along the road called Eliot Vale, which later becomes Eliot Place.

Many of the buildings on this stretch date from the very late eighteenth or very early nineteenth centuries, and show how the heath was being enclosed in a most urban manner. The tall, fashionable houses reveal much about the changing residential and social character of Blackheath during the wars with France in the years after 1792. While in much of London the hostilities brought about an economic downturn (see p. 270), in Deptford they caused an explosion of speculative house building – in large part down to the military build up along the Thames in Deptford, Greenwich and Woolwich. It brings to mind an evocative image. There must, for a few years, have been a regular military and naval community here, with militias training on the heath, and ordnance booming as ships' crews and garrison troops went through gunnery exercises.

The best house on Eliot Vale is number 9, which is dated 1805 and takes the form of a brick box flanked by lower brick wings. It has a glorious geometrical semicircular arched door, flanked by two most strange, narrow, projecting brick-built piers that rise higher than the house's parapet – and which, on closer inspection, are each topped by a diminutive chimney pot. When viewed alongside the elongated first-floor window, what comes to mind is the work of Sir John Soane (see pp. 174–5), who had an obsession with the compositional potential of chimney stacks, and with well-lit staircases. Could Soane have been involved with the design of this small house, or, more likely, was it just his influence at work?

Number 9 Eliot Vale, replete with a wonderfully geometrical fanlight.

As you walk east along Eliot Place, the houses tend to get older because the street was expanding to the west throughout the 1790s and early 1800s. So, numbers 2 and 3 were built in 1805, number 6 in 1796, and 7 and 8 in 1792. And an even earlier relic is at the end of the row. Where the Hare and Billet stands there has been a pub or coaching inn since at least the seventeenth century; opposite is a small pond that is nearly as old, having been a watering place for cattle being taken into London. On Samuel Travers's 1695 map – *A Survey of the King's Lordship or Manor of East Greenwich* – the pond and the area around it is called 'Beggers Bush'. The name suggests this was an ancient gathering place for tinkers, itinerant street-people and vagabonds making their way in and out of London – a reminder that the heath was once a hunting ground for highwaymen and footpads and a refuge for all manner of outcasts. Walk around the pond to the east and look across its still surface to the Hare

A glimpse into London's past through the shrubbery around 'Beggers Bush'.

and Billet, framed by trees and bushes on the water's edge. It's a splendid little vignette, a glimpse into London's past.

Our route is to the south-east. A few metres after the Hare and Billet, a street curves off to the right. Arranged around an informal grassy square, essentially a field, are terraces and groups of houses that form an irregular crescent. Most are Georgian of various dates, with the street jutting out to the north-east called Grote's Place, those on the northern part of the crescent called Grote's Buildings, and those to the south Lloyd's Place. Houses have been springing up here since mid Georgian times.

Of the three streets, Grote's Buildings packs a particular architectural punch. The three-house composition at numbers 3 to 5 is very powerful. It comprises a central four-storey house flanked by lower houses of the same width. Details are simple and uniform and the matching semicircular arched doors reveal this building to date to around 1771–4, when this type of front-door design was fashionable. Lloyd's Place is generally slightly

later, formed by a collection of much-altered eighteenth- and early-nineteenth-century houses. Particularly good is Lindsay House, a splendid large brick-fronted detached house of around 1790 – notice how the centre is emphasised not by the front door but by a window, set within an arch and framed with stucco. Most inventive and charming.

————◆•◆•◆————

From Lloyd's Place walk south, along Tranquil Vale, into the heart of Blackheath village. A sense of its building history soon emerges. There are a few early-eighteenth-century village buildings, then the first wave of coordinated and large-scale expansion from the late eighteenth century and through to the end of the Napoleonic Wars. Then there is the expansion from the early 1850s following the arrival of the railway, when tall houses and shops were built.

The result is a portion of the walk that offers a history of Blackheath in miniature. First, to the south of the Crown public house, stands a small but fascinating building that is a charming reminder of a Georgian vernacular tradition now all but lost in London. Number 47 Tranquil Vale is of timber-frame construction, with its frame – no doubt of softwood – clad with overlapping horizontal boards, known as weatherboards or clapboards. It is only two storeys high and one window wide. Understandably such modest buildings, of fragile, economic and transitory construction, have generally been swept away in schemes of urban improvements or fallen easy victims to fire and neglect. So a type of building, once common in the poorer parts of Georgian London, or on the edges of the city, is now very rare and very precious. A similar vernacular style is visible behind the timber-frame building, in the diminutive Collins Square – now no more than a cul-de-sac – on the west side of which are three very small weatherboarded cottages. *The Buildings of England* dates these to the late eighteenth century, with 1798 being generally agreed. Some retain simple original interiors, with a front parlour entered directly through the front door, and two doors on the parlour's inner wall – one leading to a winding staircase and the other to a small closet. These cottages were probably built as homes for agricultural workers serving the Collins family, who gave the square its name.

Back south along Tranquil Vale, you soon come to another good group of eighteenth-century houses on the west side. The most visually striking is Vale House, six windows wide, stucco clad and with an early-nineteenth-century Tuscan porch. The building probably dates from around 1700. Immediately to its north is what must be one of the smallest Georgian houses in London – a sliver of an infill between larger Georgian blocks. Number 29 Tranquil Vale can't be more than a couple of metres wide. In fact a large portion of its white-painted front belongs to a three-window-wide house to its north – number 31 – which probably dates from around 1730.

These eighteenth-century buildings now stand in the midst of houses and shops that were constructed after the arrival of the railways. A little to the south there is a good Victorian railway station, with the track passing through the village in deep cuttings that enter long tunnels at either end (the one running north-east is a mile long) – a dramatic reminder of the heroic and often ruthless nature of the first railway age. Making these cuttings and tunnels, and the station's low-level platform in the village centre, must have been vastly disruptive and not a little disquieting for many. The railway arrived in Blackheath in 1849 and the platform-level architecture dates from then, as does most of the higher-level ticket office, which was extended from 1875–8.

Number 47 Tranquil Vale, built in a vernacular tradition that is now all but lost in London.

Just south of the station is an excellent example of another phase of building, as the village grew during the late nineteenth century and expanded into adjoining villages and communities. The Blackheath Halls in Lee Road, dating from 1895, is a most significant piece of Victorian architecture. It claims to be London's 'oldest surviving purpose-built cultural venue' – something of a bold claim, considering it is not as old as, say, the Albert Hall, but never mind. The building says a lot about the cultural aspirations of late-Victorian Blackheath. Faced with red brick and terracotta, crowned with gables, and built in a free interpretation of the early seventeenth century Flemish Renaissance style fashionable at the time, the Blackheath Halls is grand, handsome and was designed to make a strong statement. It still does.

⬥•◆•⬥

The final section of the walk takes us up to one of the great achievements of Georgian architecture in south London: the Paragon, built in 1794 to 1807. It marks one of the high points of the classical language of eighteenth-century design, and serves as a distillation of the ideals of much of the architecture we have seen on this walk.

First, though, north from Blackheath Halls, turning right on to the road running to the north-east. At first called Montpelier Vale before becoming Montpelier Row later on, it contains a number of pretty late-eighteenth-century houses. The terrace on Montpelier Row was built in stages between 1794 and 1805 on land owned by the local entrepreneur and politician John Cator.

Cator was, in many ways, an archetypal late-eighteenth-century MP. After a failed election bid at Gloucester in 1768, he set his eyes upon Wallingford – one of the country's most notoriously corrupt boroughs. In 1792, the English historian Thomas Oldfield wrote of it that 'the highest bidder is always chosen', with the electors perceiving bribes as part of their birthright: the poor 'regarded any attempt to bring about a reformation of the borough as an attack upon their vested interests, deserving of determined, if not vindictive, opposition'.[2] For Cator, who was a millionaire thanks to his successful Southwark timber business, it seemed like a good opportunity: first elected in 1772, he was returned in the general election of 1774. His ambitions, though, were not merely political. Cator had a long history of buying and developing land on the peripheries of south London – first the mansion now known as Beckenham Place, and later land ranging from Croydon to Chingford.

In 1783, Cator acquired a 250-acre country-house estate in Blackheath, which he promptly divided into building plots. So, while much of the road we now walk along had already been developed by mid century, it took its current form – charming late-Georgian houses looking out on to the heath – in Cator's time. It reveals that speculators thought money could be made running up fairly ambitious houses on the south edge of the heath. And this was, of course, because there was a market here for homes, despite the significant distance from central London, or even from the Thames-side villages.

A few houses in particular are worth looking out for. First, we come to 22–23 Montpelier Row, a large semi-detached pair conceived as a single composition dating to 1798. Most interesting are the loggias – that is, the open-air galleries, with that to the west divided up with columns – which lead to the front doors. The pavilions, which adjoin on either side, are very different in detail but seem designed to complement the loggias on the inside in a most picturesque manner. The dominant architectural feature, though, is the two groups of large-scale uniform terraces of the 1790s. The smaller, more westerly portion at 12–14 (now part of the Clarendon Hotel) is the more architectural, with tall first-floor windows of double-square proportion, with more squat second-floor windows and nearly square attic windows. It's a nice essay in simple but effective proportioning.

Several of these houses were designed by Michael Searles, Cator's preferred architect and – as we have seen in West Grove – one of the masters of late-Georgian neoclassicism. He is a fascinating character, a designer of great skill who drew on the standard repertoire of late-eighteenth-century architectural details to create a distinctive style – one that became the vernacular model for much of south London. Searles liked bold, urban compositions, noted for their uniformity and symmetry. This often manifested in buildings with striking silhouettes, grandly arched ground-floor windows and, above all, minimal but exquisite detailing – all characteristics embodied by the next few buildings we encounter.

As soon as you turn east into South Row, you come across the first of Searles's major works. This is Colonnade House, set back in its own

Michael Searles' Colonnade House, arguably one of the most satisfying Georgian houses in London.

modest grounds and reached via large, squat gate piers. Built in 1804, it has a three-window-wide and three-storey-high centre block flanked by lower and narrower side blocks. Although large, this was a single detached house, as revealed in its single central front door, leading to a spacious entrance hall containing an elegant winding staircase of minimal construction. The design is made especially memorable by the truly splendid colonnaded veranda that runs along the front of the house, and projects slightly beyond each end. The Doric columns forming the colonnade are beautifully detailed, as is the related ironwork – notably the lamp holders and the rail on the top of the colonnade, which renders its upper surface a first-floor balcony. The design of this building, and its location on the edge of the heath, in its own grounds, in front of a small pond and looking slightly to the west and evening light, surely makes it one of the most enchanting Georgian houses in London.

Further east on South Row is Paragon House, a free-standing house also designed by Searles, and dating from 1794. It's a splendid and monumental piece of work. The side elevation on Pond Road contains the main front door. The delicate neoclassical door surround is in the slightly earlier style of Robert Adam, the Scottish architect responsible for grand country houses like Syon House in Middlesex and Kedleston Hall in Derbyshire. This is because it comes from a row of long-destroyed houses Adam built with his brother, John, off the Strand between 1768 and 1772. The houses, named Adelphi Street – Greek for 'brother', after their creators – were tragically demolished in the 1930s, but this door surround was salvaged and added to Paragon House in the 1950s during the repair of war damage.

There were other houses, almost certainly by Searles, standing between Paragon House and Colonnade House, but these were damaged by bombing in 1941 – and rather than being repaired or rebuilt were replaced in the late 1950s with architect-designed and modernistic flats by the Span house-building company. These flats are good in their way, and now something of a period piece. They have large windows lighting their main living rooms, and so I suppose respond to their splendid site by offering prospects over pond and heath. But, like most products of the modernistic 'International Style', they feel generally placeless, having little or nothing to do with Blackheath's rather distinct and admirable building traditions. At the time, the Span buildings were vigorously opposed by a local heritage organisation, the Blackheath Society, which wanted Searles's houses recreated. The battle, though ultimately un-successful, was a long one, with the Span buildings only being approved after a government inquiry. But while these Searles's buildings have been lost, his greatest work, thankfully, still survives. Immediately to the east of Paragon House is the crescent that gives it its name: the Paragon.

The Paragon is a large-scale, sweeping crescent formed by three-storey blocks, each of simple uniform design and each comprising a pair of houses linked by colonnades that rise just one storey above ground level. It is magnificent. The delicate setting in the landscape, with a wide swathe of lawn to its front to counter-balance the urbanity of the crescent's composition, makes it a wonderful expression of the notion of *rus in urbe*, one of the keynotes of late-eighteenth-century informal and picturesque planning, which sought to place terraces within a park-like environment. Indeed, in many ways the Paragon epitomises the late-Georgian urban and residential idea. Although formed with semi-detached pairs, which give the Paragon a varied silhouette, it also has a long and sustained frontage thanks to the colonnaded link-blocks that unite the pairs of houses into a single composition, almost sublime in its scale.

The Paragon, a timeless work of art by accident.

Tragically the Paragon was seriously bomb-damaged in the Second World War, but it has been very well repaired and restored (although you might notice that some of the ground-floor interiors now look alarmingly modern). On the other hand the small end pavilions, with their arched windows and white corner blocks, look utterly right and charming – but are in fact inventions of the 1950s. Sometimes restorers not only get things right but can also make things better. But this is very rare indeed.

In its scale, simplicity and sophisticated detail the Paragon has the feel of a great work, created by an enlightened public authority in one of the

world's grand classical cities like St Petersburg or Helsinki. But it wasn't. This is, in many respects, the paradox of Georgian London: despite being largely the creation of ruthless speculative builders working with money-grabbing private landlords such as Cator, much Georgian urban architecture is of sublime quality, with commercial creations like the Paragon being timeless works of art almost by accident.

In order to grasp quite how far London's architecture had changed over the course of the preceding century, it is worth walking a few metres beyond the Paragon. Cross Morden Road and go along St German's Place. Here stands one of London's more magical buildings, which tells us much about late-seventeenth-century architecture – and, through its contrast with its surroundings, even more about how much that style had changed by Michael Searles's time.

The building is Morden College, one of the best of the capital's relatively large and architecturally distinguished collection of late-seventeenth- and early-eighteenth-century almshouses – a couple of which we encountered in the Greenwich walk. Many of them were designed in the economical but ornamented 'vernacular' style of brick with Portland stone or white lime-rendered dressings. Morden College is no exception – but what is exceptional is its larger-than-usual size and general generosity and high quality of its detailing. The College was founded in 1695 by Sir John Morden and intended to house 'decayed Turkey merchants' and allow them to live out their days in some comfort, style and gentility. Morden himself was, naturally, a Turkey merchant and, as a class, these were most interesting people. The Levant or Turkey Company was a chartered company formed in 1581 to trade with the Turkish Ottoman empire and so had 'factories' in such places

The entrance elevation to Morden College.

as Constantinople, the Levant, Damascus and Aleppo. Indeed it was a physician attached to the English merchants' factory in Aleppo – a Dr Halifax – who in 1693 travelled into remote central Syria and wrote one of the earliest descriptions of the ruins of the ancient classical city of Palmyra. Turkey merchants must have seen many of the wonders of the ancient world first hand, and have been to fabulous, distant and almost mystic places: Cairo, Baghdad and of course Jerusalem.

Naturally one would expect an almshouse designed for such exotic veterans to be somewhat special – and Morden College does not disappoint. This is partly because it was designed by men of talent and, I think, because it was intended to carry a specific message. The mason who built the College was Edward Strong, one of Sir Christopher Wren's favoured tradesmen and close colleagues, who played a key role in the construction of St Paul's Cathedral, worked on a large number of Wren's City churches and on Greenwich Hospital. Subsequently, in 1705, he won the chief mason's contract to work on the Vanbrugh-designed Blenheim Palace in Oxfordshire. Strong was no doubt capable of designing the College but there is a more compelling possibility. Morden was on the Greenwich Hospital Commission with Wren and it is, as *The Buildings of England* puts it, 'more than likely that Wren designed the building'.[3]

Consequently Morden College has all the hallmarks of some of Wren's most accomplished buildings. The entrance elevation is memorable and a masterpiece of the red-brick and white-stone vernacular that we have already encountered at, for example, Flamsteed House (see pp. 99–100). And, as in so many of Wren's designs, Morden College is filled with symbolic allusions, which take some time to unravel. The first clue lies on the small keystone that is placed in the centre of the arch of the main

Not just any old cherubs: the keystone above the door of Morden College.

portal set in the middle of the College's front range. It shows the heads of two chubby cherubs, facing each other and almost kissing, with their feathered wings wrapped ornamentally around each of their necks. But as we saw in St Stephen's Walbrook (see pp. 144–52), to Wren these were unlikely to be any old cherubs, and are best interpreted as seraphim, the six-winged angelic guardians of the Ark of the Covenant in Solomon's Temple.

Such Solomonic references continue in the square-plan inner court around which the College's ranges are organised. On one level the court, in its form and style, relates to the courts in Greenwich Hospital and – ultimately – to those proposed by Inigo Jones and John Webb for the abortive Whitehall Palace (see pp. 149–51). But in referring back to these buildings, it also places itself in a long tradition of Solomonic architecture, drawing on the biblical emphasis on the square, cubical, 2:1 and 2:3 proportions.

So there could be much more to the cosy architecture of Morden College than might at first seem the case. But you can also simply enjoy the building on a simpler level – as a small masterpiece of English domestic architecture, wrought in its Golden Age when characterful individual craftsmanship combined with erudition and elegance to create haunting beauty. Considered alongside the other, later treasures of the walk, it sheds light on over a century of extraordinary change to London's domestic architecture: a period in which the religiously infused, individually crafted buildings of Stuart England gave way to the altogether more secular, almost industrially produced and consciously simple and repetitive late-Georgian style.

Kew Gardens

A journey to Kew is easy from central London and can be most pleasant, rattling along on the District Line to Kew Gardens station. And the reward when you get there is tremendous. The gardens remain an exquisite pleasure ground – at moments almost a fairyland – locked within the vast suburban sprawl of south-west London.

In the mid eighteenth century there were two royal residences in what is now Kew Gardens. There was a large villa called the White House and near it, to the south-west, the striking, red-painted, brick-built Dutch House – now known as Kew Palace. This had been built in 1631 for a City merchant, but had been leased by the royal family since the late 1720s when Frederick, Prince of Wales – the son of George II – settled in the park. Born in 1707, Frederick was left in Hanover when his father moved to England in 1714 at the accession of the Hanoverian dynasty. And in Hanover Frederick stayed until 1728, when, soon after the coronation of his father, it became obligatory for him finally to show his face in the nation in which he was heir to the throne.

These fourteen years of independence, during which Frederick developed his own ideas about life and kingship, were no doubt the root of his inability to get on with his father on any issue whatsoever. Soon Frederick established his own court in opposition to his father's, in which he encouraged the arts (particularly music), favoured politics and politicians that were counter to the king's inclinations, and set about building himself into the fabric of his new country in the manner that he found agreeable. He took up cricket – already the country's favourite team sport and, like horse-racing, a focus for gamblers – and arranged matches at Kew, becoming not just an enthusiastic and knowledgeable supporter but also a skilled player. In 1736 the prince married the sixteen-year-old Augusta of Saxe-Gotha, who became one of the stalwarts and visionaries of Kew and of its transformation from royal pleasure ground into a botanic garden of international importance.

In his architectural taste the prince followed the Hanoverian court style that emerged during the second decade of the eighteenth century. Architecture was politics by other means. In 1712 the Whig Protestant artistic pundit Lord Shaftesbury argued in a 'Letter' for a 'rational . . .

national taste' in architecture, in opposition to what he perceived as the French-influenced, Catholic and Tory-tainted Baroque architecture of Sir Christopher Wren and his circle.[1] Baroque, the argument went, was the house-style of the Roman Catholic Counter-Reformation and of the absolutist French monarch Louis XIV. So for Whigs of Shaftesbury's stamp, who fancied that the Tories favoured the return of the Catholic James II and the Stuarts, to build Baroque was virtually an act of treason.

Soon after the Whig-orchestrated installation of George I, a neo-Palladian movement got under way that – in the logical simplicity of classical design – reflected Shaftesbury's appeal for a 'rational' style. This was the context in which the Palladian architecture we saw in Walk 3 developed. It was argued that the bold, masculine simplicity of the Palladian was in accord with the British character and, of course, was seen as artistically the opposite of the wilful, feminine Baroque. One of the ironies – not to say confusing oddities of this political manipulation of architectural styles – was that in the early seventeenth century Palladian architecture, introduced in consistent manner into England by Inigo Jones (see p. 80), had become the court-style of James and the Stuart dynasty, whose absolutist ambitions were precisely what the ascendant Whigs set out to oppose. But by the early eighteenth century Jones had been recast by the Whigs in patriotic manner as the father of British architecture – the 'great master' who had 'outdone all who went before' and proved that in 'most we equal, and in some things, surpass our neighbours'.[2]

The movement took hold with terrific speed. But initially there appears to have been some confusion over the meaning of art. George I himself seems to have jumped ship in dramatic fashion even as he was being painted in around 1720–22 by the Baroque artist Sir James Thornhill, as part of a heroic family group in the Painted Hall of the Wren-designed Greenwich Hospital. Thornhill, made Sergeant Painter to the king in 1720, assumed that more royal commissions were on the way – and indeed they seemed to be, when he was asked to paint interiors in the revamped Kensington Palace. But even before the Painted Hall project was completed, Thornhill was dropped by the king in most unceremonious fashion. In his stead William Kent, the protégé of the key advocate of neo-Palladianism, Lord Burlington, was appointed to execute the Kensington Palace scheme. The new movement's leading lights soon

A 1769 engraving of the White House (or Kew House), George I's foray into the newly fashionable style of Palladianism.

established themselves in royal and aristocratic quarters. And so in 1731, when the Prince of Wales wanted a new house in the gardens at Kew, he turned to Kent. The result – the White House, earlier known as Kew House – was a simple cubic box with a pediment and lower wings.

Frederick died suddenly in 1751, from a lung infection that might have been caused by being struck on the chest by a cricket ball. So when George II died in 1760 Frederick's eldest son ascended to the throne as George III. He reigned for sixty years and proved a most complex man and monarch. His mishandling of the reasonable complaints of the American colonists bred a ferocious patriotism that – combined with the stupidity and arrogance of some of the politicians George chose to advise him – led to the humiliating loss of the colonies. If not for cricket, perhaps Frederick would have lived and ruled as king to a ripe old age, and, being a far wiser man than his son, the problems with the American colonies would no doubt have been resolved in amicable manner.

Frederick's widow, the Dowager Princess Augusta, meanwhile settled into a comfortable retirement at Kew. But she was not out of the public eye for long. By the 1760s, rumours circulated that she was having an affair with the prime minister, John Stuart, 3rd Earl of Bute – the man her husband had once employed as tutor to the future George III. It was a scandalous allegation. John Wilkes, sometime radical and popular champion of liberty for the working man, published an article in 1762 in

his magazine *The North Briton* that referred to the 'feeble pretensions of a court minion' whose rise to power involved 'the prostitution of royalty'.[3] It was easy to read between the lines – Wilkes claimed that Augusta and Bute had usurped power to rule the nation, while the stupid and weak George III did nothing. Unsettled, the king orchestrated Bute's dismissal in 1763.

Economic botany in action: the Palm House of 1844.

Nonetheless, the short-lived political ascendancy of Lord Bute would have a long-term effect on Kew. In the early 1760s, Augusta promoted an idea first put forward in 1759 by Bute: that Kew should become a specimen garden containing 'all the plants known on earth'. But Kew's most obvious monument to Bute and Augusta's close relationship is the gardens' tallest structure. The Great Pagoda rises ten storeys high and, as well as being intended as a prominent and exotic 'eye-catcher' in the gardens, it was also designed to offer a bird's-eye view over the enchanted terrain. It was built in 1762, as a gift from Bute and his government to Augusta. The architect was Sir William Chambers, who we met earlier (see p. 192). He used the westernised style of Chinese architecture that had been popular in England since the 1740s for capricious and picturesque creations. Initially the Chinese designs were in the Rococo spirit – playful, asymmetrical, witty, slight and seemingly ephemeral. But Chambers being Chambers – a man dedicated to solidly built neoclassical design – this piece of Chinese fantasy is a heavyweight affair. It's a functional brick construction, octagonal in plan and with strong semicircular arched openings. With its oriental trim, including gilded dragons and lacquer-red timber, the pagoda looks rather like a utilitarian lighthouse decked out in fancy dress.

George III shared Augusta's love for Kew and its plants. After her death in 1772 he increased his ambition for the gardens. The king aimed to give this paradise a practical purpose, and this took tangible form after a meeting with Joseph Banks. James Cook had made the first of his great journeys of exploration between 1768 and 1771, during which time he explored, among other places, Tahiti and the islands and landmass that were later named New Zealand and Australia. Banks, a gentleman of wealth and education with a fascination for botany, paid for a passage on the voyage, during the course of which he made observations about the places and people he saw, and collected specimens of many plants. But for Banks this was not just to do with science and the quest for knowledge. He realised that his specimens had potentially vast financial value. If Britain or its colonies could grow their own supplies of valuable plants – for example, tea, coffee and mahogany – then the country and empire could become far more self-sufficient. Very quickly upon returning to England in 1771, Banks met with the king, who became an avid supporter of the notion of 'economic botany' – and what better place than Kew Gardens to store and nurture specimens brought back from the journey?

In the early days George III loved the experiment so much that he shared it with the public. Kew was open on a weekly basis and those who bought a ticket could see not only exotic plants but also had a good chance of seeing the king and his family in most homely manner, pottering about the grounds, their house or garden. Charlotte Papendiek, a lady-in-waiting to the queen and later an Assistant Keeper of the Wardrobe, described the scene in 1776:'Kew is now become quite gay . . . their Majesties were to be seen at the windows [of their house] speaking to their friends, and the royal children amusing themselves in their own gardens . . . The whole was a scene of enchantment and delight, Royalty living among their subjects to give pleasure and to do good.'[4]

This idyllic world did not last long. George III's first bout of instability came in the summer of 1788, with his long-standing eccentricity rapidly giving way to severe mental illness. For some time he was confined at Kew, occasionally secured in a straitjacket and locked in the White House. After he recovered in February 1789, the king seems to have taken a form of vengeance upon Kew – and the house in which he had been imprisoned in the most humiliating circumstances. He had the White House demolished in 1802. Now, nothing survives beyond its plan marked on the ground, its kitchens and its elegant orangery. In 1810 George III lapsed into terminal mental illness that increased gradually in intensity until his death in 1820. His son, George IV, had no interest in Kew as a royal residence, and by 1818 the Dutch House had ceased to be a royal home.

But the institution of the botanic garden at Kew had grown beyond direct dependence on royal patronage. By 1840, when it was taken on by the nation, it had become one of the world's most important scientific bodies. Its structures are worth studying in some detail. Between the kitchens of the White House, the Dutch House and the Great Pagoda – as well as later works like the pioneering Palm House (designed in 1844 by Richard Turner and Decimus Burton, and the first building in the world to incorporate the large-scale and structural use of wrought iron) – Kew reveals much about the Enlightenment spirit of the eighteenth century, and its long legacy in the industrial age.

WALK 6

The Regent's Canal

The rise of the waterways

The Regent's Canal is one of London's greatest and most overlooked assets. Conceived in 1802, it was immediately recognised as lucrative investment for it would form a crucial link between the Thames and the Grand Junction Canal – thus linking London directly with Birmingham. It was designed to roughly skirt the west, north and east edge of London in the first decades of the nineteenth century, running for 8.6 miles from the

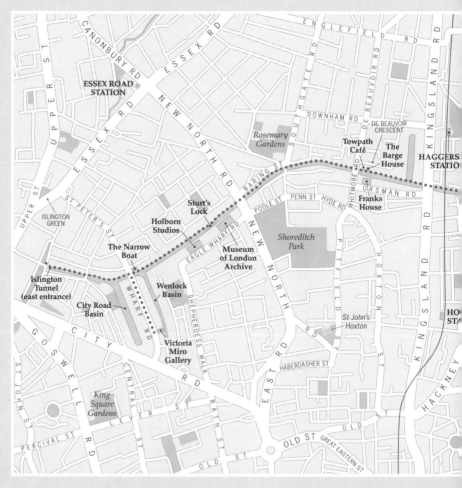

Thames at Limehouse Basin. From here it runs north-west to Mile End, via Hackney and London Fields, up to Camden Town, then on to Maida Vale and the basin, where it joins what is now the Grand Union Canal and branches south to the Paddington Basin, where it terminates.

The proposal came at the end of half a century of increasingly frenetic canal construction. A hundred years previously, there had been no easy way to transport goods across the countryside – roads were unreliable, and horses with carriages could not carry large amounts of materials. As one speculator lamented in the late eighteenth century, 'The great expence [*sic*] of land carriage will ever deprive us of many useful and desirable articles, particularly mines and minerals, which must lie dormant in the bowels of the earth.'[1] The joy of canals, on the other hand, was that barges could

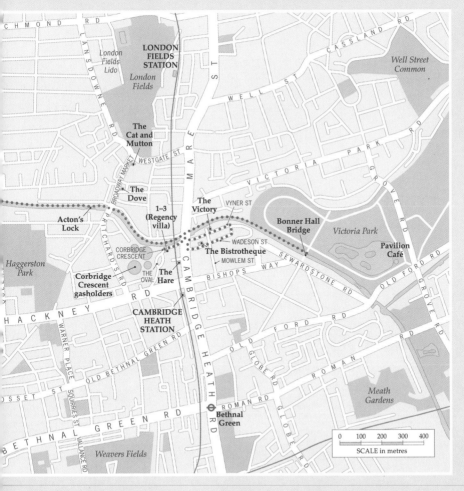

carry huge volumes of materials, and relatively quickly. The first people to realise this were entrepreneurs in the North West – notably Francis, 3rd Duke of Bridgewater, who in 1763 opened a canal that could transport coal from his mines in Worsley to the growing town of Manchester. The success of these early ventures sparked a wave of canal speculation: by 1835, England and Wales had 4,000 miles of navigable waterway, the majority of which were canals.[2] By 1793, one excitable commentator was able to write that the canals had 'in effect, converted the internal parts of our island into coasts'.[3]

Such projects contributed to an extraordinary transformation of the British economy. This was the age of Richard Arkwright's mills and James Hargreaves's spinning jenny – and of the consequent boom in industrial output. By the early nineteenth century, there was a certain swagger to

Barges line the edges of sections of the canal.

Britain's industrialists. 'It is impossible to contemplate the progress of manufactures in Great Britain within the last thirty years without wonder and astonishment,' wrote the Scottish merchant Patrick Colquhoun in 1814. 'The facilities afforded to the great branches of the woollen and cotton manufactories by ingenious machinery, invigorated by capital and skill, are beyond all calculation.'[4] William Huskisson, the President of the Board of Trade, put it more simply a few years later: 'I know of nothing in the history of commerce – I am not acquainted with anything in the history of our manufacturing prosperity – that can at all compare with this.'[5] Britain was at the peak of its Industrial Revolution.

In this context, the Regent's Canal seemed an assured speculation with which nothing could go wrong. After nearly a decade of planning and raising finance, an Act of Parliament for the canal's construction was passed in 1812. John Nash, the architect favoured by the Prince Regent,

became a director of the canal company. Since 1811 he had been the Crown's master-planner for the transformation of its farms north of the Euston Road into Regent's Park. The canal was to be a picturesque ornament to the park, which would contain villas and be flanked by palatial terraces, some enjoying a prospect of the new waterway. As with the realisation of Regent's Park, Nash delegated much of the design work – in this case to his assistant in the Department of Woods and Forests, James Morgan, who was appointed chief engineer to the canal company and proved a most able and talented designer.

Work started in October 1812 and the first section from Paddington to Camden Town was opened in 1816. This included a 251-metre-long tunnel under Maida Vale, a 48-metre-long tunnel under Lisson Grove and a long stretch within the Regent's Park as well as several basins for loading and docking barges. Indeed these mighty works – in their bold engineering and construction, executed by gangs of 'navigators' or navvies – anticipated the vast tunnels, cuttings and embankments of the coming railway age.

This was an architectural achievement as much as a commercial one. In Regent's Park Nash and Morgan succeeded brilliantly in making what was in effect an industrial thoroughfare a positive visual enhancement. One reason for the success is that the canal sits in a cutting – quite deep in places – meaning not only that sections are secreted within richly planted banks but also that it is crossed by handsome bridges. The best, a small masterpiece in its way, is Morgan's Macclesfield Bridge of 1815–16, which has carriageway supported by two rows of massive cast-iron Grecian Doric columns made in 'Coalbrookdale' – as lettering above capitals proclaims. Located in Shropshire, Coalbrookdale was one of the heartlands of the Industrial Revolution. This bridge was severely damaged in 1874 when a barge carrying gunpowder very unfortunately blew up as it passed beneath. But the ranks of columns survived and the reconstruction was faithful, although incorporating hard blue engineering bricks – unknown in the early nineteenth century – for arches.

And then, as this first phase of the canal was being completed, the whole project nearly collapsed in humiliating disaster. Thomas Homer, the visionary who had first projected the scheme in 1802 and who was its head of finance, was in 1815 accused of embezzling funds. He was arrested and eventually brought to trial, found guilty and transported – but the scheme, always underfinanced, was left in chaos. There were other problems, including, peculiarly, a shortage of water, as well as the failure of the pioneering hydropneumatic lock at Hampstead Road designed by the military engineer William Congreve. The lock had to be rebuilt in 1819. The scandals helped further delay the construction, which was already taking longer than had been anticipated. The second leg to Limehouse was not opened until August 1820, by which time the building costs had risen from the initial estimate of £400,000 to £772,000. All in all, the cutting of the 8.6 miles of canal had taken eight years.

When, at last, the second leg did open it proved well worth the wait. It included a number of heroic enterprises – most notably the excavation of the 878-metre-long tunnel below the Angel, Islington, the City Road Basin and the large Regent's Canal Basin (now known as the Limehouse

Macclesfield Bridge of 1815–16, subsequently damaged when a boat full of gunpowder exploded nearby.

Basin) that was used to transfer cargo between barges and seafaring ships. Soon, though, the canal began to function in a manner not anticipated by its backers. Rather than being an artery to transport goods between Birmingham, London and the open sea, it became most useful as a means of moving goods around London – principally coal and building materials – with the City Road Basin becoming the focus of activity. This was the context in which additional basins, such as the Wenlock Basin of 1826 near the north end of the Islington Tunnel, were added.

This change in function would contribute to the canal's unusual longevity. Because it prospered by serving London rather than by linking London to Birmingham, the creation of Euston station in 1837 and the arrival of the London and Birmingham Railway did not deal it a death blow. The railway could transport goods more quickly between the two cities than was possible by canal but could not – at least initially – transport goods to any great extent within London. So for a while the new railway and the Regent's Canal worked in happy harmony, and indeed the tonnage of coal transported within the capital by the canal actually increased.

Of course, this could not last forever. As the railway network grew and as roads improved, the canal system could not compete. Use of the waterway dwindled. Several attempts were made to use its route for a railway, and in 1883 it was sold to the Regent's Canal and City Docks Railway Company with this aim in mind. The project stalled thanks to intense opposition from the Crown, which could not abide the idea of trains puffing their way around Regent's Park. Instead the company raised money for dock and canal improvements and in 1904 renamed itself the Regent's Canal and Dock Company. The canal – merged with the Grand Junction in 1929 to form the Grand Union Canal – prospered until the late 1940s. It was then nationalised as trade rapidly diminished. This time it seemed decline was terminal. In 1969 it closed to commercial shipping.

In recent years, however, the Regent's Canal has undergone an extraordinary renaissance. Today it is used not as a highway of trade and commerce but of leisure and pedal-powered transport with, in the summer, a waterbus plying between Maida Vale and Camden. The canal – now owned and operated by the Canals and Rivers Trust – can never have looked better; its locks work, its basins and many parts of its banks are lined with barges, and its towpath is thronged with walkers and bicyclists. It is also the location of some of London's best cafés, restaurants and art galleries. In short, it is an excellent place for a stroll to ponder London's long-lost industrial past, in which one never has to forgo the pleasures of the twenty-first-century city.

THE WALK

Our route starts at the south side of Victoria Park, at Bonner Hall Bridge – best accessed by getting the Tube to Bethnal Green, a ten-minute walk away. The first portion of this route offers clues about the nature of east London before the arrival of the Regent's

Canal, taking in several buildings that predate the waterways, and whose fates were inexorably changed by its arrival.

Before moving on, take a moment to reflect on Victoria Park. In the eighteenth century, this was all open pasture, interspersed with the odd brick kiln and market garden. The one notable feature was Bonner Hall, so called after the sixteenth-century bishop of London Edmund Bonner. All this was to change in the nineteenth century. As London expanded, calls for public parks grew; in 1840, Queen Victoria was presented with a petition signed by 30,000 residents. The Crown estate purchased 218 acres in the area and, over the next few years, converted it into Victoria Park. The park shares a family resemblance to Regent's Park at the other end of the Regent's Canal – no doubt down to the fact that its designer, James Pennethorne, was a protégé of none other than John Nash.[6]

The view south-east from Victoria Park's Bonner Gate.

When I first knew the park – many years ago – it was a fairly rough place. In particular the Pavilion Café, a few hundred metres to the east of Bonner Hall Bridge, was a grisly affair, best avoided unless one wanted to experience the stark reality of East End cuisine. Now, like many in east London, it has transformed into one of the best cafés mentioned in this book. It makes a splendid place to begin the walk if you're in need of a bite to eat or drink.

For those ready to plunge into Georgian industrial architecture, however, it is best to walk to the western end of the park and through the canal gate on to the towpath. Here, one can begin to imagine the feel of the canal in its early days: the canal side adjoining Victoria Park is used as moorings for barges, mostly residential, while across the waterway (which, as is usual, has a towpath – intended for the horses required to tow barges – generally on only one side) are the gardens of houses. This must be a delightful place to live, especially for the nautical-minded. Houses soon give way to light industrial buildings of various dates, many now serving as homes or studios.

The decaying Regency charm of The Oval, now accompanied by two Victorian gasholders.

When one crosses under the bridge carrying Cambridge Heath Road, everything changes. You are thrust into a splendidly gloomy vista, but one with a moving if modest grandeur. Immediately west of the road bridge is a series of wide, shallow arches and a mighty brick pier, presumably all part of a now-lost wharf or small basin that once ran south of the canal – complete with a small window in the pier suggesting that this massive piece of brick construction is inhabited. Above these works, and parallel to the road bridge, rises the metal bulk of the Victorian railway bridge. The view westwards is enriched by the prospect of a three-storey stucco-clad Regency villa, embellished with no fewer than three full-height bows that offer a charming sinuous frontage to the canal. And looming over all, to the west of the now sadly decaying villa, are the tall and stark skeletal structures of a pair of nineteenth-century gasholders.

It's well worth clambering off the canal here to take a closer look at this threatened piece of industrial and once ornamental London. Go up the stairs to the east of the bridges, cross the Cambridge Heath Road/ Mare Street bridge to the south side of the canal and head down the grandly named Corbridge Crescent towards the villa. Several things now happen, and they are all most rewarding. A narrow alley – Grove Passage – lurks below the crushing form of the railway viaduct, and Corbridge Crescent suddenly exposes its early granite setts which, during my last visit at twilight, glistened with moisture and led to a strange and exotic world that unfolded around and in front of the Regency villa. This section of the canal was constructed between 1816 and 1820 and the villa appears to date from around then. Upon closer inspection, it is – despite mutilations – not in such bad condition as it first looks. The cornice has gone, and the front door been butchered, but windows are in reasonable order and a light shines from one. It's inhabited, at least in part. To the rear is a large, red-brick wing. A notice is fixed next to a small door, which offers a flashback to the old East End: 'Soup Kitchen . . . open weekdays 10 to 2, Saturdays 10 to 1, Sundays 11 to 1.'

This marks the end of Corbridge Crescent, which now leads to The Oval – a small piece of neoclassical town planning that incorporated an elongated circus, somewhat in the Nash manner of Regent's Park. What high ambitions these names evoke. The crumbling villa is the solitary survivor of a crescent, perhaps ruined by the arrival of the railway. Or it was perhaps the fault of the canal itself. Crescent and Oval – located just off the Hackney Road – were new creations in 1820 when the canal arrived but were, in the words of *The Buildings of England*, 'hopelessly compromised' by the social transformation brought about by this industrial thoroughfare.[7] Today, all that's left of The Oval is its form, now defined by a scattering of low and mostly mean twentieth-century industrial structures and by its central island, still framed by robust granite kerbs, but no longer planted – just an oval of beaten earth littered with urban detritus. Only a short distance away, on Hackney Road, there are still substantial rows of early-nineteenth-century terraces and semi-detached villas.

Such lofty Georgian ambitions stand in stark contrast to the use of The Oval now. The villa, the land and later buildings that surround it are occupied by Empress Coaches. Everywhere are coaches, campers and buses of different types and sizes, being serviced and cleaned. It has its own surreal charm: in the yard next door, fellows go about their business; one chap with black and shiny hair, in an outsize jacket, ambles around smoking a cigarette. Everything looks like a flashback to the 1950s. This magical, individual and living piece of workaday London is, of course, under threat. Instead of coaches and oily workshops all is to be cleared away for a 'mixed use' development containing over 500 square metres of 'commercial floor space' and 116 flats. Consent was granted by Tower Hamlets Council in December 2008. So all this now exists on borrowed time – indeed demolition might have taken place by the time you visit. This is how cities die and how character is lost: gradually, stealthily, bit by bit.

Towering over the villa to the west are the pair of gasholders. This portion of the Regent's Canal has been home to gasworks since the Georgian period. The pioneering Imperial Gas Light and Coke Company, which had been founded in 1812 to supply gas to light England's streets, gained control of the current site of Haggerston Park in 1821, at a time when the canal was still largely surrounded by open fields.[8] The second decade of the nineteenth century had witnessed an extraordinary growth in the amount of gas lighting in Britain. In 1812, there was only one gas company; just fifteen years later, every town with a population over 10,000 had a gas supply. The resultant change to urban life was enormous

The solitary survival of a crescent of Regency houses on The Oval.

– suddenly, nightfall ceased to represent the end of the day's work or ambling, and became a new opportunity for labour and pleasure-seeking.

The gasholders on Corbridge Crescent are somewhat later. They reveal the wonderful way the mid-nineteenth-century mind – intoxicated by the thrill and pomp of the past – could, with only a little appropriate ornament, turn even a functional industrial structure into architecture stamped with the cultural pedigree of history. The smaller of them has vertical stanchions fashioned as two tiers of sixteen classical columns – denuded Corinthian over Doric – evidently calculated to evoke the power and form of the Colosseum in Rome. Interestingly this type of classically embellished rotunda was pioneered for a now-demolished gasholder built on this site in 1856; the current smaller one dates from 1865 and was designed by Joseph Clarke, with the columns cast by the famed Staveley Coal and Iron Company of Derbyshire, and the neighbouring taller but simpler gasholder constructed in 1888–9.[9] Now, these gasholders no longer inflate and, if a battle is not waged, are probably not long for this world. Their majestic and sculptural forms, which make a vital contribution to the scene, are due to be demolished, despite protestations by the local heritage group the Hackney Society.

Before returning to the canal, cross to the east side of Cambridge Heath Road and into Vyner Street, running parallel and immediately south of the waterway. In the early nineteenth century this cobbled thoroughfare was on the outskirts of a conurbation that sprawled north, up to the area around London Fields. But everything changed with the arrival of the Regent's Canal. Vyner Street – at that time called John Street – was cut off from the land to the north, and began to develop a rather different character.[10] Two centuries later this small street became the unlikely heart of east and north-east London's burgeoning art scene. New galleries set up here to show not the established trends or artists, nor the 'mainstream', but an eclectic mix of what was 'upcoming' and experimental. But as is the way with such spontaneous eruptions, the peak is soon passed as corporate interest muscles in. The low rents have now spiralled up, so the vibrant little art world here has become something of a victim of its own success. Some of the pioneering galleries have moved on – mostly west to Fitzrovia – and the art scene of Vyner Street has itself become part of East End history.

Nonetheless, at the time of writing there are still some galleries worth visiting, especially on the first Thursday evening of the month when many host events. There are also a few pubs nearby that are more than decent, and where local artists gather: the Victory in Vyner Street, the Hare at 505 Cambridge Heath Road (a modest three-storey mid-nineteenth-century building that retains much of the atmosphere of a Bethnal Green local) and the Bistrotheque at 23–27 Wadeson Street. This is a sophisticated bar and restaurant housed in battered but large-roomed former industrial buildings, which hosts erudite talks and, famously, outrageously camp cabaret evenings. The Bistrotheque has been going for some years now, remains popular and seems ever-expanding, but was initially amazing simply for being here at all, stuck down a Bethnal Green backstreet and secreted amongst anonymous post-war factory buildings.

When you've had your fill of the pleasures of Vyner Street and its environs, walk back to the north bank of the canal and continue west. After a short while you come to another bridge, which carries a road leading to Broadway Market and then to London Fields. This is an old market street that now has two good pubs – the Dove, and the Cat and Mutton – said to have occupied the site since 1790.[11]

Acton's Lock. The lock-keeper lived in the house on the right until the 1980s.

But when I first explored it twenty-five or so years ago, Broadway Market was a desolate place. Most of the array of shops – including one splendid Regency affair – were run-down or closed, sitting alongside a few old-time cafés, a pie and mash shop, and a couple of rough-looking pubs. All has now changed, and Broadway Market has become one of the most sophisticated and popular Saturday markets in London, with its down-at-heel shops and cafés reborn as exquisite eateries and delicatessens.

Back on the towpath, the walk continues west, and we now get a better sense of how Regent's Canal would have felt in its industrial heyday. The first treat comes in the form of a splendid pair of operational locks which manipulate the water level, allowing barges coming from the Thames to navigate the higher ground of north London and to pass beneath a bridge carrying Queensbridge Road. This is Acton's Lock, so called for William Lee Acton, on whose land this portion of the canal was built. Until the 1980s, the lock-keeper's family lived in the neighbouring cottage.

These days, being generally operated by relaxed holidaymakers who have hired their barges, it is easy to forget the extraordinary feat of engineering the locks represent. One Victorian description of a trip down

Regent's Canal, by the writer and theatrical producer John Hollingshead, does a good job of reminding us. His friend tells him

> how our frail bark, the *Stourport*, will be admitted into a deep, narrow, oblong, brick well; and how, as soon as we are in the dreadful trap, two massive iron-bound timber gates will close behind us in such a manner that the more the pressure is increased from behind, the tighter will they bind themselves together. Then he draws a fearfully vivid picture of the two gates in front of us – a single, slender barrier, that alone opposes the advance of an ocean – a hundred thousand tons of water forty feet above our heads, fretting to be at us, like a bear looking down from his pole upon the tender children outside his pit.[12]

Such reflections do a good job of conjuring the nineteenth-century awe at the industry and scale of the waterways. It is something we are reminded of again by a structure a little further to the west. After a short stroll we pass below another bridge, this one carrying the Kingsland Road – the Roman Ermine Street linking London to Lincoln and York – which runs due north from Shoreditch. Immediately to its west, on the north side, there is the long and narrow Kingsland Basin – now tranquil but once bustling with barges loading and unloading. It illustrates how the canal operated in its prime. Barges were pulled by horse-power to strategically placed locations such as this – many adjacent to a main road – where goods were transferred between barge and dray. Very close by a large timber merchant was located, presumably here because once it received its wares by barge.

The south side of the canal at this point is lined with late-nineteenth and early-twentieth-century buildings, many rising almost directly from the water and offering a fine medley of simple functional design – the early ones in brick, the later in reinforced concrete, or white-rendered blockwork, with large steel-framed windows. These are typical of the industrial and utilitarian buildings that, in north-east and east London, grew up along the banks of the canal. The buildings were served by the canal and confirmed its purpose. But here industry has long gone and the canal is now no more than a glorious ornament and place of pleasure. The buildings now mostly contain flats and artists' studios and, when I strolled along the canal, on a sunny weekday afternoon, the activities were more than just the expected. There were, of course, the dog-walkers, joggers, bikers and oddball fishermen who really could not have hoped to catch much that was edible. But also an array of ambitious contemporary architecture and one anonymous industrial-looking building called Franks House that is, of all things, the store for the British Museum's Ethnography Department. Located at 38–56 Orsman Road – parallel to and south of the canal – the building's fine art-deco

An early twentieth-century warehouse on Orsman Road backs on to the canal.

form is revealed, with its striking strips of glazing and asymmetrically placed corner tower.

Back on the north side of the canal, opposite the museum store, is the Barge House restaurant, created within the ground floor of a recent building that fronts on to De Beauvoir Crescent. But immediately to the west of it is something that seems much less but is, in fact, so much more. This is the Towpath Café, composed of just a couple of holes in the basement wall of the large and bulky industrial building that rises along the canal. Outside each slit-like hole is an array of simple chairs, a few tables and perhaps a bowl or two of water to quench the thirst of passing dogs. It's the perfect place for a canal-side walker to grab a coffee, a freshly-pressed fruit juice, a sandwich or cake and – if the weather is right – a wonderful place to sit. When I first found Towpath I was hungry and thirsty from a long walk and it really was like coming upon an oasis. During the past few years it has expanded, and now colonises a wide stretch of canal-side structures, with lots of exterior seating.

The building that rises high above the café was built as a printworks, but is one no longer, and eased itself into local legend in the 1960s and 70s by becoming the powerhouse for that lost generation of erotic magazines filled with scantily dressed young women. These publications have, of course, been superseded by far sterner fare. But back when the presses were in full production, the towpath became the haunt of cavorting and noisy boys who were determined to get the irritated printers to stone them with bundles of 'adult' magazines. The former printworks is a fine piece of 1930s architecture, with a bow-fronted staircase tower.

———— ◆ ————

On the next portion of the walk, the towpath becomes wider, the feats of engineering more ambitious. We are, it seems, entering one of the heartlands of the late-Georgian industrial metropolis. The first sign of the increase in scale is the brick-arched Whitmore Road bridge. These early canal bridges really are fine pieces of early-nineteenth-century engineering. They are made in traditional manner of traditional materials – essentially Roman in inspiration – and are robust and handsome in their utilitarian simplicity. They also sometimes have a strikingly if unintended picturesque quality. The gently curving arch of this bridge frames splendid views along the canal and, because of its generous width, reflections from the water are able to ripple and dart within its dark and cavernous interior. The passage within it is dank and echoing: a strange and alarming underworld through which bikers and pedestrians rush from sunshine to sunshine. The apparently wider girth of the canal after the bridge is, in fact, an illusion. The increased sense of space is suggested by the buildings, which are generally lower and more distant because of the wider path. This sense of scale and seriousness is reinforced by the mighty Sturt's Lock a few hundred metres later, accompanied by a towering former pumping station that once regulated the water levels of the canal.

The industrial feel of this portion of the walk is reinforced by a stark, functional building just west of the New North Road bridge, on the south bank. This is the store of the Museum of London. It is an Aladdin's cave of wonders, many not simply archived away or stashed in filing cabinets but displayed splendidly in glass cases. In my view some of the museum's most intriguing objects are kept here, hustled out of the main City building by showier pieces calculated to appeal to popular taste. Again,

Reflections dart and ripple across the top of Whitmore Road bridge.

as with the British Museum store, this Eagle Wharf Road repository can be viewed by appointment, and for some it could be a rewarding termination to this walk. That would be a shame, for there is yet more to see.

Take, for example, the group of nineteenth-century industrial buildings that stand a hundred metres past Sturt's Lock. This striking complex was once home to the Regent's Canal Ironworks – the foundry of the master ironworker Henry Grissell. Along with his cousin Samuel Morton Peto, Grissell became one of the leading public-works contractors of the early nineteenth century – contributing to structures ranging from Nelson's Column to Clerkenwell Prison, and designing ironwork for the gates around Buckingham Palace and the British Museum. The site, complete with a tall brick chimney, is nearly a sixth of a mile in length and rises above its own 'marina' walkway that offers moorings for boats and barges.

Some years ago the complex was converted into the Holborn Studios, made up of photographic studios and a pleasant water-side restaurant and bar called the Commissary. The Studios have long been recognised as an exemplary piece of regeneration, in which old buildings have been retained and new life created. Now all is under threat. The owners want to 'develop' the site as flats and 'commercial space', which could mean the destruction of some of the old buildings, the loss of jobs and the closure of the Studios. It all seems incredible – and very sad. The Holborn Studios is exactly the sort of place that gives the canal character and creative energy, and is a great example of the ways in which buildings can change and adapt. This is, in general, a most sensible approach. Existing buildings represent 'embedded' energy that it is a crime to squander – something that many developers rarely seem to appreciate.

As we contninue west, we begin to approach the final walkable stretch of the Regent's Canal. A little further along we come across the long Wenlock Basin, where ranks of gaily painted barges nestle below a canopy of trees. It's now hard to believe that this was ever a working wharf. It was, of course, once considered a mighty and daunting feat of engineering –

The Narrowboat pub viewed from City Road Basin, shielded from view by the outsized parapets on Wharf Road bridge.

and one that very nearly failed. In 1826, while still being constructed, the dam across the entrance collapsed, causing the main canal's water level to drop by 13 inches and halting traffic on the waterway.

The dauntingly industrial atmosphere these waterways must once have had is proven by another structure, further to the west. At the Wharf Road bridge, a steep flight of stairs rises to road level and to a modest early-Victorian pub – the Narrowboat – which seems to totter at street level on the very edge of the shallow towpath cutting. But most striking of all are the parapets of the Wharf Road bridge – in particular, their height. They are far too large to see over. The design is a reminder that, in the early nineteenth century, the canal was not regarded as an ornament but as an industrial highway, at best a place of drudgery and at worst a realm haunted by queer canal folk. In the nineteenth-century imagination, these canal-dwellers came to be seen as the lowest and most alien of people – worthy of pity or even disdain. Take the following description from an

1888 novel *Life in the Cut*, in which one character describes a ten-year-old child who lives on a canal boat as 'dreadful, so dirty, starved and stunted, she scarcely seemed a child, more like a wicked hobgoblin; though she did not look wicked either, only wretched and forlorn, nursing another fearful-looking, more uncanny atom than herself.'[13] The canals and their inhabitants, it seems, were to be greatly feared.

Now, of course, precisely the opposite is the case – as demonstrated by the archly high-end art gallery that we now approach. On Wharf Road – running parallel and to the west of Wenlock Basin – stands the Victoria Miro Gallery, located in a nineteenth-century furniture factory. The interior offers a vast and minimal space reminiscent of warehouse galleries in New York, but some original elements have been suffered to survive, including a few roof timbers and worn floorboards. The architect is Trevor Horne, a specialist in such stripped-back contemporary design, often with retained, although greatly adapted, old buildings. The garden backing on to the Wenlock Basin was created by the artist Ian Hamilton Finlay, and the gallery itself houses works by Chris Ofili, Grayson Perry, the Chapman brothers and Peter Doig. The whole affair offers a fascinating perspective of the upper-slopes of the London 'art scene'. Confident, wealthy and brilliantly contemporary without being overtly brash – and a million miles from the gritty industrial aesthetic the building originally possessed.

———◆◦◆◦◆———

We now approach the final, glorious, industrial crescendo of the walk. Rejoin the canal towpath and just a few metres west from the bridge is the stupendous City Road Basin, covering one and a half hectares in area. The waters here are wide and the view to the south tremendous. Standing on the wide quay the City seems to open up, with the water of the basin a highway to its heart. You can see the obelisk spire of the 1730s St Luke's church on Old Street, the serrated profile of one of the Barbican towers and – as now with so many viewpoints in London – the soaring, tapering and somewhat surreal silhouette of the Shard next to far-distant London Bridge station.

Opened in 1820, the City Road Basin became the heart and soul of the canal in the 1890s. Goods and materials were offloaded to be dispersed around the surrounding area, and products loaded for transportation

An engraving of City Road Basin from 1828 offers a glimpse of the late-Georgian industrial metropolis, with St Luke's Church obelisk towering in the distance.

around London and Britain or for export abroad via the docks to the east. There were flower and timber wharves, coal depots – even Pickfords, the house-removal company, had a depot here. The surrounding buildings are varied, nineteenth century and modern, but most are tough and big-boned. It's a pleasing place to loiter and contemplate the city, with the atmosphere of urban industry still present but transformed into something less grimy and challenging. When I was there one of the barges, moored nearby on the north towpath, offered home-cooked Slovakian food.

The last short leg of the walk has a very different character. The waters now move between streets lined with salubrious early-nineteenth-century terraces, many with well-planted gardens. The canal-side becomes bucolic, with houses glimpsed through the rich array of trees. Suddenly we are in a kind of Eden, a splendid example of the late-Georgian obsession for creating *rus in urbe*, with stern and uniform terraces framed and softened by informal clumps of trees and gardens. We are in the heart of the city but it feels like we are walking through glades and groves. The canal becomes a place of fantasy, of heavy engineering inspired by the romance of history. Here the imagination is inflamed by low-arched and antique-looking bridges – utterly Roman in feel – and by secret bowers, with their chairs and tables manipulated to ideal positions by the nearby terrace-dwellers.

The theatrical entrance to Islington Tunnel, designed by James Morgan.

And then the canal narrows and feeds into a deep, dark tunnel that carries it for 878 metres below the heights of Islington and the Angel above. There is no towpath so the walk ends here, in front of the splendid tunnel arch, designed in heroic style by James Morgan in the visually powerful Baroque manner of Sir John Vanbrugh. The opening is in a gentle catenary curve – a much stronger shape than a semicircular arch – and there is a heavy keystone and two squat and tough-looking Grecian Doric pilasters. It looks like the theatrical opening to some operatic dungeon. But despite its ornamental appearance, the tunnel was in its day a great feat of practical engineering. It was built between 1815–18 by navvies using horse- and manpower and explosives, with the spoil carried away in wheelbarrows.

When the canal opened bargees had to 'leg' their boats through the tunnel – in other words, lie on their back and punt the barges through by pushing with their legs against the tunnel roof. This hideous, back-breaking work was necessary until a steam tug was installed in 1826 that heaved barges through in a continuous chain. In other tunnels, legging was necessary until well into the nineteenth century. John Hollingshead witnessed the system on another canal in 1860, and described the moment two boats passed. 'It was necessary to leave off legging, for the boats to pass each other, and the leggers waited until the last moment when a concussion seemed inevitable, and then sprang instantaneously, with singular dexterity, on to the sides of their boats, pulling their narrow platforms up immediately after them,' he wrote. It was, in his rendering, a peculiarly beautiful scene.

> The action of the light in front of our boat produced a very
> fantastic shadow of our recumbent boatman-legger upon the side
> wall of the tunnel. As his two legs stuck out horizontally from the
> edge of the legging-board, treading, one over the other, against
> the wall, they threw a shadow of two arms, which seemed to be
> held by a thin old man – another shadow of the same substance
> – bent nearly double at the stomach, who worked them over and
> over, as if turning two great mangle-handles with both hands at
> the same time.[14]

The only way to reach the other end of Islington Tunnel, if not travelling by barge, is to ascend to the street and continue west overground. That, though, is another walk. For now, merely take a moment to look back east and reflect on the extraordinary achievement of the late-Georgian waterways, and the way they transformed the British economy.

It was a feat that contemporaries were highly conscious of. The English poet and essayist Anna Laetitia Barbauld captured the optimism of the canal age in a 1773 poem, 'The Invitation', which reflects on the remarkable changes that the waterways had brought to the English landscape:

> Here smooth canals, across th' extended plain,
> Stretch their long arms, to join the distant main:
> The sons of toil with many a weary stroke
> Scoop the hard bosom of the solid rock . . .
> The traveller with pleasing wonder sees
> The white sail gleaming thro' the dusky trees;
> And views the alter'd landscape with surprise,
> And doubts the magic scenes which round him rise.

The British Museum

The British Museum is a temple to the arts embedded within the Georgian terraces and squares of Bloomsbury. These, although now badly battered by twentieth-century interlopers, remain in themselves a monument to the arts of harmonious urban design and living. Exploring Bloomsbury and the museum, then, is a journey to the very heart of civilisation.

To understand the British Museum, it is necessary to understand the area in which it was built. The main entrance is on Great Russell Street, which until well into the eighteenth century marked the north-western edge of the continuously built-up area of London. Until various estates – notably the Bedford estate (see p. 493) – started to grant leases to speculative house builders in the late eighteenth century, the prospect from the north of Great Russell Street was almost exclusively rural. All that could be seen were some gardens and meadows, a few detached buildings, and the distant villages of Hampstead and Highgate.

Approach Great Russell Street from Holborn to its south-east, which takes you through Bloomsbury Square, started in the early 1660s by the Earl of Southampton, and united with the Bedford estate in 1669, when the son of the Earl of Bedford married Southampton's daughter. Some early houses survive on the west side of the square, all now radically altered. Much of the square, though, is mid to late Georgian. On the north side, where Southampton's mansion once stood, is a pair of tall, uniform, plain and repetitive terraces built very soon after 1800. The rich and picturesque planting of Bloomsbury's squares, and of the communal rear gardens, helped create the visionary late-Georgian ideal of *rus in urbe*.

Great Russell Street runs west from the north side of Bloomsbury Square. One of the grandest buildings along its north side was Montagu House, built in 1686 to the designs of the natural philosopher Robert Hooke and a little-known French architect named Pierre Pouget, and free-standing in its own extensive grounds. In the mid eighteenth century the avid collector of objects and specimens of natural history, Sir Hans Sloane, determined to bequeath his collection to the nation to form the core of a national museum. He intended for his museum to be housed in perpetuity in the Tudor manor house he had bought and occupied in Chelsea. But after Sloane died in 1753, plans evolved, and rather than leaving his collection in outlying Chelsea the government purchased Montagu House and adapted it to house what became known as the British Museum, which opened to the public in 1759.

From the outset, Sloane's collection was complemented by two libraries: the Cottonian – which comprised a number of ancient works collected by the Elizabethan antiquarian Robert Cotton – and the Harleian – bequeathed by Robert Harley, Earl of Oxford, and containing an array of medieval illuminated manuscripts. It was a fine basis for a national museum. But this was not the British Museum as we now know it. While it paid lip service to the ideal of public access, from the outset it was keen to limit precisely who was allowed to see its treasures. In 1755, as plans for the museum started to come together, the trustees decided that their goal was 'to prevent as much as possible persons of mean and low Degree and Rude or ill Behaviour from Intruding'[1] – and, as such, it needed stringent entry requirements. In the early years, you could freely access the library if you were a trustee, a museum officer, a fellow of the Royal and Antiquarian societies, a member of the Royal College of Physicians, or a professor at Gresham College – anyone else required a reading-room ticket, which could only be acquired from a trustee. 'By these Regulations,, argued the trustees in 1756,'no one, that can have any pretentions to come to read or consult the Books or MSS, can have any difficulty to acquire that privilege, & none but improper persons can be

The staircase of Montagu House in 1845.

excluded.'[2] The galleries, meanwhile, were nominally open to the public but only during the working week and so were largely inaccessible to all but the leisure class.

The original museum, then, was an exclusive affair. But all would change in the early nineteenth century. In the decades after its foundation the museum made further acquisitions, through gift or through purchase

– notably the 65,000 volumes of the King's Library assembled by George III and gifted to the nation in 1822 by George IV; the Townley Collection of antique sculpture, purchased in 1805; and Lord Elgin's collection of sculpture, or 'Marbles', from the Parthenon in Athens, purchased in 1816. By the second decade of the nineteenth century it was clear that the adapted late-seventeenth-century Montagu House was an inadequate location for the display of a national collection, ever increasing in quality and quantity. A new building was essential and, as it happened, this urgent requirement coincided with an international movement for the creation and design of national museums open to the public. This was not pure altruism on the part of governments but reflected a growing belief that a more cultured and educated workforce was also a more satisfied, stable and able workforce, better equipped to utilise the manufacturing potential offered by the new technology of the Industrial Revolution.

The first major architectural expression of the conviction that great states should collect and display art is the Glyptothek in Munich. It was founded by the Bavarian King Ludwig I to house the state collection of Greek and Roman sculpture and designed in 1816 by Leo von Klenze in a Greco-Roman style. It established the principle that these great public museums, ornaments to their nations, should be conceived as solemn, inspirational and imposing Temples of Art designed in noble classical manner. They were to be not only monumental public buildings, giving focus and beauty to their urban setting, but were also to evoke the virtues of ancient learning and civilisation.

Such buildings had interesting pedigrees. Great families or institutions had previously created private museums within palatial buildings, which can be seen as the partial models for the first great public museums. For example the Uffizi, started in Florence in 1560 for Cosimo de' Medici and designed by Giorgio Vasari, contained offices (as the name implies), but also works of art displayed in galleries and an octagonal Tribune. And in England good examples are Holkham Hall, Norfolk, designed in the early 1730s by William Kent and Lord Burlington, which incorporates a gallery Tribune-like room for the display of paintings and antique sculpture, as well as Dulwich Picture Gallery in south London. Designed in 1811 for private clients by Sir John Soane in Dulwich, it was the world's first free-standing picture gallery that was open to the public. Although architecturally sophisticated, this gallery was relatively small and certainly not designed to be a public Temple of Art. By the second decade of the nineteenth century, the notion of public museums was gaining momentum: the next significant development after the Glyptothek was the Altes Museum in Berlin – arguably the masterpiece of the great Prussian architect Karl Friedrich Schinkel – designed in 1821 or 1822 to house the Prussian art collection.

This was the cultural, architectural and political context for the design of the current British Museum, a vast temple inspired in its detail if not its form by the Parthenon and Ionic Erechtheum (both on the Acropolis in Athens), as well as by the Ionic Temple of Dionysus at Teos. The stimulus for what turned out to be a vast building project that would last over a quarter of a century was the gift in 1822 of the King's Library. It was recognised that this acquisition would require its own home in Bloomsbury and Robert Smirke – the eminent designer of a wide range of public buildings – was commissioned in 1823 to design an extension to the existing museum to house the library and a picture gallery. As work on the extension – essentially a long open gallery, of double-height proportion and fitted with most elegant bookcases – reached completion, it became clear that a radical rebuild of the museum could no longer be avoided. The demolition of Montagu House commenced and proceeded in stages. In 1825 Smirke was commissioned to produce a master-plan for the new museum, which in essence took the form of a huge quadrangular court defined by ranges of buildings, with the King's Library forming much of the east range.

The appearance of the museum towards Great Russell Street evolved in odd manner. Its centre is dominated by a vast Grecian portico – the epitome of an antique Temple of the Arts. But Smirke organised his plan somewhat pragmatically because the portico is framed by wings that break forward in a seventeenth-century Baroque style. And all is linked by columns that perch on a podium evoking the sense of a Grecian agora in the heart of the city. The large size of the project meant that Smirke's museum was not completed until the 1850s, by which time the dour and academic brand of the Greek Revival that it embodied was hopelessly out of fashion in an age increasing dominated by the artistic and ethical principles of the Gothic Revival (see pp. 365–9).

The majestic Great Russell Street entrance front to the museum.

Having ascended the outer steps and passed through the southern portico, you are in a noble Grecian entrance hall – recently repainted in bright colours to simulate Smirke's initial scheme, which sought to imitate the bright colour palette of ancient temples. In the court beyond is the circular and domed Reading Room, designed in 1854 by Smirke's younger brother Sydney. This expansive court, once open to the sky and then gradually filled with an ad hoc warren of rooms and corridors serving the

library, was transformed after the British Library moved to St Pancras in 1997. It is once again a single open space, bathed with light beneath a glazed domed roof – designed by Foster + Partners – that wraps in splendid fashion around the Reading Room. It was opened in 2000.

The former King's Library can be entered directly from this court. After the volumes were moved to their new home, this huge gallery, full of outstanding early joinery, was made into a vast cabinet of curiosities – in a sense a taster for the museum as a whole. It's a great success. The corresponding range to the west is stupendous in a different way. The robust and spare architecture of its galleries is now juxtaposed with authentic art, artefacts and sculpture from Assyria, Greece and Egypt.

Today, with the stylistic battles of the nineteenth century a distant memory, it is possible to see the museum for what it truly is. A perhaps unlovely work of architecture, but one that is immensely powerful in its simple and solid logic. Smirke took an emerging building-type – the temple-like, state-owned, public museum – and gave it one of its earliest and most memorable expressions, realised on a huge scale with the help of iron and concrete as well as brick and stone. The museum is, in many ways, a pioneering modern building.

WALK 7

King's Cross
to Barnsbury

The late-Georgian estates

In 1934, the eminent architect and academic Steen Eiler Rasmussen wrote a book called *London: The Unique City*. Rasmussen had grown up in Copenhagen, and had become something of a wunderkind in his native Denmark when he won three national architecture and planning competitions by the age of twenty-one.[1] But his most influential insights only came when he visited London in the late 1920s, and spent several months lecturing, travelling and talking to Britons.

According to Rasmussen, London was unique because it was not the product of absolutist power or of undue state interference or bureaucracy but, instead, was developed in an almost organic manner by private enterprise creating family homes on leasehold estates – yet somehow magically achieved a unifying sense of harmony. It was a city built by private citizens, responding to market forces, and yet – with its handsome squares and noble streets – achieved the virtues of public architecture. In this sense, London was different to the capital cities of the Continent, many planned from above by monarchs:'The commercial city, London, became the antithesis of Paris, the city of absolutism.'

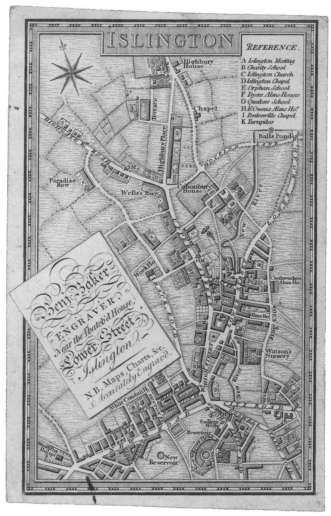

This engraver's trade card of c. 1798–1800 offers a glimpse of Islington just before estate building began in earnest.

The streets that made Rasmussen think like this were, above all, concentrated in the small patch of London around Canonbury, Barnsbury and Bloomsbury. The fact that the generally harmonious and quintessentially civilised portion of London covered by these walks was achieved by a disparate mix of private landlords and speculating builders remains astonishing. The main concern of these men was to build for profit, with the fundamental principles of sound construction and the disciplined hierarchy of uniform urban design imposed only in most informal manner by estate regulations or by a number of London Building Acts, notably that of 1774, which sought to codify house building to achieve sound- and fire-proof construction. A work of sophisticated urban art was created – but almost by accident, and certainly not in response to any authoritarian master-plan. The estates and builders simply got on with the creation of their components of a shared but never declared urban and social vision.

The speculative building system was, in theory, simplicity itself. The estate leased building plots, usually for around eighty years and for a low ground rent, to speculating builders who constructed houses at their own expense (and in conformation with the stipulations of the Building Acts or the estate steward or surveyor) and then sold on the lease – hopefully for a healthy profit – to the first occupier. Slight variations included the possibility of easing the speculator's capital obligations by allowing a 'peppercorn' rent – essentially a rent-free period – for a limited time at the beginning of the lease, and the option for the builder to construct only the shell of a house, leaving the first occupier to finish to suit their own taste and pocket.

In this system, if all went well, the estate had its land developed virtually for no cost to itself, and although ground rents were initially low it took possession of the houses when the first leases fell in. Speculating builders had low ground rents to pay and could, if they sold on their leases or let their houses advantageously, make a handsome profit and continue their speculative enterprises, ideally at an ever-increasing scale. The first occupant acquired a handsome home at a relatively low cost, with a low ground rent. In theory, then, everyone was a winner – although, as we'll see in some of the houses on this walk, it didn't always go to plan.

A good illustration of how, in practice, this worked comes early on our route. In 1815, Thomas Cubitt – a pioneering building contractor, ambitious speculating builder, and architect – took a lease on a large parcel of land owned by the Calthorpe family, in an area that is now to the south-east of King's Cross station, between Gray's Inn Road and King's Cross Road. Despite its proximity to central London, it was still mostly open land. But not for long: in 1814 Lord Calthorpe had obtained an Act of Parliament allowing him to grant building leases on the estate and the first significant beneficiary was Cubitt, who on 1 November 1815 signed agreements to construct extensive offices and workshops for his building business and, immediately to the north, to lay out and build two streets.[2]

These were named Frederick Street (after Lord Calthorpe) and Ampton Street (after an estate in Suffolk associated with the Calthorpe family), which were connected at their west ends by a short terrace along Gray's Inn Road. Construction of the terrace and streets started in 1820, and, although development was gradual, in 1823 Cubitt enlarged his leasehold interest in the estate, allowing him to build the north side of Frederick Street and extend both streets to the east to the estate boundary and to connect them with a short additional street named Ampton Place.[3]

And yet this was not just any old piece of commercial speculation. What's striking is the variety of details and of approaches to the elevations. The houses are almost experimental in the range of their architecture and are the epitome of metropolitan taste on the cusp of change from simple brick-built late-Georgian style – much of which we saw in Walk 5 – to the more ostentatious stucco-clad palatial compositions of the early Victorian period.

Thomas Cubitt was a remarkable man. He was one of a family of builders and by trade a master carpenter, but in 1815 he set up business as a building contractor offering a wide spectrum of services to clients. This was pioneering because, by tradition, Cubitt – as a carpenter – would have subcontracted to other trades. But he offered a one-stop service, which was far more efficient. This changed the London building world forever. As well as a building contractor Cubitt operated as a speculator and as an architect, and on an ever-increasing scale. He built Eaton Square on the Grosvenor family's Belgravia estate, much of Pimlico, and during the 1840s the entrance front of Buckingham Palace and Osborne House on the Isle of Wight for Queen Victoria and Prince Albert.

Thomas Cubitt's work on the Calthorpe estate serves as an excellent introduction to the main quest of this walk: to reveal what made Georgian and early-Victorian London an architecturally exemplary

Sedate architecture enlivened by exquisite detail: Gibson Square, laid out in the 1830s.

city. It offers a case study in sedate and simple architecture that is often enlivened by erudite and exquisite detail, and combined with a sure grasp of the picturesque principles of urban composition. This mastery of space and planning seems to have been intuitive, or based on generations of tradition and trade practice, because often the designers were not architects trained in urban planning but simple (and clearly most able) builders – of whom Cubitt is the great example. Generous squares open off narrow streets, wide straight streets of terraces offer sublime vistas, and these are juxtaposed with bucolic planting, and a variety of house forms – notably terraces and villas of different types and sizes – set within a uniform aesthetic of brick-built architecture. All is rooted in the classical language of design, with only the very occasional dash of Gothic.

The route is an L-shaped affair that starts in the streets around Gray's Inn Road, goes more or less directly east to Myddelton Square and then north – in a pretty direct line – to end in a fanciful loop around Barnsbury Square. It has been chosen not because of the size or family connections of the estates on which these buildings stand, but because they were built upon in the years soon after 1800 in a manner that is, in many ways, the epitome of London's very distinct domestic architecture. In these streets, it is indeed hard to disagree with Rasmussen's assessment of London as a 'unique' and exemplary city.

THE WALK

Our route begins with Cubitt's development of the Calthorpe estate, which lies only a few minutes' walk south-east from King's Cross and St Pancras stations. From the front of King's Cross, walk south along Gray's Inn Road, and within 250 metres on your left (east) is Frederick Street.

It is immediately clear that Cubitt had grand ambitions for the Calthorpe estate. The north side of Frederick Street, constructed between 1823 and 1827, is particularly fine, and reads almost like an advertisement, with Cubitt seeking to demonstrate his talents as an urban designer. The houses are three and four storeys high, most with simple brick elevations above ground floors that are stuccoed and intended to read as podia, as in Roman temples. Others have façades that are fully stuccoed. Some of these are dressed with pilasters with ornate and unusual capitals, combining several Greek Revival motifs and seemingly inspired by details on the Choragic Monument of Thrasyllus of 320 BC, which stands on the west face of the Acropolis in Athens.

These stuccoed and architecturally ornamented elevations are used to organise the terrace of separate houses into a uniform, symmetrical composition so portions could – with a bit of poetic licence and imagination – be viewed as a single urban mansion. This was a familiar concept in London terrace architecture from the early seventeenth century onwards (see the Piazza, Covent Garden, on pp. 493–5) – and Cubitt's Eaton Square from 1827 is a superb and monumental example. But rarely was this urban ideal achieved with such subtle and economic means.

The style of the time was whimsical and often witty. Take the tent-like canopies on the first floor of the stucco houses, which are made of metal

The whimsical 'Trafalgar' balconies on 48–52 Frederick Street, designed to look like canvas awnings.

but were no doubt intended to read as canvas awnings. They were likely painted with broad stripes of dark and light green so that they appeared as tent-like as possible. Such designs are known as 'Trafalgar' balconies, perhaps because they came into fashion around 1805 – or because they were perceived at the time to have something of a jolly, nautical appearance reminiscent of the awnings used to cover the decks of men-of-war. In the same theatrical spirit, the pine-made window sashes on the houses and the front doors were probably grained to look like oak, or even mahogany, the stucco colour washed or 'frescoed' to look like Bath stone, while bronze-green paint was applied to the area railings and to the cast-iron balconies that did not have canopies. Some details might even have been painted to look like ebony. The street, when completed in the late 1820s, would have appeared gay indeed.

Ampton Street is also fascinating. The houses were built between 1820 and 1823, with those at the centre of the south side relatively simple – each only two windows wide, brick-fronted above stuccoed ground floors. To the west is one group faced entirely with stucco, and with only

The simple stuccoed houses on the north side of Ampton Street.

one wide window per floor. But the slightly later houses that survive to the east, also stuccoed, are ornamented with a finely detailed cornice, moulded window surrounds and porches with Doric piers supporting pediments ornamented with stylised honeysuckle motifs. The houses at the west end of the north side are different again: all very plain, with brick above stucco ground floors but with the elevations of the centre four houses stuccoed to create a central feature in the simplest way possible. To the south would once have stood Cubitt's large and state-of-the-art builder's yard, and, although precious little survives, the site now hosts a most agreeable public park called the Calthorpe Project.

These streets speak volumes about Cubitt and the development process in late-Georgian London. Having started a large building business, Cubitt had to keep his workforce employed, so if commissions didn't come to him he had to create work through speculative building – and that is how the Calthorpe estate development got under way. And, of course, speculation was helped if the product was given added value through design. If the design echoed the wayward pulse of fashion then it would initially attract attention and then attract tenants. So Cubitt's fashionably picturesque and erudite design gave his speculation a competitive commercial edge and appealed to discerning custom in a marketplace awash with new housing.

It worked at first but only twenty years after Cubitt built them, these streets would enter a decline. This was in large part due to the arrival of the railways in the area from the 1840s onwards, and the construction from the 1860s of the underground and rail route through and near the east ends of Frederick and Ampton Streets. The process remorselessly transformed the district around King's Cross from a semi-rural retreat with enclaves of salubrious housing to an ever more intensely occupied and industrialised quarter of London, with often dubious lodging houses and hotels and noisome workshops. The cutting is visible from Acton Street, immediately to the north of Frederick Street. A high brick wall now screens it, so it is easy to miss, but look over the wall (you'll need help to do this because it's high and – of course – caution is necessary) and you'll see a deep and cavernous cutting – its sides supported by closely-spaced horizontal cast-iron restraining bars that span over the track. The line leads to Farringdon station, which opened in 1863 as the terminus of the newly completed Metropolitan Railway that formed the initial phase of the world's first passenger-carrying underground railway.

Further along, the tracks lead into a tunnel below the east end of Frederick Street. This is a good example of pragmatic rather than heroic Victorian urban railway engineering: while some sections of the route were tunnelled or left open, most were cut and then covered with a deck, set at street level, which was then built upon. In this way the urban scar was healed and the damage forgotten. The construction of this route entailed the destruction of some of Cubitt's fine houses – only thirty or so years old at the time – which were replaced by new buildings. The most impressive of these second-generation buildings is a fine mid-nineteenth-century Italianate public house named the Carpenter's Arms. Go for a drink and you can feel the trains moving beneath you.

———◆•◆•◆———

Cross King's Cross Road – heading east – and you enter a different estate and a more expansive world, characterised by sustained terraces of simple, repetitive design set amongst – and occasionally within – gardens and plantations of trees. And the terrain is very different, undulating as the ground rises to the east of the course of the now lost – or at least completely invisible – River Fleet, which once flowed along the sites of King's Cross Road and Farringdon Street to the Thames. The estate, which stretches from King's Cross Road in the west to St John Street in the east, was once owned and developed by the New River Company. It is one of London's most interesting.

The New River Company was established by Royal Charter in 1619 with the aim of supplying fresh water to the capital. The water came via an artificial waterway – the New River – that was created between 1604 and 1613 that ran to the City of London, north London and the East End, partly in cuttings and partly by means of aqueducts, principally from the River Lea, Chadwell Spring and Amwell Spring. The river was a complex example of hydraulic engineering. Water flowed the 30-mile route thanks only to gravity, with a fall limited to 5 inches per mile; there was a constant fear that it would gather in quagmires rather than flow as planned to the 'New River Head' reservoir or 'Round Pond'. This consisted of an 'Inner' and an 'Outer' pond and was located on the high ground of Islington, near the site of Sadler's Wells. From here the water could be fed under naturally achieved high pressure to the streets of the lower-lying city. The technical mastermind behind this scheme was Sir Hugh Myddelton, who was also the company's first governor, with a major local landowner Sir John Backhouse being the principal trustee. His family had owned land in Islington that until the Reformation of the 1530s was part of a vast Knights Hospitallers estate – the knights of St John of Jerusalem – and it was Backhouse land, together with land owned by Backhouse heirs the Lloyd family, which was acquired to form most of the New River Company estate.

The estate amassed by the company – with the 'Round Pond' at its heart – was initially used to further its water-supply business, since it was evident that additional reservoirs would ultimately be required as London's population increased in size. Indeed in 1709 the 'Upper Pond' was constructed on what is now the central garden on Claremont Square. In addition the company – from the start a commercial as much as a public-spirited concern – realised that property holdings could generate significant additional income by the satisfying fashion for using the various springs rising in Islington as medical spas.

Sadler's Wells Theatre, with the New River coursing alongside, depicted in 1792.

In this scheme, the New River Company was drawing on a long Islington tradition. Sadler's Wells itself was a former monastic spring – believed to possess medicinal properties – which in 1683 was joined by a theatre or 'Musick House', the second public theatre to be opened in London after the Restoration of 1660. The project was the brainchild of Richard Sadler, who from the start made a point of selling his spring water as hard as his theatrical performances. Such establishments, set in the environs of London where parish restrictions were relaxed and regulations against the running of bawdy houses hard to enforce, soon became centres of London's vast sex industry. Perhaps as a cover for the large numbers of female prostitutes who presumably thronged to the Wells, Sadler insisted that his water was particularly beneficial for the cure of female ailments such as 'fits of the mother, virgin's fever and hypochondriacal distemper'.[4]

Agriculture was the main money-making activity on the company's land, but that income was not enough and by the early eighteenth century it was struggling. In the 1730s it became embroiled in a long legal dispute with the Reverend John Lloyd – the adjoining landowner to the south – who complained that the company's building projects and its leaking supply pipes running below his fields were damaging his estate. Eventually the company was obliged to pay Lloyd £525 in compensation and a perpetual annuity to his estate of £362 10s 0d in return for 55 acres of, presumably, 'damaged' land.[5] This annual payment was a continual burden to company revenues, especially from around 1800, when it went into seemingly terminal decline as a number of newly established water companies further reduced its income.

With revenues from water supply in apparently irreversible freefall, building on the estate became, as the *Survey of London* observes, 'the obvious solution' to the company's woes.[6] The decision to go ahead was reached around 1810, when speculative house building on land to the north and east appeared to be progressing successfully and when the war with Napoleonic France, although far from resolved, was much less financially destabilising than five years earlier. In the summer of 1811 the company's new surveyor – William Chadwell Mylne – was directed to prepare a plan for building 'First Rate' houses on the eastern portion of the estate. Presumably the development was to start here because water-pipe replacement and rationalisation, for which Mylne was also responsible, was not completed in the western portion of the estate, and would not be until 1819.

No plan for the initial estate layout appears to survive, although one would surely have been essential if only to ensure that reorganised water-distribution pipes ran along the routes of proposed streets and avoided potential building plots. However, some contemporary documentation and the estate as eventually developed offer strong hints about the company's intentions. For example Mylne's instruction to prepare plans for the construction of 'First Rate' houses for ground near Sadler's Wells reveals that the estate had high ambitions in 1811. 'First Rate' houses were the best type of terrace houses specified in the 1774 London Building Act. London houses were to be of four 'Rates', with each rate determined by size of ground plan and width of frontage (the number of floors was not significant), and each had to conform to minimum standards (and costs) of construction, floor-to-ceiling heights and volume. The provision of the post-Great Fire 1667 London Building Act, which sought to relate height of house to width and grandeur of street, was relaxed in the 1774 Act but, in practice and to reflect the urban tastes of the time, First and Second

Rate houses were invariably located on wide principal streets and squares, Second and Third Rate houses on secondary streets, and Third and Fourth Rate houses on minor streets.

The strategy underpinning Mylne's plan appears to have been pretty straightforward. A partly commercial street, furnished with groups of shops, was to run as a curvaceous spine through the centre of the estate, connecting at its south end to existing streets and ultimately to the ancient St John Street, while in the north it fed into Pentonville Road. This street, lined with lower Rates of houses, was named Amwell Street, after the location of one of the springs feeding the New River. The area to the west of this north–south spine was to have a large square at its heart – named Myddelton Square after the Company's first governor – that would serve as the location for some of the estate's best houses. Other grand houses were to be located on wide existing thoroughfares like Pentonville Road, and buffered from the road and traffic by gardens and planting. Connecting these First and Second Rate houses were streets lined with smaller houses offering accommodation to less wealthy tenants. This not only ensured that the estate housed a wide social spectrum but also meant that builders had the widest possible range of options on offer when seeking occupants for their speculations. What made good social sense and led to a well-balanced community also made economic sense.

The estate, as built, has only a most informal version of the grid plan that tended to dominate British urban design for most of the eighteenth century. This presumably reflects the triumph of existing field boundaries and pathways over architectural and urban ambition for, no doubt, such existing boundaries provided a convenient and easily comprehensible way to divide the estate into the different plots to be let to different speculation builders. River Street, for example, joins Myddelton Square at a curious angle, which probably follows the diagonal southern boundary of the large Robin Hood's Field that once occupied neighbouring land. Fortunately for the designers, such informal and asymmetrical urban planning was coming into vogue in the early years of the nineteenth century.

The first buildings on the New River Company estate encountered on this walk are among the last constructed during its first phase of development. The short western arm of Great Percy Street leads up

Even the lower-rate New River Estate houses contain erudite detailing – as with this fanlight at 77 Amwell Street.

from King's Cross Road to Percy Circus. Round or oval urban features have always been an oddity in London's development. The first notable example – inspired by French Baroque planning – was Seven Dials, built during the 1690s on Mercers' Company land on the north edge of Covent Garden. More recently, in about 1812, John Nash had conceived a vast circus for the Crown estate as part of his Regent's Park scheme – it ended up as the scaled-down Park Crescent, linking the park to Portland Place. And then there was the long-lost Polygon, a circus of outward-facing semi-detached houses in Somers Town – just north of the Euston Road – built in 1793 and originally rather smart. The speculative builder responsible was Jacob Leroux, who was described by one disappointed client as a 'gentleman with a dastardly speciousness … which a Hyena might envy'.[7] Leroux was probably typical of many of the men who built Georgian London, which makes the artistic excellence of their corporate creation more wonderful and more unlikely in equal measure.

Given this exclusive and curious pedigree, Percy Circus is of considerable interest. On an estate that is in general – in theory if not always in practice – dominated by the right angle and straight vista, the presence of a circus is something of a surprise. And this sense of wonder is enhanced by the fact that Percy Circus was placed on steeply rising land so that you look up to Great Percy Street that leads to the north-east and into the heart of the estate, and down to the short section that leads to the south-west and which forms the foreground to a vista west over King's Cross with Bloomsbury beyond. The picturesque effect of the circus and its prospects is heightened by the tall, luxuriant plane trees that now grow in its centre, giving it the sense of a mini park engulfed in urban sprawl.

The architecture of the circus is, for the estate, also something of an oddity. It was constructed in 1841–3 and its houses are far more Italianate than the earlier ones on the estate. What this means is that the Percy Circus houses are in line with a prevailing fashion of the time for giving classically-inspired architecture a sixteenth-century Italian Renaissance trim. When I first got to know the circus, in about 1970, three of its five segments were more or less intact. Now only two survive. The segment that has gone during the intervening years was, historically and socially if not architecturally, the most interesting because it contained the house in which Vladimir Lenin lodged in 1905, by which time the circus, along with most streets in the area, had become a netherworld of boarding houses and cheap hotels, largely serving the nearby railway termini. The block was replaced in 1972 by a poorly detailed replica, but at least if you squint it more or less blends harmlessly into a general prospect of the circus. And to the north-east stands another expression of the changing fates of the circus, in this case from affluent private households to public-authority flats: Bevin Court, the block of flats with a Y-shaped plan rising behind the circus, is one of the most impressive post-war modernist housing projects in London. It was built from 1952–6 to the designs of Skinner, Bailey & Lubetkin, with Lubetkin being among the more significant continental modernist architects to settle in England before the Second World War.

The route of the walk now leads past Holford House up to the eastern portion of Great Percy Street. This is one of the architectural showpieces of the estate – both for its sustained, almost sublime, scale and bold simplicity, and for its apparent unity. It was planned in 1818, got under way soon after 1820 and was named for Robert Percy Smith – the man who became governor of the New River Company in 1827, by which time

A mini park amid urban sprawl: the view west along
Great Percy Street from Percy Circus.

much of the street was complete (although construction went on until the
early 1840s). For example numbers 21–39 were not built until 1839–43,
but still under W. C. Mylne's control and still, generally, in visual harmony
with the earlier terraces.

The terraces in Great Percy Street, as is common with all the domestic
architecture on the New River Company estate, achieve their grandeur by
the most solemn and economic of means. There are no central pediments
or columns of pilasters; instead all is achieved through proportion,
through the relationship of window to wall, through a studied hierarchy
of window sizes, and by the sparing use of often exquisite details such
as fanlights, front doors, balconies and area railings. This minimalism
is artistically most satisfactory but also makes clear that from the start
economy of construction was a key concern for the estate and for its
builders. Pediments and columns were a luxury that could not be afforded.

Contemplation of the details in the facing terraces in Great Percy

Street is a rewarding and enlightening experience. The houses on the northern side – designed or approved by Mylne – are four storeys high above basement level, but only two windows wide. This means they are Second Rate houses, very similar to the standard Second Rate house illustrated by Peter Nicholson in 1823 in his *New and Improved Practical Builder and Workman's Companion*. But while all is most uniform, if you look closer you can see that these are the product of speculation. Look hard and you will see straight joints in the brick elevations between some of the pairs of houses, which is a pretty sure sign that they were constructed by different speculating builders, working under Mylne's overall control, with access to only enough money to each build pairs or small groups of houses.

On the south side of the street – eighteen houses in two ranges (numbers 28–72) – much is subtly different. This is because it was part of a different estate, overseen by different speculators: the Lloyd Baker estate. Interestingly, the two ranges – built from the late 1820s into the early 1830s – are unlike the rest of the architecture on the estate, which we will see in a moment. The reason is, presumably, the architectural good manners that prevailed in 1820s London. Harmony was more important than dogma or strident self-expression, so for this site the Lloyd Bakers approved a design to conform to the New River Company estate house-style and match the houses opposite. And so, despite the fact that the Lloyd Baker terrace is one storey lower than the New River one opposite, there is an overall sense of visual harmony.

But more telling is the fact that the terrace is more regimented, the houses more strictly repetitive, with the only visual variety coming from the manner in which those at the west end are obliged to step up the hill. The sense of visual unity is emphasised by setting first-floor windows within a blank arcade, with arches that transfer the weight of the wall above the first floor on to the brick piers between the first-floor windows – which in turn allows the windows themselves to be as large as possible. This very distinct motif – used only sparingly in the eighteenth century (see, for example, Michael Searles in Blackheath in the late 1780s, pp. 201–3) and inspired by Roman and Renaissance examples – enjoyed a huge vogue in England during the 1820s, particularly among London builders, as the later phases of this walk will make abundantly clear.

Many of the houses in Great Percy Street were long ago converted to flats so interiors can be disappointing. But the better preserved examples confirm the notion that late-Georgian speculative urban architecture was a 'refined industrial product', as Rasmussen approvingly observed in the 1930s. Details are finely designed but evidently largely mass-produced, creating a sense of general uniformity, and most are – as illustrated by Peter Nicholson's 1823 model designs for Second, Third and Fourth Rate houses – of simple geometric form. Uses within such houses had become pretty standardised by the early nineteenth century, notwithstanding the whims and eccentricities of individual households. The front basement room served as the kitchen, with the rear basement room used for servicing and the location for the water supply. Lavatories were generally located at the rear of the ground floor, with water-flushed 'water closets' generally replacing privies set over cesspits. The ground-floor front room was generally the best dining room. Consequently ground-floor front rooms in these terrace houses are often furnished with a recess for a buffet and possess decorative plasterwork and fire surrounds ornamented with details, such as grapevine motifs, associated with Bacchus and conviviality. The ground-floor rear room could be a breakfast parlour or study, the first-floor front room usually served as drawing room with perhaps a library or bedroom to its rear, with the floors above serving as family bedrooms. Servants would be disposed around the house, sleeping wherever was convenient – including in the kitchen or on landings – and by the 1820s would be summoned by the family by a steelwire-and-spring-operated system of bell.

Turn south from Great Percy Street into Cumberland Gardens and you enter a very different architectural vision. The east side – developed in the late 1820s – marks an edge of the Lloyd Baker estate, around 32 hectares in extent, where building started just a year or two after the New River Company commenced its operations.

The former monastic land acquired in the mid sixteenth century by the Backhouse family passed by inheritance to the Lloyd family, coming into the possession in 1719 of the Reverend John Lloyd – the man who was to enter into prolonged dispute with the New River Company. In the mid eighteenth century the estate passed to Lloyd's daughter who in 1770 married her cousin, the Reverend William Baker. As was the law at the time, Baker took full possession of his wife's inheritance and it was perhaps in recognition of this valuable windfall that he changed his surname to Lloyd Baker. In 1806 Lloyd Baker, with his son Thomas John, started to contemplate the development of their fields – by then used mostly for brick and tile making and as a 'military ground' for archery and for exercise by the local Light Horse Volunteers, with a militia barracked on Gray's Inn Road. As with the trustees of the New River Company, the Lloyd Bakers had observed neighbouring estates being

The pedimented villas along the east side of Cumberland Gardens represent a sharp break with the architecture of the New River Estate.

profitably developed by speculative builders and felt the time was right to act.

An estate plan was produced in 1806 by a speculating builder and surveyor named Henry Leroux, but this proved a false start when Leroux collapsed into bankruptcy in 1809. Perhaps this Leroux was related to the 'dastardly Hyena' of the Polygon; indeed it's possible he was one and the same. His bankruptcy, combined with Napoleon's continuing military successes on the Continent, seems to have sapped the Lloyd Bakers' resolve. Speculation became an ever more uncertain prospect as the nation retrenched for a long-haul war and money was husbanded rather than boldly invested in building. This made the Lloyd Bakers most cautious.[8] So plans went on hold for the duration of the war and it was only in 1818 that things got on the move again when a middle-aged local surveyor named John Booth – a bricklayer's son, in 1821 master of the Drapers' Company and a commissioner of sewers for Holborn and Finsbury – was appointed to make a plan and proposal for developing the estate. Ultimately Booth's suggestion was broadly accepted and, as a stroll down Lloyd Street makes clear, he came up with something more artistically surprising than his conventional trade background might suggest.

Evidently Booth and the family had been looking around and came to the conclusion that the local housing market was awash with plain-fronted and uniform three- and four-storey Second and Third Rate brick-built terraces. Presumably they thought they could attract speculating builders and residential tenants if something different was offered. What they came up was – essentially – a piece of city built to romantically escapist picturesque principles, with rows of pedimented villas: two-storey detached houses of ornamental design, generally linked together by entrance blocks and set, in reasonably informal manner, amongst generous plantations of trees. The escapist aspect was that the speculative villas should appear as idyllic pavilions scanted within a well-leafed and bucolic landscape. The standard villa-type Booth came up with is well illustrated by the street parallel to the east of Cumberland Gardens, Lloyd Street – two storeys high and linked visually into pairs by a shared pediment and connected to adjoining pairs of villas by a screen of Doric piers. Details vary – some houses have ground- and first-floor windows set within arches, as around the corner at Lloyd Baker Street, for example – but the general feel is the same. All are unified by a loyal adherence – in detailing – to Greek classical architecture rather than Roman. This was the fashion of the time, when the Greek Revival was in full swing.

Where did John Booth get the peculiar idea that the estate should be developed as a series of seemingly individual Greek Revival villas? It is hard to say but the usual suggestion is that it was, in fact, the idea of his well-educated surveyor son, William Joseph Booth. He had studied at the Royal Academy School in 1819, then made a Grand Tour to Italy and Greece, and in 1822 exhibited drawings of ancient Greek buildings at the Academy. This explanation seems likely since he clearly had an enthusiasm for Greek architecture, and was already assisting his father by 1819, eventually succeeding him as the estate's surveyor.

The Greek feel continues at the end of Cumberland Gardens, on Lloyd Square – in fact more a blunt-nosed pyramid than a square in shape – whose picturesque informality is accentuated by the tall, thickly planted trees that now ornament its central garden. Although the central urban feature of the estate – where villa construction started in the early 1820s – the square was probably entirely practical in origin: the estate had to be kept open here to allow access to New River Company distribution pipes that interconnected in this area. The view west from the square's junction with Lloyd Street is not to be missed because it shows the estate's characteristic architecture – and sloping setting – to best advantage. The pediments of the square's villas are continued, as if to infinity, by the long row of similar villas on Wharton Street. And beyond is the panorama of west London.

The pseudo-Grecian oddity of the Lloyd Baker estate has ensured that it has been noticed. But the responses have been mixed – ranging from bemused incredulity and patronising contempt to charmed delight. In a sense, it seems, the architecture has proved to be something of a mirror in which different ages have seen a reflection of their own attitudes to the use – or abuse – of history. In 1895 Arthur Machen – the extremely oddball author of niche horror tales – failed to see the charm of the estate, with its double villas 'shaped in a manner to recall the outlines of the Parthenon', and in his 1895 novel *The Three Imposters* dismissed it as 'hideous in the extreme'. But then, of course, Machen was – as his often cringingly horrible stories make clear – more of a Goth than a classicist. The usually penetrating architectural critic, Ian Nairn, also lost his sense of humour when it came to the estate and took a disapproving and puritanical modernist stance in 1966 when he dismissed Lloyd Baker Street as a 'parody of the Greek Revival'.[9] It was left to the architect Hugh Casson – who had been the mastermind behind the architecturally eclectic 1951 Festival of Britain – to see the point of the estate. In 1983 he argued that Lloyd Square was 'one of the nicest squares in London', where the villas stood 'linked arm-in-arm . . . guarding their well-kept simplicity' from the roar of nearby traffic.[10]

———————•◦◆◦•———————

From the south-east corner of Lloyd Square, walk east along Lloyd Baker Street, which soon comes out on Amwell Street. Here the Lloyd Baker and the New River Company estates meet and, as with Great Percy Street, integrate in comfortable and most civilised manner. This border street – almost entirely built on New River Company land – was evidently seen by both estates as the commercial thoroughfare for their respective residents, with shops congregating in its central portion. The evidence of this original use can still be made out and the street remains something of an oasis, with cafés and shops serving its hinterland of houses and flats.

To the south-east of Amwell Street are gardens and a curious collection of early industrial buildings known as the New River Head. This is where the early-seventeenth-century circular 'ponds' – more properly reservoirs – were located and so was, once, the beating heart of the New River Company estate. The main building now is the tall Engine House that once contained a large steam-powered pumping engine, installed in 1767 by the pioneering civil engineer John Smeaton. The object was to improve upon nature and increase the flow of water beyond that achieved by mere gravity. Near the Engine House is the base of the windmill that was constructed in 1708 to pump water into the 'Upper Pond', the site of which is now framed by the terraces of Claremont Square.

Our route is east along River Street, made up of seemingly fairly standard Third or Fourth Rate houses of the 1820s. The increase in scale and architectural ambition at the junction of River Street and Myddelton Square is a typical example of the social and architectural hierarchy of

A 1797 view of the New River Head. Sadler's Wells Theatre is in the distance on the left.

Georgian town planning. As a rule, the practice was to have relatively minor houses, for less affluent tenants, in streets leading to squares, around which the best houses would be located. Also by the 1820s it was usual – as here – to have houses of the same scale and status, and loosely uniform in design, united in the same street rather than – as a hundred years earlier – to mix groups of houses of differing status and design. Essentially, by the 1820s speculative house building was bigger business, with the product more mass-produced and execution more streamlined. So, in the short distance from Amwell Street to Myddelton Square, you pass through three areas that, in the early nineteenth century, would have been subtly but distinctly different in their class or types of occupants.

Myddelton Square is one of the most satisfying of London's late-Georgian squares. Built from 1822–43, it looks intact but is not quite original, since much of the north side (numbers 43–53) was rebuilt in very decent and faithful manner in 1947–8 after wartime bomb damage. The square was intended to be the central architectural set-piece of the estate and the pin-wheel around which its streets revolve. There are a couple of most revealing details to note while you contemplate the square's terraces. Look first at the windows. Until the late eighteenth century it was usual for windows on all levels to align, but soon after 1800 the practice changed when it came to the design of narrow, two-window-wide houses like those around Myddelton Square. Instead the fashion took hold to create one centrally placed and often slightly wider window to light the ground-floor front room. This meant that the front-door opening also had to be pushed to one side so that – contrary to all earlier ideas of sound design – the ground-floor openings did not align with those above.

This design represents a profound change of attitude. In the eighteenth century, the usual practice had been to design the façade to look as good as possible, even if this created awkward interiors – essentially, buildings were designed from the outside in. But by the time of Myddelton Square, the approach had reversed. The ground-floor front room was, in smaller houses, the main room of the home – the dining room or even the best parlour – and so demanded a large window set in the centre of its front elevation. The resulting sense of asymmetry on the outside – reflecting the requirements of function over mere appearance – expresses the principles of the picturesque and even anticipates the spirit of the coming Gothic Revival, both of which rejected forced symmetry in favour of the asymmetry found in nature or that is the simple response to functional requirements. These seemingly simple houses, then, capture the architectural world on the cusp of profound change, with design increasingly inspired by practicality.

Look now to the corners of the square. Two are closed and two are open. A closed corner – where terraces meet at right angles – increases a square's sense of enclosure, exclusivity and separation from the rush and noise of the surrounding city. But designing the right-angular junction between two terraces can be tricky. Here the speculators clearly didn't think about it too much, and seemingly Mylne was in no position to insist on a bit of finesse. Visually the terraces simply abut, with no attempt to design special corner buildings to fully fill the available space, or to modify the design of the end-of-terrace houses. This is made more odd by the fact that, although the terraces are broadly similar, they are of slightly different scales and designs, so that first-floor arcades and adjoining balconies are at varying levels and the rustication at ground level collides in uncomfortable manner. The effect is disconcerting and reveals only too clearly the hand of the speculator, working as fast and cheaply as possible.

The misaligned closed corners at the south-east of Myddelton Square reveal all too clearly the hand of the speculator.

Another curiosity of the square's layout is the narrow passage, flanked by houses of distinct design, in the centre of the south side. This represents a plan gone wrong. It was intended to be a street leading to Sadler's Wells, but for reasons best known to themselves the theatre owners objected to the new street, the building boom of the 1820s deflated and it failed to materialise. The wide gap in the centre of the south side of the square must have been a depressing reminder of failure, but between 1841 and 1842 the estate managed to reduce it to the size of a narrow alley by the construction of the pair of existing houses. Slightly taller than their 1820s neighbours and of different design, the house was built by a New River Company employee named Richard Saywell, who managed to give them the sense of being sentinels, as if guarding entry to a special domain. A charming conceit, of course. The houses guard nothing of value because the alley led only to a service road – now Myddelton Passage – set parallel to the terrace, which now leads only to a bin store.

But perhaps it is not quite correct to claim that this alley led to nothing at all. For over the decades Myddelton Passage – perhaps because of its secluded nature yet proximity to sparkling theatreland – developed a sordid and malevolent character in stark contrast with the respectability of the occupants of the neighbouring square. George Gissing, in his sometimes startling, often lurid and certainly disconcerting 1889 novel *Nether World*, uses Myddelton Passage as the setting for a vicious ambush. The novel is set within the context of London's remorseless and – for Gissing – corrupting poverty and, presumably, when it was being written the passage must have had a sinister reputation. He describes it in dark terms, evoking a sense of tomb-like claustrophobia: it was 'narrow' and set between 'walls seven feet high' over which the branches of yet taller trees loomed. To one side of the passage was the New River Head and to the other 'small gardens behind Myddelton Square'. Within the wall screening the gardens were doors, which 'seemingly never opened', and at night all was illuminated in 'feeble' manner by just a couple of gas lamps.

In his narrative Gissing mentions a policeman trudging along the passage with an 'echoing tread'. This bit of colour is much to the point. Myddelton Passage, quite understandably, seems to have been a place the local police dreaded to walk; in fact, there is evidence to suggest that walking it represented a rite of passage for the local force. Once you had walked its bounds you had something to be proud of. The gloomy garden walls behind Myddelton Square and the tall trees have long gone, but the wall securing the New River Head survives. The wall was built in 1806, and from the mid nineteenth century it became covered in graffiti by policemen, who almost invariably carved only their collar number and a letter representing the Metropolitan Police Division in which they served. Most carved G, for the Finsbury Division based in King's Cross Road.

The one name carved is Robinson. This could be a clue. Perhaps this was a very intimate place of memorial, by police for police, because on 17 October 1888, a Detective Sergeant Robinson of G Division was stabbed while on duty.[11] The stabbing, which took place in nearby St Pancras, took place in the midst of the Jack the Ripper Whitechapel murders. Robinson had a man under surveillance who, for reasons now unclear, was considered a potential suspect. Robinson was in disguise, dressed as a woman and loitering in the street. This was presumably to attract the interest of the suspect, but instead he attracted the interest – or rather suspicions – of two 'cab washers' who challenged his behaviour and strange costume. A fight quickly erupted and Robinson was stabbed. The case went to trial, but because the sergeant's disguise was odd, because he had not shown his warrant card and had perhaps struck the first blow, nothing much came of it – beyond, I imagine, a certain amount of embarrassment and annoyance for G Division. But, because Robinson survived the case with only minor injuries, it raises the tantalising possibility that it was he who engraved his name in Myddelton Passage.

———————◆———————

Soon after it was conceived, Myddelton Square became the spiritual hub of the area, because in 1818 the commissioners for the new Church Building Act suggested that a church be included in this newly envisaged piece of city. The Act offered a pot of £1,000,000 for the creation of new churches, in response to the rapid urbanisation of a number of parishes around Britain – which meant that in some areas there was only one church for hugely expanded populations.

This Act had been passed as part of a national celebration to commemorate the successful conclusion of the Napoleonic Wars. The Tory government of Lord Liverpool deemed it patriotic and Christian to furnish the country with new churches in which the population could thank God for their victory. It was also politically expedient. Social and political unrest increased rapidly after 1815, initially in the wake of the imposition of the Corn Laws that, going against the prevailing notions of free trade, prevented the import of cheap foreign wheat to protect the profits of farmers at the expense of the working population. The government's reaction to unrest was harsh and took shameful form in 1819 with the 'Peterloo Massacre' in Manchester, when yeomanry and regular cavalry were unleashed on a crowd demanding reform of Parliamentary representation. What's more, there was mounting tension due to the prospect of full Roman Catholic emancipation and the increase in Nonconformity.

Building new churches was part of the government's response. These 'Waterloo' churches – as they were soon called – were not just triumphalist expressions of the established religion, but also proclamations of the state's presence and control. The Church Building Commission turned to the government's Board of Works to get the ball rolling and to devise architectural guidelines and models. What this meant was that the Board's three 'attached' or advisory architects were charged with the job of giving

The south side of Myddelton Square, with an alleyway leading to the claustrophobic and ominous Myddelton Passage.

this vision a physical form. Unfortunately, these men – John Nash, John Soane and Robert Smirke – did not get on particularly well, nor did they share architectural or professional convictions. All three had dabbled in whimsical Gothic but were, in essence, classicists, and consequently were outside the growing movement for a return to authentic Gothic design and construction.

There was another problem. While the ambitions for this building campaign were significant, the money to realise it was not. Costs per church were capped at £20,000. So although many were constructed – by 1856 something over 600 around the country following budgetary top-ups – they are often desperate and frugal affairs. The early designs for the Commission – classical or Gothic – have a penny-pinched feel. Quite simply money was lacking for grand or generous gestures, and the churches that were built as a result of the 1818 Act tend to have a gimcrack and etiolated quality, even after 1824 when the Commission's initial budget was increased.

Myddelton Square makes an interesting case study. It was agreed by the estate's trustees and the Commission that the centre of the then proposed square would include a church and churchyard, as well as an ornamental garden intended for use by residents. The key conditions that the New River Company trustees imposed on the commissioners was that the churchyard be enclosed with railings and that burials would not take place within it. They further requested that Mylne himself design the church, and the Commission agreed, merely stipulating that it was 'of a plain Gothic character'.

In 1822 Mylne got to work on St Mark's – as the church was named – and he must have been somewhat challenged. He had to provide a building that would ornament the new square and accommodate 2,000 people with, in this case, only £15,000 from the Commission to spend. And in addition, he was probably not too sure what the Gothic style involved. At the time of building, little solid research had been undertaken into authentic Gothic, and only in 1812 had Thomas Rickman identified the structural and decorative development of English Gothic architecture – through three distinct stages from the early twelfth to the sixteenth century, which he termed Early English, Decorated and Perpendicular. Architects of Mylne's generation had been trained and had worked in the classical tradition and to them Gothic appeared to be a generally unlearned style; they were blissfully unaware or unconcerned with its governing structural innovations and their profound implications for building.

The best that Mylne and his late-Georgian generation could do was to pluck their Gothic designs from existing examples and compose for dramatic and picturesque effect. And, in many respects, Mylne was surprisingly successful. Construction started in 1825 and it is evident that much of his thought and money was spent on the tower, which closed the vista into the square along Inglebert Street from busy Amwell Street and was clearly intended to be something of a landmark in, and ornament for, the estate. It is a fine piece of work. It's tall, clad in Bath stone, and reasonably correct and consistent in its Perpendicular detailing that, as the *Survey of London* points out, appears to be based on prototypes in Gloucester and Somerset, where Mylne had worked as a young man. With its Bath stone and Gothic detailing, the 28-metre tower stands in pleasing contrast with the brick-built classicism of the surrounding terraces. It's only when the side elevations are discovered that one's heart sinks a little. The body of the church is brick-built in an almost industrial manner, with a nod to Gothic in its puny supportive buttresses and pointed windows. It is the style of ignorant pasteboard Gothic that the movement's greatest evangelist, A. W. N. Pugin (see pp. 367–9), would rail against only a few years after the church was completed in 1827.

———•◆•———

Cross Myddelton Square and now walk north along Mylne Street, which leads to the next, and indeed in some respects the best, square of the estate. Claremont Square is, like Myddelton Square, a fascinating study of diversity – some intended and some the result of the exigencies of the speculative building system – within an overall sense of harmonious uniformity.

The west side was built first – between 1815 and 1824 – and looked out over the 'Upper Pond' of the New River Company. Since the terrace here arrived before the square was set out (or perhaps even conceived), it was named Myddelton Terrace and built as an adjunct to the already existing Pentonville Road. Evidently Mylne and the New River Company trustees intended this terrace to function as a model for later developments and it introduced a number of ideas that were to become the norm – notably stuccoed and rusticated ground floors, first-floor blank arcading, first-floor cast-iron balconies, and arched front-door openings fitted with fanlights and framed by quadrant columns with Grecian Doric flutes.

This was already becoming the standard vocabulary for house building in London, but nevertheless these dwellings on the west side of Claremont Square are an advanced and fashionable model for 1815 that was meant to ensure that the estate was developed with some visual cohesion. The apparent uniformity of the terrace conceals the fact that it was built by a dozen speculators over a period of nearly ten years. The twelve houses to the north (from the demolished numbers 1 and 1a to 11) came first, from 1815. By 1820, Myddelton Terrace was extended to the south, after it was decided to create a square at this location – organised

Claremont Square. The taller house was built as the home of John Scott, the archly respectable developer who embezzled £10,000 of parish funds.

around the 'pond'. Numbers 12 to 17 were added between 1820 and 1824, and a straight joint between 11 and 12 shows where work stopped for five years.

The penultimate house in the terrace (number 16) has slightly higher floor levels than its neighbours, is ever so slightly wider and has an extra storey added. Its grandeur is owed to the fact that it was built and occupied by one of the estate's more important speculators. John Scott was a brick maker by trade who, by 1821, when he built his house, had made and sold over 3 million bricks on the estate. Scott lived in his grand house for over a decade, becoming, according to an 1834 newspaper report, 'one of the most opulent and respectable men in the parish'.[12] In that year, however, his world fell apart. It was revealed that for no less than fourteen years he had used his apparent wealth and high standing as a means to gain trust and embezzle £10,000 of parish funds. This was a truly colossal sum, more than enough to have built one whole side of Claremont Square.[13] Clearly, by the end, Scott was concerned that his scheme would be discovered: he made his will in May 1833, presumably anticipating his imminent fall and possible execution, and a copy survives in the National Archives.[14]

The east side of Claremont Square got under way in 1823, and the south side was built between 1826 and 1829, completing the charming three-sided square looking out on to the 'Upper Pond'. Today, though, no such pond exists. In 1855 it was transformed into a roofed reservoir, which now takes the external form of a large and stunted grassy mound rising in an almost sinister manner in the midst of the terraces. Internally the reservoir is a masterpiece of mid-Victorian brick-vaulted engineered architecture of sublime scale. It's like a dream of fabled catacombs of ancient Rome.

Our route is north, to Pentonville Road. The road was created by an Act of Parliament of 1756 that envisaged a wide new road around the north edge of London, from Paddington in the west to St John Street in the east, for the use of drovers taking cattle and sheep to Smithfield meat market. The idea was to protect the smart residential areas expanding in Marylebone from the dirt, smell and congestion that vast herds of livestock caused and to keep Oxford Street open for coach traffic and promenaders frequenting its shops and places of pleasure and resort. The New Road, to be at least 12 metres wide with no buildings within 15 metres of its edges, was administered by turnpike trusts which recouped costs by charging a toll. This early bypass, set just beyond the north edge of west and central London in the mid eighteenth century, was constructed in stages, with the east portion (now named City Road), extending beyond the junction with St John Street to Moorgate, not being completed until the 1760s. It was only in 1857 that the Islington section of the New Road was renamed Pentonville Road, after Henry Penton, the local landowner who developed much of this land.

The terrace that survives to the east of Claremont Square is one of the best-preserved examples of the domestic architecture that initially rose along the New Road. The houses are large and well detailed, revealing that the site along the new thoroughfare was regarded as prime. Houses here would be light and airy, enjoy generous prospects over London and its environs from this high ground, and the sight of drovers and their beasts

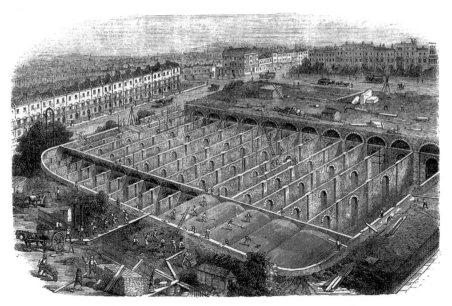

The Upper Pond in the midst of its transformation into a reservoir in 1856.

– kept at a distance – was obviously not, in these open circumstances, regarded as a problem. The expansive front gardens, a response to the Act's requirement to set buildings back 15 metres from the edge of the new road, would once have been a standard feature of the houses lining its edge. The road must have, at first, been delightful, with the country to the north, the city to the south, and the thoroughfare itself providing a fine and animated prospect.

—•◆•—

The Pentonville Road forms the north boundary of the New River Company estate and when you cross it you enter a noticeably different world. Gone is the measured, if often compromised, hierarchal order that you will have experienced from the start of this walk from Frederick and Ampton Streets off the Gray's Inn Road. Now the feel becomes more organic, more varied and less planned – indeed more ancient. In part this is because the essential urban grain is the western hinterland of the old village of Islington centred on Islington High Street and Upper Street. The village, until the seventeenth century known as Isledon, is pre-Norman in origin, with Upper Street, and its northern continuation, Essex Road, probably being Roman.

But there is another reason for the change in atmosphere. For the estates north of Pentonville Road were built in a rather different manner to the New River Company and Lloyd Baker estates. The land here was owned and developed by a larger number of smaller estates – or by their lessees – than south of the Pentonville Road. The result is that, while the houses are evidently of similar date, ambition and detail, all is more informal and more irregular. And there is more experimentation with different house forms than on the New River Company estate.

The first of the smaller estates we visit is the Cloudesley estate. Walk north from Pentonville Road along Baron Street, and you come to a delightful street market, Chapel Street Market – one of only a handful of the old street markets surviving in London that still feel authentic. The buildings forming the backdrop to the market are a mixed bag, and their garish shopfronts and alteration mean you have to work hard, but when you get your eye in it's like unlocking the secrets of Georgian London. Most of the houses – certainly on the north side – are eighteenth century, and some are very good indeed. The long irregular terrace at numbers 9 to 23 (continuous) is formed almost entirely by Georgian houses of different dates and mainly of individual design, but most earlier than 1800. Among the best are numbers 15, 16 and 17 – the latter being a tall pair with a neoclassical plaque set at its centre (the plaque seems to show a draped

Chapel Street Market is overlooked by Georgian houses.

maiden, carrying a cornucopia, but who unfortunately has lost her head). Number 19 is the best of all. It has semicircular arched first-floor windows, a handsome and usual feature, and must date from around 1790. Its rear elevation (easily seen from the street to the north) has a lovely, bulbous, full-height bay, with three windows per floor wrapping around its ample curve. These would have served drawing rooms and bedrooms and once have offered spectacular views over the countryside and gardens lying to the north.

Continue north a short distance along White Conduit Street to Tolpuddle Street, then north along Cloudesley Road. The origin of the estate development of this area north of the Pentonville Road goes back to January 1517 with the will of Islington resident Richard Cloudesley, which dictated that 14 acres of land, 'called the Stony Fields', should be used to fund religious and charitable bequests. This action was – no doubt – intended as much for the good of Cloudesley's soul as for the living who would benefit from it. He was, as was the practice of all wise and affluent Christians at the time, laying up his treasure in heaven to speed him through the pains of purgatory. This legacy became the Cloudesley estate and charity.

The land Cloudesley left, to be administered by the parish of St Mary Islington, consisted of two large fields, in an area called White Conduit Fields. These fields had long been cow pastures because, for centuries, what is now Liverpool Road was a drovers' track, known as the 'Back Road'. The cattle and sheep herded along this track would be left to recover from their journeys and fatten up on the land west of Islington village before being driven down to Smithfield for sale and slaughter. In the early nineteenth century, when increasing land values and the demand for housing made the transformation of these fields into streets unstoppable, the presence of the past was enshrined in a street layout that largely followed field- and land-ownership boundaries and the routes of ancient pathways. The boundaries of Cloudesley's fields, and of his land ownership, are now marked (clockwise from the south) by Cloudesley Place, Cloudesley Road, Richmond Avenue (the north boundary) and Liverpool Road – the old 'Back Road', given its new name in honour of Lord Liverpool who became prime minister in 1812.[15]

Cloudesley Road, especially north of the junction with Cloudesley Place, is sensational, with its sustained vista of tall 1820s terraces. Although the architectural language – stucco ground floor, arched doors with delicate fanlights, and cast-iron balconies – is the same as the New River Company estate, the feel is very different. This is not least because many houses here have small front gardens, giving a more rural feel. The road bends slightly and so the vista of the marching terraces and leaping arcades avoids monotony and gains some mystery. As the architectural prospect gradually disappears out of view, it seems it could go on forever. The sublime personified.

To realise the potential value of the two fields forming the 'Stony Fields' or Stonefield estate, the trustees of the Cloudesley's charity and the parish vestry that owned the land gained an Act of Parliament in June 1811 to permit development. They resolved to 'let' the fields 'for the purpose of building' and with the money made 'ease the inhabitants of the rates'.[16] Nothing happened immediately, but in 1817–18 the first parcels of land were let to the speculating builders Richard Chapman and John Emmett. Chapman was to go on to build the monumental south side of Claremont Square, and the proximity of the two estates and the overlap in builders working upon them explains why the Myddelton Terrace model development of 1815 – with its stuccoed ground floor and first-floor blank arcades – perhaps also served as the prototype for the development of the Cloudesley estate. Perhaps the trustees thought visual unity with the New River Company would be commercially advantageous, but more likely Myddelton Terrace – for a short while standing in splendid isolation on the fields south of the New Road – was a convenient reference point. Builders wanting to work on the Cloudesley estate could simply be referred to this terrace and told to follow its pattern. Such rule-of-thumb working practice was typical of the way in which Georgian London was made.

Cloudesley Street, with its two-strong linked villas set in gardens, runs north of the more urban Cloudesley Place. It leads to Cloudesley Square, which is the architectural jewel at the heart of this small estate. Whoever it was – and it remains uncertain – who laid out the elongated oblong that is the Stonefield estate, it must be said that they got it right. The layout is simple and strikes a good balance between the creation of

Number 34 forms half of the east side of Cloudesley Square.

a large number of building plots and some sense of architectural show
and theatre. The oblong is defined by four streets and is crossed by four
streets and where they meet in the centre of the estate is Cloudesley
Square. Cloudesley Street runs into the square from the south and its axis
is continued north from the square as Stonefield Street. The pair of much
shorter east–west streets also share the same axis and, given their brevity,
are both simply named Cloudesley Square.

The first thing that must be observed about Cloudesley Square is that,
as with Myddelton Square, the Church Building Commission contrived,
in collaboration with the parish and the estate, to squeeze a large new
church within the garden at the centre. The church was started in 1826 –
the square had probably been laid out a year or so before, and the architect
was Charles Barry. At that point in his career Barry was a decided classicist.
From 1834 he became the architect of the earliest major Gothic Revival
building in nineteenth-century Britain – the Palace of Westminster (see

pp. 297–303). But in 1826, and for the coming decade or so, his significant buildings were classical, either Greek-inspired or Italian Renaissance in spirit, notably the Manchester City Art Gallery of 1824, and the Travellers Club of 1826–31 and the Reform Club of 1837, both in St James's. But for low-budget parish churches for the Church Building Commission, Barry developed a somewhat thin and not particularly archaeologically correct Gothic style. Being generous, the model for the Cloudesley Square church might have been King's College Chapel in Cambridge. But the main building material is brick not stone and details are spare indeed.

Construction of the square itself began in the mid 1820s, largely under the control of Emmett and Chapman. It follows the standard vocabulary of the time, but, as usual, there is much pleasing variety in details – notably in the ironwork and fanlights – which make it clear that many builders and tradesmen were involved. These probably included not just Emmett and Chapman and builders taking subleases from them, but also tradesmen completing the carcasses of houses raised by speculators that had gone bankrupt or had to sell their interests to raise money quickly for other projects.

From Cloudesley Square walk east, and cross the old drovers' road of Liverpool Street. Take the east–west road a few metres to the north, Theberton Street. You are now on another small estate, this one created by Thomas Milner Gibson when in the early 1820s he leased the land from William Tufnell, then the 'Lord' of Barnsbury Manor. Its centrepiece – the remarkable Milner Square, built two years into Queen Victoria's reign – represents the magisterial end point of late-Georgian architecture.

Gibson was not a traditional landlord developing his inherited ancestral land: he was a leasehold landlord and in it mainly for the money. His fortune came from sugar plantations in Trinidad, and appears to have been built up by his father while serving as an infantry officer on the island.[17] This was, of course, money earned from a slave-based economy and, as slavery came to an end in the British empire (the slave trade had been outlawed in 1807 and slavery itself was banned in 1833), Gibson appears to have resolved to diversify his commercial interests and invest money in other enterprises – including speculative house construction in London. He also became an active and successful politician, supporting free trade, being elected as a Liberal MP in 1841 and from 1846–8

The final destination of late-Georgian architecture: the sublime repetition of Milner Square.

serving as Vice President of the Board of Trade in Lord John Russell's administration.

Milner Gibson's leasehold estate was laid out in 1823, with building starting in Theberton Street, named after the family seat in Suffolk, in the late 1820s, and Gibson Square itself, to the north, constructed during most of the 1830s. The architect responsible was Francis Edwards, who was one of Sir John Soane's star pupils in the first decade of the nineteenth century. Edwards seemed to be set to achieve great things – he had the talent, the education, the connections – and vast opportunities were on the horizon for bright young architects in late-Georgian London. But it didn't happen. Edwards designed one Church Building Commission's church – rather better than most, the large neoclassical St John's Hoxton – and laid out and designed many of the early buildings on Milner Gibson's estate. And that is almost it. He got involved with the brewer Thomas Godington for whom he completed Wellington Square, Chelsea and the Lion Brewery, Lambeth, and then, seemingly, something went wrong. Probably drink, as was often the case with Georgian architects.

So how do Edwards's Theberton Street and Gibson Square houses rate? The most obvious point is that these developments were more architecturally ambitious than the terraces and square designs you have seen so far on this walk. Milner Gibson and Edwards favoured not only the usual sedate classicism and architectural uniformity but also palace-fronted designs in which numerous terrace houses were organised to create single palatial compositions. On three of its sides, for example, the three end houses are dressed with two-storey Doric pilasters and there is a central cornice to make them read as a particularly grand single composition. Clearly Milner Gibson and his architect were attempting to achieve an estate architecture ratcheted up a few notches in comparison with developments taking place on neighbouring estates, presumably with the aim of attracting a more elevated and affluent class of tenants.

From Gibson Square move north along Milner Place into Milner Square. The design dates to 1839 (two years after Victoria's coronation), and was produced by Robert Roumieu and Alexander Gough. They were a most interesting choice. In the late 1860s, they would produce one of the nation's strangest examples of Gothic Revival architecture, 33–35 Eastcheap in the City of London. That building breaks most of the rules of Gothic design and construction to achieve a sort of super-gothic: it topples forward, strewn with pointed arches and adorned with Gothic detail so that it almost seems to leer and confront the passer-by. It is a Gothic nightmare more than a dream. And some of this strange and inventive quality – the distortion of standard architectural elements to achieve a surprising and emotive effect – was anticipated by Milner Square. Here the architectural language is classical not Gothic, but the design approach is comparable – for although the architectural language is familiar, the way it is spoken is almost alien. Broadly, the four-storey houses have the

Pilasters cluster together at the corners of Milner Square, creating a sense of restless movement.

usual stucco-rendered ground floor with one wide window and front door. The first- and second-floor windows above are divided by sections of brick wall that are most curiously detailed and that, with the blinking of an eye, can be seen in two different ways. First they appear framed by elongated pilasters at the edges of the windows. But look again and they can read as a giant order of broad pilasters between which tiers of windows are set. It is all very clever, and highly theatrical.

Most memorable are the square's corners. Those formed where the different sides of the square meet at right angles are all closed, which creates a powerful sense of enclosure, and separation from the wider world. Those corners formed by the two roads entering the square – from the north and from the south – are also highly significant. They are characterised by generous areas of wall and by pilasters that cluster together to give a feeling of restless movement, while stucco capitals and entablatures break backwards and forward in what seems an exaggerated manner.

Despite its sophisticated architecture, Milner Square soon slid down the social scale so that by the late nineteenth century houses had become multi-occupied and decayed. And there were mutilations – notably porches were removed. In recent years, however, the square has been repaired, to serve almost entirely as flats for a wide social mix of tenants, and on sunny days it now sparkles almost as new. There is a strange disconnection between the square's flat-dwellers and its fantastical architectural aspirations.

Overall, though, Milner Square remains a brilliant demonstration of the way in which the classical language of architecture possesses – at least potentially – a powerful and abstract sculptural quality. This is architecture of the most active kind. It surely never occurred to the architects that their role was simply to create a pleasing and neutral backdrop for the theatre of daily life. In their vision of city living, architecture plays the lead role and sets the tone. In a sense, then, the square represents the destination that Georgian urban domestic architecture had been heading for the previous sixty years or so. In its uniformity, in its minimal use of the classical orders of architecture, in the dramatic play of light and shade and the sublime repetition on a large scale, Milner Square is a late-Georgian (or early-Victorian) architect's dream.

———————◆◦●◦◆———————

The final portion of our walk takes us north-west, to a more incongruous – indeed bizarre – manifestation of early-nineteenth-century speculation. Barnsbury Square is the only square on this walk that is, in part, an expression of an ancient past – and as a result it has a form quite unlike any other in this part of London.

To reach it, leave Milner Square by its north side, which comes out on Barnsbury Street, and head west – crossing back over Liverpool Road – until you come to the Drapers Arms on your right (north). This is a fine and somewhat monumental public house of c. 1839. It dominates the scene in a most satisfactory way, with its tall first-floor windows and grand Doric pilasters. The name refers to the Drapers' Company, who built the square to your left (south). Named Lonsdale Square, it is an oddity and reflects a fleeting moment in taste, in the late 1830s and 1840s, when there was a vogue for houses designed in an approximation of the early-sixteenth-century Tudor Gothic style. What this meant, as in this design by R. C. Carpenter, were lots of spiky gables and bays, plenty of four-centred arches, and a faint asymmetry of composition. The general effect is indeed picturesque – especially when the silhouette of the terraces is seen from the square's leafy garden. But this attempt to apply the artistic principles of the early phase of the Gothic Revival to domestic terraces is curious rather than convincing. The fact is that the Tudor Gothic, derived largely from country-house architecture or institutional buildings, sits somewhat uncomfortably within the setting of a London square. The style did not really take root in the early-Victorian house-building market and is compromised by the fact that Gothic, even of the simplified late-Tudor sort, is really too individual and rich in hand-crafted detail to be successfully mass-produced for speculative houses.

Continue west along Barnsbury Street to Thornhill Road. The road name refers to an estate a little to the west, planned by George Thornhill from 1808 – an early date for the area – and designed in part by Joseph Kay, who we last met as the man who redesigned the centre of Greenwich (see pp. 109–110). Most notable is the church in Thornhill Square, designed in 1852 by Francis Newman and John Johnson in the 'Middle-pointed' or 'Decorated' Gothic style of the late thirteenth century. It is, in the words of *The Buildings of England,* 'like a medieval village church transported'[18] – not just a romantic evocation of the past but a scholarly and authentic essay in Gothic design and construction, with plenty of external buttresses, gabled transepts and apparent chantry chapels, and a buttressed tower with a very handsome stone spire.

But our route is to the north, along Thornhill Road, to one of the great oddities of this walk – and indeed one of the most bizarre squares in London. Barnsbury Square is best approached from the west: so turn to the west on to Lofting Road, and after about 200 metres head north up Barnsbury Terrace. On the west side of Barnsbury Terrace is a pair of large, stuccoed houses of the 1840s, with ornate classical decoration. Barnsbury Terrace is modest and narrow and these palatial buildings make little sense until you realise that they were designed to act as a pleasing view-stopper from Barnsbury Square, which lies immediately to the east.

Barnsbury was once a large medieval manor – owned by the Berners family since the Norman Conquest – and the moated manor farm once

One of the stucco-clad villas on Mountfort Crescent.

stood on what is now the west side of Barnsbury Square. This no doubt partly explains the square's extraordinary, indeed unprecedented, form. Its west side is dominated by a pair of houses that are designed to look like one grand villa. They were probably built in 1834 by William Whowell, who was then the most active developer on what is known as the Bishop's estate. To the north of this villa is an uncompromisingly modernist house, white with lots of glass, which has the virtue of being honest – almost brutally so – in its architectural aspirations and allegiances. But, that said, it does rather break the spell of this strange early-nineteenth-century leafy enclave, and one can't help but wish that the creator of the building could not have been persuaded to express his honesty elsewhere.

But the highlight of the square are the closes to the north and south of its west side. Each contains early-nineteenth-century houses arranged, amidst much planting, around a circular road and garden. They are what give Barnsbury Square such individuality. The close to the north, Mountfort Crescent, is framed by semi-detached pairs of stucco-clad villas of the 1830s and 1840s, most of which sport charmingly bulbous bows. That to the south, Mountfort Terrace, is a trifle more damaged and down-at-heel but it does possess an elegant Italianate terrace, also of the 1840s.

The names of both refer to the ancient manor farm, Mountfort, which was acquired in the early nineteenth century by William Tufnell, who started the process of leasing manor land to a variety of speculative builders, including Whowell. The Tufnells, a large and well-connected landowning dynasty, are most significant in the story of the nineteenth-century development of north London. Tufnell's uncle, also named William Tufnell, was granted the manor of Barnsbury in 1753 by his father-in-law Sir William Halton; it spread far and included land to the west of the Holloway Road, which was to be developed from the mid 1840s into the 1880s when this portion became known as Tufnell Park. This was where the manor house was located, standing approximately on the site of the Odeon on Holloway Road. Still standing on Tufnell Park Road, running west from Holloway Road, is a pair of gate piers that look rather grand and now hopelessly at a loss with their surroundings. They are said to mark one of the points of entry to the grounds in which the manor house stood – entirely possible, although the piers look nineteenth century rather than eighteenth century in origin, so perhaps they were rebuilt as a kind of memorial to the lost manor.

As you leave Barnsbury Square – heading north-east if you want to get the Tube from Highbury and Islington, or west if you are looking for a train from Caledonian Road and Barnsbury – take a moment to ponder what its story says about early-nineteenth-century London. Its stucco-clad villas represent a charming high point of early-nineteenth-century style, built by the speculative developers who had been transforming north London over the previous half-century. And yet, even here, the medieval past is present – combining to create a picturesque, a sort of Eden marooned in the Regency suburbs, that is unlike any other in the capital.

The Palace of Westminster

To many people the Palace of Westminster lives more powerfully in the imagination than in the humdrum of reality. The palace is now hedged around by heavy traffic and an increasingly baffling and alarming array of security devices, the most obvious of which are the layers of concrete barriers at the west end around the Victoria Tower.

But within all this is one of the most historically important and architecturally bewitching set of buildings in the British Isles – as beautiful as it is fundamental to the sense of the nation's pride and identity. Within the tower at the north end – now known as the Elizabeth Tower – is the mighty bell named Big Ben. Along with its fellows, since the mid nineteenth century it has been the very voice of Britain in times of stress. When in 1940 the United Kingdom, its Empire and Commonwealth stood united but alone against Nazi Germany and its allies, these bells became the chimes of freedom – ringing out from clandestine radios around Europe bringing hope to conquered, occupied and beleaguered nations. And below the tower, within the walls of the palace, is the crucible of Parliamentary democracy: the chamber of the House of Commons.

The physical character of this chamber has evolved in pragmatic manner through the centuries, as has its companion chamber serving the House of Lords. Their form has given this mother of Parliaments a most distinct character that has not only influenced its function and the dynamics of the debate held within, but have also provided a model for parliaments throughout the world. Parliamentary democracy can only work efficiently and effectively – indeed arguably can only work at all – when individual members of Parliament unite within parties and when the party works in a unified manner to gain majorities when legislation is voted upon. If majorities cannot be gained in consistent manner – usually through the party forming the government – then laws cannot be passed and chaos reigns. But government utilising the party system is only acceptable within the ideals of democracy when there is an opportunity for vigorous, visible and testing debate. This debate can be time-consuming and bruising. At its worst, it merely follows and confirms party ideologies, but it can also bring with it the safety net of checks and balances.

And, almost by chance, the Palace of Westminster has provided the ideal physical forum – almost the theatre – within which this debate can take place and flourish. It has become a demonstration of democracy in action. The system has its flaws, but over the centuries it has worked more often than it has not. More to the point, it is a system that has accommodated reforms so massive that, in many essential ways, the system of democracy now enshrined by the Commons Chamber is quite different to the system in place when the current chamber opened for business in May 1852.

Traditionally, suffrage in Britain was limited to those with wealth and property – in crude terms, to those with a vested interest in the management of the country. Even the famed Parliamentary Reform Act of 1832, which extended the vote to more people, did not extend it very far. The electorate increased by 60 per cent after 1832 to around 650,000 people, but that was still a small percentage of the population of around 23.9 million. Women were still excluded and men still had to own property worth at least £10 to qualify – so the working class remained disenfranchised.

It was this exclusion of a huge number of able and socially motivated men from the means of expressing their political preferences and opinions that led, from 1838, to the Chartist movement. The Chartists argued that suffrage should be extended to all men aged twenty-one or over, provided they were of sound mind and not undergoing punishment for crime; all property requirements were to be abolished. The Chartists failed to win their fight but their ideas took hold and gradually things did change

An early-twentieth-century photograph captures the House of Commons chamber before it was bombed during the Blitz.

through further Acts of Reform. But it was not until 1918 that all men aged over twenty-one could vote and, for the first time, women, though only when aged over thirty if they met property-ownership specifications. It was only in 1928 that women got the vote on equal terms with men. So when the chamber in the House of Commons first came into use in 1852 very few people could vote, and the landed interest of the nation still dominated Commons business. The political heart of the Palace of Westminster – the chamber of the House of Commons – has changed significantly, if perhaps not fundamentally, in its function.

In its form, however, it has changed very little. After the chamber was seriously damaged by bombing during the Second World War, the decision was taken immediately to rebuild it, largely as a replica of its former self. This was, of course, highly symbolic. The expression of continuity was important because it bolstered stability – even when great change had palpably taken place – and the organisation of the chamber, with parties confronting each other in adversarial fashion, was seen as fundamental to the British brand of Parliamentary democracy. The chamber of the House of Commons was an arena for politicians and for the cut and thrust of sometimes brutal and bruising confrontational debate, and not a place intended for cosseted statesmen to chatter in almost diplomatic dignity.

The story of the form of the debating chamber is central to the story of the Palace of Westminster. And it is, in its way, emblematic of the wider story of the palace. The tale starts in the mid eleventh century, when King Edward the Confessor built a palace on the Thames-side marshes of Thorney Island and at the same time rebuilt the late-tenth-century Benedictine Abbey of St Peter's. This larger abbey became known as the west minster – that is the minster of the west of the City of London – and the name transferred to the area. King Edward's palace, because of its location on the river near the City, soon became one of the monarchy's principal and permanent places of residence.

The Normans, after their conquest of 1066, embellished the palace, with William II adding the stupendous Great Hall in 1097. It was a heroic display of power and prestige: measuring 73 by 20 metres it was one of the largest halls in Europe, and far too large for practical daily use, so smaller halls had to be built nearby to allow the monarch to live and eat in relative comfort. The hall was also, in its width, beyond the technical abilities of the age to cover in a single span. It is still not known how it was roofed in the eleventh century, and no evidence of an internal colonnade, which would have supported the span, has been found. The existing hammer-beam roof, an astonishing display of brilliant and inventive engineering, was added in 1393 by Richard II, whose white hart emblem adorns the roof and interior. The work was undertaken by the king's master mason Henry Yevele and the master carpenter Hugh Herland. These men were true and great structural engineers. The scale of the roof was unprecedented in northern Europe. It is strong, and it is stunningly beautiful: appropriate because the room was a symbol of kingship and of just and wise rule. The Norman *Curia Regis* – or Royal Council – had met in the hall and was, in certain ways, a predecessor of Parliament.

The other structure that is central to the history of Parliament is the Royal Chapel of St Stephen. Essentially this was a large and lofty building of ornate Gothic form, constructed in the late thirteenth century and replacing an early thirteenth century chapel. It was not finally completed until 1297 during the reign of Edward I. The chapel was for the use of the Royal family, but incorporated a lower (or undercroft) chapel – also ornate – for the use of the wider Royal Household. The idea for the building is said to have come from Henry III, who in 1248 was present in Paris for the inauguration of the Sainte-Chapelle. This magnificent jewel-like building, alive with light that floods in through huge windows, was evidently the inspiration for St Stephen's. Because St Stephen's was a chapel not a church, and because there was no need to accommodate parishioners, seating within it was arranged as in the chancel or choir of a church or in a college chapel. The congregation sat in tiers of stalls set against the north and south walls, facing each other across a central sacred space, with the altar and priests at the east end. There was a screen located towards the west end of the chapel, against which, no doubt, the monarch's throne was set to face the altar. As in the late-eleventh-century Chapel of St John in the White Tower (see p. 30), this organisation probably symbolised the temporal world of the monarchy in balance and harmony with the sacred world represented by the altar and clerics.

In Tudor times the function of this unusual structure would change dramatically. This was a period of great significance for Westminster. Early in his reign, Henry VIII made much use of the palace, embellishing it after a serious fire in 1512 and incorporating it into his scheme to create a vast royal quarter along the Thames, from Westminster up to Charing Cross and the Strand. This plan involved the acquisition in 1530 of the disgraced Cardinal Wolsey's grandiose York Place, which became Whitehall Palace. Henry's embellishments at the Palace of Westminster, meanwhile, included the creation in 1526–9 of the exquisite Cloister Court, near St Stephen's chapel, in a late-Gothic style incorporating beautiful fan-vaulting in the cloister walk.

Upon Henry VIII's death in 1547, the role of the chapel was transformed. The Palace of Westminster ceased to be a royal residence and Edward VI – more fervently Protestant than his father – approved the 1547 Abolition of Chantries Act, which de-sanctified St Stephen's. The young king immediately handed it over to Parliament as a debating chamber for the House of Commons. This is where the English love of tradition and continuity, and suspicion of change, becomes a key aspect of the story. The function of the chapel changed completely – from royal shrine celebrating the sacred mysteries of kingship to a place in which to conduct political debate about worldly affairs. But its form did not change, at least initially, nor did the ritual of its daily use. The banks of choir stalls once occupied by the royal family became the seats of politicians, who organised themselves through common cause and allegiance and so could confront and stare down their opponents in almost gladiatorial manner. The Speaker's chair was placed on the altar step, symbolising his exalted status and presumably the reason Members still bow to the Speaker, as in the past they would have bowed to the altar. The 'Table of the House' replaced the lectern; while the choir screen, with its two entrances, inspired a mechanism for voting, with MPs passing through one of two doors into 'Aye' and 'No' lobbies.

This complex world of change and continuity was almost completely destroyed by a fire in 1834. What survived – miraculously – was Westminster Hall, the thirteenth-century undercroft of St Stephen's chapel and Henry VIII's adjoining cloister. The rebuilding of the palace is one of the epic architectural stories of the nineteenth century. A competition was held, and Parliament specified that the design had to be late Gothic or Tudor in style to be in sympathy with the nearby Henry VII Chapel at Westminster Abbey – also because Gothic was regarded as a national style and in some peculiar sense patriotic (see p. 367). The competition was won by Charles Barry, who happened to be a celebrated master of classical design, but the potential problem was resolved when he hired as his assistant A. W. M. Pugin, the then great authority on Gothic architecture and the most vociferous champion for its revival (see pp. 367–9).

The building Barry and Pugin designed, through years of committee meetings and with the participation of many, could have been a monster. But it is not. It is a highly complicated and intensely modern building – accommodating many uses and pioneering services – within the brilliantly and picturesquely composed and detailed garb of history. The heart of the old Palace of Westminster – the chamber of the House of Commons – was not reconstructed. Or not directly. Its location and key dimensions were commemorated, on the site where it stood, in the corridor named St Stephen's Hall. But Barry did create a larger version of the lost St Stephen's chapel to serve as the new Chamber of the House of Commons, complete with choir-stall seating and Speaker perched on 'altar' step. It is set on an axis with the Chamber of the House of Lords and this axis, from north to south, passes through the Central Hall, at right angles to the axis of St Stephen's Hall. It is all very rational, and very symbolic.

From the Central Hall it is possible – on a good day, when crowds are minimal and doors are open – to look into the chambers of both the Lords and the Commons, a visual connection that seems to represent a sense of unity and balance. The axis linking the chambers is not open to the public – but St Stephen's Hall and the octagonal Central Hall to which it leads are. Access is, naturally, not as easy as it was, but well worth the trouble: this site, just a short walk from the public entrance at St Stephen's Porch – from which there is a spectacular view of Westminster Hall – is one of the greatest architectural experiences London has to offer.

WALK 8

Notting Hill

The Victorian middle class goes west

I first got to know Notting Hill in the late 1960s when it was central to London's sudden emergence as the self-made city of oddball fashion, social revolution and inspirational music. On the streets around Portobello Road, strains of nostalgia mixed fruitfully with a heady optimism about the future and 'white-hot' technology: it did not seem strange that while some teenagers paraded around in pensioned-off Guardsmen's red jackets others donned the automaton-like, 'space-age' clothes of André Courrèges, Pierre Cardin and Mary Quant. The road and pubs of Notting Hill became one of the great gathering places of the youthful denizens of this pulsating London. And at the heart of the newly vibrant Notting Hill was Portobello Road, especially on Saturday morning when its markets were in full swing.

Amidst that vibrant atmosphere, it was difficult to conjure up the Notting Hill that had existed a century before. Perhaps surprisingly, Notting Hill was once one of the great failures of nineteenth-century commercial development: a tale full of optimism and disappointment, of grand designs that went sadly wrong, of dreams that failed. First proposed in the 1820s, it was meant to be a spectacular new town to the west of Tyburn – now Marble Arch – which in the early nineteenth century marked the western end of the increasingly built-up city. But the developers overreached themselves – the elite of London had no interest in living in the then outer edges of the capital, and the area instead became home to the middle classes, before descending into poverty during the first half of the twentieth century.

The name is itself curious, recorded as 'Knottynghull' from at least 1356, an imprecise area that seems at one time to have also embraced nearby Campden Hill.[1] The 'Gate' was added in the late eighteenth century when a gate was built across the road – roughly where Bayswater Road now becomes Notting Hill – to collect tolls for

the Uxbridge Turnpike Trust. Quite where Notting Hill Gate begins and ends, and what part it forms of the larger area of Notting Hill, remains a question open to debate.

The main landowner here in the early nineteenth century was James Weller Ladbroke, the heir to a family of fabulously wealthy bankers who made their fortunes in the City during the eighteenth century. In 1821 he obtained an Act of Parliament for the development of his estate and commissioned the architect and surveyor Thomas Allason to lay out a salubrious residential suburb around what is now the junction of Notting Hill Gate with Ladbroke Road and Pembridge Road. At the time, this portion of Bayswater Road was lined with a few terraces, with Hyde Park, Kensington Gardens, and the royal Kensington Palace nearby – but at Notting Hill there was little beyond a few farmhouses, cottages, gravel pits, brick and pottery kilns and piggeries. Ladbroke proposed an estate that extended the city to the north-west, reaching as far as what is now Westbourne Park Road and Holland Park Avenue.[2] He was following the lessons that had been learned by speculating builders over the previous 200 years. As ever, the inspiration was the Earl of Bedford with his Covent Garden estate (see pp. 493–5), where in the 1630s he created a self-contained miniature town organised around a forum-like square of grand houses – the Piazza – with smaller houses, shops and taverns on subsidiary streets. Such a vision remained relevant for the creators of Notting Hill, even though the fashions in urban form favoured more sinuous crescents and the taste in elevations had become more ostentatious.

By 1823 Allason's master-plan was complete. A rising star of British architecture, he had made his name with a series of sketches of ancient ruins drawn during a visit to Pula, in modern-day Croatia. For Ladbroke's estate, he proposed the creation of a huge circus, framed by terrace houses, seemingly inspired by John Nash's plans for Park Crescent, near Regent's Park, realised in 1812. But Allason also added a twist: inspired by the example of the Bedford estate, Bloomsbury, his terraces and crescents would not only front on to communal garden squares, but also include large gardens at the rear. These gardens, or 'paddocks', would be generally accessible only by passing through the houses that surrounded them. This layout was intended to give the projected new suburb a very special quality. It was to be near enough to London for its inhabitants to enjoy the pleasures of residing in a great city, while the communal gardens and rural setting also gave residents the pleasure of country living.

Unfortunately, the financial troubles that beset the nation in the late 1820s and into the 1830s meant that the initial development of the Ladbroke estate soon faltered and relatively little was built. Perhaps this self-contained little town was just too far from the city to attract enough interest. Those buildings that were constructed and which survive, such as numbers 2–6 and 24–28 Holland Park Avenue constructed in 1828, are the only hint of the late-Georgian architectural flavour the estate might have possessed. Indeed, between 1834 and 1838 no building leases were granted by Ladbroke at all.[3]

Having witnessed his grand project stall, Ladbroke settled on another option. In 1837 an entrepreneur named John Whyte proposed to turn a large part of the estate into a horse-racing course. Ladbroke agreed, and shortly afterwards an irregular curving track was laid out around the shallow hill forming the highest point of the estate – just north of what is now the junction of Holland Park Avenue and Notting Hill. It was intended that spectators would congregate on this hill while horses galloped the long course around it. On paper, it was an excellent idea: the nearest existing racecourse was at Epsom, Surrey, and there was a great public appetite for horse-racing. The scheme also had an evocative antique pedigree, recalling the hippodromes of Rome. To make the point, the racecourse was indeed christened the Hippodrome but, alas, classical allusion did not protect the enterprise from biting criticism. When the Hippodrome opened, the *Sunday Times* sniffed that 'A more filthy or disgusting crew than that which entered, we have seldom had the misfortune to encounter,'[4] as the hoi polloi of London descended on Ladbroke's land. Yet this ambitious scheme, too, was destined to fail. The Hippodrome closed in 1842, no doubt adding to the general gloom that had consumed the area.

This moment was the nadir in the development of Notting Hill. From the early 1840s, with the economy thriving once more, London again came under pressure to expand. The plans for the district got back under way, and in Ladbroke's case with greatly increased architectural ambition. By the early 1850s this new suburb, formed by Ladbroke's estate as well as the Norland estate immediately to the west, promised to be an

An 1844 map depicts Notting Hill at the western edge of London, complete with Hippodrome.

opulent 'City of Palaces' – again aimed primarily at the affluent classes – in the manner of the Chowringhee area of Calcutta. Its crowning feature was the Royal (originally Norland) Crescent, a palatial terrace that was constructed in a semicircle opposite Notting Hill Road in the 1840s. Its designer was Robert Cantwell, who also laid out the estate.

This time around, the ambition was even greater. Allason's plan for the Ladbroke estate was extended so that the terraces or crescents defined blocks that, for London, were exceptionally large in area, just as the rows of houses were unusually tall. They became known as 'superblocks'. But there was something other than size that made these blocks super. They were intended to possess a high degree of convenience, privacy and comfort, each with the possibility of becoming almost a little residential village within the city. Typically, superblocks were formed when four tall terraces met to define a 'paddock', as suggested in the 1823 plan, that could only be reached via the houses or though discreet archways – like that in Kensington Park Gardens – which appear to be leading to magic gardens. The houses themselves were provided with small private rear gardens because the paddock was to serve as the communal garden for all the residents of the block. In addition, the best of the superblocks were to look out towards garden squares, which were also well planted and could be shared by all the blocks surrounding it.

Around Ladbroke Grove, the proliferation of gently curving crescents of such superblocks – Blenheim Crescent, Elgin Crescent and Lansdowne Crescent among them – are said to echo the curves of the lost racetracks and spectators' enclosure of the Hippodrome. The Ladbroke estate set the pattern for development elsewhere in Notting Hill. A large portion of the land further north, mostly to the west of Portobello Road, had long been two farms. There was Portobello Farm and the rather grandly named Manor of Notting Barns Farm. Portobello Farm had been owned since 1755 by the Talbot family and was approached from the south by a lane heading towards Kensal Green. The lane was called alternatively Green Lane or Portobello Farm Lane – it's now Portobello Road – and it formed the spine of the farm's landholdings. The Manor Farm, meanwhile, had been owned since 1767 by the St Quintin family, whose property stretched as far east as the central portion of Portobello Road, and as far west as what became the junction of St Quintin Avenue with North Pole Road. By the mid nineteenth century both families appreciated that the agricultural days of their farms were over and that their futures – and the family fortunes – lay in property development. So the farms were recast as the Portobello estate and the St Quintin estate, both ready and willing for business.

And yet, even when building in Notting Hill picked up, it could not challenge Mayfair or Belgravia as the location for the richest, grandest, most powerful or most fashionable of the London elite. It is true that the area's southern portion, essentially the Ladbroke estate near Bayswater Road and Notting Hill, was eventually well-occupied. But the streets and squares to the north often ended up being more modest – and even gimcrack in their construction. Rather than becoming the domain of the

The view east along Stanley Gardens to St Peter's church.

landed aristocracy and powerful financiers and statesmen, Notting Hill instead became home to well-to-do, but not fabulously wealthy, artists, scientists and explorers. This was the world of Thomas Hardy, who lived in Westbourne Park Villas in the 1860s, and of Thomas Machen, the author first of decadent and then of romantic stories of the supernatural, who lived in Clarendon Road in the 1880s and evoked aspects of Notting Hill in his strange 1907 novel, *Hill of Dreams*. Successful residents? Of course. But the intended super-rich clientele they most certainly were not.

Having failed to reach the heady heights of London's social ladder, Notting Hill had not so far to fall to reach the lower depths of deprivation. By the late 1880s, the great taxonomist of Victorian poverty Charles Booth (who we meet again in Walk 9) was able to categorise some portions of Notting Hill as home to the 'Upper-middle and Upper classes'; but other areas were 'mixed', while some – namely Golborne Road – were suffering from 'chronic want'. And the area became even poorer in the twentieth century. After the crippling expense of the First World War, followed by recession and economic depression, fewer families could afford the large numbers of servants needed to run the area's bigger houses, so they became hard to market and were subdivided into smaller and cheaper apartments. This pattern continued into the 1960s. It was not, of course, entirely a bad thing. The cheapness of Notting Hill's housing is part of what made it so appealing to Caribbean immigrants after the Second World War, helping to create the vibrant and diverse district I first encountered in the 1960s (it is, after all, the home of Europe's biggest street carnival).

It is inescapable, though, that Notting Hill's developers had aimed to create one of the most affluent sections of the city, and ended up with one of the most impoverished. The story illustrates the organic, unpredictable and unforeseen way in which cities grow, especially when they are the product of speculative developments on privately-owned estates. Today, one can see the smart suburb Notting Hill was intended to be, complete with jaunty coloured stucco houses and forests of mature trees. But a brief dip into its Victorian history reveals a darker story – a parable about the unwise, unprofessional or unprincipled aspirations of greedy developers and landlords.

THE WALK

Head to Notting Hill Gate tube station, during the working week if you can. The area has, for me, always felt most alive on Friday mornings, when the market shops are open and the street stalls in place, but the crowds are less intense and overpowering than on a Saturday. Little has changed here – physically at least – in the fifty years since I first visited. The most noticeable differences are the shops, but then shops always change in a vibrant city. Predictably, however, a certain individuality and eccentricity has been replaced by shops and businesses that are more bland and corporate – and of course more expensive.

Immediately upon leaving the station and walking north along Pembridge Gardens, one is thrust towards some of the grandest domestic architecture in Notting Hill. The mid-nineteenth-century buildings of the more opulent portions of the district reflect the dominant fashion of the time for domestic design. It had already been displayed in spectacular manner in the mighty terraces being created in South Kensington, under the approval of Prince Albert, near the site of the Great Exhibition of 1851 and of the future Albert Hall. These buildings took the architectural language established by John Nash in the early nineteenth century at Regent's Park, Regent Street and Carleton House Terrace, and pursued by others in the 1830s, but gave it a subtle new accent. Rather than being Greek or Roman in their inspiration, the new compositions in and around Notting Hill were more eclectically classical – often with Renaissance details, and in what became known as the Italianate style pioneered in the late 1820s and early 1830s by such erudite architects as Charles Barry (see p. 287). But, as with Nash's early composition, these later, grand essays were generally realised in stucco and Roman cement that concealed the brickwork and were intended to suggest more heroic acts of masonry.

Pembridge Gardens is a good example. The houses are stucco clad, the classical detail Roman rather than Greek, and with the composition of the elevations inspired by Italian sixteenth-century urban architecture. The street is formed largely of monumental detached villas, each separated from the other by a sliver of space that is just enough to assert independence. A few are linked in discrete manner to form semi-detached blocks and there is also a short terrace of five houses. Most are adorned in the then-usual way with porches sporting detached Doric Columns. The houses were constructed in the late 1850s on part of the 28-acre estate of former agricultural land owned by Robert Hall. For the development of this portion of his land Hall worked with builders named Francis and William Radford. To the north of the Gardens is Pembridge Square, developed by the same team, but a few years later. Here the stucco villas are a trifle larger and there is a delightful central garden, railed off from the outer world to form what is essentially a small private park for those fortunate enough to live around it.

This garden square emphasises the ideal to which, from the early 1850s, the landlords and builders of the more ambitious portions of Notting Hill aspired. The vision was for grand stucco-clad classical architecture to rise, in informal manner, out of lush and picturesque planting. It was a permutation, with additional gusto, of late Georgian *rus in urbe* planning that characterised building in Bloomsbury from the 1790s ands a little later in the squares of Barnsbury (see p. 244).

The Notting Hill Italianate architecture is far from uniform. The style varied between and within the various estates, depending on who was responsible for individual terraces or urban blocks. As previously

Victorian middle-class homes with a touch of the Italian Renaissance: the villas on Pembridge Gardens.

mentioned, some of the best stand a little to the west, on the Ladbroke Estate. Here, the architect Thomas Allom partnered with developer C. H. Blake to create the area around Kensington Park Gardens in the first half of the 1850s. Blake's own house by Allom, the free-standing 24 Kensington Park Gardens of 1853–4, is a magnificent palazzo that forms part of a striking composition with similar large-scale houses on the adjoining corners with Ladbroke Grove and Stanley Crescent. But it is Allom's terrace compositions that are most memorable, particularly those around Stanley Gardens, Stanley Crescent and Kensington Park Road. It really is exemplary work that shows how urban beauty can be created even in conditions governed by the ruthless exigencies of speculation. As the *Survey of London* explains, 'The design of houses, streets, gardens and tree-planting is seen with a painter's eye, so that each turn and every vista is composed in a picturesque manner . . . It says much for Allom's brilliant scenic display that his strange sort of grandeur is still evident in spite of all the damage that the twentieth century has done.'[5]

The prospects along Stanley Gardens, also a few hundred metres to the north-west of Pembridge Gardens, are particularly memorable. Looking west the view is terminated by a symmetrical composition framed by prospect towers and flanked by colonnades. A most impressive treatment for what is only a semi-detached house. The vista to the east – Kensington Park Road – is closed in time-honoured fashion by the portico and tower of a most charming classical church, St Peter's. Like Stanley Gardens and its terraces the church was designed by Allom and built at roughly the same time (1855–7) and here he seemed intent in creating a striking urban image, of the sort that might be found in Rome. This perhaps explains the design of the church. As the *Survey of London* points out, 'this is one of the very few Church of England churches to be built in London after 1837 in the classical style.'[6] By the 1850s Gothic was the overwhelmingly dominant style for churches but Allom resolved to give the congregation of this new parish a scenically charming classical church. Perhaps he wanted to conjure up memories of the Italian Grand Tour or – since the church has a rather solid Georgian character – do no more than confer upon this new suburb some pedigree of the past. Allom's urban planning is brilliant, his architecture varied but balanced, with details that are bold and at times glorious. But perhaps most extraordinary is the lush planting of the private garden worlds that these superlative and quintessentially urban elevations define. The permutations of the superblocks are particularly pleasing, with that between Kensington Park Gardens and Stanley Gardens particularly large and largely enclosed on three sides.

The houses on Pembridge Gardens form part of a similar, although far more modest, urban plan. They form the west side of one of the most enigmatic and secret of Notting Hill's 'superblocks', one that seems to have come about almost by chance and arguably more putative than actual. The block's southern elevation is remarkable, formed by an irregular terrace of Georgian houses, 52–64 Notting Hill Gate, of varied dates, most set well back from the existing road frontage behind single-storey shops, some with ranges advancing towards the road to form courtyards and some with curved bays. These houses no doubt represent the core of the hamlet that once stood on the Bayswater Road, before the area's nineteenth-century transformation, and that perhaps originally faced north, away from the main road. The other sides of this informal block reflect the ambition of Notting Hill's mid-nineteenth-century developers. Linden Gardens, which forms its east side, is made up of tall brick and stucco blocks of Italianate style. But all is most loosely composed, suggesting several developers were at work and that speed was of the essence. Linden Gardens does a loop around a central block – most unusual – and on the west side of the loop are mews' approached by arches, one of which adjoins a deep trough which offers a glimpse of the trains hurtling along on the Circle Line.

It's a strangely thrilling experience, and a reminder of the shallowness of the cut-and-cover trench system that was used in the 1860s to construct London's pioneering 'underground' railway. The Metropolitan Railway opened its station at Notting Hill Gate in 1868. Originally, and most poetically, the sides of the cutting were embellished with balustrades. One has now crumbled, and typical of our utilitarian age, been replaced by chicken wire. Beyond the mews and the cutting are the gardens at the centre of the block, They can be glimpsed through the slivers of space between villas in Pembridge Gardens. Large and well ordered, they are a remarkable oasis – but mostly large, private gardens rather than a single communal one.

After you've explored this early and almost ad hoc superblock, walk back past Notting Hill Gate tube station to the neighbouring street, Pembridge Road. This south-east portion of the Ladbroke estate was in large part constructed in the 1840s by a Southwark builder, William Chadwick.[7] Chadwick's architecture is generally good, relatively simple and brick-faced – much more in the late-Georgian Greek Revival manner than in the early-Victorian Italianate stucco-style that came to dominate much of Notting Hill. A good example stands a little way along Pembridge Road, at the architecturally splendid Prince Albert public house. This – thank goodness – is still a pub, and indeed a most handsome one. With its pair of full-height gently curving bays, which must once have looked on to a large garden and offered a fine prospect of open fields that would soon be transformed into Kensington Park Road, this pub would have been a convivial beacon in the early days of Notting Hill's development. Many meetings must have taken place here, and deals brokered, between the disparate adventurers – builders, financiers, landowners, surveyors and architects – who wanted to make a utopian urban dream a reality and, in the process, make themselves rich. For their scheme to work, they realised they were not just to construct mansions for the rich but also more humble homes, shops, workshops, warehouses, and places of worship.

Typical of Chadwick's domestic architecture is the uniform three-storey terrace, across the road and a little to the north west of the Prince Albert: 8 to 28 (even) Kensington Park Road. It is given central emphasis, in the most minimal manner possible, by raising the parapet above the central house into a shallow and stunted pediment. This hardly makes

William Chadwick's bull-nosed corner at the junction of Kensington Park Road with Pembridge Road.

the terrace appear palatial in the manner of uniform and pedimented Georgian terraces, but is an interesting continuation an earlier urban design tradition into Victorian speculative house building. Opposite is Horbury Crescent, developed in 1855 by Chadwick's son, W. W. Chadwick, which is far larger in scale and decidedly Italianate in design. It's a good marker of how the Family's ambitions and architectural taste changed as the area's fortunes picked up.

Chadwick the elder terminated the south end of 8–28 Kensington Park Road with a splendid bull-nosed corner and then proceeded north with another terrace, 13 to 55 Pembridge Road, which runs at a slight angle from the junction with Kensington Park Road. This terrace, also built from the mid-1840s, is only two storeys high and seemingly was always intended as a commercial row, with tradesmen living above their shops. Once again Chadwick toyed with details in an attempt to give visual interest to a long uniform terrace – but without spending too much money. There are raised and panelled parapets over the two central houses and the end houses, and shallow parapet pediments placed in

the centres of the long intermediate elevations. These hedges against monotony are a little too subtle to add much, but the idea is interesting.

Where this Pembridge Road terrace ends Portobello Road begins, sidling in from the west and instantly curving to the north-west, before gradually curving more to the north. This junction is one of the more subtle architectural pleasures of our walk – a symphony of convex curves that seem a direct reflection of Portobello Road's origin as an informal country lane. The curve from the terrace of shops on Pembridge Road is shallow and generous and incorporates another good and early pub, the Sun in Splendour, built by Chadwick by 1852. The convex curve to the north, and nearly opposite, is an interesting act of sympathy because it was realised by a different builder, on a different estate.

Now the first stretch of Portobello Road awaits. In the first half of the eighteenth century this road was known as Green's Lane and was a rural route that led from the gravel pit around what is now the junction of Notting Hill and Bayswater Road, north to Kensal Green by way of Portobello Farm, located near to what is now Golborne Road. Gradually – casually – the name of the farm gave its name to the lane leading to it, so Green's Lane became Portobello Lane, now Portobello Road. But why was the farm called Portobello? The answer opens a window into an extraordinary, if now generally forgotten, moment in British history. The farm was named to commemorate a famous victory in the War of Jenkins' Ear (1739–48) – so called because it was sparked by the Spanish coastguard's decision to punish a British sailor, Robert Jenkins, for smuggling by cutting off his ear. In November 1739, Admiral Vernon seized Puerto Bello in Panama from the Spanish empire, an action that led to the penning of 'Rule, Britannia' the following year. Of course, the fate of the hapless Jenkins was merely the excuse for a commercial adventure in which Britain sought to gain control of valuable raw materials in the Spanish New World, notably silver, mahogany and the trade in slaves. The failure of the British forces to achieve the political and economic aims of the government – and specifically the humiliating reverses suffered in spring 1741 by a British invasion force seeking to capture Cartagena de Indias in what is now Colombia – led to the fall from political power of Britain's first and longest-serving prime minister, Sir Robert Walpole. Arguably the whole affair had only started thanks to Walpole's personal obsession with mahogany, with which he had panelled the study and bedroom of his newly built home, Houghton Hall in Norfolk, in the 1720s. Within four years of the Cartagena fiasco Walpole was dead, seemingly a victim of his vice for this insuperable timber.

Today, the story is commemorated in the name of the most characterful route through Notting Hill. Portobello Road has never been the architecturally grandest street in the area, but has certainly long been the liveliest and, with a history as a rural lane, just about the oldest. A journey along it offers not just a cross section through the society that it serves – and the contrasts were far more dramatic fifty years ago than now – but is also a highway right to the heart of Notting Hill's identity.

The first portion of the road as you walk north can be both faintly thrilling and rather disappointing. There is no street market here, very few shops, and most of the west side is formed by tall and gloomy interwar apartment blocks fronting on to Kensington Park Road. All to the west is on Ladbroke estate land, but the east side of the street is built on land that was part of Robert Hall's estate, here developed from 1844 in conjunction with civil engineer W. H. Jenkins. The buildings constructed in the mid-1840s by the Hall–Jenkins Estate largely survive and are most charming. They form a sustained and loosely irregular terrace of two-storey stucco cottages.

They are mainly now painted in a variety of gay colours – something of a Notting Hill speciality of the last thirty years or so, perhaps inspired by similar paint schemes in Positano or parts of San Francisco (a US city that is in many respects Notting Hill Gate's soulmate). Needless to say, such jaunty colouring is historically incorrect in London and a long way from the tradition that, externally at least, houses should be simple and unassuming. More to the point picking-out individual houses in lurid colours can make nonsense of terrace designs that are uniform and architecturally coherent. But, that said, and to judge by tourists' clicking cameras, the area's colour-spectrum streets are popular and are pleasant and playful if you are in the mood. George Orwell lodged at number 22 for a while in 1927, after he gave up being a policeman in Burma. What he would have made of the lilac and peach and beige elevations of his terrace it's now hard to say. He probably would have loved it, since the wide spectrum of colours certainly suggests a bid for liberation from the control of Big Brother.[8]

The first intersection with Portobello Road, Chepstow Villas, marks a threshold. To the west are large stucco terraced house of flamboyant and varied design with the vista terminated by a tall bay on an Allom-designed house, which stands at the corner of Kensington Park Road with Kensington Park Gardens. But in Portobello Road to the north there are more modest houses and shops. Those on the road's west side, three storeys high, loosely uniform and with stucco classical ornament around their windows, stand on the Ladbroke Estate. They were constructed in the late 1840s and through the 1850s under the control of Thomas Pocock, a City attorney, and various financial backers and associates. Pocock had initially been involved in the completion of some of the grander streets on the estate such as Kensington Park Road, but evidently believed that modest terraces of shops were appropriate for the ancient, undulating and utilitarian former farm lane of Portobello Road. These Pocock buildings, with wonderfully large windows that must make their pinched interiors less claustrophobic, are now painted a kaleidoscope of colours and currently house a wide variety of what are, to be charitable, antique shops, although much of what they display as antiques are of relatively recent manufacture and charmingly patinated.

--- ◆ ---

Running to the east off this portion of Portobello Road is Denbigh Terrace. This is an interesting road. It is the meeting place of two estates. The south side of the terrace marks the north boundary of the Hall–Jenkins Estate and to the north was the 10-acre Archer–Bolton estate, developed from 1846 in generally cramped and mean manner by the landowner G. A. Archer and his developer and builder partner T. J. Bolton.

The south side of Denbigh Terrace, built for Jenkins between 1852 and 1855, is a charming affair with its stucco façade now also a rainbow of differing colours. The houses are small, mostly two storeys above a raised basement, and loosely uniform although a group towards the centre of the terrace rise an extra storey. The details of the houses are simple, boldly and sensibly in the robust Doric idiom which was cheap to execute and easier to maintain. The west prospect from Denbigh Terrace, towards the similarly simple elevations of the Portobello Road terrace, is particularly charming because of the informal way in which the pretty classical tower and spire of St Peter's Church raises itself above the humble rooftops. This vista was presumably unintended, or at least hit upon largely by chance, and is in consequence the more pleasing – it has the quality of urban ensembles found in Tuscan hill towns.

The north, Archer–Bolton, side of Denbigh Terrace has been obliterated. This entire portion of the estate – which stretched north just beyond the north side of Lonsdale Road, and a block and a half east along Westbourne Grove – was swept away soon after the Second World War for large and ugly free-standing blocks of public housing and for the westward extension of a widened and slightly re-aligned Westbourne Grove. These dismal blocks of public housing were completed and occupied when I first knew Notting Hill and now, as then, come as something of a shock. They completely disregard the established scale, materials, forms, urban grain and architectural spirit of the area. Presumably the modest houses that stood on this ground had fallen into very serious decay by the 1950s or had even been bomb damaged, and so a hole was torn in the very heart of Notting Hill to create a run-of-the-mill council housing estate. Thank goodness this experiment in radical surgery and social manipulation was not continued in this area on this scale.

One building that endured this onslaught is the Earl of Lonsdale public house, named after the popular sporting earl who gave the noble art of boxing its most highly prized trophy – the Lonsdale Belt. This pub, standing on the south-east corner of Portobello Road and Westbourne Grove, was built as a speculation in 1847 by W. K. Jenkins using T. J. Bolton as builder. The design is solid and simple, less Italianate and more Palladian in feel, with tall first-floor windows emphasised with architraves and square second-floor attic windows.[9] In the mid-1960s, this pub became the heart of the suddenly fashionable hotspot of Portobello Road. The main, cubical block of the pub has a single-street extension to the south, along Portobello Road, which must have served originally as a lounge bar, dining room or even billiard room. Here, the fashionable heroes of the clubs of London would sit occupying sofas for much of the afternoon: not the grand and great of the commercial music or fashion industries, but, more likely, what used to be called lower-middle class and working-class boys who had, magically, concocted a very distinct and stylish aura. If it was too full – as was usually the case – it was customary to display oneself along the Portobello Road frontage of the pub, draped on, or corralled behind, the railing that gives the pub a miniscule forecourt and defend the slightly depressed path of entry to its rear parts.

The interior of the Earl of Lonsdale has been somewhat reconstructed in recent years but it remains a fine example of a Victorian pub interior, probably a remodelling of the 1880s. As with most good, large, late Victorian pubs, the Earl of Lonsdale offers a vista into Victorian society with its varied bars created for different classes and types of drinker, segregated by timber screens, with each discreetly arranged compartment or bar entered through its own specific door. There would have been a public bar for working men, a saloon bar for bosses (furnished with more comfort and with pints costing a trifle more), and private and snug bars for women or those wishing to drink alone or in more sedate or intimate manner with their companions.

On my recent visit, I roamed around inside, trying to conjure up the sizzling atmosphere of so many years ago. Impossible, but for all that it still proved a very pleasing place, with low doors surviving in some of the screens (for the pot-man to move quickly from bar to bar collecting glasses). There is also a good earlier staircase, suggesting that originally the pub possessed a first-floor room for functions, grand dining or even for musical turns, which were partly the origin of the music hall.

To the north of the Earl of Lonsdale, across Westbourne Grove begins – each Friday and Saturday morning and afternoons – the bustle of Portobello Road street market, which defines the next portion of our walk.

———◆•◆•◆———

By the 1960s, Portobello Road street market – stretching north from the junction with Lonsdale Road – had long been established as a fruit and vegetable market for the working-class population of the area. Traditionally these stalls operated all week but, on Fridays and Saturdays, were joined by additional vendors at the road's northern end peddling old clothes and assorted 'junk'.

When I first knew the road its central and northern portion and the surrounding hinterland had long fallen upon hard times, with its bourgeois aspirations stymied not long after it was constructed during the second half of the nineteenth century. In this area – at some point christened North Kensington – there were large, itinerant and poor West Indian and Irish populations, generally residing in mid- to late-nineteenth-century houses owned by unscrupulous private landlords, often made grotesque by their faded glory. Built for the aspiring mid-Victorian middle class, these houses stood with stucco façades disintegrating, their pompous columned porches often crudely truncated, and their pretentious classical ornament crumbling back into dust and sand.

Many streets around here were more or less slums, if what that vague and emotive word defines is physical decay, overcrowding and a sense of desolation. It was in Notting Hill, of course, that in the 1950s the notorious landlord Peter Rachman amassed his property empire, based on the intimidation and eviction of sitting tenants, the exploitation of

Market stalls sprawl northwards along Portobello Road.

vulnerable new tenants (in large part recently arrived immigrants), and the subdivision of houses into tiny but high-rent rooms. His abusive operations became legendary and led to a change in housing law with the Rent Act of 1965, which gave more security to tenants but which also inadvertently made private accommodation more scarce and more expensive.

But the southern portion of Portobello Road and its surrounding streets fared somewhat differently. Although much of this area had also become the domain of shabby lodging houses by the time of the Second World War, there remained well-occupied large houses in, for example, Kensington Park Road and Lansdowne Crescent. It was into the southern portion of Portobello Road that the street market expanded in the early 1960s, but as a very different creature to the long-established market. Around the junction with Westbourne Grove there had been a scattering of antique shops since at least the late 1940s and now this trade expanded with a strange and extraordinary energy. Shops, street stalls and then covered markets or galleries of stalls proliferated and stretched from Lonsdale Road and the veggie stalls to the north, down Portobello Road as far south as Chepstow Villas, with outriders of market activity along Westbourne Grove.

When I first knew it in the late 1960s the antique market was a wonderland through which to roam, with objects both unexpected and bizarre as well as obviously rare and valuable. All manner of things were on sale – paintings, furniture, glass, porcelain, jewellery, books, prints, old weapons and odds and ends picked up by Imperial travellers. I was young, neither particularly acquisitive nor well funded, so I bought little in this part of the market. But when I penetrated to the seedier northern portion, beyond the portal of the elevated Westway, the roaring urban motorway that was constructed between 1964 and 1970, I often found myself sorely tempted. Here, tossed among the detritus of the rag-and-bone men's barrows, I often stumbled upon wonderful things, going for only a few shillings. Purchases were made and most of these acquisitions I have with me still.

On the Friday that I walked along Portobello Road, antique stalls still went as far north as Lonsdale Road. It was wonderfully animated, with a French female busker purring romantic airs. On the corner with Lonsdale Road is one of those eating establishments that characterise London's gastronomic renaissance. Within a tall and handsome mid-nineteenth-century structure on the Portobello estate – perhaps once a pub – is a branch of Gail's, the kind of cavernous coffee-bar-type chain-restaurants in which the leisured middle classes seem to lounge for inordinate amounts of time chatting, petting babies and reading newspapers. The place is crowded with, on warm or sunny days, its customers spilling on to chairs on the wide pavement.

While such chains no doubt bring money to Portobello Road, they also threaten it. One cluster of antique shops in a fine Pocock-built terrace, on the corner of Portobello Road and Westbourne Grove opposite the Earl of Lonsdale, has been ousted for a chain clothes store. AllSaints imposes the same ersatz quirky and slightly grungy sweatshop look on all its stores throughout Britain, from Cheltenham to Spitalfields. When I was last there, the ploy was to pack the windows with old sewing machines gathered, no doubt, at great cost from around the world, presumably to astonish, delight and attract would-be customers. Such are the commercial conventions of the highly competitive fashion industry and chain-store consumerism, in which it is now common for businesses to assume the pose of edgy individualism in the most uniform and repetitive manner imaginable. In this case, a hive of enterprise has been replaced by a generally place-less and essentially bland clothes shop, and the established and much-loved character of this corner of London has been seriously diluted.

There are still, though, recurrent hints of an older world. Just north of the corner with Westbourne Grove there is a yard leading off Portobello Road. Reached through an arch, Vernon Yard perhaps predates the houses that surround it by at least a century. The name commemorates the hero of the aforementioned War of Jenkins' Ear, Admiral Vernon, who captured Puerto Bello in Panama. A charming reminder of the history of a street currently changing beyond recognition.

<hr />

To the north of Lonsdale Road, much of the best architecture is slightly later than that to the south – and brings with it a subtly different atmosphere. Turn east on to Colville Terrace and to your left are the Colville blocks, developed on the Portobello estate during the 1860s and early 1870s by George Frederick Tippett. North of the tall stucco buildings of Colville Terrace are, to the east, Colville Gardens and, to the west, Colville Square.

The tall stucco terraces of Colville Gardens front to the east over a garden, and present their rears to a street named Colville Gardens. Bizarrely, the houses on the west side of Colville Gardens are in fact named Colville Square and face to the west. Sounds complicated? That's because it is. And it is also incompetent because this arrangement leaves Colville Gardens/Square in something of a predicament. The unfortunate street is framed by terraces that both present it with their denuded rear elevations. It is through these informal elevations that the houses are entered. Really most odd, and artistically far from satisfactory. The Colville Square terrace facing west looks on to a communal garden – once private and so conceived in the spirit of the superblocks on the Ladbroke Estate – while the square's terrace to the west has to its rear a small yard so that its rear rooms look directly into rear rooms of houses along Portobello Road.

No doubt because these blocks are squeezed too close together, this would-be majestic development seems to have proved undesirable and

Above: Jaunty-coloured houses at the intersection of Portobello Road with Colville Terrace.

Right: The gaunt and spireless All Saints church, glimpsed from Colville Road through the trees lining Colville Gardens.

soon fallen upon hard times. In the late 1960s it was renowned as one of the more squalid and dismal parts of the Portobello area. I remember going into a second-floor flat in the Colville Gardens block where about eight rooms of differing sizes and functions – divided by a windowless and utilitarian corridor – had been created within the volume of what would once have been a couple of generous bedrooms. The fortunes of the Colville blocks have changed again and they are now once more desirable and expensive homes, with, as to the south, rainbow colour schemes enlivening the scene and gently undermining the pomposity of the terrace's unified and palatial compositions.

Before moving on, look to the north-east, through the trees of Colville Gardens towards the strange Gothic tower of All Saints church. This is one of the more romantic and pleasing vistas in Notting Hill. The

elongated, somewhat Flemish-style tower of the church – designed in 1852 by William White – looks peculiar because it was supposed to support a tall stone-built spire that never managed to rise more than a few metres. This was down to the financial failure of Dr Samuel Walker, one of the most adventurous and unfortunate developers in the area, who gave the land for the church and planned to fund its construction, no doubt in the belief that such a pious action would benefit his immortal soul and reduce his suffering in purgatory. Sadly this plan to amass celestial treasure foundered in 1855 when Dr Walker's stock of earthly treasure became exhausted and he was obliged to hand over control of all his land to trustees. Seemingly unimpressed by Dr Walker's Godly work, the trustees stopped all his building projects, including the construction of the spire. The church, a gaunt and spireless runt of a building, fell into the possession of its builder in lieu of unpaid bills and so it stood for over five years, unfinished, increasingly derelict, surrounded by the carcasses of incomplete houses and christened by jovial locals 'All Sinners in the Mud'.[10] It was not until 1861 that it was finally consecrated, but still – as today – without its spire. This unlucky church proved unlucky again during the Second World War when it was twice hit by bombs and much of its interior was damaged or destroyed. The nave and aisles survive, though in a sadly denuded state – but its tower, even without its spire, is a noble sight. Perhaps this splendid structure does indeed assuage the sufferings of Dr Walker's eternal soul.

———◆•◆•◆———

Head back to Portobello Road, which north of Lonsdale Road is for much of the week the preserve of fruit and vegetable stalls, with occasional interlopers selling other types of food. The buildings on each side of the road are almost entirely mid nineteenth to early twentieth century, and while most are unexceptional there are a few that are notable and one in particular that is outstanding. This is number 191, the Electric Cinema, which opened in February 1910 and is one of the earliest purpose-built cinemas in London and certainly the least altered internally. It's small in scale and lacks the ostentation of a theatre. In fact you can see a new building-type emerging because, like many later art deco cinemas, its façade is tile-clad although the ornament is still in the Edwardian Baroque manner. The auditorium is expressed by an arched roof and a small but exotic dome above the entrance proclaims the picture palace's presence in the street. The architect was Gerald Seymour Valentin. After decades of shady existence it now functions once more as one of London's best cinemas, albeit as part of a private members' club.

This portion of Portobello Road has changed relatively little physically over the last fifty years or so. The individual shops and cafés I remember in my youth have all long gone, but the general atmosphere remains much the same and reassuringly the pubs are still with us in spirit as well as body. On the junction with Elgin Crescent is the Duke of Wellington, which is one of the more handsome buildings on this stretch. It was built on the Ladbroke estate, probably by Dr Walker, and is in the same bold and simple Palladian style as the slightly earlier Earl of Lonsdale. On the corner with Talbot Road is another fine, Italianate former pub – now a gin house calling itself the Distillery – and on the corner with Westbourne Park Road there is yet another, named the Castle.

Portobello Road changes its nature now – as fifty years ago – as it passes below the Westway. After this come the market stalls displaying the gleanings of house clearances and arrays of seemingly random collections of odds and ends. The architecture too becomes bolder and blander. On the east much is recent building. The most memorable structure is on the west, and is somewhat unexpected: large and gaunt brick-built convent buildings that were constructed in the 1860s for Franciscan nuns and since 1897 have been used by Dominicans. The most notably thing is a tall and forbidding brick wall and the large, abstract form of a huge semicircular bay. This in fact is the apse of the convent chapel, designed in 1863 by Henry Clutton. It's worth looking inside because the chapel is a powerful space, designed in the thirteenth-century French manner, accompanied by a charming cloister.

And then, just as things seem to be petering out, Golborne Road is reached. This is one of the area's high points, with its own very distinct identity that seems charmingly out of time with the bustle of much of city life. Walk east, and you come upon a street lined with a mix of shops and houses, mostly built in a sedate classical style in the 1870s and early 1880s on the Portobello estate. It is now home to a community comprised of long-established Irish families and old 'cockney' families (celebrated at 314 Portobello Road by 'Cockney's Traditional Pie 'n' Mash & Eels'), with a strong dash of Moroccan and Portuguese migrants. It's all most cosmopolitan, and given extra interest on Fridays and Saturdays by the open stalls wandering in from Portobello Road. The shops and cafés are fascinating, and include two excellent Portuguese cafés selling good coffee and cakes to the far-from-pretentious local community. The Lisboa Patisserie, at 57 Golborne Road, is squeezed into a small terrace house, while the Café O'Porto, just to the west at 62 Golborne Road, occupies a more modern building and has a large, light interior and sells delicious almond paste and custard tarts.

Many of these shops still retain the original feel of the street. Take number 86. What it now sells is not the reason to visit; instead, look out for the sensational late-Victorian shop fittings – of high quality and well preserved – that include a fine counter and tiled wall with a magnificent frieze featuring a repeating pattern of giant thistles. What could this splendid interior have been created to purvey? Outside there is a clue. Emblazoned in delicate lettering on the shop board above the door is the legend 'Universal Provider'. Of what it does not say. The tiles suggest hygiene was important, so presumably food of some sort – perhaps a butcher with the thistles representing Aberdeen Angus beef.

A few doors down – at numbers 96–98 – was, until very recently, a veteran greengrocer's, a rare survival in central London. As the name on its shopfront proclaims, it was owned by the Price family, and day in, day out there sat Mr and Mrs Price, in their habitual places, barricaded in by crates of potatoes and other wholesome vegetables. This pair of shops offered a vignette of an unchanging world, a glimpse into a lost London. Mr Price told me the shops were last overhauled in 1937. But when I last returned to the street, on a Friday morning in the summer of 2019, Mr and Mrs Price had gone, one shop was shuttered-up and the other housed a 'pop-up' selling the usual array of 'vintage clothing, furniture and more'.

<hr />

At the north-east end of Golborne Road there is a bridge, and this marks one of those unofficial barriers that divide the capital. Golborne Road continues for a little beyond the bridge but it is fragmented, partly laid waste and now overshadowed by the Westway. It was different before

Ernest Goldfinger's Trellick Tower looms over Golborne Road.

the motorway was built. The bridge crosses the broad tracks of the Great Western Railway, which follow the route marked out in the mid 1830s by Isambard Kingdom Brunel. Just beyond the tracks there is another man-made boundary – the Paddington branch of the Grand Union Canal that opened in 1801. Little survives of the early fabric of this truncated area, with all now dominated by the lurking concrete beast of Trellick Tower, whose presence can be occasionally glimpsed from the leafy and stucco heart of Notting Hill.

Trellick Tower, completed in 1972 to the designs of the Hungarian-born Ernö Goldfinger, was built to serve as council housing, an enlarged version of his slightly earlier Balfron Tower in Poplar. Goldfinger came to England before the Second World War, and was a member of the architectural avant-garde, intimate with Le Corbusier and other figures in the modern movement in architecture, and a talented proponent of Soviet-style Constructivism. All of these influences are apparent in the tall, sculptural slab of Trellick Tower, with its slightly detached lift tower that's separated by only a changing and most intriguing sliver of light.

I got to know Goldfinger quite well in the early 1980s when I was an architectural journalist and he was a grand old man of architecture. We would meet at the home he had created for himself in Willow Road, Hampstead and chat about the past. Goldfinger had an unenviable reputation as a ferocious character and an intolerant employer who was inclined to be impatient and bully lesser mortals. I suppose this single-minded confidence – even arrogance – does come across in his architecture. But with me he was the perfect host, mixing strong cocktails and telling tales about the big names in modernism. I'd caught him in his mellow old age when, I suppose, he wanted his stories recorded for posterity by an evidently receptive young journalist. These included snippets about Trellick Tower. When it was completed in the early 1970s it was not popular because taste had moved well away from high-rise public-housing schemes. But Goldfinger would not take this criticism (or any criticism for that matter) or admit that high-rise housing was wrong. To make his point – and extol the virtues of his scheme – he put his money where his mouth was, and moved into a flat in Trellick Tower. He didn't tell me how long he stayed, but I should think only briefly, for the comforts of Hampstead were great. He was, of course, right to stick to his guns, for tastes do change. Trellick Tower is now a Grade II*-listed building of historic and architectural interest, and its flats are regarded as highly desirable when they become available. And as for Goldfinger's house in Willow Road, it's owned by the National Trust, jealously preserved and open to the public as a national monument.

This walk can connect with Walk 9 around Kensal Green cemetery and Chamberlayne Road, just to the north-west. But perhaps more rewarding is to return to Notting Hill Gate and Bayswater Road by a route east of, and parallel to, Portobello Road. This offers a slightly different perspective on Notting Hill. Cross back over the bridge on Golborne Road, but turn south down St Ervan's Road and pass beneath the Westway and over the underground railway – which starts to burrow east after its bridge across the Portobello Road – and then continue south down St Luke's Road, which marks the eastern boundary of the old Portobello estate. These streets were the heartland of the area's Afro-Caribbean community in the late 1950s and 60s but are now largely the preserve of smart shops and expensive homes. Keep an eye open for 40 St Luke's Road with its squat tower. This was the home of W. H. Hudson – the Argentine-born novelist, ornithologist and naturalist – who moved to London in the 1870s and lived here until his death in 1922. It was described by the painter Ford Maddox Ford as 'fantastically gloomy', no doubt partly because Hudson's wife ran it as a boarding house. [11]

Continue south to Westbourne Park Road, then go east and then south down Ledbury Road, which was mostly built in the late 1840s partly on a detached portion of the Ladbroke estate. The atmosphere is now very high-class, with the Ledbury restaurant, on the corner with Talbot Road, being very good and very grand indeed. Architecturally more amusing is the Walmer Castle, a purpose-built pub with a very jolly façade. Ledbury Road leads south into Westbourne Grove, which at this point is one of the area's smartest, if most mainstream, shopping streets. It, like Ledbury Road, was once the domain of oddball and one-off antique shops. These are mostly all gone. Instead high-street clothes stores, belonging to one chain or other, tend to dominate. More useful is the Daylesford organic farm store from Gloucestershire offering meat and bread. Such decidedly upmarket establishments attract the clientele that the ambitious developers of Notting Hill had in mind when they built the area – they might have been concerned, though, that such clients arrived 150 years too late.

Embankment

A few steps to the south-east of Charing Cross station, nestled among the chain restaurants and corporate offices on Villiers Street, you will find Gordon's Wine Bar. Occupying the ground floor and basement of a nineteenth-century building, the bar contains an ancient world of vaults and stout piers below ground level. These probably date from the 1670s building on the site but could just, in part at least, be fragments of the older York House (see p. 498). Gordon's dates from 1890 and is still run as a family affair, and if you time your visit carefully – perhaps late afternoon on a day early in the week – then the often-overcrowded bar can be a place of subterranean bliss, where you can enjoy your wine and a plate of cheese, biscuits and pickle. The real treat, though, is on the outside. If you sit on the terrace, before you to the south-east are Embankment Gardens.

Until the mid 1860s this was part of the foreshore of the Thames and the building above the wine bar was a riverside warehouse. At high tide water would have been at your feet, but at low tide there would have been a wide expanse of mud, stretching as far as the modern river's edge, occupied by an array of structures, including beached boats – the workplaces, even homes, of river-folk who made their strange livings along the banks of the Thames and by harvesting its waters. There were boatmen and ferrymen, as well as mudlarks, who searched for lost or discarded things. There were also scavengers of other sorts. Charles Dickens wrote about some of them. *Our Mutual Friend*, published in 1864 – essentially a novel about the river and river life – starts with characters fishing in the Thames for corpses: a commodity that was potentially of considerable value. Many died in the river in those days, largely because so many people worked or lived on the Thames and because accidents happen. But there were also suicides. Waterloo Bridge was a particularly favoured location: in the 1840s, 15 per cent of London suicides were jumpers from the bridge. It probably developed this morbid role because in the early days it was a toll bridge and not much used, so those embarking on their final lonely task could be fairly certain there would be no passers-by to intervene.

The nature of the Thames would change, however, in the 1860s. The Embankment, built between 1865 and into the early 1870s, was in part inspired by the desire to clean up the river after a series of serious cholera outbreaks, for which tainted river water bore a heavy responsibility, and partly to modernise services and communications in London. So the Metropolitan Board of Works (MBW), founded in 1855 to oversee the city's major infrastructure projects, came up with a radical plan. Its lead engineer, Joseph Bazalgette, proposed pushing a stretch of the north bank into the river towards the south bank – initially between Westminster Bridge and Blackfriars Bridge and in the early 1870s extended in the west to form Chelsea Embankment. In the space created the MBW could insert not just a sewer system, designed to interrupt the flow of raw waste into the Thames and carry it off for treatment, but also gas mains and telegraph cables and – below the eastern portion of the Embankment – tracks for the newly started underground

Until the arrival of the Embankment, ramshackle warehouses and homes rose directly from the Thames – as captured in this watercolour by Walter Greaves of the water's edge in Chelsea.

W. Greaves

A cross section of the Embankment at Charing Cross Station, as it appeared in 1867.

railway network. And, when roofed over, this below-ground-level space, protected from the Thames by a retaining wall or embankment, could support a major new road, tree-lined like a Parisian boulevard. In most sections of the Embankment's length, when local conditions permitted, the former foreshore could be raised and planted to form riverside gardens.

The garden in front of you, planted in 1874, is the largest, stretching uninterrupted from Hungerford Bridge to Waterloo Bridge. Because the Thames here was wide and slow-flowing, Bazalgette was able to push the edge of the river to the south-east by around 135 metres. Of course, appropriation of about a third of the river bed had a dramatic effect on the Thames – changing its ecology, speeding up water flow, and potentially making surviving stretches of water deeper and more dangerous both to people and to structures like bridge piers. But none of this seemed to worry most contemporary observers. Charles Dickens Jr, the son of the novelist, published a *Dictionary of London* and in the 1893 edition remembered the 'squalid foreshore' with its 'tumble-down wharves, and backs of dingy houses, which formerly abutted on the river', and praised 'the beautiful curve of the Embankment, majestic in its

simplicity, with its massive granite wall, flourishing trees and trim gardens'. This, he argued, was 'an unspeakable improvement . . . conductive to health and comfort'.[1]

Bazalgette's scheme was brilliant in its way. Indeed this heroic exercise was so greatly admired that it was soon honoured with the name Victoria Embankment, and thus given quasi-royal status, certainly royal approval, as a piece of civil and social engineering. Not only did the Embankment improve services and communication in the city but it also replaced the 'tumble-down wharves' and unsightly 'dingy houses' of the poor riverside workers and residents with a boulevard and a garden, soon peopled with statues of Victorian heroes.

But the legacy of the Victoria Embankment, and of Chelsea Embankment to the west, has proved deeply problematic for the city. Both these works have done what they were intended to do. But they have also, in most dreadful manner, cut off the river from the life of London. Buildings that rose on the river's edge, or from the water like Somerset House (see p. 485), have been marooned behind a thundering road. And at Chelsea, the ancient riverside gardens have been landlocked, and a marvellous array of riverside wharves, taverns, homes and paths along Cheyne Walk swept away with stunning brutality.

The great leafy riverside boulevard that the MBW created no doubt initially looked wonderful with picturesque horse-drawn traffic and promenading pedestrians. But sadly times have changed and the boulevard has only too easily become a polluted urban motorway. In a way the doleful legacy of the Victoria and Chelsea Embankments has been to encourage London to turn its back on its great river, even to ignore it – rather than to use and enjoy it. This is a sad fate for the people of a great riverside metropolis, which was historically almost a water-city like Venice or Amsterdam.

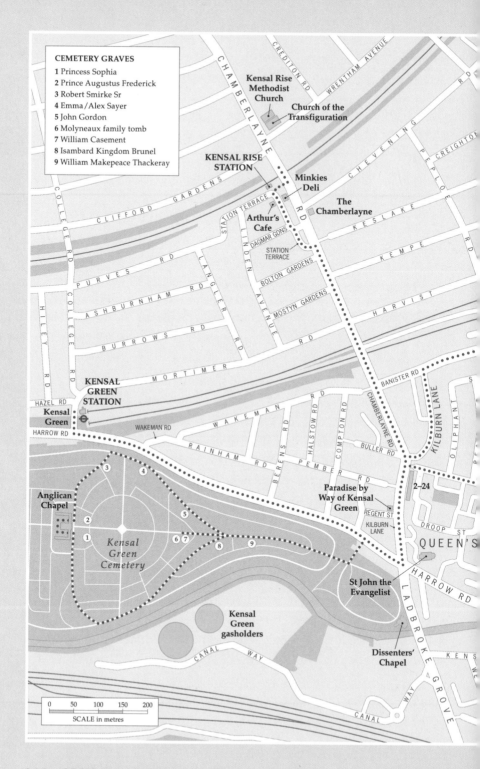

CEMETERY GRAVES

1 Princess Sophia
2 Prince Augustus Frederick
3 Robert Smirke Sr
4 Emma/Alex Sayer
5 John Gordon
6 Molyneaux family tomb
7 William Casement
8 Isambard Kingdom Brunel
9 William Makepeace Thackeray

WALK 9

Kensal Green and Kensal Rise

*Life and death in the
Victorian city*

In the 1830s, Kensal Green was a rural hamlet a mile or so from the edge of the capital. By the turn of the twentieth century it would be a bustling London suburb, complete with some of the most progressive working-class housing in the country. The change was brought about in large part by a single groundbreaking enterprise: the Cemetery of All Souls, which in 1832 became London's first great suburban burial ground. And yet, despite this most specific history, the transformation of Kensal Green is part of a much broader story. Through the nineteenth century, sleepy villages on the edges of the city were gradually engulfed by the city, as it became home to an ever-growing industrial working class – and giving birth to the sprawling metropolis we know today.

Any walk through Kensal Green must begin with the cemetery that has been so integral to its shifting fortunes. All Souls is the pioneer – and arguably the most astonishing – of London's 'Cities of the Dead'. Previously, generations of the capital's dead had been packed into small

A city of the dead: looking west along the main avenue of Kensal Green cemetery.

city-centre burial grounds and churchyards and into the vaults of the city's churches. Gradually, as these receptacles became ever more crowded, it became apparent that something was terribly wrong. In the early 1830s no one quite understood how disease spread, but it was nonetheless evident that the dead of the city were killing the living. In response, in 1832, Parliament authorised the establishment of commercial cemetery companies in the remote and healthy fields around London. Kensal Green was the first to open – and as the cemetery boomed, so did the population of the village.

This transformation from quiet hamlet to bustling cityscape was largely complete by the 1860s. Helped along by the construction of several railway stations and waves of Irish immigration, by 1871 the parish next to the cemetery was home to 2,138 people living in just 264 houses.[1] And, as so often in Victorian London, urbanisation brought with it overcrowding, squalor and disease. Soon Kensal Town, just to the east of the new cemetery, had a reputation as the archetypal west London slum, nicknamed 'Chelsea-in-the-Wilderness' thanks to its isolation (both geographical and cultural) from its more affluent southern neighbour. An 1868 newspaper report from a landlords' meeting gives a sense of the poverty in which the inhabitants lived:

> It appeared that in Kensal New-town there is a large number of
> cottages let to very poor people at weekly rentals, and that the

landlords have very great difficulty in obtaining their rents
. . . It would be an absurdity to employ a broker, because in
nine cases out of ten the 'few sticks' in the houses would not
be worth distraining for . . . Generally speaking the tenants in
Kensal New-town were a migratory class, 'here today and
gone tomorrow'.[2]

The buildings we encounter on the second half of this walk, then, were largely a response to concerns about the state of Kensal's poor. The local landowners were uniquely well placed to deal with these problems. The area north of the cemetery had, in theory at least, been managed with a sense of *noblesse oblige* for centuries. In the first half of the fifteenth century the land here was acquired by Henry Chichele, a most inspirational and influential Archbishop of Canterbury. In 1438, with King Henry VI, he founded All Souls, Oxford – a college whose key purpose was to pray for all who had died, and indeed for all who were still to die, in the Hundred Years War – and before his death bestowed to it the fields that now make up Kensal Rise. The control of part of the land fluctuated in Tudor times, for a while being in the possession of Lady Margaret Beaufort and of Henry VIII's last wife Catherine Parr, but All Souls remained involved until the area was developed in earnest in the late nineteenth century. As you might hope All Souls took some benevolent interest in the way its land was used.

When you wander through the vicinity today, the effects of this benevolence are clear. The terraces around Kilburn Lane, built from the mid 1870s onwards, offer a vision of working-class life that couldn't be further from the slums that once made up the area. They reflect one of the great preoccupations of many members of the late-nineteenth-century philanthropic movement: that providing decent housing or the bare essentials of life was not enough. The poor, it was thought, had to be given beauty, education and culture to inspire them, and to help them rise from the shrunken world of despair and spiritual poverty. Much like the public-parks movement, getting fully under way in the 1860s, with the aim of providing healthy open space, the developers of Kensal Rise and Kilburn wanted to provide housing that was not simply a barrack-block but comfortable and handsome.

It was an approach that would earn many admirers. Decades later, in 1901, Walter Besant, a typical late-Victorian polymath who churned out novels and popular history packed with social criticism, observed of the East End that the most pressing problem was not poverty or crime but soul-destroying ugliness and 'meanness'. The houses of Kensal were designed to forge another path: one that overcame squalor by offering working people a hearth and home to be proud of.

THE WALK

Travel to Kensal Green station – a somewhat gloomy stop on the Bakerloo Line – and ascend from its open-air platform to Mortimer Road. Head south on to Harrow Road, and proceed east. Within a few steps a tall wall, with lofty trees behind, will appear to your right. This is the boundary to Kensal Green cemetery, which you should follow east along the road.

Take a moment to ponder Harrow Road. This is one of the city's ancient thoroughfares – perhaps originating as a pre-Roman track or trade route – that now cuts a revealing cross section through the communities of west and north-west London. It runs from Paddington Green and Edgware Road (another ancient track, parts of which the Romans incorporated into Watling Street), north-west to Harrow. The age of the road is only hinted at by a few buildings grouped along its north side, which confirm that in late-Georgian times it must have been a pleasant rural thoroughfare. All appear to date from the 1820s, and although modest in scale were no doubt respectable retreats for the mercantile class and for rural artisans of superior means. From west to east, there is a terrace of tall brick-faced houses (numbers 856–850), then a detached villa (842) with a pretty fanlight, followed by another terrace, now stuccoed (840–836), a long row of cottages (834–822), and a free-standing house of strange composition, formed with a tall and narrow centre portion flanked by lower wings (818). This group is most picturesque, with admirable variety in scale and form.

Further along Harrow Road, to the south, is the triumphal entry to the realm of the dead: our first introduction to Kensal Green cemetery. Its classical design was a controversial choice. When the creation of the

The restrained classicism of the existing entrance to the cemetery (above) is in stark contrast with the Gothic alternative that was nearly built (right).

burial site was first mooted, a competition was held to find a design for this ceremonial entrance, resulting in a miniature but bitter episode in the ongoing 'battle of the styles'. The founder of the cemetery, the barrister George Frederick Carden, wanted its architecture to be in the Gothic style. Unfortunately, the chairman of the General Cemetery Company set up to run Kensal Green, a banker named Sir John D. Paul, did not. He wanted Grecian architecture that, with its temple associations, he felt was more solemn and appropriate. Carden's preferred Gothic design was duly swept away. Not long after, so was Carden.

Fortunately, the bile of the long-ago battle does not affect the building's charm. The great, arched gate contains rooms for the porter and is embellished with giant Grecian Doric columns that support a noble entablature. It is a fine and fitting piece of work – reflecting a muscular although not unromantic approach to the grim business of death. It was perhaps partly designed by Paul himself, with the advice of the architect John William Griffith, a partnership that would be responsible for all of the cemetery's main buildings and layout.

The prospect of the 29-hectare cemetery from the gate is also gratifying, if a little surprising. Avenues stretch in various directions that, replete with richly planted trees, create a picturesque park. The general artistic ambition of the place – to create a sacred ground that could make death almost a thing of beauty – was inspired by the world's first great suburban cemetery: Père Lachaise, constructed in Paris from 1804 with the blessing of Napoleon. From here, though, one realises that London's great cemetery is rather more oddball than Paris's. The vista not only offers a prospect of early-Victorian death – in all its pomp, glory and decay – but also a fine vision of early-Victorian industry. Through the trees of the cemetery rise the skeletal forms of a collection of large gasholders, standing on a site acquired in 1845 by the Western Gas Company. From its earliest days, this theatre of death was accompanied by the very worldly business of coal-fired gas production.

There are many paths through the cemetery, but the central road – reached by taking the first right (west) after the gate – is the most magnificent. Adorned by the earliest, most important and most opulent monuments, the avenue suggests that the early cemetery was an exclusive venue. The proprietors, the General Cemetery Company (founded in 1830), hoped that high fees for plots would not only boost their income in the short term, but also foster a high-class atmosphere that would attract even more wealthy clients in the long run. So, from the start, the cemetery was a contradictory creation: both a spiritual site built to celebrate the dead, and a rather calculating money-making exercise.

For a while, the founders' gamble looked like it might fail. There was no English precedent for park-like Valhallas, and the Victorian middle class didn't know what to make of it: was being buried here the done thing? But after a few grand and fashionable interments set the tone, the venture took off. In 1843 Prince Augustus Frederick, a son of George III, was buried in the cemetery, and a few years later, in 1848, he was joined by his sister, Princess Sophia. Suddenly, to be interred there was to join the company of royalty. The cemetery was made, and the bodies of the great and good of Victorian Britain flooded in. By 1853 nearly 20,000 people had been buried here.

In these early years, the cemetery established a reputation as the final resting place of architects and engineers, artists and writers. As you wander the avenues, keep an eye out for the graves of Isambard Kingdom Brunel, buried 1859, and his father Marc, buried ten years earlier; the writers William Makepeace Thackeray, buried 1863, and Anthony Trollope, buried 1882; and the illustrator George Cruikshank, who despite being a born-again temperance fanatic managed to father eleven illegitimate children and died in 1878 (his body was later moved to St Paul's Cathedral). More recent burials and interments of ashes include the playwrights Terence Rattigan in 1977 and Harold Pinter in 2008.

These recent burials are a crucial part of the cemetery's story. Many of the large suburban burial grounds that followed Kensal Green became full to capacity, lost their money-making potential and ceased trading. This usually proved a disaster: without income, it was impossible to maintain them, and some fell into scandalous disrepair. This never happened at Kensal Green. It seemingly filled up years ago, but the company has somehow always managed to accommodate fresh burials – usually by squeezing new graves between the old. The result is some truly strange juxtapositions between the graves of the long-dead and the graves of the recently deceased. The modern aesthetics of death are another world in comparison with the tastes of the nineteenth century. Add to that the extraordinary diversity of tastes even within Victorian high society, and you get a quite dizzying array of tombs. Along the main avenue, almost jostling for room and attention, are monuments in Greek, Roman, Renaissance, Gothic and Egyptian tastes. Clearly death was, from the artistic point of view, a very eclectic business.

Just a handful of examples will make this point clear. First, for fans of the classical, comes a remarkable monument to Major General Sir William Casement, on the southern side of the avenue. The place of columns is taken by male caryatids that stand sentinel around the general's draped sarcophagus, on which sits his plumed commander's hat. The caryatids are turban-topped – presumably a reference to Casement's time in the Indian civil service. This splendid confection dates from 1844.

An array of styles: the tombs of William Casement (above) and John Gordon (right).

Nearby stands a strikingly Gothic tomb: a large, octagonal affair, with each face treated like the elevation of a gabled shrine, which is one of the most architecturally ambitious structures in the cemetery. It was created in 1864–6 by John Gibson – a leading architect of the time – for the Molyneux family. This tomb gives us some idea of what the architecture of the cemetery gate would have been like if Carden's taste had prevailed: ornamental, and battered by time, which tends to be a problem with the delicate detail on Victorian Gothic buildings. Often too much care went into making it spindly and unworldly, and not enough into the problem of how to make it survive the buffets of time. Paul was right: the simple, block-like Greek is far more robust, and can easily take a few generations of neglect in its stride.

Over the avenue to the north, and in striking contrast, is one of my favourites: the tomb of John Gordon, built in 1840. It's purely architectural and wonderfully bold – just four tremendously stout, tapering square piers, topped by simple Tuscan capitals that carry an entablature and four plain, flat-faced pediments framed by curious Egyptian faces. It's all so elemental, seemingly making a point about the eternal and unchanging beauty of pure and robust classical architecture. People live and die, through the millennia, but architecture endures for all time.

To match the range of architectural styles, the cemetery also hosts a charming array of symbols. Broken columns signify a life cut short, upturned torches symbolise the extinguishing of the vital spark, and anchors represent belief in resurrection after death. Such a diversity of images doesn't reflect a diversity of beliefs: while Roman Catholics could technically be buried here and Dissenters have their own chapel in the east of the cemetery, almost all of the major monuments are Anglican. Nevertheless, non-Anglican imagery abounds, much of it appropriated from pagan traditions. The most popular pre-Christian images are, predictably, the many strange and wonderful motifs in the creation of Egyptian tombs and mini mortuary temples. Spotting and enjoying these often incongruous little essays – often wonderfully archaeologically ill-informed – is one of the many pleasures of exploring the cemetery.

Once my eyes adjust to the aesthetic eclecticism of the monuments, I often like to indulge in a little *Schadenfreude*. Many serve as a profound representation of the transience of worldly power and greatness. In the sixteenth and seventeenth centuries, tombs were generally intended to serve as memento mori: reminders to the living of the constant imminence of death and decay. Centuries later, many of the Kensal Green tombs would come to function as splendid memento mori – even if this was not the original intention. Take the monument to Robert Smirke, 'Academician of the Royal Academy of Arts in London', who died in 1845 aged ninety-one and is buried to the north-west of John Gordon. The father of the great architect Sir Robert Smirke, who designed the British Museum, Smirke Sr was himself no lightweight, rising to be an admired portrait painter and book illustrator. But in death he is sadly diminished. The grave is surmounted by a large headstone embellished with a badly carved and now weather-worn visage of the deceased. It's all very melancholic and a sobering reminder of the ultimate futility of attempts to gain immortality (especially when, as in this case, the funerary art is of such mediocre quality and realised in such ephemeral material).

A little to the east, near the boundary with Harrow Road, is another somewhat overwrought monument. It consists of a tall pedestal topped by an outsized declamatory statue, right arm raised, which towers above cavorting cherubs. This is said to personify 'Faith' or – rather more charming, in its implied uncertainty – 'Hope'. On the base of the pedestal, in large letters, is inscribed the rather abrupt legend 'To Her'. But who can 'Her' be? Presumably the person with long flowing hair, shown on a Van Dyck-style bas-relief bust on the side of the pedestal. This is Emma Jones Soyer, who died in 1842 aged twenty-eight, 'due to a miscarriage induced by her terrible fear of thunderstorms'; her husband, Alex Benoît Soyer, was heartbroken and erected the monument for her. Benoît Soyer was another Victorian famous in his lifetime: a renowned chef in mid-nineteenth-century London who brought French excellence to the kitchen of the Reform Club when it opened in 1841, cooked for Queen Victoria, did his best to feed the starving during the Irish Famine of 1848, set up a soup kitchen for the poor in Spitalfields and took an efficient field kitchen to the Crimea to help nourish poorly fed soldiers. Like Smirke, he is now largely forgotten, memorialised only in this enormous family tomb.

Between them, the array of tombs reveal much about the Victorian attitude to death. They speak not just of the religious ritual of burial, but also of the fear and mystery that then surrounded the simple act of dying. Perhaps the greatest fear was of premature burial, which became something of a hysteria in the late nineteenth century. Some years ago I investigated this nightmare and discovered that there was a regular periodical, *The Premature Burialist*, which, well into the twentieth century, published evidence that premature burial was not only possible but even likely. The belief seemed to have rested on an unscientific but deep-rooted belief that a person could appear dead, even with their heart stopped, but in fact be in a deep trance or state of 'suspended animation'; Edgar Allan Poe, in his 1844 short story 'Premature Burial', blamed all on a pseudoscientific and wildly exaggerated interpretation of catalepsy. To the Victorian mind, one way to avoid this horror was embalming, which involved the removal of so many organs that even Christ himself would have a Herculean task bringing about reanimation. Alternatively, there was the option of a 'safety coffin': a contraption that offered a way for the 'corpse' to signal that it had been buried alive. Kensal Green has some of the finest examples still in existence: look out for tombs that are topped by bell towers, whose pulls lead directly down into the coffins – ready to be rung by any 'corpse' finding itself conscious. These monuments serve as another reminder, were one needed, that the Victorian way of dying was not as close to ours as we might think.

Walk back round to the western edge of the main avenue. Here presides the Anglican chapel, also designed by J. W. Griffith: a splendid building that takes the form of a four-columned Grecian Doric temple, flanked by long low wings that extend west to define a courtyard. I always find the chapel moving because it is virtually a half-sized version of the long-lost and continually lamented Euston Arch – the first monument of the railway age, completed 1837 – designed by one of the tenants of the cemetery, Philip Hardwick, and infamously demolished in 1961 to make way for the rebuilt Euston Station. Before it stand the monuments of the cemetery's two most illustrious incumbents: the royal children of George III. Neither tomb is too ostentatious but evidently it suited their family (and the cemetery company) to give these memorials the best, and most visible, locations. Of the two, only that of Princess Sophia manages to make itself memorable, largely through the high quality of its materials and workmanship. It consists of a tall pedestal supporting a larger-than-life-size, and rather ornate, 'Quattrocento' ('four hundred', i.e. in fifteenth-century style) sarcophagus on legs.[3]

Inside, the chapel is a sparse but elegant affair, with a charming ceiling decorated with a Greek key motif. The centrepiece of the room is the catafalque: the altar-like structure that lowers coffins down into the catacombs below. In the 1830s this device was operated manually using a screw jack, but it was prone to malfunction, either emitting loud groans or simply stopping moving at crucial moments in funerals. So, in 1844, a new hydraulic lift was installed. The upgraded version was a high-tech piece of machinery, able to lower the entire catafalque (rather than merely a coffin) into the catacombs. After years of disuse, in 1995–7 it was restored to its original glory; it is still in use today.

The Anglican chapel designed by J. W. Griffith.

The real highlight of the chapel complex, though, is what lies beneath it – the catacombs. To visit them, one must book into one of the tours given each Sunday. It is well worth the effort. They are, of course, eerie beyond belief: dark, dusty, echoing and packed with coffins, many covered in once plush but now mouldering red velvet, peeping out of the shadows of the many dank and lonely recesses. I remember seeing one body that was in a very strange predicament. Its coffin was wrapped in brown paper embossed with stamps and postmarks, which made it clear that this unlikely package had arrived from Bombay at some point in the 1930s. But nobody had claimed it, or even unwrapped it. Here the body waits, like a piece of abandoned left-luggage, perpetually in transit on its way to the world to come.

To the west of the chapel, in the open-roofed cells around the courtyard, are a few early sculptural monuments. But if the truth be told, the general standard of sculpture at Kensal Green is not high, and certainly does not bear comparison with the great Continental cemeteries. Take

the tremendous Staglieno cemetery in Genoa, founded 1851, which is much like an open-air sculpture museum – the Genoese evidently realised that one's name would last longer in memory if commemorated by a striking piece of art, preferably in bronze or marble. Curiously, this is a lesson hardly ever learned and applied by the patrons of Kensal Green.

The poverty of artistic execution stands in stark contrast to the pretensions of many of those commemorated here. From the start, the venture was criticised for its hubris. As *The Builder* put it in 1854, the cemetery was a 'rendezvous of dreary inanities', only notable for its 'ponderous coxcombry'.[4] It's something to bear in mind as you meander back through the graves –

some artful, more entertainingly pompous – to the great Doric gate to the east. For all the wealth and ambition in nineteenth-century London, there was one thing that the Victorian upper-middle class couldn't buy: taste.

<hr />

The brash riches of All Souls Cemetery are even more striking when compared with the gloriously understated architecture that surrounds it. Kilburn Lane offers a glimpse of some of the greatest architectural achievements of Victorian philanthropy, offering beautiful and cheap homes to London's labouring classes. First, though, you must endure a truly lamentable church. Pass back through the Doric gate, turn right along Harrow Road and, in a few metres, you come across St John the Evangelist.

Completed in 1844 – seemingly on the cheap, to judge by the mean use of industrial-looking buff brick and flint – St John was described by Nikolaus Pevsner as an 'atrocious' building with a 'barn-like' interior.[5] He had a point. This thoroughly unlovely church is an example of how badly wrong Kensal Green could have gone, had the tides of architectural fashion flowed slightly differently: its architect, H. K. Kendal, was the man behind the competition-winning but rejected Gothic designs for the cemetery arch and chapel. It represents one of the losing sides in the mid-nineteenth-century 'Battle of the Styles': the Romanesque. Fashionable at the time, particularly in Germany where it was called the *Rundbogenstil* because of the abundant use of semicircular topped arches, the Romanesque was promoted in England by the German-born Prince Albert. But it made little headway in the face of the strong challenge offered by the Gothic and the classical traditions. Thank goodness for that.

St John sits on a crossroads. To the south is Ladbroke Grove, running straight and true to the heart of Notting Hill; to the east, Harrow Road goes on to Paddington; and to the north lies Kilburn Lane, and this is the route we follow. Things start to look up as, almost immediately, Kilburn Lane turns dramatically to the north-east; if you carry straight on, you enter Chamberlayne Road, which now contributes much to the increasingly vibrant life of the neighbourhood. It also serves as a boundary between two subtly different urban quarters. To the west is Kensal Green, while to the east is Kensal Rise, an area characterised by large swathes of late-nineteenth-century streets.

Before plunging north-east into Kensal Rise, it's worth looking a little more carefully at the buildings on and around the southern end of Kilburn Lane. Most obvious is a truly splendid pub, dated 1892 and resplendent with its array of Elizabethan-style lofty gables, which stands on the west side of Kilburn Lane, at the corner with the grandly named but extremely short and modest Regent Street. The pub is now called 'Paradise, By Way of Kensal Green'. It is a rather ambitious reference to a poem of 1913 by G. K. Chesterton, which sings the virtues of 'The Rolling English Road' and concludes with a reference to the cemetery:

> For there is good news yet to hear and fine things to be seen,
> Before we go to Paradise by way of Kensal Green.

The pub's current name is proclaimed by a striking board recently set on its bevelled corner. It shows a naked figure, its chest and shoulders wrapped in a wind-blown cloak but its naked posterior and legs exposed to public gaze (the 'way' to 'Paradise', perhaps?). It's all a bit baffling. The side door gives a clue to the pub's original name: above it is an image of a plough. The original inn on the site, the Plough, was established in the sixteenth century, and offered a charming pun on the pub's location – just above the Harrow Road.

The interior is equally fascinating, with a heady mix of the art nouveau and Tudor classicism typical of the 1890s. The Paradise is now a local landmark and one of the stalwart markers of the new Kensal Green and Kensal Rise. Fifteen or so years ago this was a working-class area with large and long-established communities of Afro-Caribbean or Irish descent. These communities remain, but are now greatly diluted by the arrival of waves of middle-class professionals. Its bars are packed with a weird and wonderfully Baroque collection of furniture and outlandish statuary on and around which the sleek new, and mostly young, denizens of the area disport themselves. Cities and their districts do evolve – that's what keeps places like London alive and interesting – and Kensal Green and Kensal Rise are currently in the grip of one of these great spasms of change. The only problem, of course, is the perpetual one: as new and richer communities move in, rents and house values rise and older, and perhaps poorer, existing communities are forced out.

The irony here is that the Victorian architecture that now attracts Kensal's ballooning middle class was quite explicitly not designed for them. Just before the north-west curve of Kilburn Lane we come across a terrace of most interesting late-nineteenth-century houses, which hint at the working-class origins of the district. This is the former property of All Souls College, an institution that, in the late nineteenth century, helped to offer decent and respectable shelter to the area's then large, and generally quite poor, working community. Many of the streets are almost utopian in their good-spirited intent.

Subtle design features give away these philanthropic origins of the terrace. It is modest in scale – each house is only two storeys high – but ornamented with erudite if economic Gothic detail. The houses are entered through handsome paired doors, each topped by gables inspired

The Kilburn Lane terrace. The gabled porches reveal that these are third-class houses.

by medieval altar canopies. And each gable contains a terracotta panel bearing, within an eight-pointed star, the date 1876 and some entwined letters: ALGDCL, for the Artizans, Labourers & General Dwellings Company Limited. This enterprise, founded in 1867, was behind all of the elegant streets that we encounter as we turn east into Kensal Rise.

———◆•◆•◆———

The objective of the Artizans Dwellings Company was simple. Its founder, a self-made and possibly illiterate builder called William Austin, had seen the squalor of London's working-class housing first-hand. In it, he spotted an opportunity. His company endeavoured to build model houses on the outskirts of cities, offering better-paid workers the chance to commute in from the tranquil suburbs. It was not a wholly charitable enterprise: the company was always for-profit, and in its early years made a number of shrewd investments in Battersea and Salford. The enterprise soon caught the eye of the great philanthropist and social reformer Lord Shaftesbury,

better known for his campaigns against child labour earlier in the century, who became its president.

The idiosyncratic consequences of the company's semi-philanthropic, semi-entrepreneurial approach are visible throughout Kensal Rise. If you follow the curve of Kilburn Lane you enter street after street of pretty Victorian working-class cottage housing. This is the Queen's Park estate, constructed by the company from 1874, which offers thoughtful architecture that, although humble in scale, does not lack ambition or serious intent. Rather than the utilitarian tenement blocks that were typical of such enterprises, here we have terraces, each intended for a single family, each with its own front door and little garden, and each emblazoned with those distinctive terracotta plaques.

The layout of the large estate is in itself remarkable. When construction began, it was conceived loosely as a right-angular grid. Most of the estate's north–south streets are numbered – from

'First Avenue' in the east to 'Sixth Avenue' in the west – whereas most of the slightly narrower west–east streets are lettered – originally ranging from A Street through to P Street. Perhaps the inspiration was New York's early-nineteenth-century grid, in which the avenues and cross streets are numbered, with the exception of an area in the Lower East Side, added to the grid in the 1840s, where the avenues are lettered 'A' to 'D'. This district – inevitably soon known as 'Alphabet City' – was first occupied by Manhattan's German community, but by the 1870s was becoming home to the city's poorer Irish, Italian and East European Jewish immigrants. Today, you could be forgiven for thinking that the Queen's Park Estate's streets are no longer lettered, but look again and you will see they are. In 1883 it was decided to make the area a little more homely by replacing the lettered streets by names, but the first letter of each new name commemorates the street's lettered origin, so O Street became Oliphant Street, N Street became Nutbourne Street, and M Street became Marne Street.

As you explore the area, and your eyes adjust, you will begin to notice subtle diversity within what at first seems to be overwhelming uniformity. One notable feature of the estate is its clear hierarchy: the avenues tend to contain slightly bigger and more ornate houses than do the streets, and within the streets occasional details give away that some houses are slightly bigger than others. This little town was designed to include five classes of houses, so that it could accommodate working people ranging from the reasonably well off to the reasonably poor.

It isn't just size that marks out the different classes of houses. Fifth Avenue was the best address, and has architectural features to match. Corner houses tend to be furnished with spires and ground-floor windows are embellished with small Gothic shafts and boldly sliced-back mouldings. In the somewhat smaller roads, such as Oliphant Street, the houses are similar but their front doors are often grouped under gables and, sometimes, under straight-topped brick lintels. These are clues to the hierarchy: gabled porches distinguish third-class houses, whereas the simpler lintel porches mark fourth-class houses, which are slightly smaller. The original plans from these houses reveal a simple but practical layout, with a back and a front room on both floors, plus a rear closet on the ground floor that contained a fireplace for cooking, a

The junction of Sixth Avenue with Oliphant Street, two of the estate's more modest roads.

'copper' in one inner corner for washing, and a sink and a lavatory in the two outer corners.[6]

The ALGDCL's architects were keen that homes wouldn't be the only thing they offered to residents. Most of the estate's corner shops were in the original plans, once serving as bakeries, grocery stores, butcher's, fishmonger's, cobbler's, a chemist, and even a fancy basket and canework emporium. There were a few public buildings, too, most notably the library at the southern intersection of Fourth Avenue with the Harrow Road. The library was a direct expression of the company's aspiration that its tenants be given the opportunity of 'self-improvement'. This Victorian ideal was vividly expressed by the influential campaigner Samuel Smiles, who wrote that 'self-education' could raise individuals 'from poverty to social eminence' but, more important, 'knowledge is of itself one of the highest enjoyments. The ignorant man passes through the world dead to all pleasure, save those of the senses.' Smiles's book, *Self-Help*, was published in 1859 to spread the doctrine of strength through knowledge, of thrift, perseverance and civility, and it was in this admirable spirit that the fine Queen's Park Library – originally Kensal New Town Library – was opened in 1890.

There was, though, one facility that the company refused to build: public houses. The estate was explicitly for the so-called 'respectable' working class – industrious, well-behaved and churchgoing labourers who were often distinguished from, in late-Victorian parlance, the 'roughs'. To help its flock on its way, the company prohibited alcohol from being sold within its boundaries: indeed in 1878 it managed to prevent a Mr Bates, with a shop at 9 Harrow Road, from selling alcohol, while in 1884 the tenant of 24 Third Avenue was evicted 'due to drunkenness and obscene language'. The company's intention was to make Kensal Rise a temperance community. Such schemes were not entirely foolproof: one 1899 account wryly noted that the absence of licences on the estate 'will account for the good business done by the "off" licenses which cluster round [its] eastern outskirts'. But it was a noble bid at teetotalism, which is reflected in the lack of pubs on the estate to this day.[7]

This all sounds most utopian, but in practice the story of the estate was rather more chequered. For one thing, in spite of all its philanthropic rhetoric, the men behind the Artizans Dwellings Company weren't exactly impeccably behaved. The nadir came near the very start of the project, and from a most unexpected quarter. The company secretary, William Swindlehurst, turned out to be most aptly named: in 1877 he, along with John Baxter Langley and Edward Saffery, went on trial at the Old Bailey for a fraud committed upon the ALGDCL. John Shaw Lowe, the deputy chairman, was also accused but seems to have fled the country. The men were charged with 'unlawfully conspiring by false pretences to obtain £9,312' from the company. They had bought land from All Souls, acting on behalf of the company, and then sold it on to the company with a large mark-up for themselves.[8] Of course, these wretched, greedy and stupid men were found out, and sentenced to servitude and humiliation: Swindlehurst got eighteen months, the other two twelve months each.

Set against the shocking example of their 'betters', the residents of the estate were impressively well behaved. The trouble that came was, by comparison, very small beer – such as one intriguingly ambiguous eviction of 1884, in which the tenants at 21 Caird Street and 32 Harrow Road were removed for using their premises 'for immoral purposes'.[9] Yet this was not to say that life on the estate was easy. Nineteenth-century census returns reveal that, even when being used as planned, by today's standards the district was shockingly overcrowded. Despite the 'respectable' professions of the residents – railway porters, clerks, carpenters, plasters, laundresses and dressmakers, many recent immigrants from Ireland or immigrants from the English countryside – they were crammed into every room. Take the fourth-class house at 107 Oliphant Street, which, in 1891, housed two families in its six rooms. The 'head' of the first was Shirley Harriet, thirty-two, from Brill, Buckinghamshire (her husband is not listed but she is not described as a widow, which suggests he was alive but not living in the house), which she shared with her brothers Joseph Pollard, twenty-seven, and Willis Pollard, twenty-two, both agricultural labourers; the second was headed by Thomas Honour, thirty-one and in a similar trade, from Boarstall, Buckinghamshire, and included his wife Sarah, twenty-seven, from Brill, Buckinghamshire, and their two sons and two daughters, all aged under five. The families' shared Buckinghamshire origin implies that these two households were connected, but nevertheless it's hard to imagine how nine or ten people occupied this small house. Presumably every room, apart from the kitchen, was used as a bedroom.[10]

The census taken ten years later, in 1901, suggests that the intensity of occupation of 107 Oliphant Street was not just an aberration. Thomas Honour was still in residence, as sole 'head' of the house, but now classified a 'General Labourer' – likely a career change induced by the increasingly urban nature of Kensal Green. But Sarah is gone, presumably having died; Thomas has a new wife, Josephine, aged thirty-eight. Three of the children from the first marriage are in residence but Percy, the youngest and less than a year old in 1891, is not listed, likely also dead. Two sons and a daughter from the second marriage are now in residence, as well as a 72-year-old widow named Charlotte Martin, born in the City of London and 'receiving parish relief', and a 27-year-old lodger, born in Basingstoke, Hampshire, and working as a 'Builder's Carman'. So ten people in all. Such records offer a glimpse of the hardships – death, poverty, overcrowding – that were often an inescapable aspect of working-class life.[11]

Even more depressing, though, is how widely accepted this quality of life was by contemporaries. Consider the account of the campaigning social reformer and philanthropist Charles Booth – a man obsessed with classifying the social status of Victorian London's districts, who we met in

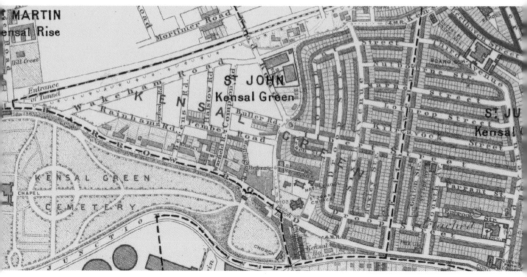

A section of Charles Booth's 1898 'poverty map' of Kensal Green and Kensal Rise. The sea of light red indicates that the Queen's Park Estate was 'fairly comfortable'.

Walk 8. He inspected Queen's Park on 16 January 1899, keen to see how the area had fared since the publication of his magisterial *Life and Labour of the People in London* from 1889. He concluded that the estate was 'purely working class', with 'no poor' in plain view. He praised the architecture, namely the 'broad [and] well paved' streets and the 'fairly built' houses (although some were 'much better than others'), whose inhabitants were 'chiefly clerks, postmen [and] policemen'. According to Booth, there was 'great competition' to live in Queen's Park and 'rents were paid one week in advance'. He grades the estate pink, the third from top grade out of the seven he used to delineate the social and economic profile of London, meaning an area that was 'fairly comfortable' and whose inhabitants enjoyed 'good ordinary earnings'.[12] Clearly, at the turn of the nineteenth century, the life we saw at 107 Oliphant Street was about as good as things got.

◆◆◆

It is only when set against the other Victorian buildings around Kensal Rise that one realises the achievement of the Queen's Park estate. Once you have had your fill of the Artizans' houses, go back to the intersection of Kilburn Lane and Chamberlayne Road, and walk north. Notice the remorseless vistas of terraces running perpendicular to the road, such as on Wakeman Road and Kempe Road. This was the dull reality of most Victorian houses for the middling and poorer classes. In their own way, many are impressive, with their serrated silhouettes of gables and the rhythmic advance and retreat of right-angular bay windows. But, in their repetitiveness, they bring the creativity and architectural flair of the estate to the east into stark relief.

Chamberlayne Road itself is lined by a rich collection of late-nineteenth-century buildings, many built as shops. These days they have diverse uses – an American-style diner at number 66, a flower shop at 76 to 78 – and express the recently acquired character of this part of Kensal Rise: sophisticated but eccentric, smart but comfortable, with what might be taken for detritus by the non-initiated being in fact a statement. London is a city of urban villages, each with its own atmosphere, and Kensal Rise is busily honing and asserting its own new identity.

Yet throughout the walk north, the Victorian heritage of the area reasserts itself. A little further on, just before an excellent gastropub called the Chamberlayne, the road starts to rise up in a gradual ramp that was constructed to take traffic over the railway tracks; if you take a left (west) on to Station Terrace, which continues at ground level, you discover a shrine to the district's old character. Arthur's Café, in particular, looks like it comes from another world when viewed from above – possible from the modernistic glass box of the exquisite Minkies Deli, which holds the high ground immediately opposite. These moments when parallel worlds meet are one of the pleasures to be savoured when walking around those parts of London in the throes of change.

It is worth taking a moment to relish this collision of old and new as you arrive at Kensal Rise station, a convenient place to end this walk. Climb up the stairs to Chamberlayne Road, and look north to the 1890s red-brick pile of Kensal Rise Methodist Church and the Roman Catholic Church of the Transfiguration, huddling together as if for mutual protection. The pair neatly distil the joy of Kensal Green and Kensal Rise: even as the area modernises, echoes of its Victorian origins abound. It is a heritage that, between All Souls Cemetery and the Queen's Park estate, marks the district out as one of the significant architectural achievements of the age.

St Pancras Station and the Midland Grand Hotel

In June 1863 the Midland Railway Company obtained an Act of Parliament to extend its line into London and to construct a terminus at St Pancras. Designed by Henry Barlow, its main feature, started in November 1867, was the stunning train shed, built primarily of wrought-iron ribs. In its scale and engineering elegance, the shed was, when completed, one of the wonders of the age. It achieved a span of 75 metres, making it the widest single-span structure in the world, and was executed in a boldly utilitarian manner where the prime ornament was the functional beauty of its construction.

Today, though, it is not the shed that first catches your eye when you visit St Pancras. In 1865 the railway company held a competition to secure a design for a large, luxury hotel and railway offices to stand on a splendid raised site on the Euston Road, just to the south of the shed. The winner was George Gilbert Scott, and, after revisions and reductions in scale, construction started in 1868. When the Midland Grand Hotel and its related offices was completed in 1876 it was arguably the most splendid, functionally complex, and structurally modern Gothic Revival building in the world. It proclaimed an architecture for the age – rooted in the past, ornamented and adorned with the pedigree of history, yet functional and fit for the very modern purpose of mass travel ushered in by the new railway age. The hotel's interior boasted elaborate Gothic decorated public rooms, as well as London's first elevator or 'ascending room', hot water radiators, modern plumbing and exposed iron construction. An indication of the brilliance and quality of Scott's creation is that, after years of neglect, and potential demolition during the 1960s, the building is once again a grand hotel, and hugely admired for its architectural panache.

To visit the station and hotel now is to enter a wonderland of mid Victorian engineering prowess and of architectural opulence – both themes combining in fantastical manner in the hotel's spectacular flying and Gothic vaulted grand staircase, which seems to defy gravity. But a visit can be something more. For it is also like entering the mind of that curious age, troubled, full of contradictions and aspiring to so much –

The vaulted grand staircase inside the Midland Grand Hotel seems to defy gravity.

notably, from the architectural point of view, to find a stylistic expression appropriate for a Christian people and for the greatest empire the world had ever seen.

The Christian aspirations were most succinctly expressed by the polemicist, architect and Roman Catholic convert Augustus W. N. Pugin, who we met in Walk 7. In the 1830s he reduced architecture to a basic moral issue. The late Georgian world of art was eclectic, with architects working in contrasting styles – Roman, Greek, Renaissance, Gothic, even 'Hindoo' and Chinese – to suit the mood of the moment, the tastes of the client, the use of the building or the character of the site. But Pugin argued that this was wrong, and even immoral. For him, there was only one way to building: the Gothic. This, he said, was Christian in origin, rooted in British culture and artistically and structurally superior and more adaptable to modern demands than 'pagan' classical architecture.

As he argued in *The True Principles of Pointed or Christian Architecture*, published in 1841, there are 'two great rules for design . . . 1st, that there should be no features about a building which are not necessary for convenience, construction, or propriety; 2nd . . . all ornaments should consist of enrichment of the essential construction of the building.' Ornament should not, Pugin emphasised, be 'tacked on' to buildings or be 'constructed' – it should be the consequence of 'the decoration of construction'; that is, to arise from the structural necessities of the building in question. It is in Gothic – or what he preferred to call 'pointed' – architecture alone 'that these great principles have been carried out'.[1]

Classical architecture was, according to Pugin, not only often deceitful – with techniques and materials of construction routinely concealed or denied rather than honestly expressed – but also structurally primitive and limited. On the other hand, in Gothic architecture construction is not concealed but revealed in 'truth', expressed and beautified, and the potential of the materials of construction fully realised and – through the use of pointed arches, ribs and buttresses – given added strength through design. In *True Principles*, Pugin used a Gothic flying buttress to illustrate his point. It has a beautiful and ornamental form but all is derived from functional requirements. For example, the buttress's crowning pinnacle gives it an elegant silhouette but is primarily a counter-weight to help it withstand the lateral thrust of the stone vault it supports. Similarly the

John O'Connor's *From Pentonville Road Looking West* (1884) captures the dreamlike quality of St Pancras at dusk.

buttress's striking stepped profile – getting larger in stages as it nears the ground – is simply a reflection of the fact that the lower portion of the buttress has more structural work to do, and more load to carry, than the upper portions. For Pugin, Gothic architecture was a rational structural machine that, through its honesty, achieved beauty that was divine.

So Pugin's polemic was not just about aesthetics and engineering, but also about the spirit of the nation and about religion. 'Christian architects', thundered Pugin, 'with stones scarcely larger than ordinary bricks, threw their lofty vaults from slender pillars across a vast intermediate space, and that at an amazing height.'[2] In Pugin's view the Gothic Revival was not just about reviving Gothic forms but about recovering the audacious Gothic spirit and emulating authentic Gothic principles of construction. This meant using, as far as practicable, traditional materials of construction in

traditional manner. All of which, he implied, were an echo of God's wisdom; to build Gothic was to build in harmony with God's Creation.

Pugin was not the only theoretical influence on the design of St Pancras. John Ruskin was another who also greatly admired the rational aspects of the Gothic – particularly its structural excellence – combined with its ability to utilise the potential offered by different building materials and its feel for appropriate ornament inspired by nature. As he wrote in *The Stones of Venice*, published 1851–3, Gothic workmen displayed a 'peculiar fondness of the forms of vegetation', which was for him part of the true Gothic spirit, defined by 'magnificent enthusiasm' that 'never could do enough to reach the fullness of its idea.'[3] Ruskin particularly admired Venetian Gothic for the way in which colour and decoration were far from superficial, but rather derived in most muscular manner from the honest expression of the materials of construction. Most powerfully this approach was manifest in the combinations of structural stonework of different colours, juxtaposed with marble, to achieve ornament that was at once enduring and part of the building's very substance. This structural polychromy was one of the virtues that led Ruskin to believe that Venetian Gothic – odd as it may seem – was the truest and most useful model for British architecture of the modern age.

As you walk around St Pancras Station and the Midland Grand Hotel it is possible to see these theories being applied in practice. Through the hands of the inspired Scott, they leap into life to dazzle, amaze and entertain. As Scott admitted in his memoirs (published after his death in 1878 as *Recollections*), it was the 'thunder' of Pugin's writings that had first woken him from his 'slumber'. This thunder rumbles on today in this extraordinary collection of buildings on Euston Road.

WALK 10

Bermondsey

The industrial heart of London

In 1869, the French artist and illustrator Gustave Doré teamed up with a journalist, William Blanchard Jerrold, to write a book depicting the lives of ordinary Londoners. Professing to have seen London both 'awake and asleep, at work and at play,' the pair set out to capture 'representative bits of each of the parts of the whole'. Entitled *London: A Pilgrimage*, and published in 1872, the book starts with Bermondsey.

Noting the district's 'representative thoroughfares of river-side London', Doré drew a city of tight and curving streets, with tall warehouses linked by bridges and enlivened with frenetic commercial activity. 'At the cost of sundry blows and much buffeting from the hastening crowds we make notes,' the pair report, as they attempt to capture the work going on around them:

> The hard-visaged men, breathlessly competing for 'dear life,' glance, mostly with an eye of wondering pity, at the sketcher, and at his companion with the note-book . . . The warehouse men pause aloft on their landing stages, books in hand, to contemplate us . . . and the man bending beneath an immense sack, turns up his eyes from under his burden, and appears pleased that he has disturbed us.[1]

Doré and Jerrold evidently thought of Bermondsey as the epitome of Victorian industry and commerce: squalid and gritty, of course, but also vibrant and colourful. A world where 'at every turn there is a sketch', because 'every twisting or backing of a cart; every shifting of the busy groups suggests a happy combination of lines and light and shade.'

Today, anyone in search of a glimpse of the industrial Victorian metropolis will still find much in Bermondsey although, of course, the place is far less vibrant and characterful than in Doré and Jerrold's

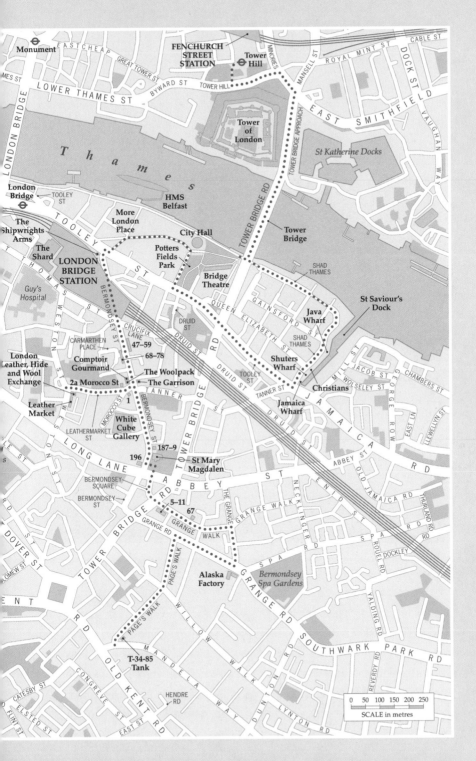

Monument

EASTCHEAP

FENCHURCH
STREET
STATION

Tower
Hill

GREAT TOWER ST

MINORIES

MANSELL ST

ROYAL MINT ST

CABLE ST

DOCK ST

VAUGHAN

EAST SMITHFIELD

MES ST

LOWER THAMES ST

BYWARD ST

TOWER HILL

Tower
of
London

TOWER BRIDGE APPROACH

St Katherine Docks

LONDON BRIDGE

T h a m e s

London
Bridge

TOOLEY
ST

HMS
Belfast

More
London
Place

City Hall

Potters
Fields
Park

Tower
Bridge

TOWER BRIDGE RD

SHAD
THAMES

The
Shipwrights
Arms

TOOLEY
ST

The
Shard

LONDON
BRIDGE
STATION

BERMONDSEY ST

Bridge
Theatre

QUEEN ELIZABETH ST

GAINSFORD ST

Java
Wharf

SHAD
THAMES

St Saviour's
Dock

Guy's
Hospital

THOMAS ST

WESTON ST

CRUCIFIX
LANE

DRUID
ST

Shuters
Wharf

MILL ST

JACOB ST

WOLSELEY ST

GEORGE ROW

CHAMBERS ST

EAST LN

LLEWELLIN ST

CARMARTHEN
PLACE

47–59

68–78

TOOLEY
ST

London
Leather, Hide
and Wool
Exchange

Comptoir
Gourmand

The Woolpack

DRUID ST

TANNER ST

Christians

JAMAICA RD

2a Morocco St

The Garrison

1

Jamaica
Wharf

Leather
Market

MOROCCO ST

LEATHERMARKET
ST

White
Cube
Gallery

BERMONDSEY ST

TOWER BRIDGE RD

187–9

ABBEY ST

ABBEY ST

OLD JAMAICA RD

SPA RD

DOCKLEY RD

LONG LANE

196

St Mary
Magdalen

THE GRANGE

GRANGE WALK

NECKLINGER RD

ENID ST

SPA RD

ROUEL RD

THURLAND RD

DOVER ST

BERMONDSEY
SQUARE

BERMONDSEY
ST

5–11

67

GRANGE RD

GRANGE
WALK

GRANGE WALK

Bermondsey
Spa Gardens

GRANGE RD

YALDING RD

REVERDY RD

TOWER BRIDGE RD

PAGE'S WALK

Alaska
Factory

DUNTON RD

LYNTON RD

SOUTHWARK PARK RD

BARTHOLEMEW ST

DOVER ST

PAGE'S WALK

WILLOW WALK

MANDELA WAY

T-34-85
Tank

CONGREVE ST

OLD KENT RD

EAST ST

HENDRE
RD

0 50 100 150 200 250
SCALE in metres

CATESBY ST

ELSTED ST

FLINT ST

'At every turn there is a sketch': Gustave Doré's engraving of warehouse workers, likely inspired in part by Bermondsey.

time. The authentic life of London's wharfs and riverside warehouses – as places of industry and trade, and repositories for the goods of the world – is long over. And it is not just life that has gone but swathes of buildings, through wartime bombing and ill-judged post-war demolitions. But enough survives in and around Bermondsey to rekindle in the imagination the world depicted by Doré – particularly towards the east end of Shad Thames where it turns south-west. Here there are still tall warehouses rising on the narrow street, gantries and bridges. And nearby St Saviour's Dock is still a strange and miniature water-world. On its east side is the location of the fabled 'Jacob's Island', engraved on the nation's collective memory by Charles Dickens in *Oliver Twist*. Generally speaking, though, all that remains is thoroughly sanitised, with warehousemen, rugged and physically demanding working life and poor dwellings long ago giving way to smart offices, studios, restaurants and luxury apartments.

For me, more moving now is Bermondsey Street south of the London Bridge viaducts. It remains a place of large-scale, mid-nineteenth-century industrial architecture – much of it raw and wonderfully utilitarian – juxtaposed with smaller, earlier domestic architecture. Everywhere there is evidence of the area's early and long-term trade in leather and hides, and beneath all are the echoes – faint but still significant – of Bermondsey's earlier life as a merchants' village on the edge of London and, in the Middle Ages, as a major monastic enclave astride an ancient route through the marshes south of the river.

In its early days Bermondsey Street was something of a causeway, cutting through the low-lying marsh connecting isolated areas of high ground – indeed the name 'Bermondsey' is almost certainly derived from 'Beermund's eye' or 'island', which was once the property of a Saxon lord. It would become the high street of the riverside village of Bermondsey, which connected the parish church of St Mary Magdalen and the huge Cluniac priory, founded in 1082, with the Thames.

Its transformation into a site of industry began in the eighteenth century, when the road became a centre for trades related to the leather industry such as tanning. This was in large part thanks to the Neckinger, one of London's numerous and now lost rivers, which ran through the marshes and joined the Thames just to the east of where Tower Bridge stands today. Now virtually forgotten and almost entirely invisible, the river was once central to powering the machinery of the leather trade. In 1857, John Timbs would state in his *Curiosities of London* that the area's leading trade was leather: in the 'great skin Market', he noted, 'are sold the skins from nearly all the sheep slaughtered in London'.[2]

One description of working life in and around Bermondsey leaves a particularly vivid impression of the leather industry. In his *Dictionary of London* of 1893, Charles Dickens Jr records:

Warehouses back on to the water at Shad Thames.

> The neighbourhood in which [the hide market] lies is devoted
> entirely to skinners and tanners, and the air reeks with evil
> smells. The population is peculiar, and it is a sight at 12 o'clock
> to see the men pouring out from all the works. Their clothes are
> marked with many stains; their trousers are discoloured with tan;
> some have aprons and gaiters of raw hide; and about them all
> seems to hang a scent of blood.[3]

The journalist Henry Mayhew, who we will meet again in Walk 11, offered
a similarly evocative description of Bermondsey's tannery activities in
1850:

What may be styled the *architecture* of the district is that rendered
necessary by the demands of its chief commerce. Long, and
sometimes high, and always black and wooden structures,
without glass windows ... irregularly surrounded by a series of
closely adjacent pits, filled to the brink with a dark, chocolate-
coloured, thick liquid ... while high above all, towers a tall
narrow chimney, throwing out thick columns of black smoke ...
these places are the tanneries.[4]

When walking through west Bermondsey the senses must have been
assaulted in a most extraordinary manner – the sight of blood on the
workmen's clothes, acrid smoke, the stench of skins being cured in pits
filled with a foul brown liquid including dogs' rotting excrement, which
was an essential product in the tanners' trade. As Dickens points out, a
trip to the area was particularly memorable 'for the unpleasantness of the
compound of horrible smells which pervade the whole neighbourhood'.[5]

While little of the leather trade remains today, its legacy can be found
in one of Bermondsey's most prominent landmarks: London Bridge
station. In February 1836 the London and Greenwich Railway opened to
herald in the birth of London's railway age – in large part to bring cattle
into the city for slaughter for their meat, hide and horns. Initially the
terminus for the railway was at Spa Road, Bermondsey, but by December
1836 the route had been extended west to London Bridge – just over six
months before the opening of Euston station, the first terminus to link
London to another British city, Birmingham.

Thanks in part to its bustling new rail terminus, Bermondsey would
gradually transform from a world of leather to a more diverse industrial
hotspot. In 1857, Timbs recorded that 'at Bermondsey, perhaps is carried
on a greater variety of trades and manufactures than in any other parish
in the kingdom', with 'paper and lead mills, chemical works, boat and ship
builders, mast and block makers, coopers, turpentine works'. And this
panoply of uses is still visible in any walk through the area today. Some
sites, like the Leather Exchange, offer a remarkable vision of London's
mercantile exuberance, capturing and reflecting the spirit of an age in
which art and commerce were happily and creatively united, the one
nurturing the other. Other areas, including much of Morocco Street, are

populated by nothing but sturdy and functional late-nineteenth-century warehouses – a splendid vision of Bermondsey's vigorous industrial past. Between them, one can glimpse just a shadow of the bustling district that Doré sketched in the 1870s, and whose buildings pepper the streets through which we walk.

THE WALK

This walk starts at one of the most famous landmarks in Britain: Tower Bridge. This bridge is a rare thing – a much-admired structure of great character, even though it was forged through endless committee meetings, compromise, contradiction, uncertainty and a fair degree of absurdity. It has a story worth considering at some length as you ascend from Tower Hill tube and stroll south across the bridge.

The tale starts in the mid 1870s, when it was argued that a river crossing to the east of London Bridge would both improve communications in the City and, by providing direct access to industry on the south bank, increase the commercial potential of the docks on the north. There was, for practical reasons, only one site possible – a strip of land just east of the Tower of London – and a competition to find a suitable design was held. This was supervised by the City of London Corporation, which grabbed the initiative to build the new bridge. There was one key stipulation. It was not to block the access of tall-masted cargo ships to the wharves at the Pool of London, immediately to the west of the tower. To protect navigation the span of the proposed bridge had to be either incredibly high or it would have to open in some way to allow ships to pass through.

Over fifty detailed designs were submitted. Most were weird and wonderful, including a swing bridge, a 'roller' bridge incorporating steam-operated sections that rolled from pier to pier, and a high-level bridge. All offered more or less workable solutions – some more expensive and complex than others – but all would visually overpower the historic tower and its setting. Many thought this far from desirable.

Debate raged and two distinct interest groups emerged, each of which believed it should be responsible for the design and construction of the new bridge. There was the City Corporation, which had organised the competition and believed the proposed bridge was its responsibility. The City did, after all, begin just to the west of the site, and it had the funds to see the works to completion. They were to come from the City's Bridge House estate, a body established in the early thirteenth century to collect tolls and rents from all using or residing on London Bridge. The City had, over the centuries, used the resulting money to buy and develop property, and build other bridges across the Thames – notably Blackfriars Bridge in the 1760s. By the 1870s the money was there to build the proposed bridge by the tower.

On the other hand there was the Metropolitan Board of Works (MBW), which had been established in 1855 to improve London's roads and sewers (see p. 336). The engineer responsible for these works was Joseph Bazalgette, and in the mid 1870s he produced a design for the MBW for a high-level bridge adjoining the tower. When the MBW submitted this scheme as part of a private Parliamentary bill, the battle lines were drawn.

Competing visions of Tower Bridge: the designs submitted by Joseph Bazelgette for the MBW (below) and Horace Jones for the City Corporation (bottom).

The City – in the person of its architect Horace Jones – objected to the proposed design and in 1879 submitted its alternative scheme. Designed by Jones himself, it solved the problems of navigation by proposing that the bridge should have a roadway which rose to allow ships to pass. This solution also offered the opportunity for the new crossing to be designed as a medieval-style drawbridge or city gate: a composition that, argued the City, would allow the new structure to sit in happy harmony with the adjoining medieval Tower of London.

The logic of this suggestion gave the City the edge in the debate and the project moved inexorably into its hands. After ironing out some technical problems – the drawbridge was originally to be raised by chains, which promised to be so slow that it would almost always be neither up nor down – a final design was settled upon, with the help of the engineer John Wolfe Barry. Jones and Barry were grilled by a House of Commons Select Committee which established that, from the technical and operational point of view at least, the City's proposal was a goer.

And then, when all seemed settled, Queen Victoria spoke up. The queen had opposed the bridge for some time: she feared that a new bridge, on the eastern edge of the Tower of London and including a carriageway overlooking its walls, would not only be an eyesore but would fatally compromise the tower's continuing role as a fortress and royal redoubt in times of crisis – a fear that was not as unfounded as it sounds in the 1880s, a decade of social unrest, Fenian terrorism and growing republicanism. In December 1884 the queen stirred herself from the torpor of her perpetual widowhood to make her opinion known. Her private secretary, General Ponsonby, passed to the relevant authorities the queen's 'deep distrust' of the bridge, and let it be known that she was 'strongly opposed' to any proposal that would undermine the defensive potential of the tower.[6] When Barry hastened to reassure the queen, Ponsonby replied, 'Bosh!'

What was to be done? The case for a new bridge was unarguable, and had on its side not only the City but also the general public. Yet the queen and the royal party stood firm in their opposition, continuing to argue that the proposed bridge would be a serious 'disfigurement'. For a moment it seemed that the proposal, if not handled deftly and in most diplomatic manner, could provoke a constitutional crisis and do irreparable damage to the British monarchy. Eventually, though, the royal party blinked. The queen and her courtiers realised that she not only risked provoking resentment but was also inviting humiliation: to ride roughshod over popular opinion was not good, but to attempt to do so and lose was to court disaster for the monarchy and fuel the growing spirit of republicanism. The Queen retreated and in August 1885 the Parliamentary bill to build the new bridge received royal asset – no doubt very grudgingly. In a wise attempt to embrace the inevitable and associate itself in positive manner with this major London 'improvement', the royal party arranged with the City for the queen's son – Edward, Prince of Wales – ceremonially to inaugurate construction in April 1886 by 'driving in' the bridge's first pile.

The bridge quickly started to take form, and a most strange form it was. In its initial years it looked astonishingly modern, being no more than a strong and utilitarian steel-made structural frame – an honest expression of the means of construction and of its function. The basic design strategy is still apparent: the twin towers rise on piers that are connected to the land by carriageways, which are supported from above by wrought-iron members that curve down to lower towers on the banks on either side. Between the tall main towers are the drawbridge sections of carriageway. Jones's original chain-drawn mechanism, ultimately rejected as too slow, was replaced by a 'bascule' or see-saw system, around which the two centre towers were built. In the bascule system, each section of road is counterbalanced by a mighty weight, which descends into a huge chamber when the bridge is opened. At first this was all powered by a cutting-edge coal-fuelled hydraulic engine, which has long since replaced by electricity. But the whole mechanism means that, like a ship, Tower Bridge has always had a crew and a bridgemaster, an engine room, a bridge-like control cabin, and vast and cavernous spaces in the bowels of the piers, rather like the holds within a great vessel. This makes the bridge like no other in London, a moving – almost a living – thing.

Of course, the fashion for the display of ruthlessly engineered construction had not quite arrived, certainly not in the City of London – although the idea of unornamented engineering being in itself a structure's primary ornament was being pioneered at the same time, far to the north, with the construction of the Forth Railway Bridge, built

The old world charm of Tower Bridge now sits against a backdrop of City skyscrapers.

between 1882 and 1890. Tower Bridge's steel frame was quickly clad with a richly detailed veneer of granite and Portland stone. These finishes, it was believed, gave the bridge the cultural pedigree to raise it above mere functionality and, in theory, to sit comfortably with the neighbouring Tower of London. It didn't quite work. After Jones died in 1887, his design was modified into an even more peculiar form by Barry. He decided to replace Jones's High Medieval – or 'Middle Pointed' – details with those in the Tudor Gothic style. Jones's architecture would not have particularly harmonised with the Romanesque details of the White Tower, but Barry's mechanistic-looking late Gothic – probably chosen to honour the Palace of Westminster designed four decades previously by his father, Charles Barry (see p. 287) – was even less visually sympathetic. The overall effect is to give the structure a more than slightly fake old world charm.

You either like such frippery or you don't. When the bridge was completed in 1894, though, Londoners showed very quickly that they did. Within a few years Tower Bridge became one of the unofficial symbols of the city – the water gate into the City from the south and the City's great gateway to the massive dock system downstream on the south bank and to Britain's vast empire beyond. Today, Tower Bridge is a London institution, its evolution and appearance an epitome of the contradictory values of the late-Victorian age: a pioneering new building designed to look old; a monument to modern capitalism that was nearly scuppered by the monarchy; a purely commercial enterprise that, through its romantic appearance, caught the imagination of the nation.

———◆•◉•◆———

Go down the steps at the south-west corner of Tower Bridge, and cross under the road. You are now standing in one of the most infamous sections of the Victorian city. To the east, a wide and deep inlet marks the spot where the River Neckinger flows into the Thames. In the late eighteenth and early nineteenth century this inlet, the stinking drainage ditches around it, and the marshy land they defined was a slum known as Jacob's Island or Dockhead.

Here was an area of intense poverty rather than useful industry, with the mounds of marsh covered with decrepit structures and slum dwellings of the meanest sort. The centre of the 'island' was London Street and Jacob Street, running parallel to each other, east from St Saviour's Dock to George Row. These streets were set alongside wide ditches, with that next to George Row emptying directly into the Thames. All – streets, houses and the ditches – are long gone, replaced by late-nineteenth-century warehouses that have since been converted into smart flats and studios.

George Cruikshank's illustration of Bill Sikes's death at Jacob's Island, published in February 1839 to accompany the syndication of *Oliver Twist*.

Nineteenth-century literature gives us a glimpse of what Jacob's Island once held. In *Oliver Twist*, Charles Dickens selected it as the scene for the dramatic demise of the murderous thief Bill Sykes, who plunged to his death in the island's Folly Ditch, also known as Hickman's Folly. The novel was published in 1838 so it is reasonable to assume that Dickens's description – although somewhat emphatic and over-drawn for dramatic purposes – presents a recognisable likeness of Jacob's Island as it appeared in the early Victorian age. There were, he observed,

> Crazy wooden galleries common to the backs of half a dozen houses, with holes from which to look upon the slime beneath; windows, broken and patched, with poles thrust out, on which to dry the linen that is never there; rooms so small, so filthy, so

confined, that the air would seem to be too tainted even for the dirt and squalor which they shelter; wooden chambers thrusting themselves out above the mud and threatening to fall into it – as some have done; dirt-besmeared walls and decaying foundations, every repulsive lineament of poverty, every loathsome indication of filth, rot, and garbage: all these ornament the banks of Jacob's Island.[7]

Dickens's description must only have added to the mythic status of Jacob's Island as the archetypal Victorian slum. Just over a decade later, in 1849, the journalist turned social observer and reformer, Henry Mayhew, described the area in similar terms: 'On entering the precincts of the pest island the air had literally the smell of a graveyard, and a feeling of nausea and heaviness came over any one unaccustomed to imbibe the musty atmosphere. It is not only the nose, but the stomach that tells how heavily the air is loaded with sulphuretted [sic] hydrogen.' The smell was no doubt largely thanks to the proximity of the leather industry, but certainly wasn't helped by the 'swollen carcasses of dead animals, ready to burst with the gases of putrefaction', nor by the shoreline's 'heaps of indescribable filth, the phosphoretted smell from which told you of the rotting fish there, while the oyster-shells were like pieces of slate from their coating of filth and mud' and the water was 'almost as red as blood from the colouring matter that [poured] into it from the reeking leather-dresser's close by'.[8] Jacob's Island was evidently seen to represent the darkest, most dismal and dangerous aspects of the city – a place where the rot of the material world seemed to be emblematic of deep spiritual malaise, and which opened a window into a world of depravity. So it is hardly surprising that eventually it would be visited by the most characteristically Victorian representation of evil, Spring-heeled Jack.

To this day few agree who or what Spring-heeled was. He first appeared in October 1837, when a servant named Mary Stevens claimed she was attacked on Clapham Common by a figure that held her in a firm grip, kissed her face, ripped her clothes and caressed her flesh with claws that were 'cold and clammy as those of a corpse'. The girl screamed, rescuers arrived, the attacker fled and disappeared without trace. The next day, he struck again in south London, causing a coachman to crash his vehicle. Passers-by rushed to the scene to see a cackling figure make a getaway by leaping over a 9-foot-high wall. Now the press started to make much of these strange stories and soon christened the mysterious miscreant 'Spring-heeled Jack'.

Public interest in the phenomenon increased rapidly and in early January 1838 even the Lord Mayor of London, Sir John Cowan, involved himself in the mystery. He tried to get to the bottom of it by holding a public meeting to explore various explanations. No consensus was reached but more cases were presented, which mostly concerned servants or young ladies being frightened practically out of their wits by the antics of a strangely garbed leaping, babbling and laughing personage. A few weeks later the most detailed and well-observed manifestations took place. On 19 February Jane Alsop was attacked at her home in Old Ford, Stepney, during which her clothes were shredded and her flesh scratched by Jack's claws, with rescue coming in the perhaps unlikely form of her young sister. Nine days later Jack struck again, this time near Narrow Street, Limehouse, when he savaged eighteen-year-old Lucy Scales who, while walking with her sister along Green Dragon Lane, was set upon by a fire-breathing fiend and terrified into a faint, but with no serious harm being done.

By the beginning of the 1840s, the appearance of this high-leaping phantom started to be agreed: he had claws, eyes like 'red balls of fire', and 'diabolical' features, wore a black cloak, tight-fitting white oilskins and some kind of helmet, and breathed blue and white flames. This was the form he took when he supposedly appeared in Jacob's Island. In 1977, the journalist Peter Haining would describe Jack's most notorious crime in a successful book, *The Legend and Bizarre Crimes of Spring-heeled Jack*. Jack, he reported, appeared at the island in November 1845, and proceeded to attack a 'bedraggled young prostitute of thirteen years old', Maria Davis: 'Huddled behind their windows, the few eyewitnesses said Jack picked the terrified girl up in his arms and with one jerk hurled her into the fowl, muddy waters below.'[9] Nobody came to her aid and she sank to her death – forgotten, it seems, until her tale was told by Haining over a century later.

Most terrifying. But Maria Davis's story could be the stuff of myth. Haining is dead and can't now defend or explain himself, but those who have attempted to verify this tale claim to have been unable to find corroborating, independent, contemporary evidence. So perhaps the dastardly slaying did not happen – or perhaps the late Haining looked and found where others have failed. It remains something of a mystery but, I suppose, in such ways urban legends are born. Besides, whether Haining embellished the history of Jack is not really the point. Certainly, in one form or another, Jack existed in the Victorian imagination. Even if his sightings were perhaps no more than a manifestation of endemic hysteria, they surely reveal a collective fear of arbitrary punishment for the unspecified but ubiquitous sins of the city, embodied by such dire districts as Jacob's Island.

By the end of the century Jack was so embedded in the lore of London that it seems likely his name inspired a later terroriser of the city's underbelly: Jack the Ripper. Indeed it is impossible to understand the atmosphere surrounding the Whitechapel murders of 1888 without knowing something about Spring-heeled Jack: both were interpreted as the embodiment of the dark spirits that were supposed to lurk in the shadows of London. And, unlike the original Jack, the blood and corpses that trailed in the wake of the Ripper made it startlingly clear that he was real enough – the culmination of a street terror that had its origins fifty years earlier.

The character of Jacob's Island as backwater of outcast London lingered through much of the nineteenth century. Eventually, though, hovels and ditches gave way to ranks of hardy and wholesome warehouses and wharves, of the sort illustrated by Doré. While his warehouse illustrations are to a degree generic – each likely a collage inspired by a number of Thames-side streets – one caption does suggest that the area provided inspiration for some of the sketches. The picture in question shows brick warehouses with loading bays set in tall arcades, a tier of three bridges linking warehouses, and much handling and loading of massive bales. Its caption refers to Miles Lane, Duck's Foot Lane, and 'not far off' Pickle-Herring Street, which was the westward extension of Shad Thames – the road running parallel to the Thames on the south side opposite the Tower of London.[10]

By the end of the century the desperate days of Shad Thames and Jacob's Island were over. A later portrait of the area is offered by the

The Gustave Doré illustration most likely to be inspired by Bermondsey, labelled as 'not far off' Pickle-Herring Street.

social reformer and philanthropist Charles Booth, who we last met in Walk 9. On 5 and 6 June 1899 Booth and his secretary walked through Bermondsey with a PC Watts, 'a thorough going policeman, heavy in build, manner and in tread'.[11] In the area around Shad Thames, Booth noted 'mostly wharves and warehouses . . . with the River at hand, but blocked out by the high buildings, and even the sky partly hidden by the cast iron bridges that have been thrown across the roadway'. While far from rich, the district was also hardly impoverished: Booth categorised many of the houses pink in his colour-coded analysis of the social and physical fabric of London, denoting homes that were 'fairly comfortable' with residents commanding 'good ordinary earnings'. Not all of the social problems had gone – nearby, Booth observed 'tumble-down houses' with 'women, loud voiced and foul tongued . . . as they flung threatening oaths at some children'; but by and large this was now a place of industry, not squalor.

What of this world now survives? The atmosphere of a working dockland has long gone, but a good number of late-nineteenth-century warehouses are still standing, serving as smart apartments, studios, offices, shops and restaurants. Many retain an array of bridges or hoists, but which are now no more than curious and picturesque urban ornaments. The best are in the arm of Shad Thames that runs south-west and parallel to St Saviour's Dock. These are robust, functional and handsome brick structures whose names, still emblazoned on their walls, proclaim the identity of their former owners or the areas of the world from which their contents came. There's Jamaica Wharf, Shuters Wharf, Christians, and Java Wharf, where sacks of exotic spices were once heaped in pungent profusion.

Much, though, has been lost. When I first encountered Shad Thames in the late 1960s, the majority of the street was framed by tall, gaunt and very utilitarian warehouses, in use mainly for the storage of tea, coffee and varied spices. Now, the eastern portion of the street is defined by the ungainly bulk of the former premises of the Design Museum (currently a café and flats). And the portion immediately to the east of Tower Bridge has the feel of a film set: at first glance it looks reasonably authentic, but much of the architecture is deceptively recent, the cobbled road surface wrong and, of course, traditional riverside life entirely absent.

A number of atmospheric alleys penetrate the bulky former warehouses to connect Shad Thames to the riverside quay that, after much campaigning, was secured for public use. These alleys are the last memory of the work pattern here, when dockers scurried through them carrying loads between ship and street. They also hint at the nature of the

The bridges between Shad Thames warehouses are a memory of the nineteenth-century work pattern.

area before its industrial development, when it was formed by a maze of narrow ditches, alleys and islands of houses.

<hr />

From the south-western end of Shad Thames, go west along Tooley Street and cross Tower Bridge Road. This portion of the walk takes us through the mercantile hub of Victorian Bermondsey – from London Bridge station, via the warehouses of Bermondsey Street district, to the centre of London's leather industry.

Our first port of call is the doleful wastes of Potters Field Park, now a windswept and unlovely public space including a somewhat trampled lawn and 'amphitheatre'. When first completed, nearly twenty years ago, this gesture seemed to be of little practical use to anyone, but recently things have changed and there is now potential. In 2017 the 900-seat Bridge Theatre opened nearby – opposite the lawn – with the splendid address One Tower Bridge, within a new apartment building. It houses the London Theatre Company, operating under the inspirational leadership of Nicholas Hytner (formerly artistic director of the National Theatre). The interior space is 'flexible' – the company has staged promenade and 'in the round' productions – so no doubt the inventive Hytner will soon find a good and creative use for this conveniently located amphitheatre.

There was anciently a street called Potter's Fields running across the site, so the park's name is logical. But it is also a trifle unfortunate. When Judas repented of his betrayal of Christ for 'thirty pieces of silver', he cast down the money in the temple and then hanged himself; the chief priests pondered the use they could lawfully and ethically make of the money and finally decided to buy the 'potter's field, to bury strangers in'. Ever since, a Potter's Field has been a burial ground of unknown or itinerant people.[12] Here, the name is appropriate. It is, in a way, a deadly place: at least it makes my spirits wither. Perhaps, in time, the presence of the Bridge Theatre might yet bring the space to life.

Hytner might consider a play about betrayal and ethics as a way of inaugurating the amphitheatre – particularly appropriate because amongst the glitzy architecture defining the 'park' presides the glass-blob that houses the Mayor of London. This building, opened in 2002, was designed by the office of the much-admired Lord Foster and is a pioneering example of the recent school of silly-shaped and 'whacky' City structures, all of weird form and all calculated to attract commercial clients by their charming and characterful excesses. The best of this breed are the 'Gherkin', also designed by Foster's office and Ken Shuttleworth, and the 'Shard', nearby at London Bridge, designed by the Genoese architect Renzo Piano. But the mayor's office is, of course, not a commercial but a public building that should in some way symbolise the majesty and dignity of London. Its ephemeral and corporate-looking 'charm' falls very short of the mark.

Walk south-west along More London Place, a geometrical and not unpleasing sliver of a passage, which leads back to Tooley

Street and the remains of a more vigorous and muscular world. Tooley Street was a great mercantile thoroughfare in the nineteenth century, lined with ware-houses, offices and railway structures related to London Bridge station which sits, at high level, immediately to its south.

Today, little of the original station is still standing – it was recently comprehensively redeveloped into its current form – but a few glimpses of its Victorian origins remain. Take the viaducts. These great arches, inspired by Roman aqueducts, not only gave the new railways a heroic antique quality but also meant that trains could sail above long-established road networks and thus cause minimal disruption. The first of these soon ubiquitous railway viaducts was constructed here in 1836. By the mid Victorian period viaducts also provided a handy income for the rail companies that owned them because the arches could be let for various uses. One of the more charming sections stands round the corner from Tooley Street, in St Thomas Street and Crucifix Lane. Here the viaduct is concealed behind a mid-Victorian ornamental screen formed of polychromatic brick arches. These are punctuated by piers whose pillars are embellished with stone-carved heads – likely the faces of the men who were creating or enlarging the station at the time.

Many of these arches look immensely strong, with barrel vaults wrought of striking and handsome bricks. They certainly are strong enough to support the trains that hurtle above. But their impressive appearance can be deceptive. During the First and Second World Wars, London's railway viaducts were used as public air-raid shelters, and more than once this led to disaster. When faced with a bomb packed with explosives, the relatively thin brickwork is horribly vulnerable and easily penetrated; on the night of 25 October 1940, during the Blitz, a bomb crashed through the roof a little to the east of this spot, at the intersection

An archly modern portion of the redeveloped London Bridge station (above), site of the lost South Eastern Railway offices (inset).

of Tanner Street and Druid Street. Seventy-seven of the people sheltering inside were killed.

The viaducts are not the only notable pieces of Victorian railway architecture to have been built in this area. One of the most exemplary was the South Eastern Railway Offices, at 64–84 Tooley Street, which once served the company that operated London Bridge station. It was a monumental work – completed in 1893 to the designs of Charles Barry Jr – the brother of John Wolfe Barry – which oozed pride in its function, in the company that built it and in the railways in general. It was a pleasure to contemplate, a message from another, sadly lost world when offices did not have to be silly or whacky in appearance but grand, dignified, sophisticated, well designed and beautifully built. Needless to say, its more recent owners, Network Rail, felt obliged to demolish the offices as part of its destructive upgrading of London Bridge station. They stood when I started this book and are now gone, replaced by a meagre open space and station entrance. Inexplicably, the building was not listed, and the frantic efforts to save it came to nothing, largely because demolition was approved by Southwark Council and supported by the London mayor's office when Boris Johnson was mayor. Writing about the architecture of London is a great pleasure – but can also be heartbreaking.

You might at this point like to repair to the splendid mid-Victorian Shipwrights Arms, which adjoins the eastern edge of the site of the lost railway offices. If you do you will find yourself walking beneath the welcoming and outstretched arms of a half-naked female figure that hovers, in perpetuity, above the main door to the hostelry – forever doing her best to stop a tier of windows tumbling on to customers below. Alternatively, follow the road to the south-east of the Shipwrights Arms. This is Bermondsey Street, which plunges underneath the platforms and tracks of London Bridge station, before breaking into the open air at the junction of St Thomas Street and Crucifix Lane. We are now in the heart of Bermondsey's historical leather-making district, a world populated by a number of sublime industrial buildings. The northern portion of the street is worth taking in slowly, if only to appreciate fully the rich mix of architectural styles that inhabit it.

Take, for example, numbers 47–59. At number 55 stands The Tanneries, a monumental Venetian Gothic warehouse, its ornamented brick-built exterior giving romantic and cultured pedigree to an otherwise utilitarian interior. Two doors down, at number 59, is a bold neo-Baroque composition of around 1900, vaguely in the manner of the 1720s. And the eclectic and variable nature of mid-nineteenth-century industrial architecture is confirmed by number 50: here, an alleyway leads down to an archetypal 'wall of glass' warehouse – very proto-modern – with the elevations to each floor formed by generous areas of glazing, including glazed doors to tiers of loading bays.

This was not just an industrial street – it was also populated by shops, houses and taverns. On the west side is arguably its most sensational architectural moment. Numbers 68–78 Bermondsey Street is a group of houses that date from the late seventeenth to the early nineteenth centuries. Look out for the wide and tall arched opening – leading to the

The monumental Venetian Gothic of The Tanneries.

cobbled Carmarthen Place – which is adorned with a river-god keystone that appears to be made of Coade terracotta or 'artificial stone', a much-favoured material in the late eighteenth century. The Regency shopfronts on numbers 68 and 70 are terrific, but the best moment comes with number 78. This late-seventeenth-century house is altogether remarkable. The pedimented oriel window set at first-floor level – generously glazed and with delightful quadrant corners – would once have been a common feature of London's thoroughfares, but virtually none are now left, and certainly none as fine as this. Also notable is its timber-framed construction with a plastered front and clapboard-clad top storey – again, a common practice for modest houses in pre-nineteenth-century London – which is now a rarity. All in all, it offers an insight into ordinary street architecture in the peripheral areas of London in the decades around 1700. It is a reminder that in this city, the most extraordinary domestic and industrial architecture can often be found side by side.

A little further down Bermondsey Street you come to a crossroads. To the left is the western portion of Tanner Street, its north side lined with an impressive array of tall, mid- to late-nineteenth-century warehouses. To the west is Morocco Street – another leather reference, because Morocco was the name of the high-quality leather used for ladies' gloves, shoe uppers and in book binding. This is the route to take, stopping first at number 2a, one of the most quietly pleasing buildings you could hope to come upon. Probably dating to the 1890s, it has a front elevation faced with white glazed bricks, a device that not only lightens the street but also means the façade can be easily washed. The original function of the building is revealed by the pair of life-size horse heads that terminate each end of the ground-floor fascia: this was, of course, a farrier's. Most charmingly of all, number 2a is not yet some gorgeous restaurant or exquisite shop, but continues in the modern equivalent of its original function. Now, rather than farriers clipping hooves and shoeing horses, mechanics mend car tyres and tinker with engines.

The prospect looking west from the farrier's is wonderful. Morocco Street curves around to the south-west and Leathermarket Street branches due west, the cusp of the division being formed by a splendid curved

The ways divide like water breaking each side of a ship's bow: the view west along Morocco Street.

warehouse around which the ways divide like water breaking each side of a ship's bow. To the left there is virtually nothing to be seen but sturdy late-nineteenth-century warehouses. And some of these warehouses are very good indeed. Number 1 Morocco Street – still proclaiming its past life as a 'Leather Factors' in large faded lettering – is particularly fine, with the light entering its upper floors maximised by having windows separated not by thick slabs of brickwork but by slender cast-iron columns. There are more treats, though, to be found by turning right, down Leathermarket Street. Enjoy the utilitarian brick-built warehouses on its south side until you reach its west junction with Weston Street.

On these roads' southern corner stands a truly remarkable building, which formed the heart of the leather industry in late-Victorian Bermondsey. The London Leather, Hide and Wool Exchange, dated 1878, was designed by George Elkington in an eclectic amalgam of historic styles – an approach beloved of mid- and late-Victorian architects intent on drawing on historic precedent to forge something completely new. It is essentially late Elizabethan or Jacobean with a dash of Flemish Renaissance, but with a twist to make it look like nothing built in Tudor or Stuart England or the seventeenth-century Low Countries. The most charming details are the giant and muscular 'Atlas' figures which hold up the entablature above the main door, and the round, stone-carved panels within the ground-floor windows, each of which illustrates a different aspect of the leather trade.

But this entrancing building is only half the story. Immediately to its south is another building, part of the same exchange, which is quite as exciting but in a very different way. This is the leather market itself, built in 1833. Where the exchange is all whimsical historicism, with naive embellishments, the market is wonderfully tough and practical, a commercial structure designed to express solidity and substance. It seems to have a resolve as hard as the granite base upon which it sits. And yet, on closer inspection, it has more than a touch of opulence. The long, low frontage – hard yellow bricks with dashes of sandstone – makes it clear that this building was a secure place and leather a most valuable material. And the windows, framed by giant Tuscan pilasters, are calculated to proclaim that this is not just a solid, working building but also a temple of commerce, expressing the solemn majesty and moral certitude of legitimate trade and industry. The complex of buildings ceased to function as a leather exchange as early as 1912 – it now houses a mix of small businesses, including a café and an excellent pub. But its architecture is evocative enough to still conjure images of Victorian craftsmen and traders heckling over pieces of leather.

<hr>

Make your way back to Bermondsey Street and continue south, past the junction with Tanner Street. Here you'll find – at number 96 – an excellent boulangerie named Comptoir Gourmand, if you now fancy a coffee and a bun. While the warehouses and exchanges on and around the northern end of the street tell a story of industry and commerce, the buildings we encounter from here onwards reveal more about leisure in the nineteenth century: there are not only some glorious houses, but also a couple of good Victorian pubs, the Garrison and the Woolpack (virtually facing each other), a church, and even a philanthropic club. Intriguingly, many of these buildings reveal that our modern-day distinction – work versus pleasure, public versus private – was remarkably permeable until late in the nineteenth century.

Take the large, brick-fronted building at number 169 Bermondsey Street, which must date from around 1800. It looks, in some ways, like a regular early-nineteenth-century house – yet it was also a shop, manufactory and warehouse. It hints at the way the industrial architecture of the later nineteenth century emerged out of the traditions of Georgian domestic design. The building's interior sports the robust timber and cast-iron construction befitting an industrial structure, yet with delicate fire surrounds suggesting domestic comfort, with one most charmingly embellished with a tablet emblazoned with a sheep or goat, referring presumably to the local hide industry. And it is beautiful, too: the widely spaced windows are each divided by a sliver of a vertical recess – a functionally unnecessary detail that elevates mere utilitarian construction into poetic architecture. The local legend is that this building once housed the London factory of the famed hat-maker Christy's, founded in 1773. Overall it evokes a pleasing impression of a finely poised machine, but with all the humanity of a residential building designed for comfort, convenience and visual delight.

This blurring of work and leisure was not just a Victorian phenomenon. Nearby is the vast White Cube Gallery, a large private commercial enterprise that seems to be posing as some sort of public museum – so a modern example of leisure and pleasure combined with hard-nosed commerce. (Virtually opposite is a recently opened café named 'Fuckoffee'. Fair comment, I suppose.) And nearby, at numbers 187–9, we see work and leisure in the early twentieth century. This building, dated 1907, was constructed to house the 'Time and Talents Settlement', as is proclaimed on the frieze in rather beautiful and curvaceous lettering. It was founded in 1887 by a group of affluent West End Protestant ladies who believed that their coddled, educated and leisured daughters ought to make an effort to help the less fortunate young women of south-east and east London. The ladies of the Bermondsey Street branch operated a 'club room' for the local girls and sought to teach them 'healthy recreations' including singing, basket-making, knitting and sewing. Here, we see how for many Victorians and Edwardians, leisure was not just about enjoyment: it was about dutifully bettering oneself, and helping the poor. Incredibly, this worthy and well-meaning but inevitably patronising enterprise – which naturally failed to tackle the root causes of Bermondsey's social aliments – continued in this building until the early 1960s. Indeed the settlement lives yet, but transformed and transported to a community centre in Rotherhithe, rather alarmingly named the Old Mortuary. Architecturally, the Bermondsey building is a curious fusion of the Queen Anne Revival, with a dash of Baroque Revival, and art nouveau – all most unusual.

The Time and Talents Settlement's peculiar attitude to philanthropy was, of course, much to do with faith. Fitting, then, that at the time the neighbouring 191 Bermondsey Street was the rectory for St Mary Magdalen church, which stands a little down the road. This is one of south London's most remarkable churches, still with a large churchyard attached. Apart from its squat fifteenth-century west tower, it was rebuilt in 1675–9 by Charles Stanton, a Southwark master carpenter who also, in the late 1690s, designed and built the body of St Nicholas, Deptford. The exterior of St Mary's was clad in stucco in 1830 at which time the Bermondsey-based architect George Porter remodelled the west front in charming, playful and utterly unscholarly Gothic manner. This gives the

The charming, playful and utterly unscholarly Gothic charm of St Mary Magdalen church.

exterior an eclectic nineteenth-century feel. The interior was modelled on Wren's St Martin Ludgate – which is to say columns advance into the volume of the building, to define a cruciform plan incorporating a chancel to the east, transepts to north and south, and nave to the west. Inside changes have been gradual and conservative, with much surviving from various periods, including the south gallery of 1794, which still retains its box pews complete with their doors.

The adjacent churchyard is guarded by a pair of early-nineteenth-century watch-houses, erected to protect the dead from body-snatchers, who at that time frequently went in search of newly-buried bodies, almost impossible to acquire but highly valued by the medical profession for anatomical study. The tombs and memorials, scattered through the churchyard, are amongst the best in central London. The first thing to observe is that a number of the handsome table or altar tombs retain their protective palisades of cast- and wrought-iron railings – very rare in London, where most have rusted or were 'salvaged' in the early 1940s to be turned into fighting material to assist the war effort.

The most striking tomb is a minuscule but perfect neoclassical affair. I've walked past it, on and off, for decades and never really noticed it until recently. This now strikes me as typical of city life when, caught in the day-to-day bustle, we see very little beyond the big, boisterous and showy. This exquisite little tomb is none of these things. It's something you could almost take home and place in your drawing room. It consists of a small Portland stone sarcophagus, less than a metre long at its base, of Roman form, with tapering sides and a surface embellished with wavy, concentric lines called strigilation. This decoration is part of the neoclassical language of death, beloved by architects such as Sir John Soane, and seems to have been used by Romans to ornament their sarcophagi either to symbolise the waters of the River Styx, over which the spirit of the dead must pass, or to simulate the lines impressed on the flesh of a corpse after its ritual cleaning with oils and fork-like scrapers. At both ends of the diminutive sarcophagus are the bronze heads of lions, one still grasping a ring in its mouth, and on its base are four stone balls. This plinth is also beautifully considered. It has gently ramped sides that rise to the small plateau on which the sarcophagus sits – presumably to represent the ascent of the soul – and at the base of each ramp is a small stone step.

For whom was this wonderful creation wrought? All is revealed by a bronze plate that remains fixed to one side of the sarcophagus. The tomb commemorates William Allen, who died in August 1762, his wife Elizabeth, who died in July 1751, and the Allens' relatives through marriage, the Beazleys, the last of whom listed is Elizabeth Beazley, who died in 1781. It looks far too pioneering to date from the early 1780s. More likely it came somewhat later, probably a little after 1800, and was the work of Samuel Beazley – no doubt related to Elizabeth Beazley – who was an architect, novelist and playwright in Regency London. Samuel Beazley, born 1786, was one of the most famed and productive individuals in London theatre, writing nearly a hundred plays and designing and enlarging a number of theatres, including two notable structures of the 1830s: the long-lost neoclassical City of London Theatre in Norton Folgate, Spitalfields, and the cast-iron Ionic colonnade that still embellishes the Drury Lane Theatre in Covent Garden. When he died in 1851, at Tonbridge Castle, Kent, Beazley was brought to Bermondsey churchyard to be buried. Presumably he wanted to be near his family.

Leave the churchyard by the gate on Abbey Street, which runs perpendicular to Bermondsey Street. You now stand opposite Bermondsey Square. Here once was the 'Great Close', or inner court, of the late-eleventh-century Bermondsey Abbey. This abbey, affiliated with the Benedictine Order and also known as the Cluniac Priory of St Saviour, was, in its day, a place of high status: it was here Henry II and Eleanor of Aquitaine held court in the Christmas of 1154, and where Katherine de Valois – the widow of Henry V – lodged and died in June 1437. The priory was closed during the Reformation in the 1530s, when Henry VIII granted it to Sir Robert Southwell, a lawyer and one of the king's able and ruthless enforcers. Southwell soon turned the acquisition to profit by selling it on to Sir Thomas Pope – a yeoman, lawyer and immensely wealthy court servant, perhaps best remembered for founding Trinity College, Oxford. Pope used his new property in Bermondsey to proclaim his status, and quickly pulled down the priory church for materials to build a grand mansion for himself, which he called Bermondsey House. But, ever the profiteer, Pope did not keep the house and land for long, selling them back to Southwell who let them out to a rich City goldsmith. It's a tumultuous history, the only surviving hint of which is the fifteenth-century tower of St Mary's, which was once part of a church that served the priory's tenants.

Bermondsey Square is now a rather strange and sad place, defined by just a small group of early-Victorian houses huddled forlornly in its south-west corner. Until ten years or so ago the square was a large and rugged open space in which, each Friday morning, the Bermondsey antique market was held. This picturesque affair moved to this site in 1950 from the Caledonia Road market in Islington, soon becoming an institution famed among dealers, collectors and enterprising tourists. Like many Londoners, I used to make a regular pilgrimage, in the early hours of the morning, to the stalls and, by candlelight and torch, found and bought some remarkable things, before retreating for breakfast in traditional cafés in Long Lane or Bermondsey Street.

This market is now almost as distant a memory as the medieval priory buildings. Bermondsey Square has been largely built upon, with seven-storey slabs of apartment blocks, hotel and chain restaurants now laying their heavy and tiresome loads where an energetic and charmingly anarchic market flourished only a few years ago. True, a Friday-morning antique market does still take place, from around 4 a.m. – but on a prim and presentable small parcel of land in the shadow of the modern commercial buildings. There has been a recent attempt to reinvigorate the market but it remains a shrunken affair that feels somewhat corporate, as if it were laid on to entertain the tenants in the surrounding apartments. It is a succinct distillation of what has become of Bermondsey Street since the Middle Ages: first semi-rural idyll, then bustling hub of valuable but largely noisome trades, and increasingly corporate and unaffordable property developments.

———————◆•◆•◆———————

As you walk south-east from Bermondsey Square, you will notice a subtle change in atmosphere. South Bermondsey is more tranquil than the frenetic buzz of the high street. This is an area that gradually transformed from priory-owned farmland to late-seventeenth- and eighteenth-century merchants' domain to Victorian city with houses and industry closely juxtaposed. The story is told by the gradually evolving architecture we encounter in this portion of the walk. The resulting area retains the ambience of a place distant from the city, in spite of its proximity to central London.

The tranquil feel of this portion of London has ancient origins. As you follow the road leading from Bermondsey Square, crossing Tower Bridge Road, you come on to Grange Walk. As its name suggests, this road marks the route from the priory to its farms (or granges) to the south and east. At the west end of this street, on its south side, is a small group of wonderful houses, dating mainly from the seventeenth to very early eighteenth centuries. Nothing quite like them survives in central London. They are a palimpsest of medieval and late-Renaissance fabric: although little of the priory buildings remains, ancient forms and functions are echoed in their current structures and plans. Such curious groups of hybrids must once have been common within the precincts of London's dissolved monasteries, where medieval structures would have been altered and retained in later buildings, but this one is now the best by far to survive and offers a virtually unique glimpse of a lost London vernacular architecture.

Numbers 8–11 Grange Walk, a palimpsest of medieval and late-Renaissance fabric.

The group consists of seven houses, numbers 5–11 (continuous). All are significantly different – reflecting their individual histories of growth – and some, such as 10 and 11 and 6 and 7, are essentially pairs carved out of a single structure. Number 5, three storeys high, is crowned by a large gable. Above the front door is a narrow window, which is a common detail of the very early eighteenth century, and probably lit a small closet. The twin-gabled numbers 6 and 7 are more intriguing still, for they occupy a structure that is presumed to incorporate part of the priory's medieval gatehouse: on number 7 one can still make out the bottom parts of a pair of pin-hinges, set one above the other, marking the position of one leaf of a large gate. Numbers 5–7 are fronted with skins of nineteenth-century stucco, which hide the evidence of their date. But the peculiar window arrangement of numbers 6–7 gives it away: the single first-floor window, along with the combined window and front door on number 7, hints at centuries of gradual change, with the original fabric retained but reused in strange and varied ways.

Visually most satisfying are 8–11. All are two-storey, although 8 is crowned by a wide gable and all retain brick fronts that appear to date from the very late seventeenth or very early eighteenth centuries. Number 9 is particularly good, with brick keystones on the ground-floor windows, while number 8 has an intriguingly narrow window on the first floor. And numbers 9 and 11 both retain doorcases with features typical of the years around 1700, such as the bold pediments of segmental form, brackets luxuriantly carved with flowers and acanthus leaves, which are in turn supported by panelled pilasters. But look closely and you will see that little is quite what it seems. Many elements are fairly new, mostly well done (with the exception of the pediment on number 9 which is a beastly affair with mouldings of incorrect profile and whole elements missing). These doorcases, like the houses they adorn, are almost living things, with their flaws and omissions being part of their remarkable and individual character.

Our tour through the history of domestic architecture continues a little further along Grange Walk, at number 67. This structure reflects the transformation of the street from rural farmland to prosperous merchants' enclave, and likely dates to the decade or so after 1715. The house is metropolitan in its architectural aspirations, while most relaxed and rural in its composition. The brickwork, in particular, is superb – look at the well-wrought segmental arches above the windows. Another hint at the nature of early-Georgian Bermondsey stands opposite. The Bermondsey United Charity School for Girls was a typical product of eighteenth-century philanthropy. A charity school for poor local boys was started within the parish of St Mary Magdalen in 1712, and enlarged to include girls in 1722. By 1819, the *Second Report of the Commissioners on the Education of the Poor* would observe that the school educated 220 boys and 130 girls – thirty of the girls 'who best deserved it' were given clothes by the charity, too.[13] The building that now remains dates to 1830. The prim and proper classical frontage indicates the affluence of the institution by that time. By then, the key and regular contribution was from a charge on an estate on Grange Road. Like so much in Bermondsey, it all came back to the leather industry: this estate was occupied by prosperous 'tan-yards', part of whose annual rent supported the school. This handsome

schoolhouse must have done much to give the girls who attended it a sense of pride and worth.

Another hint of the ubiquity of the leather trade sits round the corner on Grange Road, a little to the south of Grange Walk. South Bermondsey never became as industrially vibrant as the high street, but by the 1860s a number of factories had cropped up in this generally residential area. The Alaska Factory, at number 61, was founded in 1869 to process the hides of Alaska fur seals, one of which – carved in stone – decorates the main gate. It's a charming object, but with a face that looks disconcertingly

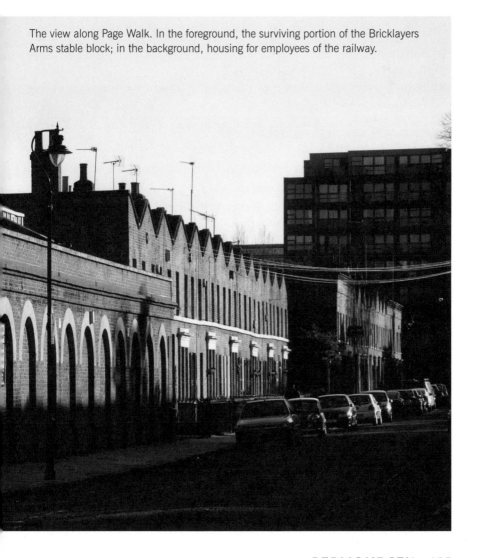

The view along Page Walk. In the foreground, the surviving portion of the Bricklayers Arms stable block; in the background, housing for employees of the railway.

human. Through the gate stands one of London's best-surviving art deco factories, built for Martin's, makers of leather clothes for aircrew in the Second World War. The main architectural feature is the jazzy tower, designed in the 1930s by Wallis, Gilbert and Partners, the British masters of commercially glitzy art deco.

The economy of this portion of Bermondsey was not, however, based on leather alone. The proof stands 100 metres to the south, at the intersection of Page's Walk with Willow Walk. Here you can enjoy one of the most sublime vistas of early-Victorian architecture still in existence: the street is wide and the buildings low, and on the south side stands a long, single-storey wall sporting wonderfully wrought brick arches. It is a surviving part of a huge stable block, whose horses once helped move the freight kept in Bricklayers Arms railway station. This station is one of the lost railway wonders of Victorian London. It stood near the south-west end of Page's Walk – just off the Old Kent Road – and was constructed in the early 1840s as the terminus for the South Eastern Railway Company and the London and Croydon Railway Company, who did not want to pay their rival to use London Bridge. Designed by Lewis Cubitt, who would later use a similar Italianate style at King's Cross, the station was a commercial disaster – it was too far from the city centre, and embedded in an area that was rapidly becoming impoverished. Within a few years the companies that had built it were incorporated with the London and Greenwich Railway. In 1852 it closed for regular passenger use.

But this was not the end of the site's railway history. Far from it. The terminus continued to be used on special occasions, as captured by an amusingly effusive 1863 article, which describes the reception of the Prince of Wales and Alexandra of Denmark in advance of their marriage at Windsor: 'The station at the Bricklayers Arms was a perfect marvel of magnificence. Wherever a garland or a human being could be put they were there,' reported the *London Review*. 'We should quite exceed our limit were we to attempt the faintest description of the display of taste and beauty which was provided at this point for the reception of the princess.'[14] Through much of the late nineteenth century, the terminus was used as one of the largest and most important railway goods yards in London. It survived well into the twentieth century, with operations finally ceasing in 1981. Today, virtually all traces of it have gone – with the exception of a few sandstone gate piers surviving in nearby Hendre Road, and the buildings in Page's Walk.

For the most observant savants, though, there are a few suggestions of the street's railway history to be found in the terraced houses to the south. The rail companies built these houses for employees and their families, and it seems likely that Lewis Cubitt or his office produced the designs. They now give the street much of its extraordinary character. The two terraces are two-storeyed, uniform and handsome in a robust way; most sport gables that express the structural form of their simple 'butterfly' roofs. The more northerly terrace has doors paired below bold, Tuscan entablatures of almost abstract form, while, in the terrace to the south, each front door is ornamented with a row of large oblong blocks, or 'dentils', set below a cornice that is no more than a slab of stone. All is very minimal and somewhat reminiscent of the work of Nicholas Hawksmoor (see Walk 3), suggesting that the designer of this group of buildings was enjoying his own mid-nineteenth-century Baroque revival.

It is only too tempting to let oneself get engulfed by the spirit of the Victorian age. However, the street has one final surprise. At its junction with Mandela Way you will stumble upon a Czech-made Russian T-34-85 tank. The gift of a local resident, it is now treated as an art piece, and regularly repainted in usually bizarre manner by diverse local artists. It's an odd urban ornament, and somewhat disconcerting if, like me, you first come upon it late at night, when it happened to be painted pink and with its trunk-like barrel rising ominously from the shadows. But in more sober moments, the tank – nicknamed 'Stompie' – is a most moving object to contemplate; with its powerful 85mm gun, an improved design of the first T-34 that was arguably integral to the Red Army's victory on the Eastern Front in 1944–5.

It's an idiosyncratic end to a walk through an idiosyncratic part of London. One is never far from the legacy of leather in Bermondsey, and the buildings and street names incessantly remind you of its industrial past. And yet it is also a place of medieval architectural treats, most decent cafés and pubs on and off Bermondsey Street, art deco towers, long-abandoned railway stations and – of course – the odd tank. Between them they create one of the most pleasingly eclectic districts of the capital.

Hampstead Garden Suburb

Hampstead Garden Suburb is the child of a utopian urban ideal that envisioned the city reborn as a place of health, beauty and the happy coexistence of home and work. All was to be realised through a renaissance of the crafts of building, through picturesque planning and through the unity of the best of the countryside with the best of the city.

This garden-city movement embraced many long-established ideas about the creation of urban areas with a flavour of country. One precursor is the late-Georgian obsession with *rus in urbe* – country in the city – which we first met in Walk 5. Another is the ideal of visionary 'model' villages and towns, which sprung up across Britain in the eighteenth and early nineteenth centuries. But the modern garden-city movement came into being with Ebenezer Howard's 1898 book *Tomorrow: A Peaceful Path to Real Reform*, reissued in 1902 with the punchier title *Garden Cities of Tomorrow.* The garden city was to be self-contained and self-supporting, to be compact with its districts small enough to allow inhabitants to walk with ease within them from homes to shops and places of work, with all possessing a beauty and sense of tranquillity – which was the antithesis of the squalor and overcrowding of the industrial city.

In parallel with the quest to create the majestic garden city as a self-contained riposte to the slum, there was also the related quest to create garden suburbs that shared many of the same ideals. The difference was obvious: as suburbs they were to be attached to existing cities, and were to be largely – although not exclusively – residential. The origin of the garden suburb is more difficult to define because, being of smaller size and almost exclusively residential, they emerged effortlessly from the tradition of model villages and idealistic artistic quarters such as Bedford Park, developed in Chiswick, west London from the mid 1870s as a comfortable and affluent middle-class enclave. And here is the key issue with the idea. The slum-dwellers who might benefit most from the garden-city and -suburb movement could not readily afford to share in this dream.

This paradox is given particular focus by London's great garden-suburb experiment. Hampstead Garden Suburb was founded in 1907 and was to be built on open high land, near Golders Green and lying at the north-west tip of Hampstead Heath (see Walk 1). The woman behind the foundation was Henrietta Barnett who, as the wife of the crusading social reformer and vicar Samuel Barnett, had spent twenty-five years in congested and poverty-stricken Whitechapel. The couple had done what they could to help, in the ways they thought best, the poor of the East End. These included bringing enlightenment – art and education, including the Whitechapel Art Gallery which they founded in 1901 – as well as more material assistance in the form of supporting slum clearance and promoting the construction of utilitarian industrial dwellings.

By 1900 the Barnetts had acquired a quiet retreat in Hampstead and became involved in calls to protect the farmland to the north-west of the heath from humdrum house building, which became a most serious threat when the Northern Line extension into the area was sanctioned in 1902. Henrietta Barnett led the campaign and in 1903 was involved in the formation of the Hampstead Heath Extension Council which succeeded in protecting the farmland and eventually adding it to the protected area of Hampstead Heath. But not all the farmland was sacrosanct. Barnett accepted that some house building was inevitable and even – if well designed and of the right type – desirable. In 1903 she proposed that a garden suburb be created on the northern portion of the farmland, primarily for housing the working classes. This, of course, was the logical conclusion of the Barnetts' East End mission. The poor were to be removed from the slums and rehoused amidst nature and inspiring beauty so that their souls could flourish and their sensibilities be refined.

The Hampstead Garden Suburb Trust was launched in 1906 to acquire the land and manage its development, with house building undertaken by co-partnership companies. This system meant that those participating bought a share, received a dividend and were involved in management. Initial shares cost £5 and so 'were beyond the grasp of the really needy and . . . possible only for skilled artisans, clerks and tradesmen'. Quickly it became clear that only the better-off members of the working class would be able to buy their way into this paradise. Henrietta Barnett, far from being concerned, seems not to have found this approach ethically unpleasing because she was 'convinced of the improving effect on the individual of investing in his own property'.[1]

Soon the plan for the suburb began to take form. From 1904 Raymond Unwin had been involved and his practice, Parker & Unwin – which had been instrumental from 1903 in the creation of the world's first garden city at Letchworth – produced the master-plan. They retained direct involvement, designing numerous houses of different types, until 1914. The plan was informal, which is to say roads tend to gently curve, and incorporated the existing clumps of trees and the contours of the land. It also preserved a small portion of wildwood in the very heart of the suburb, now known as the Big Wood. It is just large and unkempt enough to beguile visitors into believing that this is indeed part of the great primal forest that once stretched across north-west London (see p. 14).

But as well as these picturesque elements, the plan also has a formal quality. At its heart lies a rectangular square, with two churches and the suburb's institute – in essence its village hall – as well as a school. The suburb was executed by a number of the nation's leading architects, with designs largely being a combination of Arts and Crafts vernacular Gothic, or in permutations of the classical tradition – in the by then somewhat dated Queen Anne Revival manner, or in versions of the then fashionable styles of neo-Baroque or neo-Georgian. The mastermind behind many of these buildings was Edwin Lutyens, who was appointed consultant architect in 1906, a year before construction of the suburb started. Then in his late thirties, Lutyens was approaching the creative peak of his career. He was awarded the commissions for all the key buildings of the suburb – both churches, the school, and a significant number of houses – mostly terraces, forming part of the perimeter of the central square. It is Lutyens's designs that dominate our route.

If you arrive from Golders Green station, you approach the suburb via Hoop Lane and a small informal crescent called Meadway Gate, located

Baillie Scott's 22 Hampstead Way, a quiet monument to 'truth to materials'.

on the junction with Temple Fortune Lane. It's a magical point of entry because in the middle of the crescent, in a small garden, is a pergola which, in season, is loaded with flowering wisteria. Passing through the pergola feels like crossing a threshold into another world. Above the pergola, to the east, rise groups of two-storey buildings – which are an inspired and cosy reinvention of vernacular domestic architecture of sixteenth- and seventeenth-century southern and eastern England. They were designed by Edwin Palser in 1910.

Walk east into Meadway, and at the corner with Hampstead Way is one of the most joyfully romantic groups in the suburb – all gables, garden, mullion, asymmetry. This is 22 Hampstead Way and 6–10 Meadway, designed in 1908–9 by Baillie Scott and a quiet monument to the Arts and Crafts belief in 'truth to materials'. As you turn north-west along Hampstead Way, which soon forks with Willifield Way, the route is awash with oriels, mullions and bays, with the houses – united by their traditional vernacular language – often taking different forms, some most striking. The Arts and Crafts architects were, in many ways, radical and experimental, especially with their plans, as they sought to evolve a modern well-lit home, with an open and adaptable layout, from the building blocks of history and tradition. Number 40 Hampstead Way, of 1909, is particularly good. Its architect, T. Lawrence Dale, made the most of the potential of the site with a butterfly-plan house, incorporating a pair of loosely symmetrical wings radiating at a shallow angle from a centrally placed door topped by a pargeted bay and gable.

A little further north along Hampstead Way is one of the most satisfying houses in the suburb. Number 48 was designed in 1909 by Parker & Unwin and is replete with all the external elements of the Arts and Crafts cosy home – garden path set between rich planting, recessed porch complete with built-in seat, mullioned windows, high-pitched roof and tall chimney stacks suggesting large fireplaces around which the family can gather. Back to Willifield Way, and a few metres north is another bit of magic to the right. A narrow path, framed by tall hedges and trees, rises up to the east. Follow the path and you arrive at a sunlit plateau. Before you is the suburb's Central Square. In the foreground is a rather minimal Lutyens-designed memorial to Henrietta Barnett of 1938; beyond it stand his two churches.

Both are packed with Lutyens's quizzical and eclectic energy. Like British architecture at the time, he was still in search of an authentic style for the twentieth century. The Gothic and Queen Anne Revivals had come and mostly gone, leaving behind Arts and Crafts vernacular, neo-Georgian and neo-Baroque. Within this rich mix, all that could be agreed was that architecture must to some degree draw on the inspiration of the past and possess the pedigree of history (these were the years before the modernism that we meet in Walk 12 took hold).

This approach can be most effective in creating buildings that possess strong, almost abstract qualities which raise them well above pastiches of the past. Take St Jude's church, to the south. It has a Gothic silhouette because Lutyens's client – Henrietta Barnett – believed in conventional late-nineteenth-century manner that Gothic was the true style of church architecture. But he achieved this Gothic spirit with an idiosyncratic mix of Byzantine and Renaissance sources, and with the outer shell – utilising Roman-style tile-like bricks – combining red and grey in early-eighteenth-century English vernacular manner. When you enter the church it is not Lutyens's mix of historical sources you admire but the sheer expressionistic form, from the timbers of the vast roof, visible in the aisles, to the exposed structural brick arches supporting the dome. The other church – the Free Church, for non-Anglicans – arrived later, with construction beginning in 1911 and not finishing until 1960. It is a simpler affair, slightly smaller and different in form, although it is part of the same architectural quest – albeit with a more overtly Renaissance appearance, complete with a dome over the crossing.

Other buildings on the square had a more classically Baroque feel. To the east, Henrietta Barnett School – begun in 1908 to Lutyens's design but not completed until 1926, by which time many other architects had altered the plans – adopts an almost pantomime rendering of the English vernacular Baroque. The tall cupola that tops the roof is set back behind richly decorated wings, all wrought in specially made red and grey bricks and Portland stone.

St Jude's church, as sketched by Edwin Lutyens in 1908 and as built.

Lutyens's terraces of 1907–14 on the north side of the square, meanwhile, incorporate a stone-built Doric arch, framed by rustication which includes a pair of Doric capitals. This is a familiar touch of Lutyens's wit, which allows the elevation to be read either as pilaster shafts with rustication, or as a simple rusticated wall. Lutyens never seemed to tire of this visual game, as we will encounter in Walk 12 (see p. 459).

To leave the suburb, head south out of Central Square, via Heathgate. You soon come to the south boundary. This is the 'Great Wall', designed by Parker & Unwin to evoke the feel of the fortifications of a medieval city. It is a masterpiece of Arts and Crafts construction, incorporating pavilion-like bastions, and arches made of tile-like bricks. Standing here, on a summer evening, the suburb appears a most idyllic place. But, of course, the initial vision of it being an uplifting out-of-town community for artisans of the working classes has long slipped away.

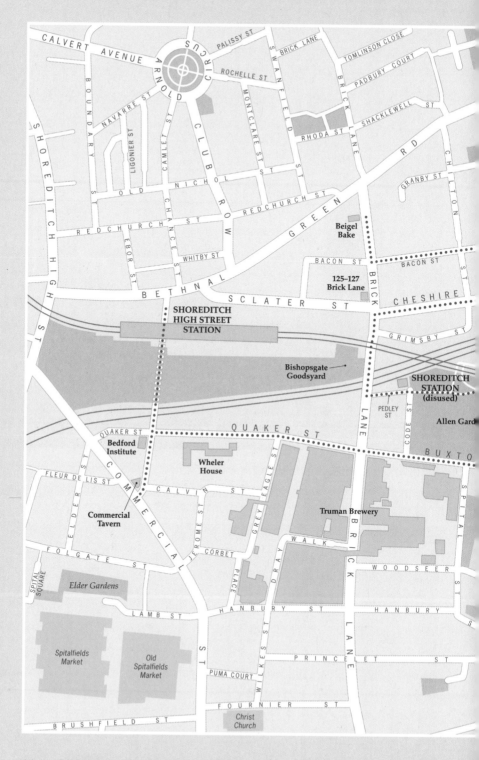

WALK 11

North Spitalfields

The last cry of outcast London

In his 1890 publication *Darkest England and the Way Out*, General William Booth, the co-founder with his wife Catherine of the Salvation Army, asked, 'As there is a darkest Africa is there not also a darkest England?' The question was in part prompted by H. M. Stanley's enormously popular book *In Darkest Africa*, published earlier in 1890, which described a disastrous voyage into the Congo in the language of Psalm 74: 'the dark places of the earth are full of the habitations of cruelty.'[1] The point Booth was making was straightforward. London was one of 'the dark places of the earth'. Why send missionaries and money to Africa or China when there was so much poverty among the London poor, and so many souls in its slums to be won for God?

Booth's perception was powerful and very influential, helping to cement further a popular attitude to East End districts like Spitalfields and Shoreditch, which were, as he knew to his horror, places that harboured abominable slums and terrible poverty. Booth's argument caught the imagination of many. In 1899 the narrator in Joseph Conrad's *Heart of Darkness*, when contemplating London from the Thames estuary, observes that 'this also . . . has been one of the dark places of the earth.'

The fact that Spitalfields was then one of the most notorious places in London has now, to a degree, been blotted out by its current manifestation as a charming, historic residential and leisure quarter, and a destination to be visited for its characterful Bangladeshi restaurants and bars and clubs. But from the 1840s until quite recently, accounts of Spitalfields were lurid and shocking. To contemporaries, they were even more remarkable because Spitalfields had once been a merchants' district favoured by affluent silk-weavers, largely descended from the French Calvinist migrants – or Huguenots – who began to move into the area in significant numbers during the 1680s (see p. 41).

Typical is the account of a dumbfounded American named David Bartlett who walked through the area in the early 1850s. 'When we first gazed at the destitution and horrible wretchedness of Spitalfields, our blood ran cold,' he wrote.

> You traverse street after street ... and see nothing but the most
> disgusting, the most beseeching poverty. There are thousands
> of men and women there who never have known what plenty
> is, what pure joy is, but are herded together, thieves, prostitutes,
> robbers and working men, in frightful masses ... the streets were
> very low and dirty [and] the odours that greeted us at every step
> were nauseating.

Bartlett concluded that 'there yawns between the rich and poor of London a great gulf almost like that between heaven and hell.'[2]

A similar atmosphere is evoked in the writing of Henry Mayhew, whose crusading *London Labour and the London Poor*, based on a series of 'letters' to the *Morning Chronicle* in the late 1840s and partly published in book form in 1851, offered some of the most disturbing depictions of life in east London. In October 1849 he visited a poor weaver's house near Shoreditch church. 'Never', wrote Mayhew, had he 'beheld so strange a scene. In the room were three large looms' and on the floor was 'spread a bed, on which lay four . . . boys . . . covered with old sacks and coats'. Next to them, for the weaver, lay a 'mattress on the ground without any covering . . . positively chocolate-coloured with dirt'.[3] This was hopeless, sordid, degrading and irreversible poverty.

These lurid descriptions must, of course, be taken with a pinch of salt. For one thing, many of the most influential accounts of Spitalfields at this time were somewhat sensationalist. Mayhew, crucially, was not trained as a historian or academic. He was a journalist and a storyteller, with an eye for the novel and the emotive. He said his books were 'the first attempt to publish the history of a people, from the lips of the people themselves . . . in their own "unvarnished" language'[4] – but the authenticity of his interviews was never fully established, and the sources are, crucially, anonymous.

What's more, many of the nineteenth-century descriptions of Spitalfields were based on its appearance from a great distance. It is difficult to overestimate the importance of the railway in shaping middle-class Londoners' understanding of the East End. When the high-level rail line was cut through the area in the late 1830s, it offered a lofty, secure and novel vantage point from which travellers could view this by now notorious area. Most, of course, did not like what they saw – and had no intention of risking their persons or property by taking a more intimate look. The view from the train, for most, offered an alarming glimpse into a parallel world that seemed incomprehensibly dark, dangerous and distressing – the world of the poor, the criminal, the vagrant, the prostitute, the insolent lounger and the professional vagabond.

Take the following description from the second volume of a travelogue, *London*, published in 1842 and edited by Charles Knight. A railway traveller describes the new experience of approaching the city from the east. Rooftops and garret windows gradually gave way to 'dismal streets in which no traveler dared to tread'.[5] George Gissing, in *The Nether World* of 1889, describes a train journey in even more shocking terms:

> Over the pest-stricken regions of East London . . . across miles
> of a city of the damned, such as thought never conceived
> before this age of ours; above streets swarming with a nameless
> populace cruelly exposed by the unwonted light of heaven;
> stopping at stations which it crushes the heart to think should
> be the destination of any mortal; the train made its way at length
> beyond the outmost limits of dread.[6]

An 1896 photo of Brick Lane from *Round London*, complete with a 'dangerous loafer in a deerstalker cap' in a doorway on the right.

Such descriptions reveal that the middle-class horror at the state of Spitalfields was rarely particularly well informed. Ever and again, when reading late-nineteenth-century books about London, the West Enders' incomprehension and suspicion of the East End leaps to the fore. This often has inadvertently comical consequences. I have long owned a book of splendid photographs called *Round London*, published 1896, which features a photo of Brick Lane – the commercial heart of Spitalfields – entitled 'a teaming Whitechapel Street'.[7] In the doorway of a closed and shuttered shop stands a man, hands in pockets and casually looking around. But in the view of the caption writer, he was 'a typical denizen

of this district – a dangerous loafer in a deerstalker cap, who was probably regarding our artist with amused contempt at the moment this view was taken.'[8] A bit harsh, perhaps.

This fear, loathing and prejudice for Spitalfields and Bethnal Green was, of course, all made far worse by the Ripper murders of 1888, which exposed to the world the poverty, the decay, the apparent barbarity and the danger of Spitalfields' streets. It seemed to be a world beyond the rule of law and beyond all decent restraint – a place that was by some deadly act of symmetry ordained to be the dark shadow of the apparently well-ordered and prosperous West End.

The Whitechapel murders would turn out to be a nadir for Spitalfields. The 1890s brought a conscious and wholesale removal of slum-housing and of ancient decayed buildings. It began with the clearance of the Nichol, located just north of Spitalfields and then one of the most notorious and desperate slum areas in London, formed largely from much-decayed eighteenth-century weavers' houses. Clearances continued wholesale from soon after the Second World War and into the early 1980s. By the time I arrived in the late 1960s, entire groups of streets were being obliterated, almost without trace, to create useful but often visually ungainly tracts of open space.

The second force to transform Spitalfields was migration. When I first got to know the area, it had been for centuries a destination for migrants: not just the Huguenot silk-masters who had largely created Spitalfields as a manufacturing quarter in the seventeenth century, but also Irish journeymen weavers during the early eighteenth century, and from the late nineteenth century Jewish families. This latter group were fleeing persecution in Russia and Russian-occupied Poland; they came in large numbers, settling mainly in the south portion of Spitalfields, adjoining Whitechapel. Despite their initial poverty and desperate circumstances, these new arrivals made a vast contribution to local life, doing much to establish the area's special and distinct culture and character. But all would change again after the Second World War. Partly as a result of the partition of India, many Muslims from the subcontinent settled in Spitalfields. They were subsequently joined by another generation of migrants, especially after the troubles surrounding the creation of the nation of Bangladesh in 1971. These migrants have, in turn, made their own contribution to Spitalfields' story, adding further levels of cultural richness and meaning.

It is now hard to reconcile the nineteenth-century Spitalfields – noted for crushing poverty and chronic overcrowding – with the present character of the area. There are still poverty and social ailments, but now often concealed from casual observation by the veneer of Spitalfields' new identity as a place of brittle fashion and ultra-expensive apartments. Of course there is a bitter contradiction in the comparison of the two Spitalfields: one of modern affluence and the other of the old evils of poverty, social despair and dysfunction. It seems almost impossible that they coexist. But they do, and it's the possibility of the simultaneous existence in the same space of opposing worlds that gives city areas like Spitalfields their compelling character and fascination.

To discover the area's earlier character you need your wits about you. And the quest can be visceral, almost elemental. There is Spitalfields by day and Spitalfields by night, Spitalfields in the light and Spitalfields in the dark – and when you walk through parts of the area at night the old Spitalfields seems not so far away. The past, always present but invisible in the bustle of daily life, returns from the shadows. So perhaps it would be best to do this walk at dusk or in the strange stillness of dawn.

There are many physical clues to be discovered, but most of the evidence of Spitalfields life as an outcast area, and of its nineteenth-century poverty, has been swept away. The more obvious and impressive historic fabric that remains dates from the days of eighteenth-century wealth and grandeur: notably the merchants' and master tradesmen's houses in Fournier Street and Nicholas Hawksmoor's Christ Church.

And so, more than with most parts of historic central London, the story of this area can now only be told with the aid of texts. Fortunately, since it has long been a place of human toil and suffering, Spitalfields caught the attention of reformers and informed observers. Their words are often powerful, penetrating and still possess the power to shock.

This walk begins in one of the most squalid parts of nineteenth-century Spitalfields – Wheler Street – before delving deeper into the history of the area, revealing the fate of its once-proud weaving community, its vibrant markets and the Jewish community. Throughout, these stories reveal another aspect of Spitalfields' current existence as two parallel worlds: there is the Spitalfields that is seen and the Spitalfields that is unseen. And, of course, sometimes it is the unseen – the immaterial – that is more real, more enduring. Only when the meagre surviving physical fragments are brought to life through texts can memory be revived, lost buildings evoked, and the ghosts of the people who once thronged these streets be given substance.

THE WALK

The first portion of this walk stretches from Shoreditch High Street overground station to Brick Lane. We have been here before on Walk 2, into the City of London. This time, though, our route is to the east – into territory that offers an insight into the squalor of Spitalfields in the late nineteenth century.

It wasn't always this way. When Spitalfields first started to expand at speed, immediately after the Great Fire of London in 1666, much of the development took place on land owned by the Wheler family; ultimately the Wheler estate would stretch from what became known as Bethnal Green Road, to the east of Spital Yard (later Spital Square) and then south to include the land on which Fournier Street was constructed during the 1720s. Wheler Street – now renamed as Braithwaite Street, the road Shoreditch High Street station opens on to – was the most architecturally important and affluent thoroughfare. It was in the houses of these streets that the more prosperous families of the area chose to live. When waves of French Protestant Huguenots began to move to Spitalfields in the

The view south through the abandoned railway arches on Wheler Street.

1680s, escaping Catholic persecution in their own land and at the hands of their own king, Louis XIV, many of the most ambitious and successful settled here.

By the mid nineteenth century, however, all of this was a distant memory. The street pattern was changed radically in this period, first by the construction of the railway from 1839, and then by the imposition of Commercial Street, a new thoroughfare, built from 1843–57, which as well as improving communication also obliterated some of Spitalfields' most desperate slum streets and courts. Wheler/Braithwaite Street retains no physical relics of its opulent seventeenth-century origins. Instead, the best buildings are Victorian. On the south-west corner with Quaker Street is the red-brick and boldly gabled Bedford Institute, built in a handsome early-seventeenth-century Flemish Renaissance style and named after a Quaker philanthropist. Built in 1893 – the date is shown in entwined numerals on the door-surround – the institute housed, amongst various admirable activities, a working-men's club and presumably did much to improve the impoverished lives of those who lived around it.

The jaunty Commercial Tavern, decked out with charming details.

Far jauntier is the Commercial Tavern, at the junction of Wheler Street and Commercial Street. It was constructed in 1863 as part of the healing process after Commercial Street had been sliced through the area and new building plots had been created. It stands on an odd, wedge-shaped plot, but the designer turned the problem to advantage by treating the wedge as an opportunity to create a bulbous, bull-nosed building – its front tricked out with lovely details – containing a well-windowed dining room on its first floor. This room allowed diners to enjoy a fine prospect of the new road and its teeming traffic, as if it had been a canal in Venice.

Wheler Street also contains five fine nineteenth-century cast-iron bollards, each with its own story to tell. One, a splendid Gothic affair, has the letters MBS cast into its base, presumably meaning the Metropolitan Borough of Stepney. The remaining four are of the more familiar cannon form, three with a 'spur' casting at their base showing they were designed to prevent loaded drays from wandering on to the pavement.

John Dodgson's cast iron bollard on Wheler Street.

One proclaims on its shaft 'St Paul's Shadwell', and so presumably was part of a paving scheme in the parish and was moved here at some later date. It also records that it was cast in 1848 by Bailey Page & Co. of 81 Bankside. Another states in large and beautiful serif lettering 'Dodgson London' – referring to John Dodgson of Lower Shadwell, registered in the Post Office Directory of 1841 as an 'iron and brass founder'. These bollards are lovely and strangely human things – the small, domed tops of the cannon-type burnished by the posteriors of generations of loiterers resting upon them, deciding whether to go this way or that or simply going nowhere at all.

The route to take, though, is the thoroughfare that intersects with Wheler Street. This is Quaker Street. On the north side is a row of gabled former railway warehouses dating from the late nineteenth century and now gutted and being converted into an economy hotel; on the south side is an early twentieth-century block of industrial dwellings, portions of the former Truman's Brewery, and a large interwar public-housing block named Wheler House. This block – standing in an open space and set back from the street – can be quite a disturbing sight, with debris littering its forecourt and its balconies bedecked with drying washing. It is at once a startling reminder of the poverty and decay that made these streets notorious in the nineteenth century, and a hint that, despite Spitalfields' renaissance as a residential area and a place of entertainment, it also contains within it some of the poorest pockets of East London.

In the late nineteenth century, the courts and alleys off the south side of Quaker Street were among the worst the district had to offer. They were, indeed, some of the darkest, most dire and most squalid buildings in the city. In the preceding decades, the density of occupation had been increased, with the construction of rows of cramped, ill-lit and tiny cottages in what were once open courts, yards and even gardens. The result was a labyrinthine urban grain, with secreted courts of tumbledown houses and of ancient large houses subdivided and neglected. So naturally, when the political and social scientist Friedrich Engels wanted to illustrate the desperate destitution of London's poor in the 1840s, he turned to the courts off Quaker Street.

For Engels the poor were the tragic victims of the ruthless and exploitative system of capitalism, and in and around Spitalfields he found evidence to support his argument that in Britain profit-driven entrepreneurs and industrialists had forged a selfish, materialist and heartless society in which the poor – if deemed unproductive – were suffered to starve. In his *The Condition of the Working Class in England*, published first in Germany in 1845, one of the most powerful moments is the story of two boys who, in January 1844, had been brought before the magistrate because 'being in a starving condition, they had stolen and immediately devoured a half-cooked calf's foot from a shop'. Upon investigating further, the magistrate discovered how they lived at No. 2 Pool's Place, Quaker Court off Quaker Street. A policeman found the mother

> with six of her children literally huddled together in a little back
> room, with no furniture but two old rush-bottomed chairs with
> the seats gone, a small table with two legs broken, a broken cup,
> and a small dish. On the hearth was scarcely a spark of fire, and
> in one corner lay as many old rags as would fill a woman's apron,
> which served the whole family as a bed. For bed clothing they
> had only their scanty day clothing. The poor woman told him she

had been forced to sell her bedstead the year before to buy food. Her bedding she had pawned with the victualler for food. In short, everything had gone for food.[9]

To push his point home, Engels quoted an article from *The Times* of 12 October 1843: 'Let all men remember this – that within the most courtly precincts of the richest city of God's earth, there may be found, night after night, winter after winter, women . . . ROTTING FROM FAMINE, FILTH, AND DISEASE.' He concluded with a call to arms: 'Let them remember this, and learn not to theorize but to act. God knows, there is much room for action nowadays.'[10]

It was an extraordinary image, and would have been unimaginable just a century earlier, when these had been handsome streets that housed a flourishing silk industry. But, through the nineteenth century, this would be the impression of Spitalfields that became embedded in the popular imagination. One of the most vivid descriptions was produced in the late 1890s and came – as ever – from the social reformer and philan-thropist Charles Booth (see pp. 310, 361–2 and 386), and his secretary George H. Duckworth. As we have seen, Booth colour-coded the streets he saw to show the economic and social status of occupiers, ranging from black for the very poor to yellow/gold for the richest. Although flavoured by a sense of compassion, his notes about Spitalfields are uncompromising, prejudiced and often scathing. New Square, off the south-west side of Quaker Street, included 'Dogs chained to each garden, thieves'; Pool Square, mean-while, was notable for having 'rough women about, Irish, one house with wooden top storey, windows broken'.[11] They noted that this square should be dark blue on the poverty map – almost the worst category.

One theme that emerges in many accounts of nineteenth-century Spitalfields is the territorialism. 'This is the last of an Irish colony,' the pair reported of Pool Square. 'The Jews begin to predominate where Grey Eagle Street is reached.'[12] There were streets, courts and small areas inhabited almost entirely by poor Jewish families of Polish and Russian origin, mostly towards Whitechapel Road, whereas other areas were almost exclusively occupied by poor Irish or poor English families. These tended to mix while the Jewish community nearly always remained separate. In this particular case, Booth and Duckworth seem to have got it wrong:

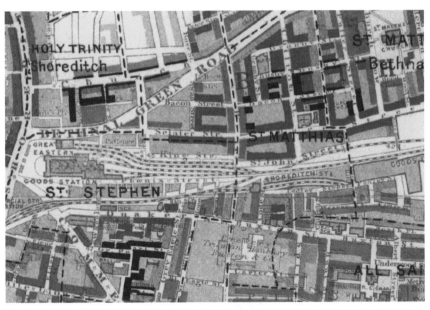

Charles Booth's 1898 poverty map of the area covered by this walk. The patch of black on the bottom left indicates that the residents living off Quaker Street were 'vicious, semi-criminal'. Brick Lane runs north–south in the centre.

they say, in a rather inflammatory manner, that the area around Quaker Street was being transformed by an 'invasion of Jews' with 'small English colonies dotted about'.[13] In fact, the census of 1891 reveals that the small cottages in these courts remained the preserve of the English poor, with most of their inhabitants born in or near the area. Even more striking is the absence of the Huguenot legacy from the census. Only a few of the names seem French, suggesting that by the end of the nineteenth century the area's once dominant French community was but a distant memory, with its members having been almost overwhelmingly assimilated or – more likely – had simply moved on.

Booth and Duckworth also tell us a little about the lifestyles of the inhabitants of this area. In their concluding 'General Remarks', they characterised the courts and streets lying south from Quaker Street and east from Commercial Street to Brick Lane as 'a thoroughly vicious quarter', made worse by the Cambridge Music Hall on Commercial Street – one of the largest music halls in London – which 'makes it a focusing point for prostitutes'. The music hall had been damaged by fire in 1896, redesigned in exotic Moorish style by Harry Percival and reopened in

1898 – just in time for Booth and Duckworth to make their observations about its evil influence – before ultimately being demolished in 1936, and replaced by the bulky, tile-clad faintly art deco factory building that still stands on the site.

———◆◆◆———

What had happened to the once-proud weaving community of Spitalfields? Clearly at some stage in the nineteenth century, something had gone badly wrong for the well-to-do Huguenots of the district. The

The view east through the remains of Pedler Street, once located in one of Spitalfields' most important weaving districts.

next portion of the walk offers a few clues. Quaker Street emerges on to Brick Lane (which we will visit later); continue straight on to Buxton Street, and you soon come to the grassy plain of Allen Gardens, much beloved by the dog-owners of the area.

It's now hard to believe, but the gardens occupy what was once one of the most important weaving areas in Spitalfields. Until the early 1960s, it retained a network of narrow cobbled streets, most lined with two-storeyed weavers' cottages, furnished on their first floors with wide weavers' windows. Indeed, until five or six years ago a significant number of these cobbled streets survived, robbed of their houses but still carrying with them evocative memories. Standing on these narrow stretches of

cobblestones, it was easy to conjure up the ghosts of their long-lost houses and the lives lived within them. Sadly most were destroyed a few years ago for the construction of the overground railway, which rises here from below and in the process slices diagonally through the route of what was Pedley Street.

The history of these streets tells of the boom years of the Spitalfields' silk industry as well as its decline. John Rocque's map of 1746 shows a short road called Fleet Street which, along with other streets probing east from Brick Lane, ended in market gardens and fields that marked the beginning of open countryside. However, by the time of a map of 1799–1819 by Richard Horwood (see p. 504), some of the market gardens around Fleet Street had been built upon. Over the next twenty years or so, they disappeared under bricks and mortar and from its eastern end Fleet Street was extended by the newly laid out Pedley Street – created in a belated burst of optimism and growth that seems to have contradicted the long-term troubles besetting the local silk industry.

This transformation of Spitalfields from semi-rural idyll to urban sprawl contributed to its subsequent transformation into a slum. As it became increasingly distanced from healthy fields by the remorseless and mean eastward expansion of London, the problems of poverty and overcrowding were greatly multiplied. By the mid nineteenth century the lives of those who occupied the small houses in these narrow streets was harsh, because the silk industry had entered its years of final decline. In the mid 1860s, the writer Thomas Archer summed up the problem: 'Unfortunately the cheapness of the French and German silk and velvet which is now exported free of duty, and the operation of the country factories as well as those of the large towns, have combined to reduce the London weavers to a very deplorable condition.'[14] The value of the industry plummeted rapidly, and the wages of journeymen weavers with it.

The fate of the weavers is well illustrated by one story of Pedley Street, commemorated by Henry Mayhew. He quotes a weaver, Thomas Heath of 8 Pedley Street, who had given evidence in 1839 to a government inquiry. Heath, the inquiry said, had been 'represented by many persons as one of the most skilful workmen in Spitalfields' and had submitted a 'detailed account' of his earnings during the last eight years. This averaged out at about fifteen shillings a week. After expenses this left Heath with an income of, on average, eleven shillings and sixpence a week. His wife's earnings were three shillings a week. What struck Mayhew forcefully was Heath's bitter and forlorn answer when asked if he had any children: 'No; I had two, but they are both dead, thanks to God.' When asked why he was pleased his children were dead, Heath replied that by their deaths he was 'relived from the burden of maintaining them, and they, poor dear creatures, are relived from the troubles of this mortal life'. Mayhew noted that if this was the feeling of a skilled weaver, earning about three shillings a week above the average wage, 'what must be the condition of the weavers now [in the late 1840s] that wages have fallen from fifteen to twenty percent since that period.'[15]

Mayhew was haunted by this desperate declaration, and so am I. Over the years I have tried to work out where 8 Pedley Street stood, as if this would somehow bring me nearer to Thomas Heath and help me understand him better. Calculating the house's location was easier before the overground railway was constructed, for this now disturbs and destroys the ground by cutting through the former junction between Fleet

Street and Pedley Street. I have, however, had better luck with the 1841 census. This is a notoriously difficult document to use – house numbers are not given, the method or order of listing the inhabitants of a street is often not clear, and handwriting can be appalling and information sketchy. But working my way through the entries for Pedley Street, in the parish of St Matthew Bethnal Green, I found Thomas Heath, and what then remained of his family.[16] He was described as a weaver, aged forty-five, born in Middlesex. He lived with his wife Ann, aged thirty – and there were no children listed.

Documents like these paint a grim portrait of the life of the weavers in the 1840s. In the same house as Heath, which can only have been small, it seems there were three other family units and eleven people all in occupation on the day of the census. What's more, the census shows that, in the adjacent group of six small houses on Pedley Street, there were forty-nine people in occupation. Add to this the number in the Heath residence and you get sixty inhabitants in a row of seven adjoining houses, meaning that on average between eight or nine people lived in each one. Of these sixty people, twenty-seven were involved in the silk-weaving or fabric industry. It must have been a crowded and squalid existence.

What was home life like for the last of the silk-weavers? The patterns of life were described by many people, often with very different manners of expression. One of the more melodramatic accounts comes from Charles Dickens, a London-obsessive and an uncontrollable romantic. In 1851 he interviewed a weaver who worked hard but lived a precarious existence, forever subject to the fluctuations of the market that were way beyond his control, and forever worried about the welfare of his family. Dickens explored the weaver's house, which quite possibly stood in or near Pedley Street, and observed that the silk looms dominated the home so that 'the children sleep at night between the legs of the monsters.' Dickens also noted that weavers kept pigeons – birds being the traditional pets of the weavers – and grew green runner beans. He ruminated that 'while birds could fly and escape, their owners could not. The bean stalk allowed Jack to escape in the fairy tale but the "Jacks" of Spitalfields will never, never, climb to where the giant keeps his money.'[17]

A far more detailed description was offered in the 1860s by Thomas Archer. He wrote not just of weavers' houses and their garrets but also of the ornaments in their homes, their characters and their hobbies. The weaver, noted Archer

> requires a 'long light', or leaden casement, so that he most frequently occupies garrets, originally designed for his trade. Poor, suffering, nearly starved, and living in a house which shares with the rest the evils of bad or no drainage, and insufficient water supply, his business requires at least some amount of personal cleanliness, for the delicate fabrics on which he is employed could never come out unsullied from the touch of coarser hands.

In these weavers' houses, claimed Archer, 'the click of the shuttle may be heard all day long while the weaver has work to do.' Archer's description of a weaver's home is particularly poignant: 'In one of these long "shops" a whole family and all their live stock will sometimes live . . . amidst the turned up stump bedsteads or the roll of blankets on the floor.' In their poverty Archer discerned a sense of family pride and the distant memory of more prosperous times. Among 'the few pieces of broken crockery, and the rickety furniture, some of which is generations old, there is often seen some sort of order and decency which is worthy of a better fortune . . . a cracked china cup, an ivory carving, a silver-keyed flute, a flawed and riveted punch-bowl . . . [or] a scrap or two of old point lace.'[18]

The street life of this weaving district is even harder to imagine today. Again, though, the historical record offers us a glimpse of what has been lost. The Old Bailey's archive includes a description of a violent robbery of September 1826. At about half past seven in the evening, a surgeon named Henry Fuller was walking along Fleet Street Hill when he was attacked by a gang of around twenty men. According to Fuller, when giving evidence in court six weeks later, two of the men pinioned his arms while another fastened them to his body by a rope. Fuller claimed that many brandished sticks to terrorise him and one shouted, 'If the b—r speaks, knock his b—y brains out.' Fuller's pockets were rifled, his surgical instruments grabbed and then he was released and the gang ran off. What happened next is in many ways more chilling, and certainly very revealing. As Fuller explained in court, after being untied and as the gang fled, 'I raised a cry of "Stop thief!"' But nobody in the street responded or picked up the cry. Eventually, 'Some persons came up and begged me to hold my tongue, saying the gang was so desperate, they would murder me if I did not.' Eventually four men were taken for the violent 'highway robbery' and tried at the Old Bailey – three were acquitted for lack of evidence but one, the eighteen-year-old James Bishop, was found guilty and hanged.[19] These streets were clearly lawless places, stalked by gangs that were bred out of the poverty and unemployment of the collapsing silk industry.

Today, the closest one can get physically to these old silk-weaving houses is by walking to the very east end of Allen Gardens. Here are the best surviving portions of early streets, with one cobbled section now serving as the entrance to the adjacent and admirable Spitalfields City Farm. On this narrow street, where weavers once walked, and on the sites of the small terraced houses in which they toiled and starved, goats now

The cobbles leading into Spitalfields City Farm, all that remains of Weaver Street, Fleet Street Hill and Bratley Street.

frolic and prize pigs wallow in bucolic splendour. The cobbled fragments include a portion of Weaver Street – which ran south of and parallel to Pedley Street – and its junctions with Fleet Street Hill and Bratley Street. These are the very corners on which unemployed and desperate weavers must have gathered in the middle of the century to discuss their plight and share their sorrows.

———————◆•◆•◆———————

In the mid nineteenth century Spitalfields was – as now – a place of opposing worlds. Even while large parts of the area were beset by poverty and despair, others were commercially vibrant, even prosperous, with their houses quite well-occupied. Along and around Brick Lane were markets, shops, manufactories, numerous pubs and, of course, the huge Truman, Hanbury and Buxton brewery. This is a side of Spitalfields that we next encounter.

Walk back via the north side of Allen Gardens, and through the narrow alleyway that still, rather grandly, calls itself Pedley Street. You come out on to Brick Lane. This is an ancient thoroughfare, and has existed with its modern name since at least 1550. On the Agas map that shows London in c. 1560–70, Brick Lane is shown clearly, but is unlined by buildings. In the early 1640s Brick Lane marked one of the boundaries of the massive earth-built system of fortifications that Parliament rapidly constructed around London. Like the Wheler estate to its west, it began to develop in the late seventeenth century; by 1703, according to Joel Gascoyne's map of Stepney, buildings lined virtually all of Brick Lane. This transformation into urban area had – along with much of Spitalfields – been rapid, almost shockingly so. In his *Tour Thro' the Whole Island of Great Britain*, published in three volumes between 1724 and 1727, Daniel Defoe remarked that, 'Within the memory of the writer hereof, all those numberless ranges of building, called Spittle Fields . . . are all now close built, and well inhabited with an infinite number of people.' Lanes that were 'deep, dirty and unfrequented' were now part of the city, and this included 'Brick Lane, which is now a long well paved street' though it was formerly but 'a deep dirty road, frequented chiefly by carts fetching bricks that way into White-Chapel from Brick kilns in those fields, and had its name on that account.'[20]

The Brick Lane before us now possesses some physical reminders of this early development, but mostly it reflects the vibrant late-eighteenth- and nineteenth-century life of the area. Most notable is the mighty bulk of the former Truman's Brewery that stands astride the central portion of Brick Lane. Truman's was, in the mid eighteenth century, one of the largest and most modern industrial complexes in the world, and it determined much of the physical character of the north-east portion of Spitalfields well into the late twentieth century. It was closed as a brewery in 1989, but the commercial, retail and leisure uses to which its retained buildings are currently put remain a major influence on life in Spitalfields.

But we walk north, towards the railway bridge. The character of this portion of Brick Lane was recast during the 1830s – and after – by the arrival of the railways. You may have noticed a small, graffiti-covered brick building on Pedley Street; this was Shoreditch station, built in 1876 to serve the Underground system's East London Line. The little station, perched above a track in the deep cutting below, closed in 2006 having been made redundant by the overground line that now sails majestically above it, to the north. The railway bridge across Brick Lane, incorporating a vast lattice-steel viaduct to its east, carries the overground railway to Shoreditch High Street station. The really significant railway works, however, lie just to the south of this bridge and run, generally out of sight, below ground level. This is the main route into Liverpool Street station from Cambridge and Norwich which, when being constructed in the later nineteenth century, wrought much havoc in this part of Spitalfields.

Take a look to the west, just before the bridge is reached. Here, behind a pair of huge gates, is a now-secret treasure trove of industrial architecture and archaeology that stretches as far as Wheler Street. This is the brick-vaulted underworld – with cobbled streets and cavernous arched rooms – of the now long-lost Bishopsgate Goodsyard. The ranges of once towering warehouses are now gone and all stands derelict, the subject of a series of much-contested proposals from developers to bedeck all with a number of residential towers. The existing structure incorporates portions of the original viaduct – dating from 1838–40 and designed by the pioneering railway engineer John Braithwaite. This viaduct, which originally led to Bishopsgate railway station on Norton Folgate, is a listed building so it, at least, should survive whatever scheme finally wins consent. The

A secret wonderland of industrial architecture: behind the gates at the former Bishopsgate Goodsyard.

redundant rail track above your head is supported by brick piers of vast girth which allow only a little light to filter into this seemingly subterranean world. The tough materials and robust brick and stone construction, the rich and wild planting cascading from above, gives it the feel of an antique ruin, like Trajan's Market in Rome. About ten years ago all of this was opened for the public's pleasure but then closed again. Such are the strange ways and vagaries of urban development.

Immediately to the north-east of the bridge is a small road, its south side now mostly occupied by the vast latticework steel viaduct of the overground railway. This was the long, once-important and well-occupied St John's Street, which was laid out in the seventeenth century and is recorded in all its splendour on Gascoyne's 1703 map of Stepney. It must have been an attractive street, lined with the late-seventeenth-century homes of Huguenots, perhaps even the grand homes of leading master weavers, since one of the area's most important Huguenot churches or 'temples' was set within a court on its north side. The street terminated with the pleasant walks of 'Hambleton's Garden', with fields beyond. This idyllic world, or rather what survived of it, was shattered when the railway arrived and most of the south side and east end of the street disappeared first below the raised viaduct and then was obliterated by the later, wider cutting. And most of what was built in place of the lost houses was in turn destroyed a few years ago for the viaduct. Now this once-grand street is now no more than the runt of a turning, seemingly heading nowhere. For some not very clear reason its name has been changed to Grimsby Street – perhaps so as not to sully the memory of St John.

The next junction, virtually a crossroads formed by Sclater Street coming in from the west and Cheshire Street from the east, is one of the most important and memory-charged places in Spitalfields – at least for those whose memory of the area stretches back for a few decades. This was the meeting place of Spitalfields' great and famous outdoor Sunday markets. Thirty years ago the markets were thriving affairs, hubs of East End life, selling all manner of wares – from cut-prices clothes and puppy dogs to old furniture and the accumulated contents of many a local attic or cupboard. It was truly amazing. All you had to do was wish to find something and, if you kept your focus, you usually would – with a lot of surprises thrown in. Now these markets are but sad shadows, although the north end of Brick Lane still puts on a reasonable showing on a Sunday morning, with street stalls selling more than cheap food and modern tat.

This junction also marks the nucleus of Brick Lane's few surviving early houses, shops and workshops. Particularly good are 125 and 127 Brick Lane, built on the corner with Sclater Street in 1778 for a Huguenot named Daniel Delacourt and with wide workshop windows. There was a sensational terrace of similarly wide-windowed weavers' houses on the south side of Sclater Street. They were built in the early 1720s, became derelict and were destroyed in the early 1970s without even a whimper. This pointless destruction – their site remains empty – was a most significant step in the fightback to save the historic fabric, and life, of Spitalfields: a fight that has been sustained for over forty years with grim determination by succeeding waves of residents.

At the west end of Sclater Street, where it faces Club Row to the north across Bethnal Green Road, was the once-famed Club Row animal and bird market. It was one of the sights of nineteenth-century London and it seemed to attract and yet repulse in fairly equal measure. There

The junction of Brick Lane and Sclater Street – in the early 1970s, and today. Many of the dilapidated Georgian buildings that once lined the street have long since been demolished and replaced.

are some memorable descriptions. Thomas Archer, writing in the mid 1860s, is particularly good because he seems to have spent some time in the area, observing 'the bird, dog, and pigeon-fanciers'. They came, he says, 'from the marshes, or from still further afield, where they have been pegging for chaffinches, or jingling robins, or netting larks'.[21] Archer writes evocatively on the character and the extravagant appearance of these bird fanciers, who were perhaps part of London's mid-Victorian gang life: 'shambling, tight trousered, sleek haired, artful,' he says, 'they are in the long run more . . . dangerous than either thief or convict.'[22] Archer also noted the more 'regular thieves' who were attracted to Club Row on market day: 'I have counted eleven as I stand here by the corner, and I know that I am the cause of their uneasy shifting hither and thither, and that they are watching me as closely as I am looking at them.'[23] Thirty years later, Charles Booth, too, had much to say about the animal and bird market: during a walk on 22 March 1898, he noted that it was a 'centre to bird fanciers' dealing in 'larks, thrushes, canaries, parrots'; they were often placed in 'small square cages wrapped up in pocket

handkerchiefs outside windows', which supposedly allowed 'new birds to pick up the right note from their fellows'.[24]

In the early 1970s, when I first got to know the area well, Club Row market was still very much a going concern. Now, thinking back, I realise I was witnessing the closing moments of a way of life. I remember entering a pub on Bethnal Green Road, one Sunday lunchtime on a summer's day. The bar room was lofty, and light flooded in through generous expanses of Victorian glazing to illuminate an atmosphere made tangible by eddying clouds of cigarette smoke. The bar was on my right, as I had entered through the door on the corner with Club Row. But it was not the bar that caught my eye. What struck me was a spectacle at once curious and distinct but also, for generations, typical in the Club Row area on Sunday market days: the room was full of birdcages, stacked one upon another, on tables, on the bar, and rising to the ceiling; indeed some were suspended from the ceiling itself. This was the last great example of a Club Row bird-fanciers' pub, where people came to trade in birds and to admire each other's recent purchases. I remember being simply amazed by the oddness of it all. What a sight – the tottering stacks of cages, the fanciers with their pints engrossed in conversation – and what a sound as the birds sang their different songs. Outside the pub proclaimed itself the Knave of Clubs, but all locals and market-goers knew it as the Bird Cage.

At that time, the rest of Brick Lane market – spreading east down Sclater Street and along Cheshire Street as far as Vallance Road – was still a proper and traditional street market, with costers, punters, vagabonds, 'dealers' and 'fanciers' of all sorts. Vans and trucks loaded with pickings from the towns and villages of Essex, north Kent, Suffolk and even Norfolk would arrive at one or two o'clock on Sunday morning. Early-rising dealers would chase the vehicles down the street and start crawling over them before they had even stopped moving, shining their

torches over the contents and into dark corners, 'sorting out' their loads and laying claim to prize pieces. I joined these romps in the small hours through truckloads of most unconventional treasures. My finds were pretty mixed – I suppose we were for the most part turning over the hauls made from house clearances, raking through the earthly remains of the newly-dead – but there were occasional remarkable and surprising relics. I once bought a late-eighteenth-century Delft tile, cracked but in a frame, with, on its back, a handwritten label recording that it came from 'John Buchan's fireplace (study) at Elsfield, Oxon'.

Even in the 1970s, the rhythm of the market owed a great deal to its ancient origins. The early start was probably due to the traditional law of *Marché ouvert* which stated that a purchaser would have title to goods – even when stolen – if those goods had been displayed and bought at a 'designated' street market. The original logic of the law seems to have been based on the assumption that most stolen goods were disposed of in markets, so it was up to the victim of a theft to go to search for their

Sclater Street market as I first knew it in the early 1970s. These 1720s weavers' houses have now been demolished.

possessions. If they found them and could prove ownership then they could reclaim them. But if the goods on sale were not reclaimed then they were the rightful possession of the buyer. By the early 1970s this arcane code had boiled down to the simple notion that if items were sold before sunrise the buyer had title. This ancient law was finally abolished in 1995. It can surely be no coincidence that the early trading at Brick Lane stopped at about the same time.

Indeed, within a few years, virtually all that made the Brick Lane markets was over. The demise of the traditional Club Row market was particularly, almost brutally, rapid. In the early 1980s animal-rights activists decided that the time-honoured trade in birds, puppies, kittens, rabbits and a few more exotic creatures was frightful and cruel. For a few Sundays protests were mounted and, in what seemed to me a very short period, this ancient East End trade was brought to an abrupt end. No doubt the conditions in which the animals were kept and sold were not good; certainly they can hardly have been fully regulated. But the market was part of the life and history of the East End, and its passing marked yet one more stage in the separation of Spitalfields and Bethnal Green from their past. And as for the Knave of Clubs, it closed long ago and its building now houses yet one more restaurant.

Still, though, one can capture a glimpse of the convivial life of the nineteenth-century East End in the pubs of Cheshire Street. Walk east, and after a few hundred metres you come to the Carpenter's Arms, a small and charming late-Victorian pub. It is now something of a haven in Spitalfields, where most pubs are packed with drinkers attracted by the area's current reputation as a place of revels. The Carpenter's Arms, on the other hand, is now run by a management that takes a pride in serving beers that are well maintained, in keeping a reasonable wine cellar, and in offering food that is mostly French. It's still possible to sit in this old-time East End boozer, drinking a good white burgundy and eating escargot.

Quite what earlier customers would have made of this is hard to know. Reggie and Ronnie Kray, who aspired to smart West End life, would surely have approved. They were born and raised in nearby Vallance Road and in 1967 bought the Carpenter's Arms for their mother Violet, who presided in the pub at weekends over a bevy of bejewelled, buxom, peroxide blondes of a certain age. The Carpenter's Arms was the convivial heart of the Kray family's 'manor', a gangster drinking paradise, its walls tricked-out with Regency-style wallpaper. The bar is said to be made out of a large piece of wood acquired by the twins from a local coffin-maker – presumably the intention was to remind drinkers of what could happen to them if they crossed the proprietors. Legend has it that the murder of Jack 'the Hat' McVitie, an East End hard man and crony of the Krays, was plotted over drinks in the Carpenter's Arms. A more certain gangland murder associated with the pub is that of local villain Ginger Marks, who was loitering between the pub and the nearby Repton Boys' Club eating chips, with a safe-breaker called Jimmy Evans, when the Krays' friend and sometime hitman Freddie Foreman drove by. This chance encounter was unfortunate. Foreman had a serious score to settle with the pair and it's not entirely clear but Evans escaped while Marks was never seen again. The police soon knew that someone had been shot, and even knew the victim had been shot in the stomach, because they found a morsel of chip embedded in a bullet hole in a wall near the Carpenter's Arms.[25]

If you turn north at the pub, you soon encounter the parish church of St Matthew Bethnal Green, completed 1746. This is a fine church, designed by George Dance the Elder (see p. 48) in the somewhat old-fashioned but economic manner of Sir Christopher Wren's brick and Portland stone churches. It is well worth exploration despite the fact that it was gutted during the Blitz. This means that when you enter nothing is quite what you expect. Instead of dark oak, columns and all-enveloping galleries, you find yourself in a light, open and airy 'Festival of Britain' 1950s fantasy, usually heavily scented with incense.

———◆•◆•◆———

In the very early twentieth century, Spitalfields would change beyond recognition. This shift was brought about, in large part, by the migration of Eastern European Jews. Their story is the one told by the streets on the last section of the walk.

In the years before they arrived, the streets around St Matthew's church were among the worst in Spitalfields. Made up largely of former weavers' houses, they had sunk into abject squalor by the time the campaigning Dr Hector Gavin visited while compiling evidence for his book *Sanitary Ramblings*, published 1848. Gavin wanted to make London a cleaner and healthier place, especially for its working people, and to do this he believed it necessary to collect evidence, street by street, to prove to the legislators at Whitehall just how lethally dirty the poorer parts of the city were. Cheshire Street – then known as Hare Street – formed one of his prime examples: Gavin recorded that it was 'abominably dirty and foul', with 'the back yards of the houses . . . in a most scandalous state'. He was particularly drawn to 'the backyard of no. 79' which was 'in a perfectly beastly state of filth; the privy is full and smells most offensively. There is a large cess-pool in it, one part of which is only partially covered with boarding; the night-soil was lately removed from it, but the stench arising from it is still very great.' He noted that in this especially foul and desperate habitation, 'a pig-stye has lately been removed . . . the wife of the present owner lately died of fever'; and 'none of the inhabitants are well', with 'three cases of fever and one death . . . clearly traceable to the abominable filthiness of this place.'[26] But in the late nineteenth century the arrival of the Jewish community meant, despite remaining materially poor, the area became incredibly rich in culture and memory. By the early years of the twentieth century Jewish people occupied about 80 per cent of the houses and tenements in the streets of south Spitalfields – particularly in and around Wentworth Street and in Whitechapel. But there were outposts of intense Jewish occupation to the east of Brick Lane, particularly in Fuller Street, north of Cheshire Street and near St Matthew's church. And in Booth's view, this growing community was more respectable than the existing English and Irish. At one stage on his walk with Duckworth, Booth gave it as his opinion that Jews tended to be honest and sober if poor, while the English and Irish poor of the area were often drunken, dishonest and dissolute. Their companion Sergeant French suggested that in one part of Spitalfields 'it was almost possible to tell where the Jews were by the houses which had unbroken windows.'

The lost life of Jewish east London can be recreated through the writings of the novelist and poet Emanuel Litvinoff, born in 1915 to Russian immigrants who had fled Tsarist persecution. He spent his early years in Fuller Street, which was present when I first got to know Spitalfields but which has now been obliterated. One can stand on its former route by taking the thin passage to the south-west of St Matthew's church. Now the site is covered by a sprawling and placeless housing estate that, in its suburban banality, attempts to give a sort of bland respectability to an area once notorious for its mean streets and poverty. But if Fuller Street had nothing else, it had soul and personality. It formed the centre of what Litvinoff called 'the ghetto of East London'.

'Life began,' writes Litvinoff, 'in bewilderment and terror at the age of three with my first coherent memory, that of moving to our two-roomed flat and tiny kitchen in Fuller Street Buildings, Bethnal Green . . . a tenement of sooty brick whose squalor in retrospect seems unbelievable', and which possessed 'an evil-smelling strangeness [that] permeated from rubbish bins and lavatories in the yard'. The family arrived with very little – 'our sewing machine and a cartload of second-hand furniture' – to be welcomed by the women of the tenement 'in a chatter of excited Yiddish'.[27] He eloquently describes the community he inhabited:

The tenement was a village in miniature . . . we sang the songs of the ghettos or folk-tunes of the old Russian Empire and ate the traditional dishes of the countryside . . . People spoke of Warsaw, Kishinev, Kiev, Kharkov, Odessa as if they were neighbouring suburbs. And the women kept the old folk ways alive; they shouted public gossip to one another over flapping laundry in the yard, screamed at unmanageable children, quarreled, wept, cursed and laughed with exuberant immodesty.[28]

The boundaries of the Fuller Street 'ghetto' were specific, its extent small, and leaving it brought risks. Running into Fuller Street was Bacon Street which, recalls Litvinoff, was 'squalid even by our standards' and a place 'until I was big and fairly robust I could only walk through . . . by making myself invisible, crediting the simple folk down there with a malicious brutality that could only be circumvented by magic.' This was another tribe, made up of poor English or Irish, 'whose wild children greeted us with the chant: "Abie, Abie my boy", and whose adults, when emerging drunk and violent from local corner pubs, would from time to time lurch into Fuller Street and scream "Christ-killers all of yer!" with a shrillness that pierced the dreams of sleeping children.'[29]

In one of his poems 'A Long Look Back', published in 1972 in his autobiographical *Journey Through a Small Planet*, Litvinoff reflected on his early life in Fuller Street, on its loss, and lamented that the old faces have all gone and that now there is 'only sometimes a ghost shuffling by, talking to the wind and lonely'.

The ghosts must be getting lonelier by the year. Litvinoff's community has gone, the houses have gone, and even Fuller Street – the heart of Litvinoff's ghetto – has been expunged with not a trace left behind. And the synagogue that stood on the north side of Cheshire Street, and that the young Litvinoff must have known well and whose galleried interior was, I remember, used in the 1970s to store mountains of old clothes, has also gone, with nothing to mark its memory. It is all most strange. With no one to mourn the passing it's as if this intense part of Spitalfields' history had never existed.

As you walk west through the bland suburban estate that occupies ground which once formed a significant part of Spitalfields' 'ghetto' – or

448 CRUICKSHANK'S LONDON

along the now almost equally bland Cheshire Street – reflect on what this part of Spitalfields has lost. You soon arrive back at Brick Lane, just 20 metres away from what are arguably the last surviving and visible relics of north Spitalfields' Jewish past. Almost side by side are two bakeries selling beigels. The most striking and characterful is Beigel Bake, at 159 Brick Lane, which is open twenty-four hours a day and sells beigels with attitude and at speed. Heaven help you if you are not quite sure what you want, or fail to have payment ready, when you find yourself at the head of the queue. It's a bit like being in New York, where everyone's a wise guy and the weak or witless go to the wall under a blast of quick-fire sardonic humour.

It's an apt place to end this walk and ponder the strange revolutions of Spitalfields' fortunes over the years, and to remember a runaway community that 140 years ago took root in these streets. This community survived and thrived but – as a living thing with a sense of tradition and continuity – has all but passed away. Only one working synagogue survives – way to the south in Sandys Row near Petticoat Lane – when once there was one or more in every major street. Now you have to come to this beigel shop to bring your memories to life and to remind yourself that there was, once, a living and breathing Jewish heartland in Spitalfields.

The junction of Bacon Street and Brick Lane, in the early 1970s and now. This is the same portion of the road as captured in the *Round London* photo on p. 420.

Oxford Street

Oxford Street is one of London's most extraordinary thoroughfares. Stretching 1.2 miles west from St Giles High Street to Tyburn (now Marble Arch), it has been an almost mythic threshold between London and the countryside to its north, and a highway of pleasure of sparkling lights and convivial taverns. But it's also been a most dark place and part of London's ancient highway of death. And as if emblematic of London's role as a place of stark contrasts, Oxford Street has been all these things simultaneously.

The street started life as a Roman road, and in the sixteenth, seventeenth and eighteenth centuries was named after the places to which it led – Tyburn, Uxbridge, Oxford. Until the late seventeenth century it was a country road, moving west from St Giles through fields. But around 1680 it began to be lined, in continuous manner, with buildings, largely as a result of the development of the estates to which it formed a border – starting with the development of Crown-owned land to form Soho Square in the 1670s, but later including the Cavendish Harley estate and Portman estate to the north, and the Grosvenor estate to the south. By 1746, according to John Rocque's London map, Oxford Street was surrounded with buildings on both sides as far west as what is now South Molton Street, just west of Bond Street. By the very early nineteenth century Thomas De Quincey, in his *Confessions of an English Opium-Eater*, was able to describe a vista along Oxford Street as offering nothing but the prospect of 'never-ending terraces'.

By De Quincey's time Oxford Street was already known as a place of entertainments – albeit entertainments of the most macabre kind. For until 1783 Oxford Street retained its ghastly role in the 3-mile ritual journey of condemned felons from Newgate Gaol on the edge of the City of London to execution at Tyburn. Here, in front of baying multitudes, the condemned were hanged from a triangular gallows erected at the informal crossroad where Oxford Street is joined from the north by the Edgware Road and from the south by Tyburn Lane – what is now Park Lane. By the early nineteenth century the entertainments had taken on a different form. When the newly created Regent Street, laid out after 1813 by John Nash for the Crown and constructed during the following decade, crossed Oxford Street, it heralded vast change. The updated function was marked by the creation of Oxford Circus that – like Regent Street to its south – became primarily a location for shops and was soon central to London's new pleasure ground, and a place of parade, convivial gathering and prostitution.

Oxford Street's role as a street of more licit entertainment reached a sudden and tremendous peak in 1772 with the opening on the Soho edge of the architecturally astonishing Pantheon. This briefly made Oxford Street London's entertainment centre. Designed by James Wyatt, the Pantheon incorporated a huge coffered dome – partly inspired by the AD second-century Pantheon in Rome but also by the AD sixth-century Hagia Sophia in Istanbul – and served as an assembly room and opera house. Initially it was popular and fashionable and after being destroyed by fire in 1792 was rebuilt in slightly reduced form. After numerous vicissitudes – including being a theatre, a shopping 'bazaar' and a wine warehouse – the Pantheon was demolished in 1937.

This long history as a place of great entertainment was the context in which Oxford Street took on its current function: as the most central of London's shopping streets. By 1890 the street contained, along its length, nineteen pubs and an almost continuous display of shops, of various sizes, manufactories and offices, housed in a dazzling array of architecture of different, dates, styles and sizes. And by 1910 something new had arrived, the US-style department store: places of monumental design and ambition, each offering its own inner world of delight housed within palatial buildings often of bafflingly rich and even fantastical design.

It is these early-twentieth-century stores that are the focus of our visit to Oxford Street. Our excursion culminates in the most famous and historically important of the department stores: Selfridges. On the way, though, there are other buildings to see. Between them, the four stores featured here reveal four distinctly different approaches to early-twentieth-century commercial architecture. Each has its own individual story to tell. But there are a few themes uniting them all: they aimed to add a touch of magic to shopping, to make it stylish, painless and enjoyable. They were designed as expansive, escapist and relaxed places, where not only all manner of goods were within easy reach but so too were a range of other services. And many stores decided the best way to achieve this

A masterpiece of muscular classical invention: the Mappin & Webb store of 1906–8.

combination of entertainment and opulence was with a grandiose look, with a nod towards the palatial.

Get the Tube to Oxford Circus – the Central Line station opened here in 1900 and the Bakerloo Line in 1906, both key dates in the creation of Oxford Street's shopping epicentre – and head east, to numbers 156–162. Here stands the former Mappin & Webb store, built from 1906–8 and designed by Belcher & Joass, who were leaders of their profession – promoters of the Edwardian neo-Baroque style and the designers in 1911 of Whiteleys in Bayswater that was, along with Harrods and Liberty's, a pioneer of the London department store. The building is one of the best in the street when it comes to muscular classical invention. This is a steel-frame structure so the external stonework – essentially non-loadbearing – can be minimal, windows large and the ground-floor stone Doric columns almost impossibly tall and slender. This is because not they, but the steel stanchions they conceal, are holding the building up. The steel-frame construction also allowed the interior to be light and open, with no internal walls necessary, and thus easy to adapt to suit changing fashions and functional requirements.

This is a most rewarding building to contemplate, with a rich array of inventive details, including the idiosyncratic Ionic capitals topping the columns on either side of the second-floor windows, which help support the high-level arcade. Note also the Michelangelo-inspired scroll pediments above the second-floor windows, the keystones branded with 'M&W' and the spindly bronze tripods – inspired by Grecian architecture and that perhaps once supported gas lamps – sitting on top of the main cornice.

The store's immediate neighbour, across narrow Winsley Street, at numbers 164–182, is presumably what Mappin & Webb felt it had to compete with. The monstrously large and architecturally ambitious Waring & Gillow began construction on this site in 1901. It raised the benchmark of palatial ambition for Oxford Street's stores and offers an insight into the staggering cultural and commercial aspirations of these early-twentieth-century retail entrepreneurs. It also reveals the depths of their pockets when it came to creating a store that proclaimed their intentions – one might say pretentions. Waring & Gillow were makers of high-quality furniture and ships' fittings, and clearly this was a company that thought image was everything. The emporium is a Baroque palazzo that could hold its own among the palazzi of Rome. It has often been said that its architecture is inspired by Christopher Wren's work at Hampton Court Palace, because its façades are made of red brick and Portland stone and because it has round windows like Wren's Fountain Court. But Waring & Gillow's store is more palatial than Hampton Court Palace, and far more Baroque. The architect was R. Frank Atkinson – who went on to collaborate in the design of Selfridges department store – in consultation with R. Norman Shaw.

The former Waring & Gillow store, more palatial than Hampton Court Palace.

The details are particularly good. In the centre, standing cherubs support the coat of arms of the City of London, presumably because the store is near the ancient Conduit Mead estate, from which water from the nearby Tyburn Brook was piped east to the City. Above the round windows are vigorously carved heads of river gods and varied goddesses. And on both corners of the building are stylised ships' prows, ornamented with cornucopia and the emblems of France and England, no doubt commemorating the firm's ship-fitting associations, its international trade and the money it was minting. Sadly, it did not last. Trade gradually tailed off and in 1980 Waring & Gillow merged with another furniture maker and gradually disappeared from the scene. Its former building now houses an array of familiar high-street chain shops and offices.

Around Oxford Circus itself, to the west, there is a great deal of twentieth-century commercial classicism on display. Nash's theatrical stucco-clad quadrant buildings have long been swept away. In their place are rather joyless and mechanical-looking essays, with giant Ionic columns. The curved portions of the buildings are hopelessly inadequate at creating a sense of enclosure, or even at making it obvious that this crossroads – where Regent Street crosses Oxford Street – is in fact a circus.

The quadrants that now stand here are the work of Sir Henry Tanner, and were built between 1913 and 1928. Instead, for more effective fare, head straight on to the west, towards the portion of Oxford Street that has long been the most commercially valuable – and consequently the most architecturally intriguing.

One of the best is at numbers 363–367, which is a most important early-modern building designed for His Master's Voice (HMV) record company in 1938 by Joseph Emberton. It was the first manifestation of modernism in the street. But it was hardly mainstream: Emberton was a somewhat idiosyncratic modernist with a strong, almost expressionistic, feel for form, texture and colour. The rather sombre façade is formed by bands of black glazed tiles, alternating with bands composed of opaque glass blocks in which are spaced simple, metal-made, casement windows. The glass-block bands glow at night when interior lights are turned on. But this seldom happens now because HMV, which dates from the 1890s, entered administration in 2018. At the time of writing its future, if it has one, remains unclear. So this seminal building, although not derelict, has been closed for a long time, with rough-sleepers now inhabiting the recessed entrance threshold with its perpetually locked street door.

And then, at last, we come to the monumental bulk of Selfridges (numbers 398–454). The design history of Selfridges is complex – partly because it was built in phases, and partly because its structure was pioneering for London and challenged building regulations and because the scale and scope of the enterprise was new. Consequently a considerable amount of brooding, consultation and experimentation was necessary – and it didn't help that the client's ideas kept changing. At one point there was to be a central tower on Oxford Street. Soon after 1906 Albert D. Millar, from the Chicago office of the renowned architect Daniel Burnham, was put in charge. The design of the elevation was then modified in 1907 by Francis S. Swales, a Canadian-born architect who had trained at the École des Beaux-Arts in Paris. After work got under way in 1908, the London-based architects Frank Atkinson and Thomas Tait were brought in because they had experience of building big, steel-frame buildings in the capital.

But all of that confusion ultimately paid off. With its giant Ionic columns marching along Oxford Street, this is history-based architecture on a massive scale. If Roman emperors had built department stores, there can be little doubt that this is how they would have done it. The emperor here was Gordon Selfridge, late of Illinois, who visited London in 1906 and spotted the business opportunity for a US-style department store – a little like Marshall Field's in Chicago, where he had worked and prospered for twenty-five years.

The building's historical allusions – visually spectacular as they may be – were only skin deep: construction materials and techniques were modern in the extreme. This was a fast-track steel-frame building process, with elements mass-produced and prefabricated off-site for speed, economy and precision and then delivered in correct sequence and colour-coded for quick and precise assemblage. This applied not just to the steelwork but also to the classically detailed stonework that, essentially, is mere cladding for the structural steel frame. Significantly, as with Mappin & Webb, this frame not only allowed fast, strong and essentially fireproof construction but also provided an open and highly adaptable interior.

A visit to the inside of Selfridges reveals a faithful commitment to the original Mr Selfridge's vision of shopping. He wanted the inside of the store to be light, airy, friendly and welcoming. Customers were encouraged to linger all day. Not only could they shop in comfort and in relaxed manner within the white-painted columned and open-plan interior, but they could promenade, take tea or luncheon, listen to music and even make travel arrangements or buy theatre tickets through agents based at the store.

The first phase opened for business in March 1909, and was a thundering success. Selfridge had adapted the US formula for London and got it right. He came up with many marketing ploys that were, for London at least, novel – including launching the idea of 'January sales' and the 'bargain basement' for less wealthy or more thrifty customers. The aim was simple: Selfridges was to have something for everyone. He also came up with the slogan – and Selfridge loved advertising slogans promoting his business – that 'the customer is always right'. And, most telling, in 1918 Selfridge published a book entitled *The Romance of Shopping*. He really believed that, if the setting was right, shopping could be a love affair. The story of Oxford Street over the next hundred years was to be the proof of that assertion.

WALK 12

Fleet Street to Trafalgar Square

London in the machine age

O n Fleet Street, a few hundred metres to the west of St Paul's Cathedral, stand two buildings. Each represents a very different approach to twentieth-century architecture.

First, on the south side of Fleet Street, is the former headquarters of the Reuters and Press Association news agency, numbered 85. Designed in 1935 by Sir Edwin Lutyens, and completed in 1938, the building is an example of its architect's inventive take on the classical conventions of architecture. But on this occasion, Lutyens has thrown in an ironic twist. For the Reuters building is imbued with a spirit of gentle mockery of classical principles. Take the main entrance. On each side of the door are downward-tapering slabs – but where these would traditionally have supported the head of a god or a satyr, they merely support very large stone balls. On either side of the podium that contains the door,

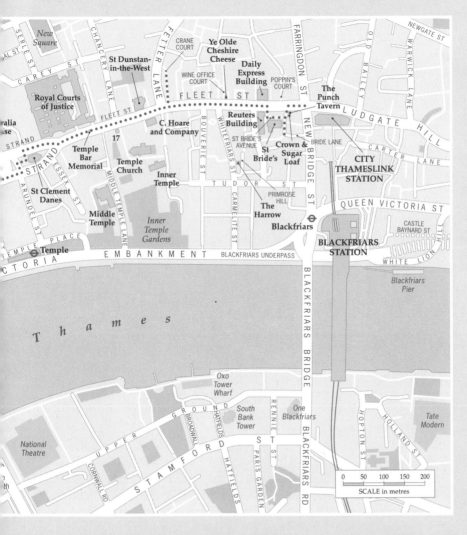

Edwin Lutyens' Reuters building, making a gentle mockery of classical architecture.

The spirit of a new age: Ellis and Clark's futuristic *Express* building.

meanwhile, there are two pilasters. But, again, nothing is quite as it seems: for, while the pilasters have moulded bases and capitals, the shafts get lost amidst the rustication – meaning that if you search for them you can see the pilasters, but blink and you miss them.

The overall feeling when contemplating the Reuters building is that Lutyens was feeling constrained by the classical language of architecture. He had worked with it, in earnest, for nearly forty years, and here seems to have been struggling to bring this familiar and well-explored language to life in an original manner. The problem could have been the context: just before he started work on this building Lutyens had completed one of his masterpieces, the Thiepval Memorial to the Missing of the Somme. This sensational and melancholic structure, with its almost abstract and sculptural presence, was perhaps Lutyens's last word on how to use and reinvent the classical language. The creative surge had perhaps exhausted him, and left him little more to say.

But maybe there's another reason for Lutyens's slightly manic flourishes in the Reuters building, and it stands on the opposite side of the road. For our second building is the black clear-glass and chrome-clad structure at 120 Fleet Street: the *Daily Express* building, constructed in 1931–2. Designed by the architects Ellis and Clark, it has more than a sense of the then-emerging art deco ornamental style – especially its lobby, designed by Robert Atkinson, which is one of the best art deco extravaganzas in Britain. However, in its pioneering reinforced-concrete frame structure, designed by engineer Sir Owen Williams, and its external sleekness, minimalism and absence of external history-based ornament, it is notably modernist – even futuristic. This was not exactly groundbreaking – this functionalist approach to design was already manifest in the early work of Continental architects like Walter Gropius. But, for a commercial building on a site in one of London's most historic streets, this design was quite something.

Perhaps, then, it was not only the Thiepval Arch that had exhausted Lutyens's creativity. He saw the *Express* building – sparkling, new and in its way revolutionary, as Lutyens had been in his youth – and realised it ushered in a new architectural order, but one which the aged Lutyens could not embrace. Lutyens would continue to defend classical architecture until his death in 1944. In January 1940 he used his post as president of the Royal Academy to organise the production of the Royal Academy plan for London, which presented 'ideal' possibilities for rebuilding and improving the capital when bomb damage was tackled after the war. Published in 1942, the plan is a bold and unfaltering defence of those artistic ideals by which Lutyens had lived for the previous forty years: the planning principles are Beaux-Arts, with lots of avenues, circuses, and vistas being created by the removal of inconvenient old buildings, with the new buildings proposed universally classical and rather grand.

In the years after Lutyens's death, the Royal Academy plan would appear the last gasp of his approach to urbanism. It would soon come to seem quaint and utterly irrelevant amidst the functionalist approach to planning that developed after the war – a world of sprawling Brutalist estates, ambitious motorway networks and archly modern public architecture. These two buildings on Fleet Street, then, represent architecture on the cusp of a revolution: the existing style taking its inspiration from the past, and the new one from the future.

This walk, which starts on Fleet Street and ends with Admiralty Arch just off Trafalgar Square, includes various responses to the great question of twentieth-century architecture: how best to respond to the unfettered capitalism, technological advancement and booming industry of Britain at the start of the twentieth century? Such considerations warranted

An idealised 'ring road through a suburban area', as depicted in the 1942 Royal Academy plan.

responses ranging from the sweeping Edwardian planning around Aldwych, to the art deco interiors of the Savoy Theatre, to the idiosyncratic modernism of Zimbabwe House.

But, of course, such modern buildings were not built in a vacuum: they were constructed at the heart of one of the most deeply historic sections of London. And so, throughout the walk, our modern buildings alternate with the more ancient structures that lie between them – the expansive late-eighteenth-century Somerset House, the twelfth-century Knights Templar church at Temple, the peculiar mid-nineteenth-century grandiosity of Trafalgar Square. The result is a walk in which ancient and futuristic architecture jostle for space, between them revealing much about the history of our capital in the twentieth century and beyond.

THE WALK

Our route begins a little to the west of St Paul's Cathedral, at the point where Ludgate Hill crosses Farringdon Street and becomes Fleet Street. You can reach it easily from City Thameslink station or Blackfriars tube. To my mind, though, the walk is best undertaken at the end of Walk 4, which finishes at St Paul's; between them, these routes reveal two very different sides to the capital.

The taverns and pubs start the moment you enter Fleet Street. Extraordinary for London now, there is a group of three, cheek by jowl, at the junction with Bride Lane. All, in their way, are good. The first you'll see is the Punch Tavern, housed in a late-nineteenth-century corner block and with a frontage on to Fleet Street. The tavern is entered through a deep porch lined with polychromatic glazed tiles and inside there is a long and utilitarian bar but also the remains of a good and once glittering – though now somewhat denuded – 1890s interior. This is clearly a hard-working pub and much lived in: as all these pubs were when journalists and print workers jostled for their drinks during Fleet Street's long reign as one of the world's great newspaper districts. The serious decline started in the early 1980s when one paper after another moved its journalists and printers to less valuable and more peripheral London sites, often in the former dockland north of the Thames.

The Punch is of ancient origin. It was originally called the Crown and Sugar Loaf but in the 1840s changed its name to honour, and attract business from, the popular *Punch* periodical that was located nearby. The ploy worked. Business boomed, and in 1894 the pub was rebuilt. Saville and Martin, veteran London pub designers, were the team called upon. In 1896 the tavern went a trifle upmarket and added a fine 'Luncheon Bar' along the Bride Lane frontage. This extension has now detached itself from its parent and is a separate drinking establishment – or at least appears to be different – which has called itself the Crown and Sugar Loaf. The interior has been handsomely repaired and restored in gin-palace style and so now rather eclipses the Punch. But, I suppose, the Punch possesses authenticity, and this an increasingly rare and precious commodity in London pub architecture.

Looming over the Crown and Sugar Loaf are the soaring stone walls of St Bride's church, perched high on its terrace or podium – a most unusual arrangement for a London church but here demanded by the dramatic fall in land from Fleet Street south and east to the Rivers Fleet and Thames. The north edge of the church's terrace is formed by a narrow paved passage, which creeps along in the shadow and is rather grandly named

St Bride's Avenue. On the corner of this avenue with St Bride's Lane is yet another pub, the Old Bell Tavern, which fronts on to the avenue, but also offers a face to Fleet Street. To judge by the avenue frontage, the building dates from the late seventeenth century. It was probably built just after the Great Fire when the church opposite was also under construction. The legend is that the tavern grew to fame and prosperity because it was much used by Wren's thirsty masons, bricklayers and carpenters. If true then the pub dates from the early 1670s.

Before leaving Bride's Lane, walk to its south end and turn the corner. In front of you there stands a most striking building: the St Bride Foundation Institute of 1893–4 by Robert C. Murray. It stands on a deeply historic portion of land between Fleet Street and the river. Immediately to the south was Bridewell Palace, built on the banks of the River Fleet, with gardens stretching down to the Thames. It was started in 1510 by Cardinal Wolsey, transferred to Henry VIII and, when complete in 1523, served as the king's principal home during the early years of his reign. His son, Edward VI, gave Bridewell to the City Corporation in 1553 as an orphanage and female house of correction. By 1556 it had become a more general prison and in the English-speaking world its name became generic for penal institutions. Tudor Bridewell was mostly destroyed in the Great Fire and rebuilt during the late 1660s as a pair of large courts framed by tall ranges of gaunt lodgings. The crowded and harsh regime of the prison, and the decay that gradually overtook its hard-used buildings, made Bridewell notorious and the epitome of brutal prison servitude. Typically Hogarth used it as the location for a scene in his *Harlot's Progress* series of 1731 (see p. 153), where Moll is shown dressed in finery but beating hemp while in the company of most alarming-looking people. Attempts were made to improve its buildings and give it a fairer face, but, as thinking changed about the nature of prisons and their design, the Bridewell proved beyond reform. It was closed in 1855 and demolished in 1863, apart from an entrance block of 1802 on New Bridge Street.

St Bride's church stands on the site of an ancient church destroyed in the Great Fire and its replacement building – on which work began in 1672 – is among Wren's earliest City churches. It was one of the finest examples of his basilica-style churches (see p. 158), with an interior well lit by large windows and with generous galleries so that the congregation could hear and see the preacher, but all was destroyed in the Second World War, leaving the church nothing but a gutted shell. Thankfully, the tower and spire at the west end survived: they are among Wren's most satisfying designs and particularly striking because he achieved a Gothic-style pointed spire in a most logical and charming classical manner, with four octagonal-plan arcades, of diminishing sizes, one upon the other, with the top one supporting an obelisk. There was one good thing that came of the wartime bombing: it resulted in the excavation of the crypt, and evidence was found of earlier churches and of a well, presumably St Bride's well, the source of water once thought sacred that gave its name to the area.

Our route is back along Fleet Street via the north–south arm of St Bride's Avenue. In front is a bland late-twentieth-century commercial building, but when I first got to know Fleet Street well in the late 1960s here was one of the alleys and small courts for which it was famed. These are memories of a medieval pattern of urban occupation – based on 'burgage plots' – when buildings tended to have narrow frontages to main

A selection of photos from Racquet Court, taken in the midst of its demolition in March 1972. The negatives have, for now, been lost, so this contact sheet is all that remains.

streets but long wings. They usually contained workshops or tenements accessed through alleys, which often led to courts around which more minor buildings were grouped. This particular alley led to the long and thin Racquet Court, at the far end of which, on the north-west corner, was a hidden delight – a five-window-wide and three-storey house of the late seventeenth century, an incredibly rare survival in the City due largely to nineteenth-century commercial rebuilding and wartime bombing.

One day, in March 1972, I popped into the court to see the house and discovered that all was chaos, a scene from hell with timbers, smashed bricks, scaffold poles and parts of buildings strewn all around. It could have been a bomb site but it was not. The demolition men were there, and my prized house was in the process of being wrecked. Its windows had been mutilated, its doorcase had been ripped off and its front door hung on its hinges. I was amazed, heartbroken. I had my camera and made my way into the house. At least I could document what survived to ensure that it was not entirely forgotten. Inside I saw good, early panelling, and the remains of a fine winding staircase with stout square newel posts. Most of the turned balusters had been removed, no doubt sold for a few pence each to some salvage contractor. Within weeks

not only had the house gone but so had Racquet Court, along with a group of late-seventeenth-century houses on Fleet Street, behind which the court shelter-ed, and the late-seventeenth-century and eighteenth-century buildings forming the west side of the adjoining Poppin's Court. All was obliterated for a bland commercial pile. Perhaps my sad photographs are the only memorial to this characterful and once-lively City enclave.

Immediately to the west of St Bride's Avenue, on the south side of Fleet Street, is the former headquarters of the Reuters and Press Association which we met in the introduction to this chapter. This, and the *Express* building opposite, set the tone for this portion of the street. Here we see how much of the ancient Fleet Street was remade in the twentieth century.

The *Telegraph* building's idiosyncratic combination of the futuristic and the classical.

A little to the west of the *Express* and north-west of the Reuters building is the former *Daily Telegraph* headquarters at 135–141 Fleet Street, built in 1928. These three corporate buildings reveal wonderfully the diversity of the London building world in the late 1920s and 1930s. Reuters is classical, the *Express* is futuristic modern and the *Telegraph* is somewhere between the two. Designed by Charles Ernest Elcock in consultation with Thomas T. Tait, it is, like Reuters, clad in Portland stone and speaks the classical language; but, like the *Express*, it possesses an art deco flourish and its classical details are idiosyncratic in the extreme.

Our next building represents a very different response to the aesthetic questions facing twentieth-century architects. Number 143–144 Fleet Street, Mary Queen of Scots House, stands on an amalgamation of two narrow sites – likely of ancient origin – and was built in 1905 to the designs of R. M. Roe for a Scottish insurance company. Roe adopted a most charming Perpendicular Gothic style with flat oriels and incorporating a bust of the unfortunate queen.

Such a melding of ancient fabric, historical forms and modern architecture is visible again and again on this portion of Fleet Street. To the west, at number 145, stands the Cheshire Cheese public house, which dates to just after the Great Fire – quite possibly to 1667 – and contains first-floor brickwork that looks to date from that period. The interior is very fine, particularly the small bar immediately to the south of the entrance vestibule off Wine Office Court. Here there is a massive chimney breast resting on bold and simple stone corbels, timber settles and a muted colour scheme of dark timber and oak-coloured plaster. Across the entrance corridor, which contains a good staircase that looks mid eighteenth century, is a dining room with something of the atmosphere of a Georgian chop house. Then, beside the Cheshire Cheese at number 147, is a very plain post-war building. Number 148, meanwhile, looks eighteenth century, though now stuccoed and much altered. To the south is Whitefriars Street, the eastern edge of the medieval Carmelite monastery that we encountered in Walk 2.

In Whitefriars Street is one of London's stranger pubs and, architecturally, one of my favourites. The Harrow, at number 22, has two faces – like Janus – and no rear. One face fronts on to Whitefriars Street and the other on to parallel Primrose Hill. The pub is evidently formed by a pair of two-window-wide early-eighteenth-century houses, now faced with stucco. When I first got to know the Harrow, in the early 1970s, it was a place of true duality. The bar off Whitefriars Street, with its lofty ceiling and open plan, was the public bar and the domain of compositors – jolly, packed and fairly raucous on certain evenings and at certain times, presumably after a paper had been passed for press. The bars off Primrose Hill offered a different world. With their lower ceilings and panelling, they were more intimate and inhabited by journalists and their 'sources'. These two different inner worlds were connected, by a flight of steps because of the different ground-floor levels, but customers rarely moved from one part of the pub to the other.

When Fleet Street was the heart of British journalism, these streets would have been awash with journalists and printers throughout the week. A relic of that time stands back on Fleet Street, opposite Crane Court. This is El Vino wine bar, once Fleet Street's smartest drinking establishment. It dates from the late 1870s and cultivated the atmosphere of a gentleman's club – I remember that even in the 1970s, women were not allowed to approach the bar and had to stay corralled in a rear room, and male customers had to wear a jacket and tie. It was a trifle intimidating, with an air of exclusiveness befitting its status as the favoured haunt of certain types of grand journalists and barristers from the nearby Temple.

Such relatively modern venues are juxtaposed with the older buildings all around. Make a point of penetrating Crane Court. It's no more than a narrow alley but at its far north end are two of the best late-seventeenth-century terrace houses to survive in the City. Numbers 5 and 6 were built in 1670 by the speculative building and property financier Nicholas Barbon. The façades of both houses were rebuilt in the late twentieth century (there was a very bad fire in number 5 in 1971) but interior details are good and both have splendid, ornamented first-floor plaster ceilings. If you can manage it, see the houses on a weekday evening at dusk when the offices they contain are in operation and the interiors are still illuminated. The lush and deeply moulded ornament of the ceilings – so rich and ambitious for such seemingly modest houses – is a wonder to behold.

———————————◆•◆•◆———————————

The next portion of the walk contains two great and deeply historic institutions, whose buildings were remade in relatively recent years. They reflect two different responses to the great architectural disputes of the nineteenth century. First, to the north-west of El Vino, stands the church of St Dunstan-in-the-West. The medieval church escaped the Great Fire – only just and because schoolboys summoned by the Dean of Westminster fought the flames most manfully; according to tradition, the fire was stopped three buildings to the east. The existing church is charmingly odd and picturesque. The medieval church – although a survivor – was evidently not highly regarded as a work of architecture. It was altered, classicised and eventually demolished in the late 1820s so this portion of Fleet Street could be widened. In 1831 work started on the new church that was completed within the year – something of a rush job.

Designed by John Shaw, the building is late Gothic in style. But this was a time before the Gothic Revival reached its earnest and archaeologically correct phase, and so Shaw adopted a rather inventive and personal approach. One of the more striking external details has little to do with Shaw and nothing to do with the Gothic Revival. The clock, set next to the tower and looking on to Fleet Street, was reused from the old church and dates from 1671. It shows Gog and Magog, the giants of the Book of Revelation that had become guardian figures of the City of

The stripped-back classicism of Jeffry Wyatville's headquarters for C. Hoare and Company.

London, who strike the clock's bells with their clubs to chime the hours and quarters. It was the first public clock in London to have a minute hand.

Our second nineteenth-century building, virtually opposite the church at 37 Fleet Street, is the bank building of C. Hoare and Company. The company was founded in 1672 by Charles Hoare and, despite ups and downs in the late nineteenth century, endures as an independent bank, still in the hands of the founding family, managing the assets of a limited number of high-net-worth individuals. In 1829 Hoare's rebuilt its Fleet Street headquarters and this is the building that survives – an early example of a purpose-designed banking house, so containing not just a banking hall and vaults but accommodation for the Hoare family, and living and working space for the 'gentlemen of the shop', as the staff were known.

The rebuilding was closely overseen by the family, who commissioned an architect named Charles Parker who had worked for Sir Jeffry Wyatville, one of the favoured architects of George IV. So committed were the family to decorum and 'quiet restraint' that poor Parker had his design pared down to bare essentials. The columns he proposed for the elevation were, for example, rejected because they 'might give too much magnificence to a House of Business'. This is odd since, at the time, even gimcrack houses being run up in London's streets were often dressed in columns and pilasters, so few would have been shocked to see their appearance on Hoare's in Fleet Street. Instead, Parker offered a design that looks neither institutional nor palatial but rather more like a private mansion. All conveys absolutely the right message for a bank: solid, authentic, and above all permanent.

———————◆•◆•◆———————

As we continue to the west, we begin to leave the territory of the journalists and enter that of the lawyers – a change reflected in the transformation of London's newspaper thoroughfare, Fleet Street, into the great legal quarter around the Strand. Number 17 Fleet Street offers the first hint of this transformation. One of the most remarkable terraced buildings in London, dating from 1610, it hosted a coffee house named Nando's from 1696, which was soon most popular with the legal profession. It might have replaced the Rainbow Coffee House that moved to 15 Fleet Street, which, founded in 1657, was one of the first coffee houses in London.

The ground floor of number 17 is occupied by a wide, stone-built arch, dated 1748 but featuring Jacobean details including banded rustication and blunt diamond motifs. The arch now frames one of the main and most picturesque entrances to the Temple, which stretches behind this portion of Fleet Street and down to the Embankment. The district is home to two of the four Inns of Court – the associations that one must join in order to be called to the bar.

The story of the Temple is vast and complex. In the mid twelfth century the land became a precinct of the Knights Templar, a military order founded in Jerusalem soon after it was seized from Muslims by Crusader forces in 1099. The main surviving physical memorial of the Templars' occupation of the site is the Temple Church, founded in 1180, consecrated in 1185 and named after the Temple Mount in Jerusalem, the location of Solomon's Temple and in the twelfth century the Templars' headquarters. The church is round in form, inspired by the Holy Sepulchre in Jerusalem and, more specifically, by the ninth-century Dome of the Rock. Built as a Muslim shrine, the Dome of the Rock's exquisite structure was used by the Templars as a church in the early twelfth century and became their signature building. The large chancel of the Temple Church was added in the early thirteenth century. This turned out to be something of a swansong, because the order was brutally suppressed in 1312, and the precinct was passed to the Knights Hospitaller, who let part to a college of lawyers. Be sure to see the Romanesque arched door at the church's west end. It's a wonderful thing. Parts are somewhat over-restored but much is well-weathered, almost crumbling, and rich with the authentic rust of antiquity. Hard to find these days, especially in central London. The door-surround is peopled with diminutive figures. Most are very decayed but some still recognisable. They appear to be Templars at prayer and chanting.

At the time of the Reformation, the Hospitallers lost the land. The lawyers were the winners. They simply expanded their occupation to form what are now Inner and Middle Temple. Much of the area was rebuilt in the late seventeenth century as lodgings and chambers – mostly for lawyers – which were organised around courts and gardens. The Temple was badly bombed during the war, including the church, but rebuilding was generally respectful and conservative so it remains a haven with a most historic feel in the bustle of the City.

Number 17 Fleet Street is not the only hint that we are entering a world of law. To the south stands a gate leading to Middle Temple Lane, and it is a most handsome affair indeed, designed in 1684 by the erudite and able lawyer and amateur architect Roger North. What North created is an inhabited Roman-style triumphal arch, which he evidently thought an appropriate way to mark the entry into London's ancient legal quarter. It is three windows wide with a large ground-floor arch for vehicles flanked by smaller pedestrian openings (as with antique triumphal arches). It really is a very pleasing essay, well designed and well built, that – by the flamboyant Baroque standards of the time – is admirably underplayed and sober. Then, a few paces beyond North's triumphal arch,

Fleet Street has transformed, with no very obvious sign, into the Strand – indicating that we have left the City of London. The only clue is a small Victorian monument in the middle of the road that marks the site of Temple Bar, which in the past was the symbolic entry into the City from the west (see pp. 166–7).

To the west is one of the great public buildings of late-Victorian London, the Royal Courts of Justice. This vast, seemingly rambling and discordant Gothic Revival complex is perhaps not everyone's cup of tea. At first glance it appears impossibly picturesque – a fairy-tale palace of towers, spires and conical-roofed bulging bays – which seems to have little to do with the dry and rational business of civil law. But on closer inspection it is evident that, behind this romantic Gothic mask, lurks a very well-organised and complex modern building in which different uses are integrated with great skill. The building has, of course, its public and its private parts. There are those sections used by advocates, by judges, by juries, by witnesses, by police, gaolers and by those on trial and those convicted. And then, most important, there are those portions used by the public. These are crucial because, by convention and tradition, the law of the land must not only be done but it must be seen to be done. The heart of the building – symbolically as well as functionally – is a huge medieval-style great hall, rich in Gothic detail, stone-vaulted and echoing in its lofty scale. This is the primary circulation space but also the initial introduct-ion to the building's aims and aspirations. New technology here was an issue, especially when it came to lighting, heating and ventilation. All these needed to be accommodated within – indeed be made subservient to – the medieval-style forms and ornament. The architect was George Edmund Street, who won the commission in 1867 through competit-ion, but with construction not starting until 1873 and completion not until 1882.

To the south-west of the Royal Courts is St Clement Danes church – rebuilt by Christopher Wren from 1682, on the site of an ancient church. St Clements now sits on an island site. It was not designed to do so: when the church was designed in the early 1680s this was the south-east corner of the Clare Market area, a place of courts and alleys and sixteenth- and

The rambling Royal Courts of Justice rising from behind 17 Fleet Street.

seventeenth-century timber-framed and plaster-fronted buildings that stood just outside the City and had survived the Great Fire.

St Clements is, architecturally, an odd church – certainly now, but also when the existing building was completed. There seems to have been a church on this site since the ninth century, probably associated with a sacred well that stood immediately to the west. By the time of the Great Fire the site was occupied by a fourteenth-century church and although it survived, many, apparently, were sorry that it did. It was evidently in a bad way structurally – some major repairs had been undertaken in the early seventeenth century and the tottering tower rebuilt in the late 1660s – and it no doubt did not measure up to the artistic aspirations or liturgical requirements of its post-fire parishioners. So in 1681 the old church was demolished and the architect of the moment, Wren, was commissioned to design a new one.

The flourish-free St Clement Danes, designed on the cheap by Christopher Wren.

The problem, it seems, was money. The fire-ravaged City churches were rebuilt using funds raised from a tax on coal imported into London. St Clement Danes was outside the City, was not damaged in the Great Fire and in the early 1680s – with many City churches under way – competition for tax money was immense. So it seems Wren and his clients chose to prioritise the way in which limited cash would be used. The existing tower, little more than a decade old, was retained but re-clad in Portland stone (its fancy spire was added in 1719 to the designs of James Gibbs) and the broad intention seems to have been to create a decent but modest exterior. There are no architectural flourishes – no large pediments, porticoes or colonnades – and significant display would have been possible since the church was essentially free-standing even though its site was somewhat constricted. The west entrance is almost domestic, and even cherubs on the external nave walls were used most economically.

But the inside is a different story – or at least it was. The church was terribly badly bomb-damaged in 1941, indeed reduced to no more than a blackened shell. Fortunately, repair and restoration when they were undertaken after 1958 were better than many post-war London church rebuildings. The plan, ceilings and even the joinery were recreated in admirably authentic and craftsman-like manner so it is now possible to discern Wren's original intentions. What seems clear is that the available funds were used primarily on the interior. It is of basilica form and its nave is particularly pretty, with generous plaster swags, abundant palm leaves and wide-winged cherubs evoking associations with biblical descriptions of the Holy of Holies in Solomon's Temple (see p. 81). This is a strangely appropriate association because the church is indeed now the Holy of Holies of the RAF, having been reconstructed as something of a museum and shrine to the service with squadron badges providing the dominant theme for the nave floor. It's a powerful interior, solemn not triumphant – as befits a church – and much to do with the pity of war. It greatly helps that the oak joinery has been darkened with all else painted off-white and key details picked out in gold. The overall impression is effective, simple yet rich.

———————◆◆◆———————

As we continue west, we encounter a spectacular example of ambitious Edwardian planning that was meant to give this part of London the feel of Haussmann's Paris. In 1898 the planners of the newly founded London County Council – the first city-wide local authority for the capital with a huge array of responsibilities – produced a radical scheme. They took the view that the surviving picturesque ancient buildings and courts around Clare Market were in fact no more than decaying hovels, standing in the way of the city's urban improvement and commercial progress.

With a pitiless lack of sentiment, it was resolved that virtually all existing buildings and complex urban grain was to be swept away and, in the manner of French Beaux-Arts planning, replaced by a broad boulevard running north-west from a massive crescent. The buildings to line these new thoroughfares were to be large, stone-faced and classical in design, although not in any sense rigidly uniform. The intention was that they would house places of resort: hotels and theatres, offices of prestigious companies, professions and government buildings. It was a most ambitious undertaking for London's new arm of local government because the objective was to give the city a major new cultural and commercial quarter, ornamented by a smattering of large and ornate High Commissions that gave all an imperial glitter. The boulevard was completed in 1905, and duly named Kingsway after being opened by Edward VII. The crescent named Aldwych, partly in memory of one of the thoroughfares it obliterated, Wych Street, was completed a few years later.

Aldwych soon became the preferred location for the quarter's most ambitious new buildings – including the High Commissions of India and Australia, the Gaiety Theatre and the smart US-style Waldorf Hotel. The architecture has a hint about it of late-nineteenth-century New York, expressed most forcefully by the tall, classical building in the centre of the north side of Aldwych. It closes the south-east vista down Kingsway with, in Roman manner, a huge and handsome recess that embraces a pair of tall piers supporting an entablature and large-scale sculpted figures. This is Bush House, built between 1925 (when this central block was completed) and 1935. The client was Irving T. Bush, a US entrepreneur and real estate investor, working with New York-based architect Harvey Wiley Corbett. It is, in essence, a skyscraper stunted to a mere six storeys because of London's tough building regulations – you can imagine it as the podium of a 1920s New York high-rise with the upper works oddly omitted. This makes sense, considering the designer: Corbett had started his career working for Cass Gilbert – the architect of the 241-metre-tall Woolworth Building completed in New York in 1913 – and in 1918 had finished the 132-metre-high Bush Tower, also in New York and also for Irving T. Bush.

But the first Aldwych building you will see when you leave St Clement Danes is the Australian High Commission: Australia House. It's a very

Edwardian London meets Haussmann's Paris: Australia House, the eastern portion of Aldwych.

poised classical building, rather marvellous and erudite in its way, but that most people today simply see through. It occupies the entire east end of the quadrant forming the Aldwych crescent and so is a rather odd shape – flat-fronted to the south where it faces the Strand, convex where it faces into Aldwych and with a blunt corner where it faces the church. The design strategy followed by its architect, Alexander Marshall Mackenzie, was straightforward: a two-storey high order of Doric columns placed on a two-storey podium, and supporting a stupendous entablature, which in turn supports further storeys. The details are bold, and tending to the Baroque – such as the large and luscious scroll keystones in the podium arcade – and all is faced in stone. This not only gives the building gravitas and an appearance of endurance, but was also an opportunity for a tasteful nationalistic flourish intended to give the design – undeniably international in its style – a distinctly Australian flavour. Various stones and timbers were imported from Australia to make the exterior a geological homage to the homeland. The podium, for example, is faced with volcanic Australian trachyte, from which the Portland stone columns rise.

Set above the main entablature is a quadriga – a chariot drawn by four horses – showing the sun god Phoebus 'driving the horses of the sea'. It is the work of Bertram Mackennal and was put in place in 1923. And on each side of a tall, central door are two sculptural groups, one depicting *The Awakening Australia* and the other *Prosperity in Australia*, both by Harold Parker. They are fair work artistically but now painfully dated in their sentiments – suggesting, of course, that Australia did not exist or thrive until Europeans arrived and seized the land from the indigenous peoples.

Despite its monumentality, the building is strangely underwhelming. I suppose it's made mute by the familiarity of it all. By the time Australia House was opened in 1918, the classical wave of which it was part had finally started to ebb, leaving this building – in which novelty and inspired invention are conspicuously absent – high and dry. Of course, it's precisely these ingredients that Lutyens sought to instil in his even later, idiosyncratic classical confections like the Reuters office.

We now have the opportunity to compare the somewhat pompous and arid early-twentieth-century classical architecture of the Aldwych with significant offerings from the eighteenth century. The difference is obvious, for the structures that dominate the next portion of our route – St Mary-le-Strand and Somerset House – are two of the most noble, notable and fascinating classical buildings in London.

Also stranded on a traffic island, St Mary-le-Strand is one of the most architecturally curious London churches, though it is often overlooked. It was designed in 1713 by James Gibbs as one of the 'Fifty New Churches', planned for areas that were either expanding or which included large populations of Dissenters or Nonconformists (see p. 111). The goal was to make manifest the power of the state through the presence of Anglican churches. But St Mary-le-Strand is an odd example of this rather nationalistic and political religious architecture. It was the first of the 'Fifty' churches to get under way, in February 1714 (excluding the 1711 rebuilding of the medieval St Alfege – see pp. 111–5). And Gibbs – the architect of this patriotic Church of England project – was in fact Scottish and a Roman Catholic.

Both of these were soon to be problematic. When Anne died in 1714 without heirs and the Protestant German George I came to the throne, with much Whig backing, there was significant opposition from

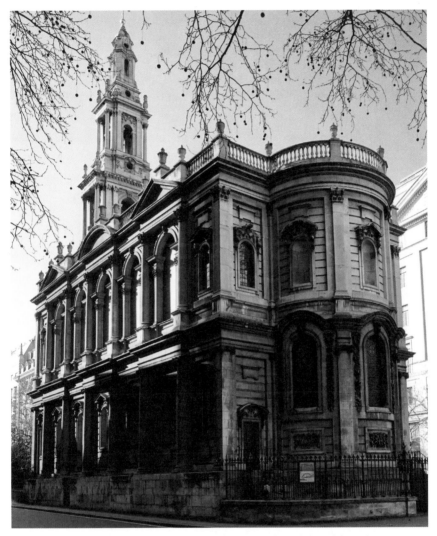

Counter-Reformation Rome comes to London: St Mary-le-Strand viewed from the east.

supporters of the ousted Stuart dynasty. Most of these supporters were Roman Catholic, Tories and Scottish, some of whom were involved in an armed uprising that erupted in Scotland in 1715 in favour of the claim of the Stuart pretender, 'James III', to the throne. Given these events, it is easy to understand why Gibbs's life as an official architect working for the Protestant Hanoverian regime became difficult in the extreme.

But at the time the plans for 'Fifty' churches got under way, all was well. Gibbs's credentials were impeccable because he was one of the very few classical architects working in early-eighteenth-century Britain who had actually travelled and trained in Italy. This direct connection to the then fountainhead of late-Renaissance design is clear in an even cursory contemplation of St Mary. It possesses a delicacy in its ornamental detail that is very different to the massive, and sculptural, contemporary churches designed for the 'Fifty New Churches' commission by Nicholas Hawksmoor (see pp. 44–6 and 111–15). Essentially St Mary's is similar in architectural feel to the exquisite seventeenth-century Counter-Reformation churches you can find down side streets in Rome. And this would have been far more the case if St Mary's had been built as designed. Gibbs did not want a dominant tower and spire, which were generally avoided by architects working in Rome, and were a non-classical Gothic feature imposed by Anglican liturgy. Instead he proposed a free-standing west column supporting a statue of Queen Anne. This, he argued, would give the church presence and, of course, an antique Roman pedigree.

Unfortunately in August 1714 the queen died before the column could be built. This proved an insuperable problem. Since the column was topped by a statue of Anne, it clearly celebrated her. But she was a Stuart and the new Hanoverian regime felt uncomfortable with this. So Gibbs was forced to lose his Roman-style column and was obliged to compensate for its loss by giving his church a conventional west tower and spire. This he did, but he never quite recovered because his perfectly balanced jewel-like design with a square-plan interior – already under way –- had to be altered in a somewhat ad hoc manner to incorporate a tower.

Despite these setbacks, Gibbs's church remains a wonderful thing and most peculiar in its use of the Roman Catholic vocabulary of church design to realise a Protestant temple. Of course Wren played the same game, but his modifications and simplifications of Italian ecclesiastical architecture were significant as he made the language of Catholic Baroque applicable to Protestant England. Gibbs, on the other hand, really did not dilute; he simply borrowed and adapted in inspired manner. The side exterior elevations – facing north and south – are particularly fascinating. After experimenting with a Roman temple-like design – with a nave flanked on all four sides with columns – Gibbs decided that the church should have two tiers of columns, like St Paul's, probably having concluded that the

The south elevation of St Mary-le-Strand, featuring James Gibbs's two-tier pilasters and large windows.

site was too constrained and intimate for the application of a full-height giant order.

As a result, St Mary's includes two tiers of engaged columns on each side elevation, set one above the other and separated by a full entablature. The upper tiers are each dominated by five large windows, set within a leaping arcade, with centre and end windows capped with large pediments. These large windows allow light to flood into the church, and especially across the nave vault. All appears to have inspired by the works of Michelangelo that Gibbs would have seen in Italy and by the mid-seventeenth-century Roman churches of Pietro da Cortona. For example, the semicircular west portico on St Mary was no doubt inspired by the portico on Cortona's Santa Maria della Pace in Rome, as indeed were the transept porticoes at Wren's St Paul's Cathedral.

The interior of the church is stunning. It consists of just a nave – no aisles and so no colonnades and no galleries. It is the only one of the 'Fifty' churches to be organised in this simple manner. But nothing else about the interior is simple. The side walls are two-tier compositions like the exterior, with paired pilasters, similar to those framing the first-floor exterior windows, placed one upon the other and divided by an entablature. The east end, with a curved niche containing the chancel, echoes the curve of the portico. Even better is the vaulted ceiling. With its dazzling display of ornate plasterwork – painted white with details picked out in gold leaf – it possesses a touch of Imperial Rome.

The church received a rough ride in the years immediately after its completion in 1724. Taste had moved from the inventive and ornamental Baroque to the simpler, more austere Palladian, whose champions thought architects like Hawksmoor licentious, wilful or ignorant (see p. 212). Gibbs, because of his potentially Catholic and Jacobite sympathies, was viewed as positively dangerous. James Ralph, a Palladian pundit, in his *Critical Review of the Public Buildings . . . in London and Westminster* of 1734 damned Gibbs and St Mary-le-Strand as an example of the fact 'that 'tis not expence and decoration that are alone productive of harmony and taste'. He observed spitefully that 'this church will always please the *ignorant,* for the very same reason that it is sure to displease the *judge.*'[1]

But Gibbs had far greater enemies than pundits such as Ralph. In January 1716 he was dismissed as a surveyor to the 'Fifty New Churches' commission, which by now was in the hands of the Hanoverian Whigs, deeply suspicious of Roman Catholics and Scots. In his letter to the commission after his dismissal, in which he successfully argued that he should be left in control of the construction of St Mary's, he revealed his hope that the completed church would 'gain me a reputation to recommend me to other business'.[2] In this his hopes were not dashed. In 1722 he was commissioned to rebuild St Martin-in-the-Fields, at the west end of the Strand. After completion in 1726, and after being promoted in numerous splendid plates by Gibbs in his *Book of Architecture,* St Martin-in-the-Fields became the most influential church design in the English-speaking world, spawning imitations and copies not only in England, Scotland and Ireland but also in the English colonies in America and eventually in India, the Caribbean and South Africa.

Almost opposite St Mary's, to the south, is Somerset House. This is one of the most architecturally important eighteenth-century buildings in Britain. It is a deeply sophisticated design with exquisite details – evidently the work of a master of the classical language – and wonderfully wrought and faced with beautifully worked Portland stone. It looks an urban palace fit for any prince but what is perhaps the most extraordinary thing about this exemplary building is that it was created not as a palace or even as palatial terrace houses but to accommodate a conglomerate of humdrum government tax offices, the Admiralty's navy office and – more suitably – the galleries and teaching rooms of the newly founded Royal Academy. The existing building takes the form of a huge court, with ranges running parallel and behind the court's east and west sides.

Design started in 1775 under the control of Sir William Chambers, who we met on Walk 5 and at Kew Gardens (see p. 216). Chambers wanted nothing to do with transient fashions, playful frippery or theatrical display with ornament run up in plaster or stucco. His passion was for the solid and time-proven gravity of ancient Rome, when architects were masters of enduring construction and when even ornament could, although sometimes exotic, possess a sense of serious purpose. Chambers favoured learning, dignity and solidity above all – and these virtues are present in abundance at Somerset House. It is, perhaps, more a petrified lecture than a building, and is certainly capable of teaching the observant student a lesson in admirable classical composition and construction. The downside is that you can sense that this is exactly what Chambers set out to do. There is not much lightness of touch about Somerset House, and of course little obvious wit. If you are in a slightly unreceptive or rebellious mood it can seem to possess a somewhat didactic character, with all apparently calculated to impress you with the genius of the architect. The north range was completed in 1780, the south range in 1786 and the east and west ranges by 1788.

The challenge of designing Somerset House was to play appropriate tribute to its long and chequered history. Before the palatial Chambers design was built, a real aristocratic and royal palace occupied the site. In 1539 Edward Seymour obtained a grant of Thames-side land from his brother-in-law Henry VIII. The Strand riverfront was a place of great prestige in Tudor and also in Stuart London. It stood between the City of London – the centre of merchant enterprise, money and ancient virtue – and the City of Westminster – the centre of political and royal power and the domain of the aristocracy. The Strand was a key part of the highway – generally followed on this walk – linking the two, and so became the preferred location for the homes or power-bases of men wanting a foot in both cities.

In 1547 Seymour was made Lord Protector to his nephew, the nine-year-old Edward VI, and promptly used his new power to declare himself the Duke of Somerset. The following year he cleared away the old monastic buildings on his Thames-side site and started the construction of a palatial Somerset Place, suited to his role as regent of England. But this great work was never to be completed as planned. In 1552 Somerset was toppled from power by scheming fellow members of the council advising the young king, found guilty of 'felony' – a vague political crime which is essentially the consequence of failing to triumph over those who would oppose you. For this failure Somerset was executed on Tower Green. Somerset Place, unfinished, was confiscated by the Crown and used briefly to house, in secure manner, Princess Elizabeth, Edward's half-sister and future queen.

When James I came to the throne in 1603, Somerset Place became the London home of his wife, Anne of Denmark, the key proponent of Palladianism in early-sixteenth-century court architecture – as we saw at the Queen's House in Greenwich (see pp. 93–4). Her architect of choice

The east range of Somerset House evokes the feel of a palatial terrace of houses.

was, of course, Inigo Jones, who from 1609 until the queen's death in 1619 worked for her on additions to Somerset Place – now Denmark House – and continued to work there in the early 1620s after it passed into the possession of Anne's son, Charles I, who gave it to his Queen Henrietta Maria. During this period Jones designed a pavilion on the Strand frontage of Denmark House – by this time rather bafflingly known as Somerset House – that, when complete, became one of the seminal buildings in British architecture, imitated time and again during the following 200 years – a design with a simplicity and majestic rationality that rapidly gave it the status of a masterpiece of British classical composition.

But this status did not guarantee the pavilion's future. Somerset House, with its tangle of buildings, was put up for sale during the Civil War but, with no buyer, was used by Parliament as a military headquarters after most of its contents had been sold off. After the Restoration of 1660, Henrietta Maria briefly returned to Somerset House but soon left for France. Following a period in the 1680s and 90s when it was occupied by Catherine of Braganza, the widow of Charles II, the palace entered a

long period of slow decline. Finally, in 1775, the Crown took the decision to clear the site for the construction of a palace for government and navy offices and learned institutions. And so Jones's seminal buildings, long-celebrated monuments of British architectural culture, were destroyed. An indication of the trauma of the moment is revealed by Chambers's design for the range built on the site of Jones's lost masterpiece. It is, in essence, a reverential copy of Jones's pavilion, updated in its classical details to reflect the prevailing and somewhat exquisite architectural taste

Canaletto's 1748 painting *London from the River Thames* captures the vista from Somerset House.

of the 1780s. When you walk from the Strand into Somerset House – through the arches of the vaulted entrance loggia – you are passing through an evocation of Jones's pavilion.

As you walk beneath the vault and between the short colonnade, observe the fine classical details, combined with Chambers's determination to express structure and even materials. This was rather a modern idea in the 1780s, when so often materials and structure were concealed. But Chambers loved structure and made a virtue of contrasting the delicate nature of the plasterwork within the vault with the more robust nature of the Portland stone around it. If you go inside to see the stone staircases – particularly that to the west which served the Royal Academy's upper-level gallery – you will see how they fly through the air with great elegance.

The central court is a magnificent affair, its ranges embellished with centrally placed screens of columns set above pedimented doors, and

with additional ornamented doors to each side. This makes the elevations look rather like palatial terraces of individual houses and is a reminder that the office block as a building type was still novel in 1780s London and struggling to find its own architectural expression.

There are many details to observe and enjoy. First, as you walk into the square, peer down into the generous light well topped by a sculpture of George III. The well, with its bold brick arches, possesses the functional grandeur of heroic Roman-engineered construction – as was very much Chambers's intention. There is an elaborate sub-structure below the court because the site, which slopes from the Strand towards the Thames, was excavated, raised and levelled during Chambers's rebuilding. There are numerous nautical motifs – as you might expect – such as mermen embracing a classical urn.

Next, advance across the square to the south range, the inside of which is mostly open to the public. A corridor runs parallel to the façade and at this corridor's west end is one of the ornamental and engineering wonders of eighteenth-century London. The Navy Staircase, once serving the offices of the Navy Board, is an astonishing feat. In the leap of vast arches, and with impossibly slender and curvaceous stone-wrought flights of steps, it reaches six levels, from the basement to the very top of the building. Completed by 1789, it is sculpture as much as architecture, presenting the observer with splendid positions from which to view and enjoy different prospects of its incredibly pleasing and open geometric form.

Finally, walk out on to the south terrace with its spectacular views across the Thames. It was from here, from the court of old Somerset House, that in 1748 Canaletto looked east to paint the City. From this perspective, with the domed St Paul's in the background rising above the broad river, London looked most like Venice, with its domed Santa Maria della Salute set beside the Grand Canal. When you stand on the centre of this terrace you are standing over the wide-arched water gate to Somerset House. It's a reminder that until the Embankment was constructed here in the 1860s (see pp. 335–9), at high tide Somerset House would have risen directly from the water like a Venetian palace.

—————————◆•◉•◆—————————

We now enter a portion of London whose recent history has been defined by the Victoria Embankment. This was a feat of engineering that was, in its way, heroic. But it also fundamentally altered how central London worked. On this portion of the Strand it precipitated the rise of new commercial buildings – hotels, theatres, shops – whose owners were keen to make use of this modern, glamorous and spacious new part of the city.

Walk to the west of the Somerset House terrace, and join the approach road to Waterloo Bridge. The great bridge designed in 1809 by John Rennie – generally regarded as one of London's most beautiful – was opened in 1817 but demolished just as the Second World War started. So the existing bridge, designed in grimly utilitarian manner by Giles Gilbert Scott and built from 1942, arose as V1s and V2s crashed into London. It opened in 1945. But if you want to see evocative fragments of Rennie's glorious bridge – which had piers dressed with pairs of huge, stone-built Grecian Doric columns – go via the nearby staircase to the Embankment below. Here, underneath the north end of the existing bridge, you will see huge stone drums of Egyptian scale and solemn grandeur that, when high-tide water laps at their bases, appear emblematic of elemental architecture emerging from the deep. These are the sad and solitary remains of Rennie's Grecian columns.

Cross under the bridge and turn to the north, up Savoy Street. Here, secreted among bulky late-nineteenth and twentieth-century structures, is a most unlikely survival – the Queen's Chapel of the Savoy. It dates from 1490–1512, and stands on the site of an earlier chapel that was part of the Savoy Palace, occupied by William of Gaunt and sacked during the Peasants' Revolt of 1381. The palace took its name from Peter of Savoy who was granted the land in 1245 by Henry III. Savoy was his queen's uncle. When the chapel was started the Savoy was Crown property so the patron for the chapel was Henry VII, who granted a charter for the adaptation and enlargement of the buildings on the site to form a 'hospital' for the poor and the destitute. By the late seventeenth century the chapel was used by French Calvinist refugees – Huguenots – fleeing persecution by Roman Catholic authorities (see p. 131). One consequence was that many Huguenots settled in south Soho, which was being developed from the 1680s as a new district of London. The chapel is still royal, or rather a 'Royal Peculiar', which means it is not under the jurisdiction of a bishop, but under that of the reigning monarch. It is simple inside – it suffered a grievous fire in 1864 – but with a large and splendid traceried east window. It's open to the public each Sunday for a traditional Anglican service, using the seventeenth-century Book of Common Prayer and the King James Bible.

Today, of course, the name Savoy has more secular connotations. For to the west of Savoy Street, set back south of the Strand, is the Savoy Hotel. Although more of social than architectural interest, its physical presence is tremendous. Standing like a brooding and overweight Parisian mansion, in what feels like its own forecourt, it possesses a somewhat exclusive atmosphere. The hotel and the adjoining Savoy Theatre – both built on land that had once been part of the Savoy Hospital – were the creation of the highly successful impresario Richard D'Oyly Carte. First came the theatre, which opened in 1881 to the design of C. J. Phipps. Now famed for its early association with Gilbert and Sullivan and their sensationally popular operettas, the theatre's brick and stone exterior was largely refaced in 1903 to match the hotel, and its interior was remodelled in 1929 in art deco manner (and faithfully restored after a fire in 1990). Happily the Savoy remains one of London's most popular live theatres.

But for most of its history it has been overshadowed by the enormous hotel next door, constructed in 1889. When it opened, the hotel was cutting edge. D'Oyly Carte had seen leading hotels in the United States, and knew the comfort and conveniences that the richest North American visitors expected – and he aimed to please. So this hotel had all the latest comforts, including many efficient lifts, and was the first in Britain to be fully lit by electric light and to have en-suite bathrooms, with copious amounts of hot water, linked to most of its bedrooms. But within months this leviathan was losing money and in trouble. Food and service were from the start seen as most important, and in an attempt to turn things around César Ritz – who had hotels on the Continent and who went on to start the eponymous London hotel – was appointed manager. He

The Savoy Hotel in 1930.

recruited chefs and staff from the best hotels in Paris and, at first, it seemed that initial teething problems had been solved. But the hotel's fortunes dipped again in the late 1890s. Ritz and his team were dismissed, D'Oyly Carte died in 1901 and the future seemed bleak. However, the Savoy endured, and its reputation grew to make it one of the best-known and most glamorous hotels in Britain. The D'Oyly Carte family's connection did not end until 1985.

The architect for the hotel and for the 1903 refronting of the theatre was Thomas Edward Collcutt. The shared aesthetic reflected their shared management: in the early years, the heady profits from the Gilbert and Sullivan productions, notably *The Mikado*, went a long way to financing the hotel. Collcutt's style was inspired by the French Beaux-Arts – most fashionable at the start of the century, as we've seen with Aldwych. Here, too, we can see some distinct New York accents. Construction was contemporary – steel-frame and as fireproof as possible with the hotel rising high – and all clad with classical detailed rendered, US style, in fire-resistant terracotta. The hope (forlorn, as it happened) was that the façades would be self-washing in the rain.

Little survives inside from the hotel's early days – like all such concerns it has been remodelled extensively from time to time. But the famed Savoy Grill continues to thrive, as does the American Bar, made-over several times yet still a decent place for a gin Martini, if you're in the mood. And if you want to experience the Edwardian Savoy, but in less formal manner, the Coal Hole public house is at hand. This is in a block of buildings immediately west of Savoy Court, on the corner of the Strand with Carting Lane, which was also designed in 1903 by Collcutt, and which retains a splendid, largely authentic interior, a strange mix of Arts and Crafts and 'Olde' England whimsy with Edwardian classicism.

———•◦◆◦•———

Behind the frontages of the Strand – now mostly made up of nineteenth- and twentieth-century building – more ancient structures survive. For example, cross the Strand and head north into Southampton Street, laid out in 1706–10, to see a remarkable survival. Numbers 26 and 27 – a fine and disparate pair of houses – were built between 1706 and 1707 and are exceedingly rare early survivals that give a good idea of the look of the domestic architecture in the main streets of London after the Great Fire. Number 27 is particularly good, with corner quoins in the form of rusticated brick-wrought pilasters, and with keystones to the windows. In 1749 David Garrick, the actor, moved into number 27.

Southampton Street runs through the site of Bedford House, the Strand palace of the Russell family that in 1550 had been granted this former monastic land by Edward VI, when John Russell was made the Earl of Bedford. The Southampton connection came in 1669 when the son of the then earl married the daughter of the 4th Earl of Southampton. The estates of these now-united families covered not just Covent Garden but also most of the Bloomsbury area of Holborn, which subsequently became known also as the Bedford estate – an estate that we have already met many times in this book. In the late seventeenth century, as the Covent Garden area became ever more densely occupied and Bedford House encroached upon by new buildings, the family moved to its house in Bloomsbury. The Russells' old Strand mansion was demolished soon after 1700.

But before this family migration took place the Earl of Bedford had made a decision that was to have a profound and influential effect on

British architecture and planning. To the north of his garden wall was open ground and in the late 1620s the earl evidently contemplated this land with a greedy eye. He owned it but could not simply just build upon it. There were certain prohibitions against the building of new houses in London, for fear of drawing country people away from gainful rural employment into the capital where they would probably fall into poverty, become a charge under the poor laws and might even foment riot and rebellion.

However, the earl seems to have had a most workable plan: to pay the king a 'fine' to secure royal approval, and to use the architect favoured by the king's father and mother and currently favoured by his wife. So, in about 1630, Inigo Jones, working down the road at Somerset House, was presumably summoned by the earl to Bedford House and commissioned to produce a design for building to the north of its garden wall.

But this was not to be any ordinary design. It was to be visionary. Jones was the master-planner for the creation of a minuscule new town, with a mix of scale and types of building, in the cool and collected Palladian classical style that was favoured by the Stuart court. And, even more importantly, most of the buildings would be paid for by speculating builders, working on leases granted by the estate with, indeed, the houses built on estate land falling into estate ownership within forty or so years. This, of course, was the approach to estate building that would define London for the next 250 years – an approach we have seen in areas ranging from Blackheath (Walk 5) to Barnsbury (Walk 7).

The key architectural ideas of Jones's plan were that the individual houses should be designed as single, simple, uniform and palatial-looking terraces to imbue the new buildings with a sense of harmony, and that the terraces should be organised around a 'square' of slightly oblong proportion. These were new ideas for London, but not for the Continent – notably in Paris, where Charles I's father-in-law, King Henri IV, had in 1605 commissioned what is now known as the Place des Vosges. It is not only organised around a square (indeed a proper square of 1:1 proportion) but also lined with uniform and palatial houses built of brick, and it incorporated arched and vaulted ground-floor loggias to serve as public walkways – all features adopted in Jones's designs. So Continental was all this, clearly connected via Paris to Italian Renaissance

Covent Garden in 1731, with St Paul's church on the left.

architecture, that the Covent Garden Square was quickly known by Londoners as the Piazza.

What is now left of this urban and architectural paradigm? Virtually nothing, beyond the outline of the piazza, the street pattern and the scale and some characteristics of the 1630s terraces echoed by later buildings, And, of course, St Paul's church. This building – designed by Jones in elemental classical style as a pedimented temple – has been restored, burnt and rebuilt during the years. But its essential temple form survives to dominate the west side of the piazza, with its pair of towering and gaunt Tuscan stone columns no doubt being original, the silent witnesses to the kaleidoscope of life that has swirled around. Since Jones's time, the piazza has moved from aristocratic quarter to being the centre of London's late-seventeenth- and eighteenth-century sex industry – when it became known as the 'Square of Venus' – and then into a sprawling wholesale fruit, vegetable and flower market, which it remained until the mid 1970s.

Head back to the Strand, this time via Maiden Lane to the west of Southampton Street, and south through Lumley Court. This is one of many narrow alleyways or courts leading off this portion of the Strand, and each has a place in London's history because they played a role in the city's rampant and financially valuable eighteenth-century sex

industry (see p. 152). In 1758 Saunders Welch, friend of play-wright and reforming magistrate Henry Fielding, observed that 'prostitutes swarm in the streets of this metropolis' and in particular 'publickly ply in the Strand and Fleet-street at noon day', leading to a pedestrian being 'tempted (it may be said assaulted) in the streets by a hundred women between Temple-Bar and Charing Cross'.[3]

The particular role of the alleys and courts off the Strand in the capital's sex industry is made most clear by James Boswell, in his *London Journal* of 1762–3: 'I picked up a girl in the Strand; went into a court with intention to enjoy her in armour [a condom made of sheep's gut intended to offer protection from sexually transmitted diseases]. But she had none, I toyed with her. She wondered at my size and said if I ever took a girl's maidenhood, I would make her squeak. I gave her a shilling.'[4] Boswell seems to have returned to the Strand again and again; it was clearly a happy hunting ground with its dark and secret courts providing him with opportunities for a rough – even disturbingly brutal – intimacy. 'In the Strand I picked up a little profligate wretch and gave her sixpence,' says one entry. 'She allowed me entrance. But the miscreant refused me performance. I was much stronger than her, and volens nolens [whether she liked it or not] pushed her up against the wall.'[5]

Alleys also survive off the south side of the Strand, and these tell additional stories. To the south-west is Durham House Street – a memory of the palace of the Bishops of Durham that long ago stood nearby – which is also a route to two other now largely lost worlds. By twists and turns, it takes you into John Adam Street that, with Adam Street to the west, contains most of the worldly remains of one of the

A Thames-side evocation of Diocletian's Palace: the Adams' design for the Adelphi, as viewed from the river.

most heroic acts of housing speculation in Georgian London. Robert Adam and his brothers John and James had done well, as architects and building entrepreneurs, during the 1760s, and in 1768 hatched a plan for a construction that, in its scale, cost and ambition, was like a great public building project. They resolved to clear away the remains of Durham House and on its site raise a vast multi-level plateau on the river bank, engineered at Roman scale with brick-built vaults, and to build upon this plateau a series of terraces of large and extremely elegant houses to be leased or sold. These would sport the latest neoclassical motifs, which Robert Adam had already forged into the immensely fashionable Adam style. One of the key inspirations were the massive ruins of Diocletian's Palace at Split in what is now Croatia. Adam had surveyed these ruins and in 1764 published a beautifully illustrated book that revealed their wonder to the world. He seems to have been taken by the way in which the huge palace, started in about AD 295, was conceived as a small waterside city of breathtakingly harmonious and erudite classical design. The Adams' Thames-side development was called the Adelphi, in recognition of the brotherly nature of the enterprise.

But from the start, things did not go to plan. The vaults, intended to be let as warehousing, were prone to flooding so their use was soon limited to the storage of coal, not particularly profitable. Then, when the project was finally completed in 1772, the prospect of war with the American colonies and perhaps with France created an atmosphere of great uncertainty. Tensions had been rising since 1765 and war did not in fact start until 1775, but by 1772 the rumbles were getting rapidly ever more ominous and for building speculators in London at that time all was most troubling. The market ground to a near halt in the mid 1770s as potential customers preferred to wait the turn of events rather than to invest, and many speculators, perhaps crippled by borrowing charges, faced bankruptcy. The Adams escaped financial ruin by a combination of loyal support from influential friends and clients and a successful lottery that allowed them to raise money by selling tickets with a number of the houses on offer as prizes.

William Chambers must have followed this tale with intense interest. Somerset House – starting just as the Adelphi was being completed – was a government project so its finances were not subject to the same terrifying fluctuations of fortune. Although he did not admire Robert Adam's playful classicism – often realised theatrically in stucco and cement rather than in stone – Chambers must have learned much from the bold engineering aspects of the Adelphi's riverside vaults.

Sadly the Adelphi has not survived, certainly not as a total work of art, which it certainly was. The pair of central terraces, set back to back, with one facing the Thames and one inland, were demolished in 1936 and replaced by the bulky and diluted art deco office that still stands on the site. And surrounding terraces have been nibbled away, but there are still fragments to see. The best individual building is the pedimented Royal Society of Arts, which survives on John Adam Street. The best sustained run of Adam buildings is the east side of Adam Street, which still reveals the way in which Adam designed the individual houses to be part of single palatial compositions – with central pediment and end pavilions dressed with giant pilasters.

To the west, John Adam Street is met from the south by Buckingham Street and ends at Villiers Street. In the early seventeenth century this was the site of the mansion of the once powerful favourite of Charles I, George Villiers, Duke of Buckingham. In 1620 he acquired York House, since 1556 the London home of the Archbishop of York, which before the Reformation had been the home of the Bishop of Norwich. Buckingham renamed this ancient pile Buckingham House and after his assassination in 1628 it passed to his son – also named George – who lost the house during the Civil War, regained it in 1660 and in 1672 sold it to a consortium of speculating house builders. They tore down the ancient mansion and laid out these streets to create building plots. But the duke stipulated, as a condition of the sale, that he should be remembered in the street names, and so it was, and so in part it remains.

Little of age survives here – beyond a few late-seventeenth- and early-eighteenth-century houses in Buckingham Street, with a couple more in York Buildings. And then there is the spectacular York Water Gate, once the ceremonial riverside entrance to Buckingham's mansion. This is a powerful classical structure of 1623–6, built just a few years before the first duke was murdered. It was probably designed by a mason named Nicholas Stone, who trained and worked in Amsterdam. Inspired more by Flemish Mannerist classicism – and the florid sixteenth-century designs of Sebastiano Serlio – than by Palladio, the gate bears the coat of arms of Buckingham and marked the edge of the Thames before the construction of the Embankment.

———————◆•◆•◆———————

To the west of Villiers Street is one of London's great railway termini. Charing Cross station had a difficult birth. It was built as the London terminus of the South Eastern Railway (SER) whose original terminus was south of the river but who in 1848 wanted to move closer into town. Finding a site and securing the necessary Act of Parliament took over a decade but in 1860 the company purchased the 1830s Hungerford Market, at the west end of the Strand, designed by Charles Fowler, and also bought the Hungerford Suspension Bridge, designed in 1845 by Isambard Kingdom Brunel. The SER destroyed both these handsome, sound and relatively new structures and built its terminus and railway bridge. All that survives on the site of Brunel's bridge are the piers from which the suspension towers rose.

The SER's engineer was Sir John Hawkshaw – who had also worked as engineer on part of what became the Circle Line on London's Underground – and the station tracks were covered by a wrought-iron shed with a single span of 50 metres. The terminus opened for business in January 1864. The wide-span roof was to demonstrate that heroic Victorian railway engineers – working for railway companies often in ruthless competition with one another and for whom time and money were always issues – sometimes took too many risks, with structures reduced to the minimum for the sake of speed and economy. In December 1905 a tie-rod in the roof broke with a loud bang and the structure started to buckle. There was panic. Trains were stopped and people cleared. The twelve minutes between the bang and the subsequent collapse was enough to save the lives of those in the station. But unfortunately this was not the case outside the station, where part of its west wall crashed into the neighbouring theatre on Northumberland Avenue. Six people were killed. A subsequent inquiry expressed concerns about the design of the roof, but blamed the immediate cause of the collapse on a faulty weld in the tie-rod that broke. If correct – and this presumably was the case – this disaster illustrates the minimal tolerances in mid-Victorian engineering. One tie-rod goes and much of the whole roof collapses in catastrophic manner. The SER's response was to take down what remained of the roof and replace it with a utilitarian and far from heroic-looking post-and-girder structure, which supports a safe but ugly ridge-and-farrow roof – like a large greenhouse.

The roof and the station concourse, also much altered, are now not of great interest, but the railway hotel, set back in a large court off the Strand, is intriguing. Admittedly it does not look much in comparison with other nineteenth-century railway hotels – for example the gloriously Gothic Revival Midland Grand at St Pancras (see pp. 365–9) and the Renaissance-style Grosvenor of 1860 at Victoria – and has been altered and extended, but it offers a few delights. The hotel opened in 1865 and was designed by Edward M. Barry, the architect in 1857 of the Royal Opera House in Bow Street, Covent Garden and son of Sir Charles Barry, who in the 1830s designed the Palace of Westminster (see pp. 297–303).

The exterior is designed in a rather quiet sixteenth-century French Renaissance style and is somewhat underwhelming. But some of the interiors possess far more punch, in particular the first-floor coffee

Edward Barry turns his hand to the Gothic at Charing Cross.

room at the east end, above the main entrance. Its details are bold and impressive, particularly the coffered ceiling. All feels like something of a reprise – in abbreviated fashion – of the Italianate Reform Club in St James's, designed in the late 1830s by Edward's father.

Edward M. Barry could also, like his father, turn his hand to the Gothic when required, as you can see by the pinnacle that stands in the forecourt in front of the hotel. The SER got it into its head to make a cultural and historic statement, no doubt to draw attention to its new station and hotel, by asking Barry to design a permutation of the so-called Eleanor Cross that had stood nearby in what is now Trafalgar Square and was demolished in 1647. The cross, erected in 1291–4 on the orders of Edward I, was one of a series of twelve built to mark the stages in the gradual transportation of the body of his wife – Queen Eleanor – from Lincoln to burial in Westminster Abbey. Barry would no doubt have studied the three original crosses that survive to come up with this design. All have tiers of niches, set one above the other and diminishing in size as they rise, topped by a spire and cross. It is a most able evocation.

Immediately to the west of the station is Craven Street, a remarkably complete eighteenth-century street, with most of its long east side surviving and a few houses on its west side. The terraces near the Strand date from the early 1730s, while the one near the Embankment is late eighteenth century, with the end house furnished with a bay that would once have enjoyed a splendid prospect of the Thames. It was developed as a speculation by the Earl of Craven. You can get inside one of the early 1730s houses because it is now a museum. In 1757 Benjamin Franklin – one of the Founding Fathers of the United States – moved into what is now number 36 as a lodger and lived and worked there for sixteen years. See the splendid panelled interior, painted and furnished in a reasonably authentic manner.

Halfway down the street, and to the east, is Craven Passage which bridges over Hungerford Lane. It is short but contains a few early buildings including a pub, the Ship & Shovell, which occupies two plots facing each other across the court. This is the only pub I know in London that comes in two helpings. The two parts are apparently linked by a common cellar.

———◆•◆•◆———

Back to the Strand, and opposite the Eleanor Cross and the station fore-court is one of the more pleasing of London's early-twentieth-century buildings. It is now Zimbabwe House, but was built in 1907 as the headquarters of the British Medical Association. The architect was Charles Holden, and it's a splendid example of the efforts made by Holden, and other talented architects of his time – like Edwin Lutyens – to forge a modern British architecture for the new century by building on, rather than by rejecting, history. This building is different in feel to architecture that went before but it is clearly rooted in the past. There are obvious references to classical composition and detailing, most creatively reinterpreted – the two-storey blank arcade forming the podium of the building, for example – and to the role of ornament in architecture. The front elevation is adorned by a series of large sculpted figures – now weathered in spectacular manner – intended to depict the *Ages of Man*. They are the work of Jacob Epstein and this was his first major commission for a London building.

Immediately to the west of Zimbabwe House is something equally fascinating, the remains of an architectural initiative that played a role in the transformation of a collection of courts, alleys, narrow streets and mews into London's premier ceremonial, and would-be triumphal, open space: Trafalgar Square. The creation of such grandiloquent public squares has little history in London, a city in which large squares – like Grosvenor Square of the 1720s – were laid out as private enterprises to provide high-class homes in delightful, tranquil and, as far as possible, private settings. But in the 1820s it was decided that London needed a vast public forum, Parisian-fashion, where national glory could be celebrated, pageantry could be indulged, and civic and cultural aspirations could be made manifest. In a sense this was to be the great national forum or agora and the epitome of the stumbling but continuing quest to make London the new Rome or the Athens of the age. It was really all pretty vulgar, not only counter to London's urban traditions but also, in its rather overtly bombastic nature, alien to the national character. Predictably much went wrong, so the story of the making of Trafalgar Square provides a salutary tale.

The buildings opposite Charing Cross station give a hint of the look the new square was to have. Of course the prevailing architectural language was to be classical and the atmosphere festive, even theatrical. The terrace facing the station is clad in stucco, now painted white but probably originally colour-washed and tinted –'frescoed', as it was termed at the time – to look like picturesquely weathered stone. It has pairs of domed round bays at each end, known affectionately as the'pepperpots', which cleverly help to turn the corners of the awkwardly shaped site. This is the 'West Strand Improvements', designed in the late 1820s by John Nash for Crown-owned land. The centre was once a pilastered pavilion but this was replaced in 1904 by a monumental stone-built column-

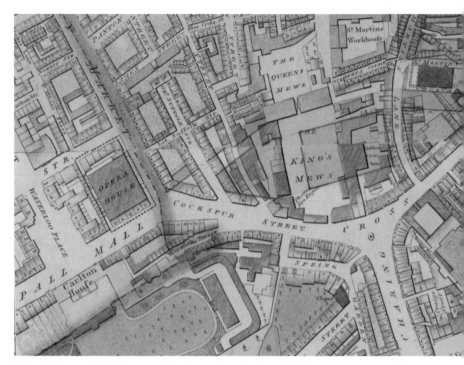

Richard Horwood's 1819 map of London depicts the site of Trafalgar Square covered in tight alleyways and narrow-fronted houses.

clad building (designed by John Macvicar Anderson), which was in turn replaced in the 1970s by the existing steel and glass elevation that is, most consciously, in striking contrast with the rest of the block. It was designed by Frederick Gibberd.

To appreciate the radical nature of the evolution of Trafalgar Square it is necessary to contemplate Richard Horwood's London map of 1799–1819. It shows the site of the then yet-to-be-built 'West Strand Improvements' covered with narrow-fronted houses and narrow courts of yet narrower houses. Nearly opposite these was a remarkable survival, the huge Jacobean Northumberland House, with its red-brick corner towers, which stood there until 1874. The Strand continued south-west, beyond the street frontage of Northumberland House, to the area that was then known as Charing Cross. This had at its centre a cast-bronze equestrian statue of Charles I, made in 1633 by Hubert Le Sueur. Remarkably the statue survived the Civil War because it was hidden by the man who Parliament had commissioned to destroy it; after the Restoration it was

purchased by Charles II and in 1675 positioned on the site occupied until 1647 by the Eleanor Cross. From here the statue of Charles I enjoys a commanding view along Whitehall, and of the site – in front of the Banqueting House – where the king had been executed in January 1649. The statue became something of a shrine to the Stuarts and to the restored monarchy and – of more practical importance – the datum point from which all distances to and from London were calculated.

To the north of the statue were a pair of large courts, the King's Mews and the Queen's Mews, surrounded by a mix of structures, many humble and utilitarian, as well as a number of smaller alleys and courts, some containing inns and stabling. Nearby was the large St Martin's Workhouse and adjoining that the monumental church of St Martin-in-the-Fields, built in 1722–6 to the designs of James Gibbs (see p. 484), but crowded by buildings and with its mighty temple-like columned portico facing awkwardly on to the narrow and curving St Martin's Lane.

The idea of a large public square, then, was a dramatic departure from what existed. But in 1826 the Commissioners of His Majesty's Woods, Forests and Land Revenues, the body behind the creation of Regent's Park and Regent Street, enlisted Nash to come up with a plan for clearing most of the buildings north of Charing Cross. Part of the plan was to liberate St Martin's church from the surrounding courts and streets and allow it to take the role of the basilica which, by tradition, was the public building that dominated Roman fora. This was a job that, by chance, St Martin's was able to fulfil to perfection because Gibbs had designed it in the fashion of a Roman temple – to be seen in the round, with pilaster-clad side elevations and a majestic columned west portico. Much of the land required for the making of this national forum was owned by the Crown, and that which wasn't could be acquired by means of the Charing Cross Act of Parliament that was given assent in 1826.

Nash had, from 1811, acted as architect and master-planner, often in association with James Burton as developer and builder, in the creation of Regent's Park, with its villas and flanking terraces, and from 1813 in the formation of Regent's Street, including Oxford Circus, Piccadilly Circus and Waterloo Place. The 'West Strand' improvement scheme was part of the vision, fuelled by George IV from the time he was Prince Regent and largely planned or executed by Nash, to transform much of West London into a stupendous urban fantasy of the ancient world, realised in brick, stucco, timber and paint, and in the process create a royal route from St James's Park to Regent's Park that would form 'a boundary . . . between the Streets and Squares occupied by the Nobility and Gentry' to the west and the 'narrow Streets and meaner Houses occupied by Mechanics and the trading part of the community' in Soho to the east.[6] Within this context, the thinking behind Trafalgar Square was clear. The creation of a large open space suitable as a location for public buildings and that would serve as a gathering place for a triumphal route west along the Mall through St James's Park to Buckingham Palace. The Regent Street royal route connected to the Mall via Waterloo Place and the Duke of York steps, to the east of which stood the Prince Regent's own royal residence, Carlton House. Buckingham Palace had been in royal ownership since 1761, and from 1826–30 was refronted, partly rebuilt and extended by Nash – at scandalous expense. These works included a marble-clad Roman-style triumphal arch, placed in front of the palace's east-facing elevation, to close the view west along the Mall. This arch made apparent to all the martial meaning of the triumphal route from the new huge square to the east. The grandiose remodelling of Buckingham Palace for George IV – monarch since 1820 – made Carlton House redundant and it was demolished in 1827, to be replaced by the majestic Carlton House Terrace, also designed by Nash. In 1851 the arch in front of the palace was moved to the junction of Oxford Street and Edgware Road and gave its name to the district now known as Marble Arch.

But the scheme for Nash's new square soon faltered. A design uniting all its sides did not materialise. At the time of George IV's death in 1830, the east side was defined by the newly exposed portico of St Martin-in-

The view north-east over Trafalgar Square towards the Strand from Admiralty Arch.

the-Fields, the entrance to Duncannon Street and a new Nash-designed building to the south, but the futures of the other sides had not been resolved. The clearance of the site moved slowly, Nash became increasingly infirm and absent from the project (he was to die in 1835), and when the next major building decision was taken the design work was in the hands of architect William Wilkins. The British Museum in Bloomsbury (see pp. 243–4) was becoming too crowded so it was decided that its paintings should be housed in a separate museum, known as the National Gallery – first from 1820 in a house in Pall Mall and then in a building designed by Wilkins for a site occupying the entire north side of the new square. Work started in 1832 and continued until 1838 and, as was standard for the time, the museum was conceived as a classical temple of the arts, with a central columned portico, including Greek

Revival details.

While the gallery was under construction the meaning of the new square was given focus. From the start it was to do with triumph, if only because it formed part of the processional route to Nash's triumphal arch in front of Buckingham Palace. But in around 1835 it was decided to call this large amorphous area, struggling to take form and find identity, Trafalgar Square. So its character of triumph was confirmed but with the focus on naval victory. This is no surprise since William IV – monarch from 1830 – had served in the Royal Navy during the Napoleonic Wars and was long on intimate terms with the conflict's greatest naval hero, Admiral Lord Nelson. So naval power, victory – and Nelson in particular – were to provide the new national focus of Charing Cross. Charles I was permitted to remain on his horse in situ – but he was about to be dwarfed.

Upon Nash's death, Wilkins, predictably, tried to grab Nash's job as master-planner for the square and produced a scheme for its completion. This was accepted but pretty well ignored, perhaps because critics had started to take a dim view of the south elevation of his gallery: with its stretched portico, squashed pediment and seemingly purposeless and greatly underscaled dome, it clearly lacked the appropriate sense of grandeur such a key site offered, and demanded. When Wilkins died in 1839, Sir Charles Barry took over the job of organising the square and trying to enhance the presence of the gallery. His main strategy was to level the awkwardly sloping site and in the process elevate the appearance of the gallery when viewed from the square. To this end Barry created the raised terrace at the square's north side and designated numerous plinths for statues of an assortment of largely military heroes. Meanwhile for the square's west side Sir Robert Smirke – architect of the British Museum – designed two visually related buildings, one of which was the Union Club, the other the Royal College of Physicians. Both were complete by 1827 and in the 1920s both were united, and substantially altered, to form Canada House.

Independent of Wilkins' and Barry's plans for the square, a committee was formed in 1838 to lobby government to build a monument at its centre to commemorate the Battle of Trafalgar, and Nelson in particular. Money was raised through public donations and architect William Railton came up with the rather obvious idea of building a Roman-style free-standing column topped by a huge statue of Nelson. Most columns of this type tend to contain a staircase so the monument could also serve the practical function of public viewing gallery, as with Trajan's Column in Rome and the columns in London – notably the Monument of 1671–7, designed by Wren and Robert Hooke, and the Duke of York's column of 1832, on the Mall, designed by Benjamin Dean Wyatt. But Railton's 67-metre-high Corinthian fluted column is simply solid stone. This was, presumably, a cost-saving exercise. It was raised by 1843, much to Barry's disgust. The column, along with its tall pedestal and podium, did fundamentally change the nature of the square from a huge open space for Londoners into more or less just a setting for a monument. The four somewhat leaden lumps of lions, designed by Sir Edwin Landseer and cast in bronze, were not added until 1867. These are British lions that, far from being rampant, have gone rather flat.

––––––•·◆·•––––––

To the south-west stands the ultimate – and final – expression of the triumphalist nature of the square and the Mall. Admiralty Arch, completed in 1912, can be seen as a ceremonial gate into the hallowed precinct of the royal St James's Park, marking the start of the processional route to Buckingham Palace. But it is also, of course, a triumphal arch dedicated, as its name makes clear, to naval victory. In this sense it possesses a symbolic role equivalent to the Arc de Triomphe in Paris. But this London arch is more. It is not just an arch symbolic of victory but also an inhabited arch within which the business of achieving victory was pursued.

The arch was commissioned in 1910 by King Edward VII and the 'grateful citizens' of Britain and its empire to commemorate Queen Victoria – who had died in 1901 after a reign of sixty-four years. It was conceived as the primary architectural monument and celebration of the Queen Empress's rule, and constructed when London was at the heart of the largest, richest and most powerful empire the world has ever seen. The arch would also come to commemorate a world that was about to end. The triumph it was intended to celebrate was to be shattered beyond recovery by the First World War.

Not only was the arch one of the great architectural and symbolic expressions of Empire, it was, in later years, a place at the centre of power,

At once deeply traditional and forward-looking, Admiralty Arch perfectly captures the peculiarities of Edwardian Britain.

politics, war and peace. Behind its public face it contained extensive and varied accommodation, intended to serve as offices for the Royal Navy and civil service and as staterooms for some of the leading figures of the Admiralty and government. The north block contained offices and private apartments for the First Sea Lord – the professional head of the Royal Navy – and for the First Lord of the Admiralty, usually a politician and civilian.

In late 1914, these key posts were occupied by two explosive characters who were crucial to the successful prosecution of the First World War – but also, as it turned out, to the conduct of the Second World War. The First Sea Lord was Admiral of the Fleet 'Jackie' Fisher, who by 1914 had done much to forge a Royal Navy, modernised and armed with a new generation of warships. The First Lord of the Admiralty, from 1911, was

Winston Churchill. It's perhaps predictable that these strong-minded and idiosyncratic men finally came to loggerheads. It is possible to imagine the heated debates that must have taken place in their adjoining staterooms and apartments.

Admiralty Arch's vital role in the nation's story is over. In 2011 the government, as part of its austerity programme, declared the arch redundant. The following year it was sold to a development company that has since obtained planning permission to convert it into a hotel, club and apartments. Works are due for completion in 2022. And yet, even with its function changing beyond recognition, the arch remains a stupendous representation of the spirit of the early twentieth century. It is a masterpiece in Edwardian Baroque architecture – the style that evolved in the last years of Empire to express the cultural aspirations of an extraordinary epoch in Britain's history. Designed by Sir Aston Webb in most ingenious manner, the Arch is, in every sense, the harbinger of the royal palace to its west – where, in 1913, Webb came up with the existing main, east-facing façade in marching Baroque manner. He also designed the grandiose fountain that stands in front of the palace. This work, which features a huge statue of Queen Victoria sculpted by Sir Thomas Brock, is known as the Victoria Memorial, and was dedicated in 1911 by Victoria's two senior grandsons: George V, and his first cousin, the German Kaiser Wilhelm II.

Admiralty Arch, designed as the portal to the palace and to set the tone for a tremendous architectural ensemble, expresses a refined and scholarly taste. It is inspired not only by the architecture of Rome but also by the late-seventeenth- and early-eighteenth-century English Baroque of Sir Christopher Wren, Sir John Vanbrugh and Nicholas Hawksmoor. Consequently it has a distinctly English character. And yet, in spite of its historic associations, it is also a profoundly twentieth-century building. With its stone elevations laid over a structural frame of steel, the arch is a spectacular fusion of ancient and modern, of old artistic values with the new virtues of pioneering building technology. It is a perfect expression of the age that gave it birth: the age of transition, when old orders ended and the modern world began.

Dagenham Civic Centre

Less than a hundred years ago, most of Dagenham was a village surrounded by open farmland, with just a scattering of dwellings, agricultural buildings and a few country houses. For much of the capital's history, it was inconceivable that this distant Essex hamlet – over 10 miles from Charing Cross, as the crow flies – would ever be absorbed into the metropolis. But absorbed it was. With ever more space required to house London's booming population, in the years after the First World War Dagenham became a bustling though peripheral suburb. This idiosyncratic urban history is integral to understanding the area's most idiosyncratic building: Dagenham Civic Centre.

To reach the centre, catch a District Line underground train to Dagenham Heathway, opened in 1932. The station debouches on to Heathway. You immediately notice the down-at-heel 1920s or 30s 'shopping parade', and the pleasingly mixed nature of the local community – West Indians, Indians, East Europeans, Vietnamese have all found a home here. On the direct walk from the station to the civic centre there is little of great interest to see. But if you have time, and are so minded, you could have a short diversion to the old centre of Dagenham: turn right out of the station and then left along Church Elm Lane which very soon leads you into Crown Street. On your right – to the south – is the parish church of St Peter and St Paul in the heart of the fragmentary remains of Dagenham village. The chancel of the church dates from the early thirteenth century but the nave and tower from 1801–5, when the collapse of the medieval tower on to the nave made rebuilding necessary. The church is a somewhat incongruous reminder that, before its interwar urbanisation, this was just another tranquil village in Essex.

Cottage housing on an industrial scale: the Becontree Estate photographed soon after its completion.

Today, though, the church is sandwiched between the two great legacies of the urbanisation of the 1920s and 1930s: the vast Becontree 'cottage housing' estate, and the huge Ford Motor Works. Becontree, lying to the north-east of the church and the old village, was the largest of all the London County Council's interwar housing estates, built outside what was then the County of London. Permission for the construction of such estates – intended to ease London's housing crisis by providing modern residences for the working-class population – was granted by the Addison Housing Act of 1919. Becontree is, in many ways, a typical consequence of this new policy. Construction began in 1921, and by 1935 just over 14,000 hectares of arable land, market gardens and private park had given way to more than 25,000 terrace houses that were homes to over 167,000 people.

These houses were of meagre construction and little or no architectural pretension, beyond a few diluted references to Essex vernacular building. Nor was there a great deal of concern about catering in convenient manner for the residents of what was, in scale at least, a new town within the outer environs of London – no significant shopping or cultural centre, merely rows and rows of winding streets of houses: in essence a vast dormitory, reasonably healthy but monotonous in the extreme. The only overt nod to history was the decision to retain Valence House (on the north edge of the estate), the much-altered portion of a medieval timber-framed and moated manor, which was used as the LCC's headquarters during the construction of the estate. The house was extended in 1928 by Dagenham Urban District Council, which had been established in 1926, to serve as its town hall, until the new civic centre was completed in 1937. But it's visually unprepossessing, rendered externally and now set within a rather dull municipal park.

From 1930, many of Becontree's residents would work within the other great arrival in interwar Dagenham: the Ford Motor Works, standing a mile and a half to the south of the village and stretching all the way to the banks of the Thames. At its peak it covered over 194 hectares. But car production stopped in 2002, replaced by the assembly of diesel engines. Since then the works have shrunk considerably, with parts redeveloped – notably the stamping plant, the closure of which was announced in 2012 and led to the loss of a thousand jobs. Demolition started in 2016 to make way for housing.

This new world of sprawling factories and terraces was the context of the arrival of the civic centre, which stands to the north. Reach it either by walking up Rainham Road from its junction with the east end of Church Street, or by getting a bus from the Heathway – a northbound number 175 takes you all the way there. The first glimpse of this long, low, brick building is astonishing. It's big, but almost dwarfed by its wide and open setting – which is now, despite generous swathes of lawn, dominated by roads and thundering traffic. The initial impression when seen from afar is that this is some sort of modernistic country house, because there lurks about it a sense of grandeur. But, as quickly becomes clear, this is a house dedicated not to the old order of the aristocratic and capitalist elite, but rather to a new order – of civic and municipal authority, and of local democracy empowered by an industrial workforce with its own ideals and aspirations.

The centre was constructed in 1936–7 to the designs of E. Barry Webber with the borough engineer E. C. Lloyd. The architecture is inspired by classical principles of the most rational kind. There is strict symmetry, a central portico of sorts – formed by four tall, thin stone piers with abstracted detail set before a large, brick-built cube, all of which conjures up an atmosphere of dominance and power. The ground floor is stone-clad and treated as the plinth of a temple, with wide and very shallow windows lighting the basement below, and wide and not-so-shallow windows lighting the ground floor. The first-floor windows are more Georgian in proportion, with vertical emphasis and just over double-square in proportion; the second-floor windows are square, in the manner favoured by early-eighteenth-century Palladian design.

The oddest thing about this civic centre is that it possesses many of the characteristics of the totalitarian architecture of 1930s Europe. In its meticulously controlled, machine-made, neoclassical perfection, its regimented symmetry and excessive scale, it evokes the architecture of the regimes of Hitler, Stalin and Mussolini. For these regimes, such architecture represented strict state control and domination, while the large scale was intended to impress supporters and to overawe and browbeat opponents. So the civic centre is, in its way, a relative of the

The peculiar authoritarianism of Dagenham Civic Centre.

authoritarian architecture embraced by the 'Thousand-Year Reich', conceived by such architects as Paul Ludwig Troost and Albert Speer. It is strange to see in the low-key setting of Dagenham.

Of course, here this type of classical architecture had a quite different meaning to the one it embodied for such megalomaniacal regimes. When the civic centre was being built the Urban District Council evolved into a Municipal Borough, but presumably the new authority did not harbour sinister ambitions of world domination. So the similarity of the ruthlessly symmetrical architecture embodies the symmetry of directly opposing ideas. In totalitarian regimes this architecture symbolised the unbending power of the autocratic state; but in Dagenham in 1937 it was apparently seen to express the benevolence of an enlightened local authority representing the interests of a new industrial working-class constituency.

Perhaps, of course, those who commissioned the civic centre didn't think of the building as carrying a political message, lofty or otherwise, and saw its style as no more than the expression of the idea that municipal architecture should reflect a sense of order and authority. Or perhaps

the civic centre is innocently following an architectural fashion embraced at the time by people and regimes of very different political persuasions. Or perhaps Barry Webber and Dagenham's local politicians were indeed blissfully unaware of the implied rhetoric of the architecture they created. But that now seems hardly possible. By 1936 war with the new dictatorships of Germany and Fascist Italy was already a reality (the Spanish Civil War broke out the year the civic centre started on site), and Troost's classical Nazi additions to the Königsplatz in Munich had been completed and widely published by the time the civic centre was designed. So what was going on in Dagenham in 1936? That is indeed something to chew over as you make your no doubt weary way home.

WALK 13

Brixton

Market forces in post-war London

BELLE

FERND

A t the centre of Brixton lies a tribute to its West Indian community. In 1948, a post-war labour shortage in Britain – particularly on the newly nationalised railways and in the newly created National Health Service – prompted the government to pass the British Nationality Act, which granted British citizenship to all living in Commonwealth countries and full rights of entry and settlement in Britain. Workers were actively sought in the West Indies. The call met an eager and rapid response: on 22 June 1948, HMT *Empire Windrush* docked at Tilbury bringing the first shipload of 802 arrivals, mostly from Jamaica. Today, this first wave of migrants is commemorated in the heart of Brixton, in the name Windrush Square.

NURSE

TUNSTA

The square was laid out in the 1990s, and is not just the civic but also the emotional heart of Brixton. On every side, there is a remarkable juxtaposition between Brixton's current status – as a vibrant, modern and rapidly changing neighbourhood – and its long and idiosyncratic history. So, to the west, the splendid Edwardian Baroque former Lambeth Town Hall – designed by Septimus Warwick and H. Austen Hall and completed in 1908 – now hosts a number of 'hot desks' for archly hip tech start-ups. Raleigh Hall, built as two houses in the 1820s, is today home to the Black Cultural Archives, near which stands a memorial commemorating the 'service of men and women from Africa and the Caribbean' during the First and Second World Wars. And the southern portion of the square is overshadowed by Brixton's parish church: St Matthew's, located in Brixton Green, is a solemn affair, designed in 1822 by C. F. Porden with funds made available by the Church Building Act (see p. 277). It is the quintessence of the Greek Revival – the height of fashion at the time – with a vast Grecian Doric west portico, and a delicate tower with an upper stage modelled on the fourth-century BC Choragic Monument of Lysicrates in Athens.

BRIGHTO

ACRE

Lambe
Town
Hall

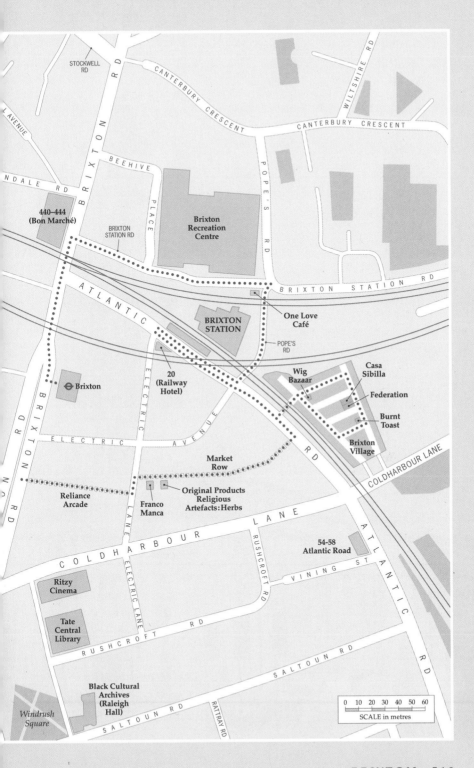

The Edwardian grandeur of Lambeth Town Hall
now hosts a number of tech start-ups.

But even this austere temple has been remade by the forces of urban history, with its catacombs now incorporating a trendy tapas restaurant and, until recently, a nightclub.

These contrasts reflect the remarkable history of Brixton over the last few hundred years. The surrounding streets have had a tumultuous two centuries, transforming from rural farmland in 1800 to dilapidated working-class suburb in the 1920s. But the most significant change to the area, as hinted at by the presence of the Black Cultural Archives on Windrush Square, was the arrival of the West Indian community in the later twentieth century. Their arrival helped turn Brixton into one of the most lively and exciting parts of south London, and gave the district its ongoing position as focal point of black British culture.

Brixton was once a place of physical transition between the Thames-side marshes of Lambeth and the highlands of Upper Norwood and Streatham. For centuries it was a place of rural obscurity, with no significant settlement. In Roman times it was simply the location of a bridge or two, notable only for carrying the road that ran from London to the south coast over the River Effra, which rose in Upper Norwood and crossed through Brixton on its way to the Thames. In pre-Norman Conquest England Brixton was probably the location of a boundary stone, perhaps placed in position by a Saxon lord named Brixi, to define land ownership or a county division. At some time in the distant past the main Roman roads were connected by a network of lanes – marking boundaries, following physical characteristics of the terrain, or simply being the results of the routes inhabitants or travellers wanted to pursue – and such was the origin of Coldharbour

Lane, Brixton Water Lane and Acre Lane. These were recognised routes by medieval times.

All changed with dramatic speed in the eighteenth century when a series of new bridges across the Thames improved connections between the populous and developed London on the north bank of the river and the fields, market gardens and pleasure grounds on the south side. The first new crossing was Westminster Bridge in 1750, followed by Blackfriars Bridge in 1769. These spurred the development of Lambeth and the St George's Fields area (now Elephant and Castle). Significant development took place along the main roads heading south to Kennington, Camberwell and Clapham, particularly along Kennington Road from the 1770s and Clapham Road in the first decade of the nineteenth century. But it was the opening of Vauxhall Bridge in 1816 that was to have the most profound influence on the development of Brixton. Admirable terraces soon lined Brixton Road and an informal town centre, complete with a green, evolved where it met Acre Lane and Coldharbour Lane. Brixton, surrounded by fields and market gardens famed for their strawberries, marshland to the north and high ground to the south, became a desirable and salubrious suburb formed of gentlemen's villas and neat terraces with, from 1822, St Matthew's church as its architectural and social focus.

In the mid nineteenth century, Brixton's pleasant situation and amiable atmosphere encouraged high-quality residential development. Take the genteel Angell Town, to the east of Brixton Road and named after the family that had owned the land since the late seventeenth century, which was first developed in the early nineteenth century but only acquired momentum in the 1850s.[1] One idiosyncratic survival of these tranquil origins can be seen in Blenheim Gardens off Brixton Hill, where a windmill – built in 1816–17 – still stands. But the idyll came to an end with the arrival of the railway. In 1862 Brixton station was opened by the London, Chatham and Dover Railway, offering connections to Moorgate, Victoria and Holborn. Gardens and surviving fields were rapidly developed to provide both grander houses along main roads and cheaper, meaner accommodation for clerks and tradesmen on minor and backstreets. As Brixton ballooned it lost its status as a high-quality residential area. It also lost its established identity as it merged with surrounding areas to form the vast and sprawling mass of south London.

But even if Brixton lost its character as a semi-rural and well-to-do suburb, it did not became anonymous or indistinct. Far from it. Brixton soon evolved a new character, and one with great and fascinating physical distinction. And at its heart was the station. The railway came into the centre of Brixton at high level and its vertiginous viaduct and bridges – with their pioneering wrought-iron girders and cast-iron piers – must have been seen as utterly modern. Immediately around the station, streets and buildings arose that were just as strident, flamboyant and, for their time, big. There is Electric Avenue, an ambitious street of shops, constructed in 1885, which – with its concave form and glazed canopied iron arcades (alas now all removed) – must surely have been a south London evocation of the quadrant-shaped and originally arcaded southern end of Regent Street. The name of the avenue celebrates the fact that it was one of the first streets in London to be illuminated with electric

Inside Brixton Market in 1952.

lights. This alone confirms the heady aspirations in the 1880s of Brixton's new business community.

Electric Avenue, which curves from Brixton Road to Atlantic Road, and its environs had by the late nineteenth century become home to a number of markets, largely housed in custom-designed buildings of the 1870s. These markets thrived and – after being joined by the 'Morleys of Brixton' department store on Brixton Road in the 1920s – established Brixton as the shopping mecca of south London. It also became a centre of entertainment, with the Electric Pavilion cinema opening in Coldharbour Lane in 1910 – one of the first cinemas in London – and being joined in 1929 by the far larger Astoria, located in Stockwell Road and given distinction by its domed entrance and ostentatious art deco interior. Gratifyingly, both these buildings survive, still rendering the delights for which they were created – the Electric Pavilion is now the Ritzy cinema, standing on Windrush Square next to the Tate Central Library of 1893, and the Astoria is now the Brixton Academy, with dancers and drinkers enjoying its intoxicating decor.

But the interwar prosperity that Brixton experienced as south London's entertainment hub was not destined to last. The middle classes moved out as it became ever more a centre of working-class life. Large houses were felled or, more usually, divided into flats or converted to commercial use, and leafy gardens were steadily built upon. By the late 1940s – as Britain struggled to cope with the gloomy aftermath of the Second World War – Brixton was dogged by increasing poverty and physical neglect. Not only were its once-delightful strawberry fields and bucolic atmosphere long gone, and its noble late- Georgian terraces eradicated or obscured, but the markets and pleasure domes of the 1920s and 30s were also in decline.

It was into this world of decaying grandeur that a new community established itself. The first West Indian immigrants arrived in Brixton in the late 1940s. For many, with no accommodation or jobs arranged, problems started immediately with a large number of no doubt baffled immigrants being given temporary accommodation in the Clapham South deep bomb shelter. This was less than a mile from Coldharbour Lane and Brixton, and near the great rail stations at Clapham Junction and Waterloo which offered employment. So, arguably, the almost random choice by anonymous officialdom of the huge former bomb shelter as a place of refuge led to the West Indian community settling in Clapham and Brixton. Gradually the district became home to waves of varied immigrants and an array of ethnic communities. Although around 25 per cent of Brixton's population is now of African or Caribbean descent, there are also many people from Afghanistan and Eastern Europe, giving the place a cosmopolitan atmosphere.

These communities have brought great cultural richness, diversity and interest. But, living in one of the poorest parts of central London, Brixton's migrant communities have also endured their share of overcrowding, conflict, grim high-rise social-housing schemes and – inevitably – crime. Over the years, Brixton has been home to a great deal of gang-related violence and drug-dealing. Intolerable tensions, and the alienation of a significant part of the community from institutions such as the police, have led to riots and an increased sense of distrust and persecution. All have, in recent years, tarnished Brixton's good name and reputation.

These simmering tensions, fuelled by economic hardships and poor housing, came to a violent head in 1981. Street crime – or perhaps rather the police's response to street crime – was the spark. During the unfortunately named Operation Swamp, officers stopped and searched over a thousand people in less than a week on the streets of Brixton on the mere suspicion that they might be in breach of the 1824 Vagrancy Act. The seemingly arbitrary nature of the stop and search tactics – and, moreover, the fact that the vast majority of those stopped were young black men – caused great local indignation and sparked riots. More than 300 people (mostly police) were injured and any vehicles were burned, as were numerous buildings in the heart of Brixton. A subsequent inquiry conducted by the law lord Leslie Scarman found evidence that the police had made disproportionate and indiscriminate use of 'stop and search' powers against young black people in the area.

Similar incidents would harm Brixton's reputation over the course of the next few decades. There were riots in 1985, when police shot a local black woman, Dorothy Groce, after entering her house looking for her son; and in 1995, after a black man, Wayne Douglas, died in police custody. And, of course, in August 2011, when unrest escalated throughout London with extraordinary speed and violence after police shot and killed a

The view north along Electric Lane in 1981, in the midst of the Brixton riots.

suspect in Tottenham. I remember that in Spitalfields most bars and shops shut suddenly, during the day, with some even being hastily boarded up. I and a few neighbours sat in one restaurant that remained defiantly open, receiving reports from fleeing pedestrians about the onward approach of the seemingly unstoppable mob of rioters. Looting became endemic, with usually law-abiding citizens ransacking shops in the extraordinary belief that – in the general chaos – they could get away with it. Mostly they couldn't. The remorseless search for the looters and the draconian, almost vengeful, sentences imposed on them became as depressing as the riots themselves. Brixton was one of the parts of London hardest hit.

This was a serious setback for the area, where tranquillity had seemingly been restored. But all has been quiet in recent years. Community leaders have done a great deal to build a sense of local pride. This is especially true of the Afro-Caribbean community, which now occupies a unique and valued place in London's diverse culture. And, it must be said, the people of Brixton make visitors welcome. Nowhere in London have so many people flashed me a smile and asked me if I was all right. It might just be me ambling around with my notepad and camera and looking every inch a visitor – and perhaps a particularly hapless one

– but I suspect this is a true reflection of the area's innate character. Most decent places in the world make strangers and travellers welcome, and Brixton is, it seems, no exception.

Certainly the evil of racial discrimination, which did so much to damage the pride and dent the identity of Brixtonians in the past, seems – for now at least – to be in retreat. Today the threat to Brixton's tranquillity is of a different kind. During the last couple of decades it has become an increasingly fashionable area in south London. Inevitably property values and rental costs have risen, resulting in pressure on the existing community from richer young professionals seeking to move into the area. Disquiet about these changing fortunes was one of the issues that ignited the 1995 riot. The word generally used for it is gentrification. This

The vibrant street life on Electric Avenue today.

is, of course, an imprecise and loaded term. It is usually taken to mean the displacement of an indigenous urban community, located within a run-down inner-city area, by affluent outsiders who covet these locations – and have the wealth and influence to get what they want. A more benign interpretation is that the incomers merely want to help regenerate a characterful area with great potential, and to contribute to its ever-evolving life. After all, Brixton's distinct character now is the product of waves of new arrivals making it their home. As you walk around, you will have the opportunity to observe, ponder and take a view.

Brixton's story is enshrined in its fabric and there is much to be explored. The walk I offer focuses on one small area – Brixton's now incredibly lively historic centre, with its bustling street life, covered markets and multicultural community. These few streets show what Brixton has been and what it has now become, offering compelling evidence to suggest that the troubles of the recent past are – although far from solved – now receding fast.

THE WALK

Travel to Brixton tube station, the final stop heading south on the Victoria Line. As you make your way to street level you may well – depending on the day – be instantly sucked into a throng of shoppers. On one of my recent visits, not too long ago, the road was packed as it was a Saturday morning, the prime market day. On weekdays, though, all is much calmer. Turn right (north) along Brixton Road and pass under the bridge. Cross Atlantic Road (to which we will soon return), and go under a second bridge, and you will arrive at the west end of Brixton Station Road, with the railway viaduct to the south.

Turn east along Brixton Station Road and after 150 metres stands one of the best introductions to Brixton's West Indian culture around: Jeff the Chef's 'One Love Café', which occupies a small mobile kitchen on the corner of Pope's Road, nestling below the vast Brixton Recreation Centre. Jeff – real name Geoff Johns – has worked on this spot since 2007, and specialises in Caribbean food: usually his dishes of the day include goat, swordfish, rice and fried banana. It was Jeff who first cooked breadfruit for me. This is a notorious food, which neatly encapsulates the bitter colonial history that indirectly led to the presence of a West Indian community in Britain in the first place. The British botanist Joseph Banks (see p. 216) observed the fruit when in Tahiti, which he visited in 1769 when sailing on HMS *Endeavour* as part of Captain Cook's epic voyage of discovery. In the 1780s, when Britain had lost access to American rice following its defeat in the American War of Independence, Banks suggested to the government that breadfruit would be a cheap but high-energy food to feed slaves in plantations in the Caribbean. The Royal Navy's William Bligh was detailed in 1787 to carry a supply of breadfruit trees to the West Indies on board HMS *Bounty*. But the trees – along with the ship – never made it: his disaffected crew mutinied, dumping the thousand or so potted plants overboard. So began one of the most famous adventures in British naval history, as Bligh and eighteen loyal men began a 4,000-mile journey to safety, in a tiny and overfull ship's longboat that the mutineers had abandoned them on.

Less well known, though, is the indefatigable Bligh's commitment to breadfruit. Four years later, in 1791, he made a second attempt at the journey and this time succeeded in getting breadfruit trees to St Vincent

A haberdashery-cum-butcher on Atlantic Road.

and Jamaica. The local population – slaves and otherwise – did not take to this new-fangled food at first. Now, however, it is regarded as an indigenous crop in most of the West Indies, and is a hugely popular part of the traditional cooking culture. A typical breadfruit is a little smaller than a football and its flesh has something of the colour, density and texture of white bread. Jeff cooks them in time-honoured manner. The fruit is cooked whole, like a baked potato, then cut into slices. These can be salted and eaten, or fried to make crisp. Most delicious, especially when enjoyed with Jeff's swordfish.

Turn right – to the south – off Brixton Station Road, along Pope's Road, and pass under the bridges. You are now back on Atlantic Road. This street – and Electric Avenue, which curves on to it – has long been the centre of Brixton's market district. From the 1870s, it was home to traders operating from street stalls, open-fronted shops and eventually from arcades. The street-trading heart has now moved to Electric Avenue, but Atlantic Road retains its market atmosphere, and some memorable and most characterful late-Victorian buildings. Most notable among these is a splendid Venetian Gothic folly of a pub, a little to the west on the corner with Electric Lane. Dated 1880 and complete with spired clock tower, this was the Railway Hotel. Having been abandoned for several years and smeared with graffiti, it has now been converted into a chain eatery, Wahaca, purveying the usual 'Mexican street food'. And so another architecturally distinguished London pub is lost. Beyond the hotel, on the south-west side of the street, stand the familiar open-fronted shops, most selling now unheard-of cuts of meat – oxtail, sheep's heads and the like – and a wide range of offal. I chatted to one of the bloodstained butchers, a cheerful and most polite young man from Afghanistan. We discussed the cuts and I tried to get pointers for making oxtail soup Afghan-style.

The tough and confident quality of the buildings in Electric Avenue and Atlantic Road, the buzz of market and street life and the high railway line with its towering iron and steel bridges, give this part of Brixton a strongly urban and strangely North American feel. This city-centre and commercial character is reinforced by some of the big stores nearby including, on Brixton Road, Bon Marché, which opened in 1877 as one of the first purpose-built department stores in England, now home to a TK Maxx.

The Venetian Gothic folly of the former Railway Hotel.

Back in Atlantic Road, at numbers 54–58, stands the former HQ of the once-mighty David Greig grocery (and latterly supermarket) chain. This store opened in 1870 and soon the Greig emporia were in mortal battle with the newly arrived Sainsbury's for the loyalty and purse of the grocery-buying British public. The Greig chain closed in 1972, gobbled up by a succession of voracious rivals, until eventually it was owned by Somerfield and the Co-operative Group. But its building survives, the name of David Greig now preserved only on pavement tiles over which the good people of Brixton tramp each day, little pondering the piece of high-street history that they trample underfoot.

On Atlantic Road, just to the north-east of the former Greig's HQ, is one of the entrances to the fast-changing world of the Granville Arcade. This building occupies a series of criss-crossing roofed passages – rather grandly named 'avenues' – that were constructed in 1937 to the design of Alfred and Vincent Burr for a speculator called Mr Granville-Grossman. When I first knew the arcade many years ago, it was a bustling bazaar packed with vendors selling Caribbean food, memorably breadfruit and Scotch bonnet peppers, along with stalls covered with a stunning variety of fish or jerk chicken, and colourful fabrics and clothes.

Now the arcade has been renamed Brixton Village and is the centre of the social and gastronomic changes sweeping through the area. Some of the traditional shops survive, with their strange fruits and fishes – and, until recently, one still selling live African snails – but many have in recent years given way to exquisite cafés and restaurants. Not all change is bad (many of the eateries are very good), but they do make you wonder if any of the old shops or snack-bars will be left in a year or two. But at least this is no place for restaurant chains. The arcade hosts a haven of inventive independent enterprise on the part of energetic gastro-maniacs. Some of the avenues now contain cafés set almost bumper-to-bumper, each almost better than the last and each most individual.

Much of First Avenue is composed of older Caribbean shops. Most sell fish, fruit or meat, but there is also the splendid 'Wig Bazaar' at number 57. Third Avenue still houses traditional market shops with only a few cafés. At every turn such establishments proclaim their individuality through striking or quirkily designed decorative schemes. Look out for number 77 Fifth Avenue, on the corner with Second Avenue: this is Federation, one of the best coffee and bun places in Brixton village. But also good is Burnt Toast, on the corner of Second and Sixth Avenues. And don't miss the interesting Italian deli on the corner of Fourth and Second Avenues, Casa Sibilla.

This peculiar clash of the old Brixton and the new exists, too, on Market Row. Standing nearly opposite the Atlantic Road entrance to Brixton Village, this covered market is slightly earlier, built in 1923–5 in simple art deco style by Andrews and Peascod. But like Brixton village it contains roofed passages, with handsome partly glazed roofs. Also like Brixton village it is packed with cafés and delicatessens, and is a delight to wander through, browsing at the few traditional open-fronted fruit or fish stalls and sitting outside one or other of the eateries, watching the astonishing variety of life passing on its way.

The joyously diverse mix of current Brixtonians is illustrated by just a couple of shops. First, at number 4, stands the original Franco Manca. It was launched a few years ago by the notorious food fiend Giuseppe Mascoli, who was born in Positano, just south of Naples, in the heart of the pizza's homeland. It has now become a chain, even sprouting a second outlet in Market Row, more or less opposite the first. So perhaps they count as one.

Reassuringly, Franco Manca remains juxtaposed with something very different at number 8, a weird and wonderful outlet of old-time Brixton. Here survives a thoroughly packed emporium selling 'Religious Artefacts and Herbs', mostly, it declares, 'from Haiti and the USA'. The images and effigies on display in the window appear to be Christian, but posters hint at something else besides. On a visit a few years ago I noticed that one proclaimed in large lettering that it is a 'Real-True spiritual shop. You name it we got it'. In smaller print, another poster confided that diverse stock on sale inside was based on 'formulas . . . passed down through generations

A weird and wonderful outlet of old-time Brixton: Original Products on Market Row.

of our ancestors', and reassured passers-by that 'our experienced and naturally gifted spiritual doctor, healer and reader is available at hand for all matters including those of an urgent nature'. On a more recent visit, while I was taking pictures, a woman appeared out of nowhere, and, with a winning smile, asked me why I was photographing her shop and whether I wanted to kill her and eat her body. Before I could reply she told me, 'The Lord is coming soon,' patted me on the nose like a dog, and was on her way. If this interlude wasn't peculiar enough, this old shop – seemingly a survivor from an earlier manifestation of Market Row – is surrounded by the ubiquitous cafés packed with youthful and affluent Brixtonites. Let's hope this wonderful establishment continues long in business.

To get a better idea of what these Brixton markets were like a few years ago, make your way to the Reliance Arcade, which runs from 445 Brixton Road through to Electric Lane and opposite one of the entrances to Market Row. It incorporates just one narrow roofed passage lined with shops – like a West End Regency arcade – and on Electric Lane has a stunning elevation inspired by ancient Egyptian tomb architecture. An odd idea perhaps, but the arcade was designed in 1924, only a couple of years after Tutankhamun's tomb had been discovered in the Valley of the Kings at Luxor and when pharaoh fever was still at its height. Inside, the small stalls lining the cramped passage are humble indeed, selling simple and useful things – electric plugs, bags, wigs – and there is a minuscule hairdresser's where, when I visited, local girls were getting flounced in an atmosphere of great hilarity.

The survival of these three remarkable covered markets is thanks, in part, to architectural conservation. In 2008, the then new owners of the markets – a property company – revealed plans that involved flattening most of them for a ten-storey apartment block, private gardens and a new market. A campaign was launched to stop the scheme, and in April 2010 the government listed all three of Brixton's covered markets as buildings of historic, architectural and social importance. No doubt this listing was also recognition of the crucial role the markets played in establishing and sustaining the West Indian community in the area. The physical protection that listing promises changed the future of the market. Rather than redevelopment, the regeneration of the existing fabric became the

Wigs for sale in the Granville Arcade.

aim, and the result now acts as a powerful reminder that not all revived markets have to end up like that in Spitalfields, which is now largely the domain of chain restaurants and bars. Chains are not, of course, always to be sniffed at. Quality can be high and consistent, and value for money good. But they are, in the end, chains, and so by their nature repetitive, uniform and usually pretty characterless. The splendid array of eateries in the covered markets is just the opposite. Being the one-off creations of inspired and usually locally-based enthusiasts, they offer genuine surprise and individuality as well as quality.

❖

Yet there's another side to this revival. The conservation of Brixton's covered markets is no doubt indirectly responsible for the demise of some of the long-standing and more humble shops. Lingering demolition threats breed uncertainty and blight and lead to low rents. A decision to conserve brings certainty, investment and increased rents. This happened decades ago in Covent Garden and, more recently, in Spitalfields market. Conservation legislation can just about preserve the historic 'body' of an area but has no real hope of saving its soul in the face of compelling market forces.

I suppose this urban law is now at work in conserved Brixton, where rents are increasing to cover the cost of maintenance and to satisfy landlords' inevitable quest for profits. But so far, the traders are holding their own. Perhaps, then, these changes are creative and no more than the healthy expression of the natural cycle of transformation that reinvigorates and regenerates an urban community. Let's hope – for the sake of Brixton and of London – this continues to be the case.

For me, the heart of Brixton offers a fascinating prism through which to view the recent history of the capital. Its architecture, like its

A shop in Brixton Village embodies the colour and vivacity of Brixton – and of London.

community, is diverse and both seem almost accidental in their evolution. Utilitarian railway structures cut and thrust through the streets around Atlantic Road and Electric Avenue, with ornamental extravaganzas like the former Railway Hotel popping up for air between viaducts and high-level walkways. And, in recent decades, people from around the world have gathered here and, against difficult odds, forged – and managed to sustain – a remarkable and mixed community. At times the community has been volatile, but always buoyant and – perhaps above all – authentic. As with eighteenth- and nineteenth-century London, much of the life of the market area of Brixton is lived on the streets: not just through the stalls of its markets and open-fronted shops, but through the characters that inhabit the thoroughfares and byways of the place. Just visit, observe, and you'll understand.

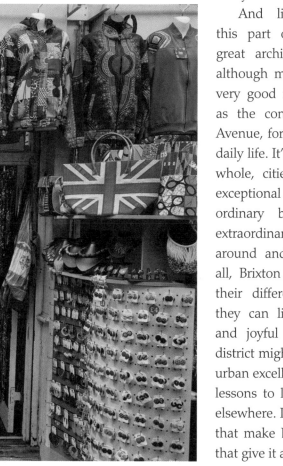

And like most of London, this part of Brixton contains no great architectural masterpieces – although many of its buildings are very good indeed, and some, such as the concave façade of Electric Avenue, form a splendid theatre for daily life. It's a reminder that, on the whole, cities are not really about exceptional buildings, but about ordinary buildings that become extraordinary through the life lived around and through them. Above all, Brixton is about people, about their differences, and about how they can live together in creative and joyful manner. To some this district might seem an odd model of urban excellence. But there are many lessons to learn here, and to apply elsewhere. It is living places like this that make London a great city and that give it a beating heart.

GLOSSARY

aedicule. A small shrine set within an enclave in a wall.

arcade. A row of arches.

apse. A niche or recess, often curved in plan, set in a wall.

attic. A storey set above the cornice, towards the top of a building.

atrium. The open central court of a building.

architrave. In a classical order, the architrave is the bottom part of the entablature, which rests directly above a capital or column. It is also the name of mouldings – derived from entablature mouldings – framing a door or window.

bay. The space between vertical features like columns or pilasters.

buttress. The end supports of a structure that carry weight to the ground. Also called an abutment.

colonnade. A row of columns, supporting a flat entablature or arches.

capital. In a classical order, the capital sits at the top of a column or pilaster and underneath the entablature.

chancel. The part of a church around the altar, usually set apart from the nave.

cornice. In a classical order, the cornice is the top section of the entablature. It is often used in isolation to ornament the top of an external elevation, usually at the junction with the roof, or the top of an internal wall at the junction with the ceiling.

doorcase. The frame surrounding a door.

eaves. A section of roof that overhangs a wall.

entablature. In a classical order, the entablature sits above the capitals and horizontally connects the columns or pilasters below. All entablatures comprise three elements: from the bottom, the architrave, the frieze and the cornice.

flute. A vertical recess in the shaft of a column.

frieze. In a classical order, the frieze is the large central portion of the entablature.

gable. The triangular portion of wall that sits beneath a pitched roof.

keystone. A wedge-shaped block at the crown of an arch, which consolidates its structure.

loggia. A room with at least one side that is open, usually defined by a colonnade, piers or an arcade.

lintel. A horizontal support across the opening of a door or window moulding.

mullion. A vertical division in a window opening, to which panes of glass are fixed.

nave. The main, central and usually highest space in a building of basilica form, normally flanked by aisles and separated from them by screens of columns, piers or shafts.

newel. The central pillar supporting a spiral staircase.

oculus. A circular and eyelike window and, more particularly, the circular opening at the crown of a dome.

order. By the Roman period there were five 'orders' of architecture – each with its own set of proportions, ornaments and attributes – which formed the basis of classical architecture. Ranging from the simple Tuscan through the progressively more ornate Doric, Ionic, Corinthian and Composite orders, each possesses its own forms of columns, capitals and entablatures.

oriel. A projecting structure containing windows and contrived to form a notable architectural feature.

pavilion. A portion of a building that is smaller than and set apart from its main section. It might be attached to the main building, or be a separate structure located nearby.

pediment. In a classical order, the pediment is the triangular or curved form set above an entablature. It marks the main entrance to, or forms the central feature of, a classical building.

pendentive. A curved triangle feature that forms the link between a flat wall and a curved dome.

piano nobile. The main floor of a building, usually a house.

piers. Vertical supporting structures on which girders, arches or trusses sit.

pilaster. The flat equivalent to a column, usually furnished with a capital, and set into a wall.

porch. A lower space in front of a building's façade, marking its entrance.

portico. A sheltered entrance or porch leading to a building or a covered way. In classical architecture often formed by the projection of a pediment or entablature, supported on columns.

quoins. The bricks or masonry blocks at the meeting point of two walls.

rustication. A type of decoration in which the edges of bricks or masonry blocks are clearly marked on a wall.

stucco. Smooth plaster used to coat walls and mould ornate architectural features.

tracery. The bars sitting between panes of glass, which offer structural support to a window.

transept. Projections set at right angles to the nave and aisles of a Christian church of basilica plan. The transepts are placed towards the altar end of the church so that, in plan, the church has the form of a Christian Latin cross.

vernacular. Buildings constructed using local materials in a traditional local style.

NOTES

Introduction
1 Daniel Defoe *A Tour Thro' the Whole Island of Great Britain* (1724–7).
2 Jack London, *The People of the Abyss* (1903).

Hampstead Heath
1 https://www.thetimes.co.uk/archive/article/1977-05-12/2/14
2 https://www.british-history.ac.uk/vch/middx/vol9/pp91-111#fnn2; http://www.esawyer.org.uk/browse/ch_date/0900.html
3 https://www.british-history.ac.uk/vch/middx/vol9/pp75-81
4 https://www.jstor.org/stable/4048139?seq=6#metadata_info_tab_contents, p. 125.
5 https://libcom.org/files/customs%20in%20common%20complete%20Part%201.pdf, p. 127.
6 C. R. Elrington, T. F. T. Baker, Diane K. Bolton and Patricia E. C. Croot (eds), *Victoria County History: A History of the County of Middlesex, vol. ix: Hampstead, Paddington* (1989), pp. 75–81.
7 Information from Jonathan Meares, Tree Manager for Hampstead Heath.
8 http://ufdcimages.uflib.ufl.edu/AA/00/00/61/22/00001/LeavesFromGerardsHerball_sm.pdf, pp. 210–11
9 From April 1817 at 1 Well Walk and from 1818 in Walworth Place, now Keat's Grove; 'To One Who Has Been Long in City Pent', 1817.
10 Elrington, Baker, Bolton and Croot, op. cit.

The Tower of London
1 William Fitzstephen, *Descriptio Londoniae* (1174–83).

Norton Folgate to Bank
1 Book of Revelation 4:2–4.
2 Dan Cruickshank, *Spitalfields* (2017), p. 20.
3 Robin Gwynn, 'The Number of Huguenot Immigrants in the Late 17th Century', *Journal of Historical Geography*, vol. 9, no. 4 (1983), pp. 384–98.
4 John Strype, *Survey of the Cities of London and Westminster*, Volume II, Book Four, (1720), p. 48 – includes a map of 'Spittlefields and places Adjacent'.
5 *Survey of London, XXVII: Spitalfields*, (1957), p. 81; M. L. R. 1724/5/67.
6 A longer discussion of the buildings on Elder Street can be found in the author's *Spitalfields*, op. cit., pp. 224–55.
7 Book of Revelation 8:10–11.
8 Raphael Holinshed, *Holinshed's Chronicles* (1577).

St Mary Magdelene, East Ham

1 Nikolaus Pevsner and Bridget Cherry with Charles O'Brien, *The Buildings of England: London 5: East* (2005), p. 266.
2 Dan Cruickshank, *Britain's Best Buildings* (2002), p. 19.

Eastbury Manor House

1 Nikolaus Pevsner, *The Buildings of England: London 5: East* (1950), p. 130.
2 *Survey of London Monograph 11, Eastbury Manor House, Barking* (1917), pp. 19–29.
3 Daniel Lysons, *The Environs of London*, vol. 4 (1795) p. 77.

Bank to St Paul's

1 https://www.britannica.com/event/Great-Fire-of-London
2 John Evelyn, William Bray ed., *The Diary of John Evelyn* (1901 edition), p. 22.
3 https://www.theguardian.com/cities/2016/jan/25/how-london-might-have-looked-five-masterplans-after-great-fire-1666
4 https://www.theguardian.com/cities/2016/jan/25/how-london-might-have-looked-five-masterplans-after-great-fire-1666
5 Lydia M. Soo, *Wren's 'Tracts' on Architecture and Other Writings* (1998), p. 133.
6 Ibid.
7 *The Wisdom of Solomon* 11:20.
8 Soo, op. cit., p. 133.
9 Nikolaus Pevsner, *Buildings of England, London 1*, (1973), p.182.
10 James Ralph, *A Critical Review of the Public Buildings . . . about London and Westminster* (1734), p. 12.
11 Gülru Necipoğlu, *The Age of Sinan: Architectural Culture in the Ottoman Empire* (2005).
12 Lisa Jardine, *On a Grander Scale: The Outstanding Career of Sir Christopher Wren* (HarperCollins, 2002), pp. 202, 415; Lydia M. Soo, *Wren's 'Tracts' on Architecture and Other Writings* (1998), p. 163.
13 Ezra 6:3–5.
14 Isaiah 6:1–3.
15 John 1:5.
16 John 12:35–6.
17 Christopher Wren and Stephen Wren, 'Upon the Building of National Churches', *Parentalia* (1750), pp. 318–21.
18 Dan Cruickshank, *The Secret History of Georgian London: How the Wages of Sin Shaped the Capital* (2010), p. 137.
19 Daniel Defoe, *Some Considerations Upon Street-Walkers, and a Proposal for Lessening the Present Number of Them* (c.1726), p. 2.
20 Mary Thale (ed.), *The Autobiography of Francis Place* (1972), p. 75.
21 *London Spy*, January 1699, Part 3, p. 14, quoted by Rictor Norton, *Mother Clap's Molly House* (1992), p. 50.

Royal Hospital, Chelsea

1 Thomas Faulkner, *Historical and Descriptive Account of Royal Hospital and Royal Military Asylum in Chelsea* (1805), p. 65.
2 Adrian Tinniswood, *His Invention So Fertile: A Life of Christopher Wren* (2002), p. 265.

Blackheath

1 Edward Walford, 'Blackheath and Charlton', in *Old and New London: Volume 6* (London, 1878) [accessed at https://www.british-history.ac.uk/old-new-london/vol6/pp224-236].
2 Lewis Namier ed., *The History of Parliament: The House of Commons 1754–1790*, vol. 19 (1964) [accessed at https://www.historyofparliamentonline.org/volume/1754-1790/constituencies/wallingford]
3 Pevsner, op. cit., p. 253.

Kew Gardens

1 Lord Shaftesbury, 'A Letter concerning the Art or Science of Design' (1714).
2 Colen Campbell, *Vitruvius Britannicus*, vol. 1, preface (1715).
3 John Wilkes, *The North Briton*, vol. I, no. 5 (1762), p. 44.
4 Mrs Vernon Delves Broughton (ed.), *Memoirs: Court and Private Life in the Time of Queen Charlotte: Being the Journals of Mrs Papendiek, Assistant Keeper of the Wardrobe and Reader to Her Majesty*, 2 vols, (1887).

The Regent's Canal

1 'A Cursory View of a Proposed Canal from Kendal to the Duke of Bridgewater's Canal' (1785), quoted in Gerard Turnbull, 'Canals, Coal and Regional Growth During The Industrial Revolution', *Economic History Review* vol. 40 no. 4 (1987). p. 537.
2 http://www.socsci.uci.edu/~dbogart/turnpike_canal_growth_may202017.pdf, p. 8.
3 John Phillips, *Inland Navigation* (1793), quoted in Gerard Turnbull, 'Canals, Coal and Regional Growth During The Industrial Revolution', *Economic History Review* vol. 40 no. 4 (1987). p. 537.
4 William Hardy, 'The Origins of the Idea of the Industrial Revolution' [accessed at www.open.edu/openlearn/history-the-arts/history/social-economic-history/the-origins-the-idea-the-industrial-revolution].
5 Ibid.
6 https://www.towerhamlets.gov.uk/Documents/Planning-and-building-control/Development-control/Conservation-areas/Victoria_Park_CAA_and_MG.pdf
7 Nikolaus Pevsner, *The Buildings of England: London 5: East*, p. 597.

8 'Regent's Canal Conservation Area Appraisal', London Borough of Hackney (2007) pp. 14–15.

9 *London 5: East* (2005), p. 598.

10 'Hackney: Mare Street and London Fields', in T. F. T. Baker ed., *A History of the County of Middlesex: Volume 10*, (1995), pp. 23-28 [accessed at https://www.british-history.ac.uk/vch/middx/vol10/pp23-28].

11 Ibid.

12 John Hollingshead, *Odd Journeys In and Out of London* (1860) [accessed at http://www.victorianlondon.org/transport/canaljourney.htm]

13 Amos Reade, *Life in the Cut* (1888), p. 10 [quoted in eprints.hud.ac.uk/id/eprint/25194/1/AOM.pdf].

14 Hollingshead op. cit.

The British Museum

1 Derek Cash, *Access to Museum Culture: The British Museum from 1752 to 1836*, British Museum Research Series, (2002) p. 27 [accessed at https://www.britishmuseum.org/pdf/2.pdf]

2 Ibid., p. 30.

King's Cross to Barnsbury

1 'Editorial Note: Steen Eiler – Ninetieth Birthday', *The Town Planning Review*, vol. 69 no. 2 (1988) [accessed at https://www.jstor.org/stable/40111797?seq=1#metadata_info_tab_contents]

2 Hermione Hobhouse, *Thomas Cubitt: Master Builder* (1995), p. 20.

3 Ibid., pp. 35–7.

4 Al Senter, 'Complete History of Sadler's Wells' (www.sadlerswells.com/about-us/history/complete-history).

5 Philip Temple (ed.), *Survey of London*, vol. 47, Northern Clerkenwell and Pentonville (2008), pp. 185–91.

6 Ibid., pp. 185–91.

7 Howard Colvin, *A Biographical Dictionary of British Architects* (1975 edition), p. 514.

8 Philip Temple, op. cit., pp. 264–97.

9 Ian Nairn, *Nairn's London* (1966), p. 172.

10 Hugh Casson, *Hugh Casson's London* (1983), p. 30.

11 Philip Temple, op. cit.,; Metropolitan Police Archives, G Division Registers; and information kindly supplied by Maggie Bird, Metropolitan Police archivist, and Guy Smith.

12 *The Weekly Dispatch*, 27 April 1834, p.1.

13 Philip Temple, op. cit., pp. 185–216.

14 National Archives, Kew, ref. 11/1816/261.

15 Cathy Ross, *Cloudesley: 500 Years in Islington* (2017).

16 Vestry book minutes, January 1811, quoted in Ross, op. cit., p. 26.

17 George Bradshaw, *Bradshaw's Handbook to London* (1862 edition).

18 Bridget Cherry and Nikolaus Pevsner, *The Buildings of England: London 4: North* (1998), p. 654.

Notting Hill

1 Ben Weinreb, Christopher Hibbert, Julia Keay & John Keay, *The London Encyclopaedia* (1983), p. 555.

2 F. H. W. Sheppard (ed.), *Survey of London*, vol. 37, Northern Kensington (1973), p. 195.

3 Ibid.,

4 Ibid., p. 200.

5 Ibid., p. 229.

6 Ibid., p. 244.

7 Ibid., pp. 214–19.

8 Ibid., p. 261.

9 Ibid., p. 275.

10 Ibid., p. 318.

11 Weinreb et al., op. cit., p. 505.

Embankment

1 Charles Dickens Jr, *Dickens's Dictionary of London* (1893 edition), p. 245.

Kensal Green and Kensal Rise

1 Victoria County History [accessed at https://www.british-history.ac.uk/vch/middx/vol7/pp182-204].

2 https://www.britishnewspaperarchive.co.uk/viewer bl/0000955/18680229/054/0003.

3 F. H. W Sheppard (ed.), *Survey of London*, vol. 37, Northern Kensington (1973), pp. 333–9.

4 Ibid.

5 Nikolaus Pevsner, *The Buildings of England: London, vol. 2* (1969 edition), p. 299.

6 Eric McDonald and David J. Smith, *Artizans and Avenues: A History of the Queen's Park Estate* (2004 edition).

7 Ibid., p. 19.

8 Old Bailey Archives, t1877 1022-761.

9 McDonald and Smith, op. cit., p. 11.

10 Census reference RG. 12/55.

11 Census Oliphant Street 1901, reference: RG 13/17.

12 Charles Booth, *Life and Labour of the People in London* (1892–97), pp. 60–65.

St Pancras Station and the Midland Grand Hotel

1 A. W. N. Pugin, *True Principles* (1841).
2 Ibid.
3 John Ruskin, *The Stones of Venice* (1851–3).

Bermondsey

1 Gustave Doré, *London: A Pilgrimage* (1872), pp. 23–4.
2 John Timbs, *Curiosities of London* (1857), pp. 49–50.
3 Charles Dickens Jr, *Dickens's Dictionary of London* (1893 edition).
4 Henry Mayhew, Letter LXXVIII, 15 November 1850, to the *Morning Chronicle*, quoted in E. P. Thompson and Eileen Yeo (eds), *The Unknown Mayhew: Selections from the Morning Chronicle 1849–1850* (Penguin, 1984), p. 548.
5 Charles Dickens Jr, *Dickens's Dictionary of London* (1893 edition), pp. 36–7.
6 National Archives, Kew.
7 Charles Dickens, *Oliver Twist* (1839).
8 Henry Mayhew, letter to the *Morning Chronicle*, 24 September 1849; from *Selections from London Labour and the London Poor* (1965), p. xxxvi.
9 Peter Haining, *The Legend and Bizarre Crimes of Spring-heeled Jack* (London, 1977).
10 *London: A Pilgrimiage*, p. 24.
11 LSE Archives, B364, p. 64.
12 Matthew 27:3–8.
13 *Second Report of the Commissioners on the Education of the Poor* (1819), pp. 142–4.
14 *London Review* (1816).

Hampstead Garden Suburb

1 Bridget Cherry and Nikolaus Pevsner, *The Buildings of England: London 4: North* (1998), p. 142.

North Spitalfields

1 Psalm 74:19–20.
2 David W. Bartlett, *What I Saw in London: or, Men and Things in the Great Metropolis* (1852), pp. 19, 39, 111–12, 116.
3 Henry Mayhew, Letter II, 25 October 1849, to the *Morning Chronicle*, quoted in E. P. Thompson and Eileen Yeo (eds), *The Unknown Mayhew: Selections from the Morning Chronicle 1849–1950* (1984), pp. 128–9.
4 Alex Atkinson and Ronald Searle, *The Big City, or The New Mayhew* (1958), pp. 11–12.
5 Charles Knight (ed.), *London* (1842), pp. 385–400.
6 George Gissing, *The Nether World*, vol. 2 (1889), p. 109.
7 *Round London* (1896), p. 125.

8   Ibid.
9   Friedrich Engels, *The Condition of the Working Class in England* (OUP, 1993 edition), pp. 41–4.
10 Ibid.
11 LSE Archives, B356.
12 LSE Archives, B351, pp. 120–21.
13 Ibid., pp. 136–7.
14 Thomas Archer, *The Pauper, the Thief and the Convict* (1865), pp. 9–10.
15 Thompson and Yeo, op. cit., pp. 126–7.
16 RG12, piece 265, folio 20, page 35.
17 Charles Dickens, *Household Words*, no. 54 (April 1851), p. 30.
18 Archer, op. cit., pp. 9–10, 17, 18–21.
19 Old Bailey Archives, t18261026-34.
20 Defoe, op. cit.
21 Archer, op. cit., pp. 21–2.
22 Ibid., pp. 22–3.
23 Ibid. pp. 26–7.
24 LSE Archives, B351, pp. 158–9.
25 Ed Glinert, *East End Chronicles* (2005), p. 281; Fergus Linnane, *London's Underworld: Three Centuries of Vice and Crime* (2000), p. 175.
26 Hector Gavin, *Sanitary Ramblings: Being Sketches and Illustrations of Bethnal Green* (1848), pp. 36–9.
27 Emanuel Litvinoff, *Journey Through a Small Planet* (1971), pp. 20–21, 170.
28 Ibid., pp. 21–2.
29 Ibid., p. 22.

Fleet Street to Trafalgar Square

1   James Ralph, *A Critical Review of the Public Buildings, Statues and Ornaments In, and about London and Westminster* (1734), pp. 37–8.
2   Terry Friedman, *James Gibbs* (1984), p. 51.
3   Saunders Welch, *A Proposal to Render Effectual a Plan to Remove the Nuisance of Common Prostitutes from the Streets of the Metropolis* (1758), quoted by Dan Cruickshank, *The Secret History of Georgian London* (2010), pp. 27–30.
4   Cruickshank, op. cit., p. 170.
5   Ibid., p. 171.
6   Bill for the Creation of Regent Street, 1813.

Brixton

1   F. H. W. Sheppard (ed.), *Survey of London*, vol. 26, Lambeth: Southern Area (1956), pp. 125–30.

KEY LOCATIONS AND BUILDINGS

100 Bishopsgate 53–4
22 Bishopsgate 60–63
39 Threadneedle Street 64–5
Acton's Lock 231
Admiralty Arch 509–11
Aldwych 477–80
All Hallows-on-the-Wall 51–2
All Saint's, Notting Hill 326–8
Australia House 478–80
Bank of England 131–9
Barnsbury 292–7
Bedford Institute 424
Bermondsey 370–407
Bethnal Green 224–231
Bishopsgate Goodsyard 437–8
Blackheath 176–209
Bloomberg London 2–3, 151–2
Bloomsbury 243–9
Brick Lane market 442–5
British Museum 243–9
Brixton 519–37
Bush House 478
C. Hoare and Company 471–2
Carpenter's Arms (Spitalfields) 444–5
Charing Cross Station 499–501
Chelsea 169–75
Christ Church, Spitalfields 44–6
City of London Club 65–6
City, The 1–7, 29–31, 47–69, 124–67, 458–75
Colonnade House 201–3
Commercial Tavern (Spitalfields) 425
Covent Garden 179, 493–6
Covent Garden market 493–5
Dagenham 513–17
Dagenham Civic Centre 513–17
Daily Express Building 461–2, 468
Daily Telegraph Building 468
Earl of Lonsdale (Notting Hill) 321–2
East Ham 71–5

Eastbury 117–23
Eastbury Manor House 117 –23
Embankment, The 335–9
Flamsteed House 99–102
Gibson Hall 63–4
Gloucester Circus 102–5
Granville Arcade 532
Great Eastern Hotel 47
Great St Helen's 57–60
Greenwich 77–115
Greenwich Town Hall 106
Guildhall 37–8, 155
Haggerston 231–234
Hampstead 9–27, 409–15
Hampstead Garden Suburb 409–15
Hampstead Heath 9–27
Heathgate House 181–3
Houses of Parliament 297–303
Islington 234–241, 283–292
Jack Straw's Castle 21
Kensal Green 341–3, 344–57
Kensal Green Cemetery 341–2, 344–54
Kensal Rise 343–4, 357–63
Kew 211–17
Kew Gardens 211–17
Liverpool Street station 46
London Bridge station 390–1
London Leather, Hyde and Wool Exchange 395–6
Macartney House 183
Mansion House 142–4
Midland Grand Hotel 365–9
Morden College 206–9
National Gallery 507–8
Notting Hill 304–33
Pagoda House 192–4
Palace of Westminster 297–303
Paragon House 203
Paragon, The 203–6

Pentonville 259–83
Portobello Road market 322–30
Punch Tavern (Fleet Street) 464
Queen's Chapel of the Savoy 490–1
Queen's House 80–6, 92–94
Ranger's House 183
Regent's Canal 218–41
Reliance Arcade 534
Reuters and Press Association
    Building 459–61
Royal Courts of Justice 475
Royal Exchange 66–9
Royal Hospital, Chelsea 169–75
Royal Hospital, Greenwich 86–92
Royal Observatory 99–102
Savoy Hotel 491–3
Shoreditch 33–47, 417–49
Somerset House 484–90
Spaniards Inn 27
Spitalfields 33–47, 417–49
St Alfege, Greenwich 111–15
St Botolph-without-Bishopsgate
    48–50
St Bride's 464–6
St Clement Danes 475–7
St Dunstan-in-the-West 470–1
St Ethelburga-the-Virgin 54–6
St John the Evangelist, Kensal Green
    354

St Margaret's, Lothbury 139–142
St Martin-in-the-Fields 484
St Mary Magdalen, Bermondsey
    397–8
St Mary Magdalene, East Ham 71–5
St Mary-le-Bow 156–9
St Mary-le-Strand 480–4
St Matthew Bethnal Green 445
St Pancras 256–9, 365–9
St Pancras station 365–9
St Paul's Cathedral 159–67
St Paul's, Covent Garden 495
St Stephen's Walbrook 144–51
Temple Bar 166–7, 475
Temple Church 472–3
Temple of Mithras 1–7
Tower Bridge 376–81
Tower of London 29–31
Trafalgar Square 504–9
Trafalgar Tavern (Greenwich) 94
Trellick Tower 331–2
Trinity Hospital 95–6
Vanbrugh Castle 98–9
Victoria Park 225–6
Waterloo Bridge 490
Westminster 297–303
White Cube Gallery 397
York Water Gate 499
Zimbabwe House 502–3